PRAISE FOR

The Big Bam

"Vivacious biography of The Bambino . . . Energetically written."
—*Kirkus*

"The right book at the right time."   —*Providence Journal*

"The best Ruth biography to date . . . [Montville's] adroit organization of the historical material—enhanced by newly studied archival material and oral history transcripts, together with his flair for marshalling undisputed facts that are intertwined with plausible speculations—has produced an engaging, entertaining, and eminently readable biography."
—*Library Journal* (starred review)

"In this day of overamped salaries, statistics, and physiques, it's useful to be reminded of the singular talent and impact Babe Ruth brought to baseball during his career (1914–35). Montville brings fresh observations to his subject [and] gives readers the measure of what made the man. Montville has also carefully sifted the factual from the hearsay, leaving us with a volume that's reliable, readable, and deserving of a place in the sports or American culture collection."   —*Booklist*

Ted Williams: The Biography of an American Hero

At the Altar of Speed: The Fast Life and Tragic Death of Dale Earnhardt

Manute: The Center of Two Worlds

Why Not Us?: The 86-Year Journey of the Boston Red Sox Fans from
Unparalleled Suffering to the Promised Land of the 2004 World Series

THE
Big Bam

THE LIFE AND TIMES
OF BABE RUTH

LEIGH MONTVILLE

BROADWAY BOOKS   New York

PUBLISHED BY BROADWAY BOOKS

Copyright © 2006 by Leigh Montville

All Rights Reserved

A hardcover edition of this book was originally published in 2006 by Doubleday.

Published in the United States by Broadway Books, an imprint of The Doubleday Broadway Publishing Group, a division of Random House, Inc., New York.
www.broadwaybooks.com

BROADWAY BOOKS and its logo, a letter B bisected on the diagonal, are trademarks of Random House, Inc.

Frontispiece photograph courtesy of Transcendental Graphics

Book design by Caroline Cunningham

Library of Congress Cataloging-in-Publication Data
Montville, Leigh.
    The Big Bam : the life and times of Babe Ruth / Leigh Montville.—1st ed.
       p.   cm.
    Includes bibliographical references and index.
    1. Ruth, Babe, 1895–1948.   2. Baseball players—United States—Biography.   I. Title.

GV865.R8M56 2006
796.357092—dc22
[B]

2006042522

978-0-7679-1971-5

[PRINT]ED IN THE UNITED STATES OF AMERICA

[9 8] 7 6 5 4 3 2 1

[Pape]rback Edition

This book is dedicated to
Jackson Nathaniel Moleux
Born: August 7, 2005

INTRODUCTION

T HE GRAND YEAR for researching Babe Ruth biographies was 1973. Five writers traveled around the country, stopping at retirement homes and suburban neighborhoods to talk to the last old men who remembered their time as teammates or friends of the greatest baseball player who ever lived. Reminiscences of long-ago hijinks and debaucheries were jotted into notebooks, impressions captured on tape recorders before the stories and the storytellers left the flat face of the earth.

The timing was important. Henry Aaron of the Atlanta Braves was on schedule to break the Babe's biggest record of all, 714 career home runs, in the first months of the 1974 season. The excitement of that moment would also turn the focus to the past, making not only the followers of baseball but the general public remember the outrageous character who had set the record in the first place. Each of the five writers figured he had found an untapped and marketable story.

The Babe had been dead for 25 years, hadn't swung a bat in almost 40. The previous biographies, including two ghostwritten autobiographies, had woven fable and half-truths around the no-nonsense statistics of the box scores and record books. The feeling was that the real story finally should be told. Get it right. Get it out. Each of the five writers had decided independently on the same course.

It was a shock when each learned he was not alone.

"I was having a very nice lunch with Jumpin' Joe Dugan," Kal Wagenheim, the author of *Babe Ruth: His Life and Legend,* says. "Joe was a teammate and a friend of the Babe. I remember him saying—after he had told some wonderful stories—'The Babe suddenly seems very popular.' I asked what he meant. He said, 'You're the third guy who's interviewed me, writing a book about the Babe.' "

"Almost the same thing happened to me," Ken Sobol, author of *Babe Ruth and the American Dream,* says. "I think it happened to all of us."

In another version of the deflating moment, New York sportswriter Harold Rosenthal, a friend of Bob Creamer's, author of *Babe: The Legend Comes to Life,* sent a message to Creamer that someone named Kal Wagenheim was writing a Babe Ruth book. Rosenthal didn't know Wagenheim and wrote, "I know what a Kal is, but what's a Wagenheim?"

Everyone was stepping on everyone else's toes. Everyone kept typing.

The strongest figure in the field, beginning to end, was Creamer. He had started first, seven or eight years before everyone else, and carried the most clout. He was a senior editor at *Sports Illustrated,* a tall and erudite man in his early fifties who already had written as-told-to books on New York Yankees star Mickey Mantle, broadcaster Red Barber, and umpire Jocko Conlon. The Ruth book was a personal challenge to see if he could write a biography on his own without the tape-recorded aid of the subject. His pace had been relaxed, the project added to his weekly chores at *SI.*

The approach of Aaron toward the record and the rumors of other Ruth books brought a call from the publisher. The relaxed pace was finished.

"My editor, Peter Schwed, asked me how I was doing, and I told him I already had 70,000 words written, long enough to be a book," Creamer says. "I also told him that at the end of the 70,000 words, the Babe was 19 years old and just starting to play for the Red Sox. Peter told me to get moving. I promised I would be finished by the fall, the date of the autumnal equinox."

None of the other writers was a sportswriter. Wagenheim had been a 37-year-old stringer for the *New York Times,* writing out of San Juan, Puerto Rico, when the plane carrying Pittsburgh Pirates outfielder Roberto Clemente and relief supplies for earthquake victims in Nicaragua crashed while leaving the San Juan airport on New Year's Eve in 1972. He covered the immediate story of Clemente's death for the *Times* and in the aftermath was contacted to write a book. His hurried effort, *Clemente!*, was a best-seller. His publisher, pleased with the success, asked him to try another baseball biography. Wagenheim picked the Babe as his subject.

Ken Sobol was a writer for the *Village Voice*. His agent called him, suggesting a Ruth book. Robert Smith, 69, was a novelist, but also gravitated toward baseball nonfiction. Reviewers had called his 1948 book *Baseball* the first true history of the game.

The fifth writer, Marshall Smelser, was an academic. He was a historian, a member of the faculty at the University of Notre Dame. His most recent book was *The Winning of Independence,* the tale of the American Revolution. Following baseball was one of his many hobbies—a large picture of the Babe had graced his office door for years. He decided to merge vocation and avocation to write "not a book for baseball people," but "a baseball book for people." The title was *The Life That Ruth Built.*

The five contenders followed separate but often overlapping tracks. Smith did little face-to-face interviewing, writing a book with a larger scope—a history of the period with the Babe's life serving mostly as touchstone and timeline. The other writers contacted teammates, family, friends of the Babe. Smelser sent a mimeographed set of questions to the former Yankees teammates of Ruth who were still alive. Sobol, looking for some negative voices, found them in the wives of former teammates. Creamer, after a lot of work, finally convinced former pitcher Waite Hoyt, Ruth's teammate on both the Yankees and Red Sox, to talk for three days in Florida about the Babe. Wagenheim found great help from former sportswriters who had covered the Yankees. Everyone rolled through miles of microfilm in his local library.

Four of the books appeared in the immediate glow of Aaron's achievement on April 8, 1974, his 715th career home run, off Al Downing at Atlanta's Fulton County Coliseum. Creamer's 443-page effort was the acknowledged winner. Its publication was preceded by a three-part series of excerpts in *SI*, and the magazine's reviewer called it "the best biography ever written about an American sports figure."

The books by Wagenheim, Sobol, and Smith, each of them solid and taking a different tack on the Babe's life, were mostly lost or disregarded in the backwash of the praise for Creamer's biography. In a few cases, one or two of the other works were compared to Creamer's effort, sometimes favorably, often not, but mostly the books weren't reviewed at all.

Smelser's biography did not appear until 1975. It was, as promised, a fat and scholarly book, 592 pages filled with footnotes. It was mostly well reviewed, but the marketplace moment had passed. Oddly, the book became a favorite of "baseball people," but not "people." Too many writers had tackled the same subject at the same time.

"It was all an education about the publishing industry," Wagenheim, who never has written another sports book, says. "In the middle of everything, you had Watergate and all the books that came out of that. I remember calling my publishers after I learned that other books were being written about the Babe. I was thinking they would arrange some big public relations campaign. What they did—immediately—was cut back the press run."

None of the books, not even Creamer's, made the best-seller lists.

More than 30 years have passed since this biographical rush in 1974. The images of *Aaron* breaking the record now seem dated: the uniforms just not right, the hairstyles odd, the film of the moment grainy and amateurish when played on a high-definition screen. Aaron's feat has been assimilated into the history of the game with the same quiet grace with which it was accomplished.

The Babe remains remarkably vibrant. He probably is even more popular now than he was when the five books were published. The long-ball approach to baseball that he single-handedly brought to the sport now dominates it. The parks are built for home runs. The players are built for home runs. A cavalcade of home runs is shown every night on ESPN's *SportsCenter* and *Baseball Tonight,* baseballs hitting off foul poles and facades, landing in the Pacific Ocean, dropping into packed crowds of spectators who spill their $7 beers and lose their designer team caps in happy pursuit.

Threaded through all of this, however, are the drumbeat questions about steroids, about what is real and what isn't, about cheating. The biggest names, the record breakers like Mark McGwire and Sammy Sosa and Barry Bonds, are surrounded by suspicion. Were their feats concocted in laboratories as much as performed on the diamond? Who took what, and when? What exactly was "the clear"? A skepticism, a lack of full acceptance, taints their accomplishments. At the least, these were men who used as much legal modern science as possible to enable them to hit a baseball a long way. They weren't walk-off-the-street human beings. At the worst, they cheated, injecting and ingesting illegal substances to make their bodies stronger.

The complications of it all—and the complications certain to arrive in the future with genetic engineering and other medical advances and God knows what—make a look back at Babe Ruth ever more inviting. Steroids hadn't been invented when he did what he did. Beer and scotch and hot dogs were his nutritional supplements of choice! He is seen as a big and natural man who did big things that are part of our culture now, each passing year oddly making their distant glow a little brighter. The Babe never sat in front of a congressional hearing trying to explain himself! He sat in front of magistrates, describing why yet another car flipped while he was behind the wheel on yet another rainy night!

This book is an attempt to tell the story again for the *SportsCenter* generation, to bring back the supposed-to-be-uncomplicated in the time of the complicated. The approach is not so much to tear down the myths that grew around George Herman Ruth as to explain how and why they developed in the time in which he lived. Why did an entire country fall in love, go gaga over him? Why was this one man so good, so much better than his contemporaries? That is a question accusingly asked in our time of steroids, and it can be asked about the Babe too. The answers are surprising and attack the well-constructed image of him as the totally self-indulgent fatso.

The authors of the 1974 biographies have been very kind. The old men they found across the country are all dead now, but they still talk in the research that these writers accumulated. Robert Creamer provided six boxes of material from *Babe: The Legend Comes to Life*. Kal Wagenheim provided tapes that he made with a bulky, first-generation recorder. Marshall Smelser, who died a year after the publication of *The Game That Ruth Built*, left all of his materials to the National Baseball Hall of Fame in Cooperstown, New York, which also supplied tapes from other researchers. Ken Sobol wanted to provide words but, alas, said, "I've moved 17 times since that book. I have no idea where everything went."

Another wonderful book, *No Cheering in the Press Box* by Jerome Holtzman, also appeared in 1974. It is a collection of oral-history interviews of sportswriters from the twenties and thirties, men who dealt often with Ruth. Holtzman, now the historian for Major League Baseball, noted in his opening that the interviews were conducted over a three-year period and totaled over 900,000 words of transcript, of which approximately 10 percent were used in the book. Did he still have those original transcripts? Yes, he did. They arrived in a large cardboard UPS box. Again, dead men talked, telling colorful tales.

Holtzman, an authority on baseball literature, says that 27 books have been written on Ruth, the most for anyone who played the game. (Jackie Robinson is second at 25.) Many of those books have been written since 1974, notably *My Dad, The Babe* and *Young Babe Ruth* and *Babe Ruth and the 1918 Red Sox*, and have further filled out the picture of the man. In addition, numerous scholarly papers and articles have been written about the Babe, especially by members of SABR, the Society for American Baseball Research. A symposium on his life and career was held at Hofstra University in 1995 on the 100th anniversary of his birth.

It is from atop this mountain of information—plus interviews, side trips, phone calls, Google-found Web sites, and the requisite ancient newspaper stories—that the typing begins again (on a computer keyboard). The job is an honor. Babe Ruth's story belongs to all of us.

CHAPTER ONE

THE LITTLE BOY *and the man get on the Wilkens Avenue trolley on the morning of June 13, 1902. It is a Friday. They are off on a trip of great dimensions. Details are important but do not seem to be available. There is so much we want to know. There is so much we never will.*

Is it really morning?

Or maybe early afternoon?

Probably not night.

The man and the boy take seats in the second row. Or maybe they are all the way in the back. The boy is on the outside so he can see the streets of Baltimore pass. Or maybe he is on the inside. Maybe he is looking at his shoes.

The jangle of nickels and pennies rolling through the conductor's coin box is background noise. Wasn't the coin box always background noise on a trolley? The ding-ding of the bell is heard when the trolley makes a stop. What is the weather? The Baltimore Sun *predicted showers and cooler. Is it raining right now? Cool enough for a jacket? Don't know. Can't be sure.*

The man is sad or resolute or perhaps secretly happy. The boy is . . . does he even know where he is going? Is the packed little suitcase on the seat next to him a clue? Or is there no suitcase? He is dressed in the best

*clothes that he owns. Or are there no best clothes? The conversation is
quiet, short sentences, the man's mind lost somewhere in the business of
the moment. Or perhaps there is no conversation, not a word. Or perhaps
there are laughs, the man talking and talking, joking, to take the edge
away.*

What?

*Imagination tries to build atop slim facts. The man is 31 years old.
That is birth certificate truth. His wife is 28 years old. That is another
birth certificate truth. Their first son, the boy, as recorded in the Office of
the Registrar of Vital Statistics, Baltimore City, by midwife Minnie Graf,
is seven years, three months, seven days old, except . . . except he will
believe for most of his years that his birthday is one year and one day
earlier.*

Why is that?

*The urge is to sketch in the rest of the picture, make judgments, add
colors and emotions and maybe a passing billboard or two. Can it be resisted? The mother has kissed the boy good-bye at the front door of 426
West Camden Street, a tear rolling down her cheek. Or she has said nothing. Or she was relieved. Or maybe she wasn't even there. The boy is sad,
crying. Or he is mute, defiant. Or he is clueless and confident, always confident.*

The biggest mysteries in the life of George Herman Ruth—and some researchers say Herman is his true middle name, handed down from his
father, and some say it is his confirmation name—are front-loaded and
frustrating. The topographic representations of most famous lives feature
well-defined peaks of public achievement, brightly lit and easily seen, but
a fog often settles over the personal life below. The fog here covers everything.

Babe?

Babe Ruth?

Behind that moon face with those small eyes, that flat nose, those big
lips that will be captured in any instantly recognizable portrait in a blue
New York Yankees cap, the boy will forever hide. He is only a shape,
glimpsed here, glimpsed there, lost again. No one has found that boy at
the beginning of it all, touched him, gotten to know him. No one ever
will. If the right questions ever were asked, the answers never were given.

Time has finished the job. There is no one to talk to now. No one is around.

He will become the Sultan of Swat, the Bambino, the Big Bam, baseball royalty, the greatest home run hitter of his time or any time, a character as interesting as Einstein or Edison or Elvis or any other twentieth-century innovator or inventor, but he will never fill in the early blanks. Want to grow up to be Babe Ruth? He will never explain how to start.

The trolley ride with his father on that June day of 1902 will always be a bewilderment. The boy will say as a man only that he was "a bad kid." Not much more than that. He was seven years old. He was an only son. He was taken to that trolley because he was a seven-year-old bad kid? How bad could he have been? "Incorrigible" was a word that was used.

There are no stories of a mother, none—good or bad or madhouse crazy. There is one picture of her, a grainy shot, pulled from a group photo of a family reunion, her famous child in her lap. Her hair is up. Her high collar is buttoned. She is not smiling.

There are few stories of a father. He was a lightning-rod salesman and then the owner of a succession of taverns. He had an anger that coursed through him. Or so it seemed. The one famous picture of father and son, later in life, shows a beefy man, striped shirt, necktie, vest of a waiter. He has a cigar in his left hand, stands behind his bar. Christmas decorations hang from the ceiling. He would like to pour you a beer.

The environment can be stitched together from history books and memoirs of local writers, but it is a broad picture of turn-of-the-century Baltimore and a bad neighborhood and working-class woes. Stevedores, sailors, wagons, horses, the many-layered bustle of business—these are the backdrop in an area of alleys and cramped brick houses near the docks on the wrong side of Pratt Street, the downtown dividing line for class and economics.

The general neighborhood, which included the house of George Herman's maternal grandmother at 216 Emory Street, where he was born, was called Pigtown. He is a boy from Pigtown. The name comes from the great herds of pigs, hundreds of pigs, that are run through the streets on a regular basis from the nearby stockyard to the nearby slaughterhouse. Residents, it is said, would open their basement windows and reach out and try to grab a passing, squealing potential Sunday dinner.

The specifics of family life are elusive. The father ran assorted taverns in the area, nine in one count, one after another, so the family moved often. The mother was pregnant much of the time, had eight children, including two sets of twins. Six of the children died early. She herself was dead of "exhaustion," the word on her death certificate, at age 39. The certificate also said she was a widow.

A widow?

That's wrong.

Isn't it?

The meager bits of information scrawled on forms and in ledgers by bored civil servants are pen-and-ink riddles as much as facts. The father was supposed to be Lutheran, the mother Catholic. They were married in a Baptist church. The boy supposedly was baptized Catholic, but 11 years later was baptized Catholic again. The word "convert" was written on the side of the official certificate. Why was that? Any mistakes made then are codified now, preserved as Paleolithic truth when found by armchair archaeologists.

The most spare anecdotes or one-liners are repeated with each succeeding retelling of the larger tale, gathering weight each time. They are repeated here. The grown-up boy supposedly told Chicago Cubs second baseman Johnny Evers of Tinker-to-Evers-to-Chance fame that his father took him to the basement and beat him with a horsewhip. Another story mentioned a billiard cue. Another said his mother beat on him in frustration.

The image that clicks into place is an embattled household on the perforated edge of poverty. Alcohol fuels discord and noise. Volatility is the one constant of every day, the smallest situations ticking, ready to explode. Love and quiet are luxuries that can't be afforded. Bills are always due. Frustrations sit in a pile that never will get smaller, life turned into existence. An unpleasant existence at that. The birth date for little George—if it is right—indicates that he was born seven months after his mother and father were married. What about that fact? Did his parents know? Was that why they were married in the first place?

Is any of this right?

A sister survived. Mary, called Mamie, was five years younger than little George. Or maybe six. She would live to be 91 years old, dying in 1992, but was of little help. She developed a mostly romanticized version of childhood, as many people do. Her parents were "in the restaurant business." Her brother was "a very big boy for his age, very good-hearted to everyone he met. He would get very angry at times, but it was soon forgotten."

She did say, "Mother was not a very well person." She didn't elaborate on what sense of "well" she meant. Physical or mental? Or both? Didn't say. At times she was at variance with things her brother said. He said he had an older brother, John, who died in a street fight. She said there was no older brother; George was the oldest. He also said their mother was a mix of Irish and English. Mamie said this was nonsense; their mother was German.

Research seems to back Mamie's side. The mother, maiden name Katie Schaumberger, was the daughter of Pius and Anna Schaumberger. They both were born in Germany; then Katie was born in Maryland. The other side of the family also goes back eventually to Germany. George Ruth Sr.'s parents both were born in Maryland. There is dispute about where his grandparents were born, either in Germany or Bucks County, Pennsylvania, Pennsylvania Dutch country. Pick one. If Bucks County is the choice, the great-great-grandparents were from Germany.

Added to the confusion are a couple of other names, "Erhardt" and "Gerhardt." These were names mentioned mostly by the boy, the son, in later years. He tried to explain, more than once, that Ruth was his real name, not Erhardt or Gerhardt. Who exactly thought his real name was Erhardt or Gerhardt was never explained. Someone—perhaps a bunch of someones—must have thought so. Why else would he explain?

In his autobiography, *The Babe Ruth Story*, ghostwritten for him just before his death, he takes care of all of this childhood material in just five paragraphs, less than 300 words. One sentence, "I hardly knew my parents," pretty much wraps up his genealogy. Another sentence, "I had a rotten start and it took me a long time to get my bearings," pretty much wraps up his early childhood.

He will never say much more. The reporters of his time never pressed, never tried to squeeze out the smallest details, the darkest secrets, the way they do now in a tell-all time of celebrity. They never fanned across his beginnings and interviewed neighbors and boyhood chums, teachers, and shopkeepers. That wasn't the style. Neither his father nor his mother told a single story, not one. There are no first smiles, first steps, first confrontations with a curveball. There are no tales of mischief or honor. No school paper has been preserved, a star pasted at the top.

Babe?

Babe Ruth?

The boy who became famous was born and existed for his formative first seven years in the wide margins between very few words. He learned his first lessons about love, life, survival. He learned about keeping secrets. He was one of the forgotten children, the same then as now, kids who are born into hard circumstance and either figure out what to do or don't. He was left alone with his questions, had to find his own answers.

He still is alone. The man who grew out of the boy very much decided to leave the boy back there. What happened? The man would never say, so the boy is seen only in outline. There he is, living in the apartment above the father's tavern. There he is, running down the street with a pack of kids, throwing something at some merchant directing a horse-drawn cart. There he is . . . where is he?

The docks of Baltimore grow darker and more threatening as they are seen from farther and farther away. Images from movies intrude: drunken sailors and longshoreman louts walking the cobblestone streets, hard women in doorways bidding them hello. Baltimore was the sixth-largest city in the country, a major port, calling itself "the Liverpool of America." Images of Liverpool join the picture. Giant schooners sit with wooden masts. An everyday covering of soot and smoke touches all objects. A drizzle always seems to be falling, a lonely streetlight losing the battle with the blackness of the alleys.

The fog settles over everything and will not leave.

Maybe the man reads a newspaper. Maybe an earlier passenger left it on the trolley. Maybe the man brought it with him to pass the time. Maybe there is no newspaper, but it is put there to establish situation and circumstance, a use of dramatic license. Maybe the man reads. Maybe he talks. Small talk.

"Orioles won yesterday," he says to the boy. "Beat the Tigers, 9–3 in Detroit."

The 1902 Orioles are in sixth place in the eight-team American League. The glories of the nineteenth-century world championships won by John McGraw, Hughie Jennings, Wee Willie Keeler, and Steve Brodie are pretty much gone. Only catcher Wilbert Robinson is around from those days, 39 years old now. He went 1-for-4 in Detroit, a double. The

Chicago White Sox are in first place, a game and a half in front of the Philadelphia A's. There is no American League team in New York.

"How about this?" the man says. "'In a baseball game between the city team from Charlottesville and the Christian Science reading room, a ground ball took a bad hop and struck Charlottesville shortstop W. Reade Jarman in the throat. He picked up the ball, threw to first to nip the runner, then grabbed his throat and fell to the ground. He was dead three minutes later.'

"Can you believe it?" the man says.

He turns from the sports page to the front. Two sergeants testified before Congress yesterday that they did, while serving in the Philippines in 1900, hold suspected "insurgents'" heads under water in order to extract information. . . . A group of striking workers fired upon a coal train in Wilkes Barre, Pennsylvania. . . . There is another big strike in Pawtucket, Rhode Island. Police fired upon a crowd. . . . A corn shortage is reported at the exchange in Philadelphia. . . . And a genuine "Porto Rican Panama" hat can be had for $2 (a $5 value) at the Hat Box in the American Building.

The man mentions the "insurgents" perhaps, but not the bargain hat. Or the hat and not the "insurgents." Or neither.

Probably neither.

There probably is no newspaper. The boy would never become a reader. Never would read an entire book in his life, not even the two he supposedly wrote. The man is probably not much of a reader either.

Probably no newspaper.

The fog will make everything greater. That is the weird beauty of the fog. The fog will be part of the magic. The fog will be the beginnings of the myth. Anyone can succeed! Uneducated, socially inept, but able to do one thing better than anyone else in the world—swing a wooden bat and hit a baseball for astonishing distances—the boy will grow up to meet presidents and kings and be carried high in the air, showered with money and kisses (a lot of kisses), and loved with a fondness usually reserved for the family golden retriever. The fog will make him forever accessible, universal.

He will be the patron saint of American possibility. In the middle of the night in small towns across the country, crowds will gather at railroad stations. Word will pass that he will be on the train when it stops to pick up coal or to add cars or to subtract cars or to change tracks. The people will gather for a sighting, perhaps a word. He will shuffle to the train's door in his bathrobe and slippers, wave from the steps, thank everyone for saying hello. The train will depart, and the people will go home satisfied, somehow fulfilled. See that? He is real.

His success will be a lottery ticket in every empty pocket. If he can do it, then why can't I? Or why can't my kids? He grew up worse than all of us. He came from the terrible, unspeakable fog. Look at him now.

His fame will be manufactured in part, packaged, kept alive by a host of inventions, but its core will be performance. He will hit his 714 home runs, be part of seven world championship teams, do things that will demand to be reported in grand, bombastic ways. For the people who never could see him on the big stage, he will bring the show to them. He will hit home runs in wheat fields and mill towns, take the best pitch of the local phenom and send it clattering off grain elevators and warehouses. Little plaques will dot the land, testimonies to where he hit a baseball farther than anyone in that particular town ever did.

His deferred childhood, extending pretty much through all of his life, will be a shared, wicked delight. No scandal will be large enough to touch him. He will crash cars, change wives, wear funny hats, curse, howl, eat, drink to excess, and belch afterward in public. None of that will matter. Hey, that's the way he is! He will be crude and rude and kind and approachable, sometimes all in the same ten minutes, and it all will be fine. He will be credited with miracles. Fine.

The two best things ever said about him will be said by teammates. The first will be a quote by Harry Hooper, an outfielder for the Boston Red Sox, talking to author Lawrence Ritter in 1965 for a book called *The Glory of Their Times*. Ritter will set up a first-generation tape recorder in the old baseball player's living room in California, and the old baseball player will remember the man who emerged almost from nowhere:

"You know, I saw it all happen from beginning to end. But sometimes I still can't believe what I saw: this 19-year-old kid, crude, poorly educated, only lightly brushed by the social veneer we call civilization, gradually transformed into the idol of American youth and the symbol of baseball the world over—a man loved by more people and with an intensity of feeling that has perhaps never been equaled before or since. I saw a man transformed from a human being into something pretty close to a god. If somebody had predicted that back on the Boston Red Sox back in 1914, he would have been thrown into an insane asylum."

The second quote will come from teammate Waite Hoyt, a pitcher on both the Red Sox and New York Yankees, in a letter to author Robert Creamer. Trying to solicit Hoyt's aid for his 1974 biography, *Babe: The Legend Comes to Life*, Creamer has written a number of letters to the old baseball player. The old baseball player, reluctant until now, will decide to talk, but still has reservations:

"I am convinced YOU WILL NEVER learn the truth on Ruth. I roomed with [Joe] Dugan. He was a good friend of Babe's. But he will see Ruth in a different light than I did. Dugan's own opinion will be one in which Dugan revels in Ruth's crudities and so on. While I can easily recognize all of this and admit it freely—yet there was buried in Ruth humanitarianism beyond belief—an intelligence he was never given credit for, a childish desire to be over-virile, living up to credits given for his home run power—and yet a need for intimate affection and respect—and a feverish desire to play baseball, perform, act and live a life he didn't and couldn't take time to understand. . . .

"There are a HUNDRED facets to Ruth's complex character, yet he was so simple as to be difficult. He was hated, derided by some—and some of the men he played against, or even with, might describe him as nothing short of an immoral boor. Could be . . . but I will argue that point."

He will be a great pitcher. He will be an even greater hitter. He will be a pied piper for children. He will be a rascal in the night. He will be a good husband, a bad husband, an indifferent husband, depending on the moment. He will be a willing but absent father. He will have a million friends. He will have very few. He will be a loner. He will farm, bowl, play golf, hunt, wear a tuxedo for Park Avenue soirees. He will be a profligate spender. He will be a very good businessman. He will never sit down.

For all of his adult years, no one will live a more public life, not even the president of the United States. His schedule will be unremitting. His hide will be tough, his energy constant. His curiosity will work only within tight boundaries. His humor will be basic. His weight will fluctuate. The reports of his death will be greatly exaggerated a half dozen times, but when the moment comes, he will be mourned as if he were a head of state. His cars will be fast. His life will be a wonder. His beginnings will be a closed book.

Why did his father take him to that trolley?

One story, maybe true, maybe not, is that a customer fired a gun in the tavern and that was that, somebody reported to authorities that this was no place for a child to be living. Another story was that the mother was always working and the father was always working and the child was running free, chewing tobacco and sampling beer. Another was that the mother was just out of it, gone, zonked. Who knows what else was taking place?

Who knows?

The early days of a man known as "the Babe" will always be missing. The irony is obvious.

It has been a long trip on the Wilkens Avenue trolley. The activity has decreased with each succeeding stop, commercial to residential, then even the end of that, the familiar row houses disappearing at the 2200 block. The city limits have been passed now, Baltimore City into Baltimore County, green grass and trees. Farms. Agriculture. Rural. Has the boy ever been out here? Have there ever been picnics? The trolley car is open on the sides. The different atmosphere intrudes. A different world. Does anyone notice?

At the appointed stop, the boy gathers his things. Or the man gathers them. Or maybe there are no things.

Man and boy walk down the aisle, go down the steps, and leave the trolley car. Boy first. Or maybe the other way around. They stand in front of the huge gray building, dwarfed by its size. The trolley stop is right in front, almost on the lawn.

"Where the heck are we?" the boy asks.

Or maybe he already knows.

The man begins to explain. Or maybe there is no need. The two of them, man and boy, walk toward the St. Mary's Industrial School for Boys. The trolley departs. The bell goes "ding-ding."

Or maybe it goes "clang."

CHAPTER TWO

ST. MARY'S Industrial School for Boys must have looked like a maximum-security prison to a seven-year-old boy. It did to everyone else. The official name, startling in itself, was St. Mary's Industrial School for Orphans, Delinquent, Incorrigible, and Wayward Boys. The main building was five stories tall, massive, faux-medieval, a gray and grim fortress that ultimately would have a chapel attached at one end, a dormitory at the other, six dark buildings in all. Entry and exit were through iron gates. A wall surrounded the premises.

The 800-plus youthful inhabitants—more than half of them remanded to the institution by local and state courts—moved through their days in military syncopation, all activities run to a schedule. Wake-up was at 6:00 A.M. Bedtime was 8:00 P.M. Obedience was the number-one virtue. The 30-plus members of the Congregation of the Brothers of Francis Xavier, the Xaverians, in charge of all aspects of daily life, walked the premises in long black cassocks, a cross on top of the Sacred Heart of Jesus sewn onto their chests, heavy rosary beads hanging from their belts.

No doubt was left about the idea that this was the end of all nonsense. The seven-year-old George Ruth had landed in an environment controlled by stern and steady hands.

"What do you do with the unruly boy?" a member of the Baltimore grand jury, which inspected the institution three times every year, once asked an unnamed brother described as "a stalwart man."

"I lay them across my knees and give them a good spanking," the brother replied.

The orphanage system in the United States had begun to grow after the Civil War, which left a need to house the children of fallen soldiers from both sides of the conflict. The concept by now had been broadened: the state was in charge of all troubled, disruptive, or unwanted children, fatherless or not, and orphanages or "homes" had sprung up everywhere across the country. Twenty-nine were in Baltimore alone.

St. Mary's Industrial School was established in 1866. The Rev. Martin Spaulding, the Archbishop of Baltimore, asked for the school in response to the state-run orphanages. He was concerned about the large numbers of poor Catholic children, often the sons and daughters of immigrants, who were put into secular homes by the courts after arrests for thievery or mischief. He worried that these children would lose their religion in their new surroundings. St. Mary's was his answer in this fight for their souls.

The Xaverians were members of a religious order started in Belgium in 1846. The order expanded first to England, then to the United States. In the 1880s, Archbishop Spaulding asked the Xaverians to run St. Mary's after the school initially was mismanaged by laymen and local priests. The brothers, though they wore the white Roman collars and the cassocks, were not to be confused with priests. Like priests, they had taken the vows of poverty, chastity, and obedience, but unlike priests, they could not say Mass or hear confession. They were foot soldiers of the Lord, the male equivalent to nuns, enlisted men on the lowest level of the Church's organizational chart.

Any middle-aged graduate of a Catholic, all-boys high school can tell tales of the brothers who taught him. No matter what the religious order, the brothers would range in personality from devout to worldly, from meek to charismatic, from kindly to sadistic. (From manly to effeminate? Yes, that too.) They usually came from working-class families and were called to the religious life for various reasons, not the least of which at the turn of the century was an opportunity for three guaranteed meals a day and a guaranteed roof over their heads.

The Catholic orphanages tended to be large and crowded. A 1904 census noted that Catholic institutions made up less than 27 percent of the nation's orphanages but housed 46.6 percent of the orphan population. Matthew A. Crenson, author of *Building the Invisible Orphanage: A Prehistory of the American Welfare System*, says that Catholic homes tended to keep their charges longer than the other institutions. The Protestant, Jewish, and secular homes would look for adoptive or foster parents, but the administrators of the Catholic homes feared that with a dearth of well-to-do members of the faith, the children would be adopted by wealthier non-Catholic couples. The institutional life also did not seem as oppressive to Catholics as it did to members of other faiths, since priests, brothers, and nuns often lived in the same kind of communal structure.

"The conditions in most of these places were far from idyllic," Crenson said. "They worked these kids pretty hard. The food was rotten. There were lots of starches, very little milk. Lots of oatmeal. Sometimes the kids drank coffee. The food was served in wooden bowls and eaten with the hands or maybe a large wooden spoon. There was no talking in the dining room.

"A lot of the orphanages featured marching drills, like you'd see in those old-fashioned prison movies. Most of them had corporal punishment, usually with leather straps. Solitary confinement up to a week was the punishment for some offenses. Reduced rations. The interesting thing is that a lot of the kids who came out of these places were still okay. Some of them led very successful lives."

St. Mary's fit well into this picture out of the notebooks of Charles Dickens. As many as 200 boys were housed on each dormitory floor, their beds placed end to end in long, perfect rows. This was barracks living with shared lavatories, showers, and common areas. Privacy was nonexistent.

Academics were not a principal consideration. When the Xaverians first took control of the school, only one brother was assigned to classroom teaching, the rest to vocational training. Students under 12 received five hours of academic instruction per day; the number was lowered to three and a half or four hours per day for students over 12. Classes overflowed with 40 or 50 students per brother, everyone working on lessons in chalk on individual slate boards. A fine white dust could be found on most sleeves at the end of classes after countless erasures.

The rest of the day was devoted to work. The trades offered were floriculture, gardening, farming, tailoring, shoemaking and repairing, steamfitting, woodworking, carpentering, baking, and glazing. Instruction also was offered in typewriting and instrumental and vocal music. The students maintained the grounds, cooked the meals, and sewed the very clothes they wore, all under the direction of the Xaverians.

A renovation program in 1912 added a large water tank for the upper floors, a clock and a flagpole topped by a cross on the main building's tower, and a redesigned entrance to the school. Students did all of this. They worked long hours and hard hours.

"I operated 16 different machines," one unnamed resident recalled about his days in the tailor shop. "On one of them, if the bobbin became empty, all 2,000 needles had to be rethreaded, a half-day's work."

Meals were held in silence. The apprehended whisperer was marched to the front of the room, where he had to stand in disgrace until the meal ended. Then he was whipped. ("The whipping didn't hurt so much," the same resident says. "The worst part was just standing there, waiting to be whipped, thinking about it.") The food, indeed, was rotten. Brother John Joseph Stern, CFX, a onetime St. Mary's resident, described the diet in the foreword to *The Young Babe Ruth*, a book written by Brother Gilbert Cairns, CFX, and edited years later by Louisville attorney Harry Rothgerber.

"The food was of the simplest and would probably edify a Trappist monk," Brother John Joseph said. "Breakfast usually consisted of a bowl of oatmeal or hominy. If we received any milk, it would have to be in the oatmeal or in the thin coffee or tea served at all meals. For variety, there was a single pat of butter or oleo on Fridays and three hot dogs, which we called weenies, on Sunday morning. We surely looked forward to Sundays. However, during the week, many a lad would bet away his weenies or promise them in return for some other consideration. I'm sure [George] would have been involved in this 'action.'

"Lunch was a bowl of soup and bread. The bread was usually home-baked and heavy, our own students being the bakers. At times it was necessary to buy regular bread, which we called City Bread. That was before the invention of bread slicing. Supper usually was more soup and bread, though again on Sunday there was a change: three slices of baloney."

Oddly, religious instruction was not a major part of the curriculum. The students attended Sunday Mass and were baptized and received their first Communions and Confirmations, but the example of the Xaverian brothers was supposed to deliver most religious lessons. The brothers delivered daily, sometimes moment-by-moment instruction in right and wrong, yes and no.

One favorite punishment was to send a disobeying boy into the yard to collect a pile of 10,000 pebbles. If a brother found the pile at the end of collection to be too small, he kicked it, sending the pebbles everywhere. The boy then had to begin counting again. He probably gathered enough pebbles this time.

One report estimated the number of severely retarded students in the school at 6 percent, adding that a greater number were "two to five years retarded" from a scholastic norm. The average stay at St. Mary's was two years. Boys were sent back to their families whenever possible and sometimes were sent off to work on farms. The ages ran from 5 to 21, when a boy could check himself out of the institution and into the outside world.

George Ruth, the newest boy, would be an exception to the average. He would wind up spending the best part of his next 13 years at St. Mary's. The "home" truly would become his home.

His nickname from the start was "Nigger Lips." He would hear the word "nigger" infinitely more times in his childhood than Hank Aaron or Barry Bonds or any African American slugger who chased his records ever did. He would hear it more than Jackie Robinson did. The word was his name, often contracted from "Nigger Lips" to "Nigger" to "Nig." Any of the permutations applied. He heard it 100 times a day.

The school was filled with nicknames. Louis "Fats" Leisman, whose pamphlet "I Was with Babe Ruth at St. Mary's" is the one student account of those days, mentions Congo Kirby and Ike Russie and Skinny McCall and Kid Mears and Loads Clark and Lefty Blake in his stories. Nicknames mostly were handed out for obvious physical characteristics, for mistakes or failings, a reach for closeness, a form of friendship through mutual embarrassment. Everybody had a nickname. The more a kid disliked his nickname, the better it fit.

The new kid disliked his a lot.

He had facial characteristics—the lips, the nose—that gave him a mixed-race look in a time and environment when a mixed-race look was not a good thing to have. His skin was "olive like our mother's side of the family," according to sister Mamie, who added that she was "lighter," more like their father's side. The new kid was a darker face in an all-white school.

His size served him well. In an environment filled with troubled kids, confrontation and petty theft and matters of respect always were part of the package. Larger was much better than smaller. His temperament also helped. He was loud and physical and outgoing. Active. He was a boy with chronic ants in his pants.

"He had ADHD, no doubt about it," his granddaughter, Linda Tossetti, suggested years later. "That would be the diagnosis today. My brother had it. He was the same way. Never slept. Two hours of sleep, three hours, that was enough. He would wake me at three in the morning to play with his toys. We would play all night, no one to bother us.

"That was the way my grandfather was. He always was moving. That's how he could eat so much, drink so much, and not be affected. He needed the energy. He would just burn it all off. That's why he would stay out all night. He couldn't sleep, didn't have to sleep."

"He was pretty big for his age," Brother Herman, one of the Xaverians, once said in a description of the 12-year-old Nigger Lips. "Not fleshy, in fact more on the wiry side, he was still an outstanding-looking boy. He had a mop of thick dark-brown hair. He was livelier than most of the boys, full of mischief. There was nothing timid about him. He was an aggressive, shouting boy who was always wrestling around with the others. He held his own, too."

The fog again settles over a lot of his doings at St. Mary's. One version has him in and out of the school a number of times. He would attempt to live with his parents at their latest address, the move would fail, and he would return. Some of the attempts would last months, some a year or two. Mamie's memory from when he was in the school was that she and her mother visited him on a regular basis, taking the Wilkens Avenue trolley on Sunday afternoons.

The Fats Leisman version is very different. Ruth pretty much stayed at St. Mary's from the time he arrived until he was 20 years old, the only exception a failed attempt at living in the St. James Home, sort of a halfway stop toward returning to the everyday world. Leisman also said that Ruth had no visitors.

"Babe would kid me and say, 'Well, I guess I am too big and ugly for anyone to come to see me,' " Leisman wrote about visiting day. " 'Maybe next time.' But next time never came."

The average St. Mary's resident tried a number of jobs before settling into one that seemed to suit him. The one that seemed to suit Nigger Lips was the tailor shop. He became accomplished at sewing shirts, eventually working in the High City Tailor Shop, which manufactured the best clothes. He would, when he made big money, always have an eye and appreciation for a well-made shirt.

His education at the school would be best expressed in his handwriting, always a Catholic school priority. He would write with his right hand, not his natural left, in an elegant script that was fashioned by assorted whacks on his wrist by a brother's wooden ruler.

Only one fight ever has been mentioned, a slug-out with a newly arrived bully, but there must have been numerous discipline situations. An active boy, a loud boy, pleasant-natured as he might have been, would have been fodder for the disciplinary system.

"They took us into a room that had straps lined up against a wall," Jimmie Reese, a friend and teammate of Ruth's with the Yankees and a visitor to St. Mary's years later, said. "They said 'These are the straps we used on Babe Ruth.' "

Again, there is much that is missing about these years. A lot of time passed. Christmases, birthdays, colds, fevers, high points, low points, school events, report cards. What happened? Did he get any presents? Did he sing any carols? Blow out any candles? Ever get an A for anything?

In 1904, two years after he was first enrolled in the school, a massive fire swept through downtown on February 7, the Great Fire of Baltimore. In 31 hours, it destroyed 70 blocks of the city, 1,526 buildings, and put 35,000 people out of work. All of this happened within four or five streets from Pigtown, where the Ruth family lived. Was he at home when it happened, nine or ten years old, terrified, wondering if the conflagration would come his way? Did everyone run to the water? Did everyone run to the fire to help? If he was at school, which was located on one of the highest points around the city, the fire certainly was visible. Was he sitting out there wondering what was happening with his mother, father, and sister? Where was he? Was he scared? Did he care? What happened?

The fog is in the way.

His mother died when he was 17 years old. Was he at home? Was he at school? Did he go to the funeral? Did he stand at the grave at Most Holy Redeemer Cemetery? Did he cry?

The fog is in the way.

He was another boy in the overcrowded system, anonymous and wounded, trying to overcome hard beginnings. He was Nigger Lips. He was ticketed to move along with Fats and Skinny and Congo Kirby and Loads and all the rest, off to find anonymous places in a society filled with anonymous places.

Except, of course, he found baseball.

The fog began to lift.

One version: he played baseball the first day he arrived at St. Mary's. Brother Herman, in charge of athletics, was putting together a game. He spotted a sad-eyed new arrival at the edge of the playground. He called the boy to the group.

"What do you play?"

"Huh?"

"What position do you play? Or don't you care?"

"I don't know. I ain't played."

Brother Herman threw him a catcher's mitt, not knowing the boy was left-handed. The boy put the left-handed mitt on the wrong hand, but was ready to go. A career was born.

Another version:

"The Babe told me that his father had no one to help him in the tavern, which made it very difficult to keep an eye on him," Fats Leisman wrote. "So, like any other boy, he took advantage of this opportunity and would often go out into the streets of South Baltimore and play ball.

"During these ball-playing episodes every now and then he and his teammates would break a window. There were so many complaints coming from the neighbors regarding this situation, and many other mischievous acts, that the Babe's father decided to place him in St. Mary's Industrial School."

The truth: probably less melodramatic than either version.

The figure who drew Nigger Lips to the game—or at least kept him there—was 30-year-old Brother Matthias Boutlier, a charismatic character from Cape Breton, Nova Scotia. He was the Prefect of Discipline, lord over all behavior, punisher of miscreants, a giant of a man, maybe as tall as 6-foot-6, weighing as much as 300 pounds. He was so large that the door to his tiny room had to be hung on the outside of the jamb rather than the inside to accommodate his bed.

He talked and the toughest kids listened. He walked and they watched to see what he would do next. He hit a baseball and their jaws dropped.

"What I think every boy who was at St. Mary's at the time will remember are the Saturday evenings after supper whenever the news got around that Brother Matthias would be hitting baseballs," Brother Thomas More Page, a onetime resident at St. Mary's, remembered in the book by Brother Gilbert and Harry Rothgerber. "Then, every boy in the school from all the five yards would gather in the upper yard, over 500 of us, awaiting the occasion. He would stand at the bottom of the steps and, with what seemed like an effortless motion, hit a ball with the fungo bat in his right hand only, while up and up the ball seemed to soar, almost out of sight, and then when it came down there was a mad scramble for it. We knew the end was coming to this extraordinary exhibition when he hit one ball after the other in rapid succession, and the balls kept falling down like snowflakes over the entire yard."

Who could resist the majesty of that performance? Certainly not the new arrival from Pigtown. He would talk for all of his days about the greatness of Brother Matthias, talk about his strength, talk about the balls he hit, talk the same way people would talk about . . . Babe Ruth.

Here was the birth of the swing that would change baseball. Fungoes are hit with a different, upward motion from the downward chop that was considered the strategic basic of the game. Here was a grand magic trick that made people ooh and aah, not applaud politely. Wouldn't it be great to do that?

Brother Matthias was an accessible hero. The new arrival soon followed the big, tough man almost as a course of nature. The brother ran, it was noticed, with a short, pigeon-toed stride. The new arrival soon ran with a short, pigeon-toed stride. The brother swung the bat in a great, upward arc. The new arrival soon swung the bat in a great, upward arc. The baseballs—when the new arrival was not so new anymore, as he grew bigger and stronger and more proficient—followed the same wondrous course.

Nigger Lips had found the perfect inspiration. He also had found the perfect place to learn and develop. Or perhaps fate had intervened. If he had been a millionaire's son and wanted to be a baseball player, if he had been willing to sacrifice anything toward that goal, he couldn't have gone to a better place than St. Mary's Industrial School for Boys. He was in a veritable baseball academy. Brother John Fidelis, describing the importance of sports at the school, once said that "playing activities is an eighth sacrament." Baseball was the basic liturgical part of that sacrament.

In 1909, for example, 28 uniformed teams played baseball at the school. Other sports were offered—football, soccer, basketball, wrestling, swimming, and boxing among them—but baseball was the winner. There were three times as many baseball teams as basketball teams, five times as many as football. Baseball, in the last few decades of the nineteenth century, had become a national obsession. Teams from different floors in the dorms played against each other at St. Mary's, teams from the different shops, from different classes, and from different age levels played against each other. An elite league had teams named after the Red Sox and other major league teams that played against each other. An all-star team from the school played against high schools and colleges.

A true baseball feeder system existed, a ladder to be climbed on merit. Equipment was not a problem, as it might have been with low-income families in domestic surroundings. The boys even manufactured a low-grade brand of baseball in the shops. Instruction was not a problem. Many of the brothers were young men and still played side by side with the kids. Other brothers, like Brother Matthias, simply coached.

The weak part of learning the game always has been the need for other people. Who will throw pitches to the young batter? Who will track down the baseballs he hits? How will enough people be found, nine on each side, to play a true game? None of these problems existed here. The number of available baseball players was almost inexhaustible. There always was someone at least to play catch or pokenans, the two-man schoolyard game between pitcher and batter.

In a Baltimore climate far milder than the northern cities on the Eastern Seaboard, the season ran for at least ten months. Games could be played into November and December, and be back again in March. Spectators from Violetville and surrounding areas would visit and watch the biggest games, as many as 3,000 spectators in the crowd. There was an importance to baseball that pumped through the school. How do you separate yourself from the rest of the collected urchins, give yourself status, hear some cheers? Baseball was one of the ways, maybe the best way.

For Nigger Lips, baseball was an everyday pleasure. He once said he played over 200 games a year at St. Mary's. He played two and three games a day. He played all the positions, including third base and short, which a left-hander seldom plays. He caught a lot with that wrong-handed glove. When he joked one day about Congo Kirby's pitching, he was asked if he thought he could do better. He pitched. He could do better.

His talent and his size had him playing with kids older than himself. He eventually played with other teams, teams outside the school. He reached a point, somewhere in his teens, where he played more baseball, practiced more baseball, than a professional. He would return to the dorm most days with the shirt torn off his back after an afternoon of baseball and wrestling and running around.

By the fall of 1913, when he was 18 years old (and thought he was 19), he was the absolute king of all of St. Mary's baseball. He was a schoolyard star.

"Ruth, one of the Stars star slabmen, allowed but one hit, that being a two-base hit," the *St. Mary's Evening Star*, the school paper, reported on a normal day, September 30, 1913. "He also struck out 22 and issued but one pass. During the game he hit safely four times."

A catcher for nearby St. Joseph's College named Jack Morgan saw Ruth play and pressured his coach to take a look at this kid. St. Joseph's also was a Xaverian institution, and the coach was Brother Gilbert Cairns. He was reluctant to make the trip, thought it a waste of time, but went to please his catcher. The good brother couldn't believe what he saw.

"Clad in a baseball uniform that was a trifle small for him, there strode up to the plate the most graceful of big men that I have ever seen," he wrote in a 1928 series for the *Boston Globe*. "There was an ease in his manner and a confidence in his gait. With a slight manifestation of nervousness the opposing pitcher turned his back to home plate and waved his outfielders back. He need not have done so; they were already on their way."

The right fielder moved so far back that he left the playing field, crossed a path, and stood in the next field, where another game was taking place. The players in that game stopped playing and stood to watch the events on the first diamond. Nobody seemed to consider this unusual.

The pitcher, finally assured that all was in place, went into his windup and delivered a low curveball. Ruth swung, hard as a person could swing. The ball jumped off his bat, flew out of the field and over the repositioned right fielder's head, caromed off a concrete wall on the side, and went well into the other field. This was a home run, the first of three on the day.

"No baseball acumen was necessary to recognize in Ruth a batter of remarkable promise," Brother Gilbert said. "A 14-year-old boy could have sensed as much."

The doors of St. Mary's were about to open for Nigger Lips. There were places he could go.

The effects of the school on the boy who became famous cannot be overstated. He always would be a child in many ways, a locked-in adolescent forever, stepping out of some weird isolation into a world of pleasures that had been just rumors, whispered after the brothers had turned out the lights. He would be naive and gullible, sometimes navigating through society as if it were a jungle in some far-off land. There were languages, nuances, that he never would understand.

At the same time, there were other languages that he knew quite well. Professional baseball—with its physical, competitive, king-of-the-mountain daily existence, with everything accomplished in the rough company of rough men—would be an extension of the life he always had lived. He was well trained for carrying a lunch box and a thermos every day, for the demands of manual labor. He knew how rough men talked and acted, knew how to draw their praise, knew how to confront their anger, knew how to react to overbearing bosses, knew very well how to survive. He never would be shy. He very well knew the basic world of work that he entered.

His wants and longings while at St. Mary's would drive much of his future behavior. A degree in psychology wouldn't be needed to see that fact. If you never have had enough of anything and everything as a child, how much is needed to fill the hole? Is there ever enough of whatever it might be—food, clothes, love, fun—to make up for all that you have missed? The trail for all of the excesses and successes in the future would be traced back neatly to the big school on the other side of Caton Avenue from Violetville.

Ruth always would speak well of the place. He would stay friendly with many of the brothers. He would buy Brother Matthias a Cadillac for $5,000 in a famous gesture in 1926, then replace it when the car was demolished after it stalled on a railroad track and was hit by a freight train. He would reappear at the school in the following years to participate in exhibitions and fund-raising drives. The story of his troubled beginnings would be served often—along with the starch-filled meals—

at orphanages around the country as a bowlful of hope for the residents. He never would argue with it. Indeed, he would appear at many of these places in his travels, walk their corridors as an orphan king of orphan kids.

The Catholic religion would stay with him, the rhythm of mistakes and redemption perfect for his life of rapidly accumulated venial sins. Three Our Fathers, three Hail Marys, and a good Act of Contrition would clear out his moral digestive system and set him back on the road. He would amaze teammates sometimes when he would appear at Mass in the morning after a night of indulgence. Three Our Fathers, three Hail Marys, a good Act of Contrition, a $50 bill in the collection basket, ready to go. He would become a celebrated member of the Knights of Columbus.

The school would continue to function for 36 more years after he left, but it would evolve into a total reform school as it took more and more money from the state of Maryland. The first two Baltimore natives to die in the coming Great War, Harry Luckman and Albert Vogel, both would be graduates of St. Mary's. Over 3,000 graduates would take part in the war, 572 of them enlisted straight from the school, many of them kids who had been there with Ruth.

The failures in the system sometimes would make headlines. A kid named Leroy Baker, 18 years old, same age and class as Ruth, was arrested in 1912 in Washington after an escape from St. Mary's. He had embarked on a burglary career in Washington, entering at least seven houses in the middle of the night, shining a flashlight into sleeping residents' faces, and holding a gun on them. He then would ask for their money and jewels. When apprehended at a rooming house, he was found reading a *Raffles*, a popular mystery series about a thief, written by Arthur Conan Doyle's brother-in-law, E. W. Hornung. He dropped the book and went for his gun before being subdued.

"I had no money," he said when asked why he had become a robber. "I was hungry."

The most notorious graduate of St. Mary's, Richard Reese Whittemore, would stay for only a year, from 1916 to 1917. Like Ruth, he was sent there as "incorrigible" by distressed parents. In later life he would form a gang responsible for at least nine murders. He would be executed by hanging in 1927 for the murder of a prison guard during a successful escape attempt in 1924.

"The Boy is ever the same," Brother Paul Scanlon, the headmaster, would say at the school's closing in 1950. "The Boy is a crude machine that develops physically from infancy to manhood. The mental growth begins about seven and continues indefinitely. To make this human machine a perfect whole it must be under the supervision and constant direction of the specialists. Every part—heart, mind and body—must have particular attention. The specialists for this are naturally, the parents and the home, the teacher, the school and the church. If these agencies cooperate and the subject is normal, the result generally will be favorable. If one or another of these is remiss it will be the exception if the product is not a failure, or at least imperfect."

For St. Mary's, perhaps imperfection was the best that could be expected. Starting with flawed materials, kids from broken and troubled homes, the Xaverians did the best they could. They tried to bang out as many dents as possible, tried to bring order to young lives that had no order. Compassion was served along with a good crack across the back of the head. The Xaverians shaped up and shipped out their charges, put young adults into the outside world. Their methods worked with some, didn't work with others.

Singer Al Jolson, the other famous onetime resident, a few years before the Babe, a Jewish kid in mostly Catholic surroundings, never liked the place. He returned to St. Mary's with his wife in 1949, more than 50 years after he left, to show her his strict beginnings. He was amazed to see the front gate open.

"It was always shut when I was here," he said. "There were bars all around."

"Was Al a bad boy?" his wife, Erle, asked Brother Benjamin, a teacher from Jolson's days still at the institution.

"He was like other boys," the brother replied. "Some boys run away from Harvard too, you know."

In 1919 sparks from a tinner's torch would start a fire during repairs on the roof of the administration building. The water pressure wasn't strong enough to reach the fire, and the administration building, a dorm, the junior building, and the old chapel were destroyed. Ten boys, trapped in the tower of the administration building, had to slide down a rope to safety, but injuries were minor and no student died. Virtually all of the school records were destroyed, including the ones that detailed the progress of the boy from Pigtown.

At the height of the fire, Brother Theodore, the head of the school, gathered the student population in the courtyard. He asked everyone to pray.

"I prayed," one student remembered. "But I prayed the place would burn down."

CHAPTER THREE

THE MAN who freed Nigger Lips from the St. Mary's Industrial School for Boys was Jack Dunn of the minor league Baltimore Orioles. He was 42 years old, a baseball man, had been a player and then a manager, and now was the owner of the Orioles. He was a bit of a baseball genius.

When he was nine years old, playing with a bunch of kids at a railroad siding in Bayonne, New Jersey, a boxcar ran over his left arm. The kids had uncoupled the car, and it started to roll slowly. As Dunn jumped to get free, his foot caught in the track, and he was thrown back and the car rolled over the arm. Doctors told his mother and him that the arm had to be amputated or he would die.

"If it makes no difference to you, I'd just as soon die with my arm on," the nine-year-old declared.

His mother agreed. There was no operation. He didn't die, was brought back to health, but the arm was left in a strange condition. Below the elbow, everything functioned fine. Above the elbow, the arm was crippled. He couldn't lift it higher than his neck. Also, a running wound on his shoulder refused to heal for the next 20 years. Surgery was prescribed. Dunn again refused. Even then he wanted to be a baseball player and didn't want to risk any further loss of motion.

With his withered left arm and its limited abilities, he still played eight years in the big leagues as a shortstop, third baseman, and right-handed pitcher. He learned tricks, ways to overcome his restrictions at both the plate and in the field. He became a conniver, a schemer, a student of the game, working all of its angles and shortcuts simply to survive. He learned extra lessons as a pitcher. Never a hard thrower, he had to study other players, figure out their tendencies, look for weaknesses and take advantage.

All of this helped when he became a manager, winning an International League pennant in Providence in 1905, and then, after mortgaging everything he had, as both the owner and manager of the Orioles. Studying players, he developed preferences for body types, for a "look." He liked big, agile, rangy athletes. (Unlike himself, it should be noted. He was 5-foot-9 and slender.) He was unorthodox and confident in his selections. He would sign players to a contract on sight alone, simply by how they presented themselves.

He would check out the player the way a trainer or potential buyer might look at a young Thoroughbred horse. If he liked the player's size, the way the player moved just walking across a room, he might make an offer. Dunn sometimes never even saw the player play a game, but the amazing part was that he seldom was wrong.

In this case, a respected referral came from Brother Gilbert. Dunn was trying to sign a highly regarded left-handed pitcher named Ford Meadows from the brother's team at St. Joseph's. The brother wanted to keep Meadows, who was a senior, for one last season. In trying to send Dunn elsewhere, Brother Gilbert suggested an alternative . . . there was this kid at St. Mary's Industrial School, you see, a left-handed pitcher who was too good to believe. Dunn already had heard about a talented kid at the school from Joe Engel, a pitcher for the Washington Senators. Engel said that he played against the kid, who not only was terrific but at the end of the game had joined the band and played a big bass drum. Dunn was interested.

There are various descriptions of what happened next. A story is told by Fats Leisman of a legendary game played solely for Jack Dunn's benefit at St. Mary's, and Nigger Lips running away from the school, then returning to pitch a shutout and sign a contract. Ruth in his ghost autobiography mentions no game, says he pitched for half an hour in a workout for Dunn before he signed. The account of Brother Gilbert and

Rodger Pippen, a *Baltimore American* sportswriter and friend of Dunn's, is much more romantic. Maybe it is even true. In this story, Dunn went to St. Mary's on a February day accompanied by Brother Gilbert and Fritz Maisel, a Baltimore native who now was the third baseman and captain of the New York Yankees. They traveled in Maisel's big-time car, which had been purchased with big league money. Dunn never had seen Ruth play.

Brother Gilbert was nervous. He had recommended Nigger Lips as a pitcher, but never had seen him pitch. The big kid was a wrong-handed catcher on that one day when Brother Gilbert saw him. Admittedly he looked like he had a very good arm, and he was amazingly adept at removing the ball from the wrong-handed mitt and rifling it to second on a line, all in one motion, but could he pitch? People said he could. Brother Gilbert didn't know.

The little group of Brother Gilbert, Dunn, and Maisel ran into Brother Matthias as they searched for Ruth. They all chatted a bit about the subject. Brother Matthias was not a flamboyant conversationalist.

"Ruth can hit," was his scouting report.

"Can he pitch?" Dunn asked.

(Brother Gilbert held his breath.)

"Sure," Brother Matthias said. "He can do anything."

And so it happened. The group found Ruth, wearing overalls, making his one fashion statement with rings on three fingers, sneaking a chew of tobacco, sliding on the ice, fooling around with a couple of kids outside the tailor's shop. Introductions were made. The calibrations, based on a lifetime of making calibrations, whirred inside Dunn's head. The numbers and memories said that Ruth, large and lean and ambitious, was the ideal baseball candidate. It was as easy as that. Dunn settled down to do business.

The man who never had seen the potential pitcher play a game, on the recommendation of a man who never had seen the potential pitcher throw a pitch, offered a contract for $250 per month to the potential pitcher. The potential pitcher, who never had seen a professional game, who never really had known that money could be made from playing baseball, accepted immediately.

It was a grand and odd transaction, all at once, and took place on February 14, 1914. The date at least was documented. Two weeks later, George Herman Ruth, the legal ward of Brothers Gilbert and Paul, under the guardianship of baseball manager and owner Jack Dunn, was on his way to spring training.

Where to begin with the new sights and sounds and tastes and smells and experiences that awaited the 19-year-old boy? The Orioles were heading to Fayetteville, North Carolina, and he went to the train at Union Station on March 2, 1914—the train, yes, would be a good place to start—in a blizzard, breathing free and different air. He had new clothes, a new suitcase, had money in his pocket, and was outside the walls and on his own for the first time in his life, heading into a horizon he had seen only from afar.

"Since I signed with you, I've played eight games," he informed Jack Dunn at the station.

This was winter. Eight games?

"And your arm isn't sore?" Dunn asked.

"No, sir, Mr. Dunn," the 19-year-old boy replied. "We had some snow this winter, and I was the commander of Fort McHenry in the snowball fights. My arm doesn't get sore."

He never had ridden a train. He never had been able to pick from a menu, then pick again and again, as much as he wanted. He never had done a lot of things. Dunn did not take the train, waiting to lead a second group of players south, including the ones who had not been able to reach Baltimore due to the blizzard. Scout Steinman, an old-timer who took care of odd jobs with the team, was in charge of the first group. Off it went.

The veterans pulled the requisite old tricks on the newcomers on the ride, and the newcomers wound up in the requisite foolish situations, guarding their shoes during the night from the porters, who surely would try to steal them, counting off the towns loudly toward Fayetteville. Ruth fell for everything. He spent his night with his left arm in the hammock over his upper berth, told that it was a special conditioning contraption for pitchers rather than a place to store clothes.

Fayetteville was a warm marvel. The temperature was 70 degrees. The men in town already were wearing straw hats in the middle of March. How can this be? Everything was a marvel. The Orioles checked into the Hotel Lafayette, where Ruth was fascinated by the elevator, riding up and down for days, leaving the door open, sticking his head out—watch it!—

pulling back just in time to avoid serious injury. He was up in the mornings at five, familiar time for St. Mary's, early for everywhere else, and down at the train station to watch the activity. He walked early to the Cape Fear Fairgrounds, where practice was held in a field next to the racetrack. He ate prodigious amounts of food at every sitting, buckwheat cakes piled into a syrup-drenched tower, gone in a moment, seconds on the way.

He was as raw as any kid who ever had stepped off any farm into this situation. He was very happy.

"He looked like a big, overgrown Indian," Fred Parent, a former big league shortstop brought to the camp to work with the younger players, said. "He really had a dark complexion. He seemed to be really a happy-go-lucky kind of kid, made acquaintance easily. He had a really big voice. You'd think he weighed 500 pounds with that voice, and it grew bigger as he grew older."

His nickname, the nice one, the one that would stick and become famous, arrived early. There are assorted versions of the story about when and how it arrived during the camp, but the one that is tidiest and, again, maybe even true has interim leader Steinman telling the veterans to take it easy with the new kid because "he's one of Dunnie's babes." Rodger Pippen and Jesse Linthicum of the *Baltimore Sun* were in camp, heard Steinman use the word, and began to refer to "Babe Ruth" in their reports. It was not an uncommon nickname at the time. The babe officially was the Babe.

Some of the first newspaper stories that mentioned his name came after the first scrimmage at the fairgrounds. The team was divided in two, the Buzzards against the Sparrows, and he played a left-handed shortstop and pitched a few innings. He also hit the longest home run in Fayetteville history.

A white post had been planted at the edge of right field to mark a spot where Jim Thorpe, the decathlon champion in the 1912 Olympics, now with the New York Giants, once had hit a ball while playing in the Carolina League. In the seventh inning against the Sparrows, Ruth hit a ball that went past the post and over the racetrack and into a cornfield. The ball was hit so far that right fielder Bill Morrisette said he refused to retrieve it unless given cab fare. Rodger Pippen, 26 years old and filling in as a spare center fielder in the game, measured the distance. He said the ball had traveled 428 feet.

"The main topic of conversation is the work of Lefty Ruth and the prodigious hit he made in practice yesterday afternoon," Pippen wrote in the *Baltimore American*. The rival *Baltimore Sun* had a two-column headline that read "Homer by Ruth Feature of Game." Notable was the fact that his first headlines in professional baseball were for hitting, not pitching.

In his free time, he still roared. He was one of the players duped in a little roulette wheel operation a local resident set up in a room in the Lafayette. He tried horseback riding. Since he never had ridden, the man at the stables gave him a Shetland pony for starters. Ruth rode the pony into the local drugstore, where his teammates were relaxing at the soda fountain. He said he wanted to buy two ice cream cones, one for himself and one for the horse. The owner said he didn't serve horses. Then there was the bicycle. Ruth convinced a local kid to let him borrow his bicycle every day. He rode it tirelessly around the town. He rode quite fast.

Jack Dunn and veteran catcher Ben Egan were standing at a street corner when Ruth came flying past, ran straight into the back of a hay wagon, was thrown six feet in the air, and landed on his back. Dunn ran to his newest acquisition and delivered some loud guidance.

"You wanna go back to that school?" he shouted. "You behave yourself, you hear me? You're a ballplayer—not a circus act."

Dunn had fallen in love with the kid. The exhibition games had started, and Ruth very much could pitch. He pitched well in scrimmages, a hard thrower with a workable curveball to back up his speed. He pitched well in relief against the Yankees. He pitched a complete game, a 6–2 win, against the Philadelphia Athletics, who had the best-hitting lineup in baseball. He also assuredly could hit. He could be fooled sometimes and look bad in striking out, but when he caught the ball, it traveled.

Talent like this did not just show up, well sanded and finished. Talent was supposed to be wild, and time was needed to tame it. Here was a kid who came straight out of school and could beat the Athletics. This just didn't happen.

"Brother," Dunn wrote to Brother Gilbert, "this fellow Ruth is the greatest young ballplayer who ever reported to a training camp."

"He'll startle the baseball world," the owner told the writers quietly, "if he isn't a rummy or he isn't a nut."

Spring training was short. Twenty-six days after he left, the boy from

St. Mary's was back in Baltimore. He was a secret no more. He was Babe Ruth. The newspapers said he was.

His first purchase back in the city was an Indian motorcycle for $115. His first trip on the motorcycle was to St. Mary's Industrial School for Boys. His first fall off the motorcycle . . . well, there were a few of them before he reached St. Mary's. The final one was in front of the school. Brother Matthias saw the whole thing. Ruth landed in a puddle next to some horse droppings.

"Oh, too bad," the brother said with a smile. "Now you're wet and dirty."

Muttering about the city's sanitation practices in regard to horse droppings, the returned world explorer went back inside the grounds looking much the same as he always did after a normal school day. He revved up his beast and proceeded to take his friends for rides, blasting around the streets with the kids from his past hanging on for dear life in his newly discovered present. Talk about satisfaction.

He embarked on his postgraduate baseball degree as the Orioles played two weeks of local exhibitions, then moved into their International League season. Every day was a new lesson.

He pitched the third of three exhibitions against John McGraw's Giants, losing 3–2 in a classic moment of miscommunication. With one out in the ninth, a runner on first, the Orioles ahead 2–1, catcher Egan gave the prearranged clenched-fist sign for "a waste pitch," a pitchout. He sensed a hit-and-run might be taking place. To Egan's surprise, Ruth delivered a pitch over the dead center of the plate that was whacked by Red Murray over the left-field fence for a two-run homer and the victory.

Egan was mad. Ruth was mad.

He thought Egan had ordered a "waist" pitch. That was exactly where he delivered it, right at the waist. Didn't the catcher know any better than that?

(A similar story was told by Fred Parent about "waist-waste" confusion in a game against the Buffalo Bisons. Parent said Bill Congalton hit that pitch for a triple. One of the stories is probably true. The pick here is Egan's.)

Ruth then pitched the second game of the season, a 6–0 shutout of the Bisons, and went to work in the regular rotation. He mixed startlingly good games with occasional stinkers, all part of learning. He hit well at times, but also had periods when he struggled. There were no Fayetteville homers. The best part was that he continued to take that big uppercut swing, and no one tried to change him.

The Orioles went on the road, and more adventures arrived in a kaleidoscope whirl. He was in Buffalo and Rochester, Toronto and Montreal, Jersey City and Newark. New towns, new country, new language. (Just the picture of him walking around Montreal is a smile.) The Orioles who had survived the final roster cuts were a veteran group, with only Dunn's son, Jack Jr., close to Ruth's age. Ruth played cards, was included in a clique of Baltimore-born players, but also spent a lot of time in his own travels.

A perfect story from Creamer's book found him sitting on the curb outside the Forrest Hotel on West 49th Street in New York at two in the morning. Outfielder George Twombley, coming home, saw him there.

"What are you doing?" Twombley asked.

"I'm waiting for a girl," Ruth replied.

"What girl?"

"I don't know. I'm just waiting. The boys at reform school said if you're in New York and you want a woman, all you have to do is wait for a streetwalker to come along."

"Maybe you should go to bed."

The team Dunn had put together was very good. On July 4, 1914, it was in first place in the International League with a 47–22 record. Ruth had a 14–6 record and was hitting long shots when he connected with the ball, which wasn't too often. Alas, nobody in Baltimore had noticed or cared. The total number of local people who had seen Babe Ruth perform in his debut year was under 5,000.

A new restaurant in the neighborhood had taken all of the old restaurant's business. Directly across the street from the Orioles' home at Back River Park was Terrapin Park, the newly built home of the new Baltimore Terrapins of the new Federal League. The citizens of Baltimore, chagrined that the once-proud Orioles had been dropped from the major leagues in 1903 for lack of support (the franchise shifted to New York, a sign that Baltimore had fallen to second-class status), saw the new league as an answer. They thought the Federal League would evolve into a third major league and the Terrapins would be a proud member. The day Ruth confronted the "waist-waste" problem, 28,000 people were across the street watching the Terrapins. Fewer than 1,000 watched him battle the fabled Giants. He later pitched a shutout against Rochester with only 11 paid customers in the stands. Even the vendors had gone across the street to work the more profitable crowd in the park that had been built in slightly more than three months, paint still drying as it opened.

Dunn estimated he was losing $1,000 per day. He was a baseball businessman, not a rich man. He had put up his life's savings, plus a $10,000 loan from Philadelphia Athletics owner Connie Mack, to buy the team. This cash drain could not continue. Faced with bankruptcy, he took a solid business approach: he decided to sell off his assets. His assets were his players.

One of the first he tried to sell, alas, was his discovery from St. Mary's. In Newark for a Sunday doubleheader, Dunn invited Mack to come up from Philadelphia to take another look at the kid who had beaten the A's in spring training. Dunn started the kid in the first game, but the kid was shaky, gone by the fourth inning. No matter. Dunn started him again in the second game. The kid pitched a 1–0 shutout.

"He's everything you say he is," Mack told Dunn at the end. "In fact, he's worth more money than you're asking. But . . ."

Mack also had financial problems and at the end of the year would sell off his own stars. Dunn had to look elsewhere.

He had an offer from the Cincinnati Reds for a package including Ruth, and John McGraw had expressed interest, but Dunn wound up doing business with the Red Sox. Owner Joe Lannin had advanced Dunn $3,000 to make a payroll, which didn't hurt negotiations. The Red Sox also were in Washington for a July 4 doubleheader, a stroke of good timing.

At the Ebbett House Hotel in Washington, Dunn and Lannin hammered out the cash deal. The announced price was $25,000 for Babe Ruth, Ben Egan, and Ernie Shore, another young pitcher who had joined the Orioles in June after graduating from Guilford College. In later years, later stories, the price was dropped to $12,500 or $8,500 plus the cancellation of the loan.

"Ring up three sales on the cash register," Dunn sadly told a friend. "I'm no longer a retailer."

He hurried back to Baltimore to catch the end of the Orioles' game with Montreal. He called Ruth, Egan, and Shore to his office when the game finished. He gave them the news that they were going to the big leagues, to the Red Sox. Egan and Shore were excited. Ruth was dumb-founded. Dunn asked him to stay in the office after the other two players left.

The owner explained his situation, that he had no choice. He told Ruth, whom he'd given a raise to $350 a month when the season started, that the figure now was $500 and that when he hit Boston that would jump to $625. He said the major leagues were the place to be, the place where the big money resided.

Ruth said he didn't care about the money; he wanted to stay close to home. This was what he knew. This was where his friends were. He still was playing baseball at St. Mary's sometimes on the same days he played for the Orioles. His team was in first place at both St. Mary's and in the International League. Boston? He had never been to Boston. He didn't know anything about Boston. With the Red Sox on the road, his departure delayed, Ruth still kept playing left field for the Orioles every day until it was time to go to Boston. Dunn wished him good luck.

On July 10, he was on an overnight train with Shore and Egan to his new home. Bill Wickes, the secretary for the Orioles, traveled with them. His job was to make sure that no agent from the Federal League offered them a contract on the trip.

In rapid succession, according to legend, Ruth stepped off the Federal Express at Back Bay station in Boston at 10:00 A.M. on July 11, 1914, said good-bye to the bodyguard, went across Dartmouth Street with Ernie Shore, ordered a breakfast of ham and eggs at Landers Coffee Shop from the 16-year-old waitress he soon would marry, stopped off at the Red Sox offices on Devonshire Street, went to Fenway Park, was fitted for a uniform, was told he was going to start that afternoon against the Cleveland Naps, then pitched seven innings to record his first major league win, 4–3. Presumably, he then ate another good meal, unpacked his suitcase at the Brunswick Hotel, and slept very well that night.

The ham-and-eggs meeting with his future bride might be shaky—other accounts suggest it took place on another day or perhaps in another situation—but the rest is true. He had an eventful arrival in the capital of Massachusetts.

A picture in the *Boston Globe* taken before the game, under the caption "New Red Sox Players from Baltimore," shows him staring at the camera with the solemn disposition of a Supreme Court justice considering an important case. Egan, who would never play a game for the Red Sox and was soon dealt to the Naps, is laughing. Shore, 6-foot-4, lanky, has a small smile. Ruth indeed looks like a young man who has just been told he is going to start his first major league game.

Behind the plate for the game was 31-year-old player-manager Bill Carrigan. A Holy Cross graduate from Lewiston, Maine, quiet and firm, he was the perfect candidate to catch the new arrival. His friend Fred Parent had advised him from Baltimore to catch Ruth, who needed more guidance, and to have Forrest Cady, another catcher, work with Shore, who was a more finished product. Parent predicted immediate success for Shore and long-term success for Ruth.

"If I remember, Babe was crude in spots," Carrigan said years later, describing Ruth's debut to *Boston Record* sportswriter Joe Cashman. "Every so often he served up a fat pitch or bad pitch when he shouldn't have. But he showed a lot of baseball savvy. He picked a runner off third base. He also cut off a throw from the outfield and threw a runner out at second. Anybody could see he'd quickly develop into a standout with a little more experience. He had a barrel of stuff, his speed was blinding, and his ball was alive."

The cutoff play came in the first inning of his first major league game. Naps leadoff hitter Jack Graney singled, then went to second on a ground ball. Shoeless Joe Jackson, the third batter, singled in front of Tris Speaker in center field. Speaker, who had a wonderful arm, fielded the ball and threw toward home. Jackson made the turn at first and started to head for second.

Ruth, 19 years old, saw in an instant that (a) Graney had pulled up at third in fear of Speaker's arm and (b) Jackson had made the turn. He cut off the throw and rifled the ball to second. Jackson stopped, retreated to first, and was followed by a throw from second. Graney made a break for home. First baseman Dick Hoblitzel threw to Carrigan, nailing Graney at the plate.

This was cerebral defensive baseball executed at a high level. It was part of what mistakenly in years to come would be called Ruth's "great baseball instincts," a term that always would make him sound like some idiot savant, some animal of nature. ("He never throws to the wrong base" would be a common remark.) The truth was that this was what he had learned, what he knew, from all of those games at St. Mary's. He had practiced this. He knew it.

"The Red Sox pulled off a clever play in the first when Graney lost a fine chance for scoring," baseball writer Tim Murane said in the next day's *Globe*. "Ruth was strong in the play."

Shore pitched the next day and threw a two-hitter, beating the Naps 2–1. Ruth had a second start a week later against the Detroit Tigers and was knocked out in three innings. Shore had a second start and beat the St. Louis Browns 6–2, giving up seven hits and striking out five. He also won the one open spot in the Red Sox rotation.

Carrigan, it seems, had given his two young arrivals a fast audition. Shore was the winner. The fact that he was right-handed helped, because top starters Dutch Leonard and Ray Collins were both left-handed, but he also had pitched better. Parent was right. Shore was the finished product.

Ruth was moved to the bench. The idea of the relief specialist, consistently coming into games in the middle or at the end, was not a part of baseball thinking. The starters started and pitched complete games if they could. The other pitchers mostly sat.

For the first time, Ruth became an extra man. The Red Sox went on the road for a long stretch, hitting Cleveland, Chicago, St. Louis, and Detroit, winning 10 of 15 games, and he never left the bench. This was a veteran team, making a midseason run at the Philadelphia Athletics. Another left-hander, veteran Vean Gregg, was acquired from the Naps, and Ruth's seat became even more secure.

He was pretty much on his own. Dunn in Baltimore had taken the duties of guardian seriously, but there was no guardian here. Egan watched over him a bit until leaving for Cleveland after two weeks, and no one else took the job. Ruth was younger than everyone else (Shore was four years older, plus a college graduate) and didn't fit. The baseball culture always likes its rookies to be quiet and appreciative of all favors. He was noisy and confident, forced his way into the rotation for batting practice, did things rookies weren't supposed to do. He found his bats sawed in half one day.

One of his nicknames among the veterans like Smokey Joe Wood and Tris Speaker became "the Big Baboon." Not a term of endearment, it was more like another statement about his mixed-race features, a cousin to "Nigger Lips." Shortstop Jack Barry, when he came to the team a year later, would say the words "Big Baboon" sotto voce every day during team meetings. Big Baboon. Big Baboon. Big Baboon. This only stopped when Ruth, tears in his eyes, stood and challenged whoever had said it to step up and fight. Barry never moved.

"I felt sorry for the kid," outfielder Harry Hooper said. "I went up to Barry afterward and told him that I knew it was him. I said if he didn't stop it, I would tell the kid who was doing it."

Ruth lived in a rooming house on Batavia Street and had to find his own friends and entertainment. He found the waitress at Landers Coffee Shop. Her name was Helen Woodford, and the fog settles in a bit around her. She lived in South Boston, was born in East Boston, maybe had lived for a while in Meredith, New Hampshire, and her parents were from Newfoundland. Or maybe Galveston, Texas. She was pretty and available. In the long tradition of lonely young men in faraway towns and bored waitresses looking for adventure, the baseball player and the South Boston girl became a couple.

"He didn't drink when he came to Boston," Hooper said. "And I don't think he'd ever been with a woman. Once he found out about it, though, he became a bear."

On July 30, 1914, an important event happened in Chicago. At the American League offices, Red Sox owner Joe Lannin made another purchase, picking up the Providence franchise in the International League for $75,000. Ruth had a place to go. He pitched and won a couple of exhibition games in Lawrence, Massachusetts, and Manchester, New Hampshire, for the Red Sox at the start of August, his first action in almost a month, and on August 18 he finally cleared waivers and reported to the Providence Grays, also known as the Clamdiggers.

He wasn't excited about the change, especially with Helen Woodford in his social plans, but Providence was the perfect place for him. He not only returned to work but returned to tons of work. The Clamdiggers were in a chase for the pennant, and he soon was pitching every third or fourth day. In his first start, 12,000 people overflowing the stands at Melrose Park, he pitched nine innings and helped win his own game with a triple in the bottom of the ninth that traveled so far that "a thousand straw hats were lost in the wild demonstration of joy that signalized the longest hit ever made at the ball park," according to the *Providence Journal*.

In six weeks he won nine games, lost three. In one stretch he pitched four games in eight days. He was 12-for-40 at the plate, a .300 average. He hit his first professional home run in Toronto, a shot that went over the right-field fence at Hanlan's Point Stadium and landed in Lake Ontario. The Grays/Clamdiggers took the International League pennant and finished with an exhibition against the Chicago Cubs at Rocky Point Park in Warwick, Rhode Island. Ruth pitched a complete game, an 8–7 win, and hit a home run that landed this time in Narragansett Bay. A small boy fell into the water trying to retrieve the ball.

And then the Babe went back to Boston.

The city was afire with baseball interest, but that interest did not involve the Red Sox. The Boston Braves, the other team in the city, were in the midst of pulling off the greatest comeback in baseball history. Losers of 18 of their first 22 games, in last place on July 4, they now were running away with the National League pennant. Their home games had been switched, with Red Sox owner Lannin's consent, to the newer Fenway Park with its greater capacity, and the team was known as "the Miracle Braves."

Ruth rejoined the Red Sox in the play-it-out stage, the A's already champs by a wide margin, the Red Sox locked into second. He pitched two games in the last week, winning one, losing the other, and was done. It had been quite a year.

The boy who had left the closed environment of St. Mary's School on March 2, 1914, to take his first train ride had now lived in three different cities and played for three different teams. He had traveled to at least a dozen cities, slept in starched sheets, sat in hot tubs and smoked a cigar whenever he wanted. He had won 26 games and lost 8 in the International League. He had won two and lost one in the American League. He had hit one professional home run, but none in the United States. Elevators no longer were a great mystery.

Somewhere in all of this he had asked Helen Woodford to marry him, and somewhere she had said yes, and he bought a car and they drove down to Ellicott City, Maryland, and said "I do" to each other on October 17, 1914. Some people said they already were married, had done the deed in the middle of the season in Providence, but that didn't matter. They were too young, 19 and 16, to get married in the first place, doomed to failure, but that was part of being young.

There is no record of a honeymoon. He and Helen went to Baltimore and—the fog comes in here again—spent the winter over his father's bar on Conway Street at the edge of Pigtown. His father? Had he made peace with his father? How had that happened? His father had remarried. Had that settled the situation? Fog.

Yes, quite a year.

CHAPTER FOUR

O N T H E N I G H T of May 6, 1915, a black-tie banquet was held at Carnegie Hall in New York City as the Civic Forum awarded its gold medal to 68-year-old Thomas Alva Edison. The inscription on the medal was "Inventor and World Benefactor." President Woodrow Wilson and ex-presidents Theodore Roosevelt and William Howard Taft sent congratulations, as did Alexander Graham Bell. Guglielmo Marconi and a host of dignitaries spoke.

The list of Edison's accomplishments ran long, from the electric lights that illuminated the evening to the movie cameras that recorded the speeches to the phonographs that sat back at every home. The white-haired old man, who declined to speak, listened quietly to the compliments delivered in the environment he had altered, if not fully created.

"He has made more men and women and children laugh than any other man, and has made it possible for more people to be amused than has anyone else in the history of the world," former New Jersey governor J. Franklin Fort said. "Nothing is impossible to Edison . . . he is an uncrowned king among men."

In the Bronx that very afternoon, a subway ride from these proceedings, the start of another advance in amusement and laughter had begun. Babe Ruth, destined himself to be another uncrowned king among men, had begun to reinvent the home run four games into his second professional baseball season.

The moment wasn't exactly on a par with the creation of the lightbulb or Alexander Graham Bell's "Mr. Watson, come here, I want you," but in the measured confines of baseball it was the start of a seismic shift that eventually would turn the game upside down. In the third inning, leading off, batting ninth in the order, no one on base, Ruth measured the "rise ball" of New York Yankees pitcher Jack Warhop and clocked it into the right-field stands at the Polo Grounds for home run number one in his major league career.

Warhop, a tiny man, was a figure from baseball's past. One writer said that he was so small the grounds crew at the Polo Grounds cut the grass down an inch and raised the pitching mound two inches just so the paying customers could see him. He was in his eighth and final big league season, 31 years old, a craftsman, a manipulator with a submarine delivery that unleashed the soft and dead 1915 baseball. He was a coy strategist, a participant in the chesslike game that baseball always had been.

The Babe—"built like a bale of cotton" was one description—was the arrival of the baseball future. Chess? He would turn the table over, let the pieces clatter to the floor. That was how he would end games. Strength and brawn had stepped to the front.

No one knew, of course, at the time of his homer—certainly not the Babe—that this was a first baby step in that direction. Like most home runs of the era, it seemed to be another odd confluence of physical forces wrapped in a good bit of luck. No one *tried* for home runs, they just happened—something like lightning striking the oak tree on the lawn.

The leading home run hitters a year earlier had been Frank "Home Run" Baker of the A's in the American League with eight and Gavvy Cravath of the Philadelphia Phillies with 18 in the National. The Red Sox as a team had hit 17. The total number of home runs in the American League was 160, an average of 20 per team.

The balls were not made for home runs. They also were scuffed up, roughed up, spit upon, and used for as many as 100 pitches in a game. The bats, heavy and thick through the handle, were not made for home runs. The mind was not made for home runs. A line drive was perfection. A fly ball was a mistake. A bunt was a grand strategic tool. Batting average was the true test of a player's worth.

"The little things of baseball are all important," F. C. Lane declared in

Baseball America in 1913, a statement of strategic thinking. "And whether or not they seem sensible to the veteran player, who is inclined to view all scientific analysis of his work as so much bunk, there is in reality no more fascinating theme in the whole range of sport."

Frank Baker, whose "Home Run" nickname came from a pair of important home runs in the 1911 World Series, never hit more than 12 in a season. He was asked years later how many he might have hit if he had played a year under the conditions that developed.

"I'd say 50," he said. "The year I hit 12, I also hit the right-field fence at Shibe Park 39 times."

The home run was such an oddity in 1913 that just that day in Boston, Gertrude Halladay Leonard, chairman of the Massachusetts Woman Suffrage Association, had issued a curious proposition for the members of both the Red Sox and the Boston Braves.

> For the two-fold purpose of showing our sincere interest in the good work of our home teams and of identifying the home teams with the equal suffrage movement in Massachusetts in the minds of all lovers of our national game, we desire to make the following offer, good for the entire season:
>
> For every home run made on the home grounds by a home player during this season the Massachusetts Woman Suffrage Association will mail a check for $5, payable to the player.

Five bucks for catching lightning in a bell jar. Five bucks for hitting a ball over the fence. The suffragettes—the "suffs"—were looking for some publicity and some support in their effort to ratify the Nineteenth Amendment, women's right to vote, which was part of the coming state elections. Little did they know they were on the first floor of a second cultural revolution.

The announcement of the beginning was in the *New York Times* the next day.

"Mr. Edison has been of great service to his country and to the world," the *Times* editorialized on page 12. "Besides his improvement in the means of telegraphic communication, the incandescent lamp, the phonograph in all its forms, and the kinetoscope, which made the moving picture possible, are directly due to his wonderful skill as an originator or adaptor."

"He [Ruth] put his team in the running by smashing a mighty rap into the upper tier of the right-field grand stand," the *Times* said on page 11. "Ruth also had two other hits to his credit."

Twenty-seven days later, back at the Polo Grounds, the confrontation was repeated, Warhop on the mound, Ruth at the plate. In the second inning, man on first, Ruth unloaded a longer, higher shot into the right-field grandstand. This was number two. Yankees manager Wild Bill Donovan ordered him walked intentionally his next two times at the plate. The amusement of men, women, and children had begun.

The May 6 game, the day he hit his first homer, also had a more immediate consequence for Ruth: it put him into the Red Sox pitching rotation. A spare part in spring training at Hot Springs, Arkansas, destined to pitch during stretches of doubleheaders and from the bullpen, he had been given the start that day owing to injuries (Carl Mays, Dutch Leonard, and Smokey Joe Wood) and ineffectiveness (Ray Collins). A well-regarded pitching staff had become vulnerable during the first month of the season.

Ruth's complete-game performance in 13 innings against the Yankees, even though it ended with a 4–3 loss, was enough to give manager-catcher Bill Carrigan confidence in him. He moved into the rotation and stayed.

The pitcher who had emerged from that first professional year in Baltimore-Boston-Providence-Boston was not a Jack Warhop stylist. The players who faced him said that he threw with an easy three-quarters delivery and threw hard. He definitely was a fastball pitcher. His fastball had a late hop, a jump when it crossed the plate. He had a solid curveball, mixed in a changeup every once in a while, and had just enough wildness to make a batter feel uncomfortable. He was not afraid to throw at a person's head—Carrigan would yell from behind the plate when it was coming—and was not afraid of consequences.

"He looked like a prizefighter on the mound," Del Pratt of the St. Louis Browns, later a teammate, said. "That was the way he was built."

The batters he faced pretty much were nameless. The ADHD meant he had trouble with names throughout his life, busy-busy-busy, never taking time to remember them. He didn't remember the names of most teammates, much less the opposition. (Anyone under a certain age was named "Kid," pronounced "keed." Anyone over that age was "Doc.") Conferences before the game, the little meetings to discuss strategies, were meaningless.

Carrigan would try, gathering everyone together, going down the lineup of a team like the Detroit Tigers. Ruth would answer how he would attack each hitter.

"Bush . . ."

"Fastball up and inside. Curveball, low and away."

"Vitt . . ."

"Fastball up and inside. Curveball, low and away."

"Cobb . . ."

"Fastball up and inside. Curveball, low and away."

"Crawford . . ."

"Fastball up and inside . . ."

And so it went.

He would recognize stances and quirks, remember who had done what in previous at-bats; he just couldn't remember the names and dates. He played the games, didn't talk about them, ran on high emotion, and, again, threw the ball hard. It didn't matter who was hitting if the ball was thrown fast and to the proper spot.

On his bad days he was troubled by wildness, and also he tired sometimes in the late innings. He was emotional too when he worked, and that sometimes got him in trouble. (The day he hit his second home run and the Yankees intentionally walked him twice, he kicked a bench in frustration. His broken toe kept him off the mound for the next two weeks.)

"[Ruth] possesses a wonderful arm and a world of stuff, strength galore, and overwhelming eagerness to be in the game," Paul Shannon of the *Boston Post* had written in a 1915 preseason analysis of the Red Sox. "The Red Sox have a splendid prospect, but one who lacks a knowledge of real 'inside baseball.' Manager Carrigan is confident that he can teach him, and if so he will be a great acquisition to the corps."

That was exactly the way the season played out.

Carrigan tried to pitch Ruth mostly against the second-division clubs in the first two-thirds of the season—part of the learning—then let him pitch against the better clubs in the final third. Ruth delivered, pitching his best baseball in a pennant drive that at one point had the Red Sox winning 19 of 21 games.

He outlasted the famed Walter Johnson of the Washington Senators, 4–3, easily beat the Browns, 4–1, pitched a terrific no-decision against the

Tigers, leaving the game with a 1–1 score in the ninth, stymied the White Sox with a two-hitter. In late September, his relief-aided 3–2 win over the second-place Tigers pretty much clinched first place.

He finished the season with an 18–8 record on a staff that had five pitchers with 15 wins or more. His ERA was 2.44. He had 112 strikeouts, walked 84 batters. He also finished with a .315 batting average and four home runs. Number three was the only $5 shot for the suffragettes at Fenway, the second-longest home run ever hit in the park. Number four was in St. Louis, the longest homer in Sportsman's Park history, over the right-field fence and across the street and through the window of a Chevrolet dealership. The league leader in home runs, outfielder Braggo Roth of the White Sox, had seven.

In the World Series against the Phillies, the home games played at newly opened Braves Field off Commonwealth Avenue to handle larger crowds, Ruth never pitched. It wasn't a great surprise, although he was said to be disappointed. The Red Sox won easily in five games, and Carrigan said years later that he never pitched Ruth because he simply had other, better pitchers at the time. He preferred right-handed pitchers against the slugging Cravath of the Phillies. He rejected the longtime rumor that Ruth never pitched in the Series due to disciplinary problems.

The manager did not say that a disciplinary problem didn't exist with the young pitcher.

The 20-year-old Babe Ruth (who thought he was 21) was a kid let loose in the adult funhouse in 1915. He was loud. He was profane. Nights ended only when morning arrived. There was no such thing as ordinary self-discipline or self-control. Joe Lannin had jumped his salary to a very respectable $3,500 for the season. Money removed the last of few inhibitions. He was off to fill in all the blanks.

Nothing mattered except the fun. Action. His first trip around the baseball circuit had been taken with bug-eyed wonder. Now he had an idea of what was out on the table—and it was time to grab.

He and Helen rented an apartment in Cambridge in the shadow of Harvard University, and the fog moved in tight around their relationship. They would do things together, be seen in public, go to bowling parties and events, but he clearly had an outside paper route too, one that did not include her. Very early there was an accommodation for infidelities. What did she think about that? Fog.

The later-distributed picture of his personal life was a mosaic of anec-dote, rumor, speculation, exaggeration, and a headline every now and then. Exclamation points usually accompanied each addition. He liked to eat! He liked women! He used three swear words in every five words he spoke! There was a question about when he started drinking—teammate Harry Hooper said he never remembered Ruth drinking in Boston; other people did—but when he did start to drink, he liked to drink!

Ernie Shore, the other young pitcher and a college graduate, did not last long as an early roommate. He said in public that he didn't like Ruth using his toothbrush all the time. He said in private that he didn't like a roommate who never flushed the toilet, who walked around naked, who never sat down, never slept. A pride for personal flatulence and exagger-ated belches also was not an admired quality.

The consumption of food was always a wonder. The emerging Babe liked his steaks uncooked and he liked them large. Helen told an inter-viewer that he would eat two large uncooked steaks at a sitting, consum-ing an entire bottle of chili sauce on the side. He would order piles of sandwiches when the train stopped in the night on the road, eat them in rapid order. He would eat six, eight, ten hot dogs at a time, wash them down with four, six, eight bottles of soda ("On Sunday we had three hot dogs, which we called "weenies . . ."). He would eat before the game, af-ter the game, during the game, until Carrigan ruled there was no eating on the bench, and then Ruth snuck food into the clubhouse. He ate every day like a man released from prison.

The stories about women were constant. He told them. Everybody told them. Not exactly shy about his sexuality, he brought profes-sional women back to his room on the road, coupling while his poor roommate tried to sleep. (In a story told in many variations, the names and places changing with each retelling, Ruth is in the bedroom of a suite with a professional, or maybe an amateur, while the roommate tries to sleep in the living room. Ruth, after each adventure, comes into the living room to smoke a cigar. The roommate the next morning counts the cigar butts in the ashtray. The number is . . . it varies. Seven seems popular.)

Third baseman Larry Gardner talked about walking into a room and finding Ruth with yet another prostitute.

"The guy was lying on the floor being screwed by a prostitute," Gard-ner said. "He was smoking a cigar and eating peanuts and this woman was working on him."

All women were potential partners. He let that be known, through word, leer, and innuendo. Not all women were charmed.

"He was a mess," Larry Gardner's wife, Margaret, remembered in Ken Sobol's *Babe Ruth and the American Dream*. "He was foul-mouthed, a show-off, very distasteful to have around. The kind of person you would never dream of having over for dinner. I suppose he was likable enough in his way, but you could never prove it by me.

"Once, on a train, he came up to me and started talking in that loud voice of his about how I had gotten him in trouble. I asked why and he said earlier on the trip he had seen a woman he thought was me and he had come up behind her and whopped her on the head, but it turned out to be somebody he didn't know. He thought that was the funniest thing he'd ever heard of."

He was a practical joker in the clubhouse, physical stuff out of second grade—like nailing someone's new shoes to the floor, slipping a piece of cardboard into the middle of someone's sandwich, using fire in creative ways. The bulk of his teammates accepted him in the way they would accept a mischievous, immature little brother. Some couldn't stand him. The team was split pretty much into two different cliques along religious lines, the Protestants and the Catholics. Ruth was with the Catholics. Veterans Tris Speaker and Smokey Joe Wood, best friends and leaders of the Protestants, couldn't stand him. Forty years later Wood would do a taped interview with Lawrence Ritter and talk about life with "the Big Baboon." Thinking about what he said, pretty much unkind, he would call Ritter back a few days later to redo the interview in a nicer fashion.

The "Baboon" nickname was in effect. "Tarzan, King of the Apes" was another. A late entry was "Two Head," a tribute to the literal size of his head (large) and the figurative size (growing larger by the day). That was a favorite of Dapper Dan Howley, a former Phillies catcher from nearby Weymouth, who worked out with the team.

Howley spotted Ruth driving one day on Washington Street, the main commercial thoroughfare in Boston. Howley started shouting, "Two Head, Two Head." Ruth spotted him, stopped his car, and started chasing him. Traffic backed up immediately. Howley hid. Automobile management was and always would be a problem. Ruth drove fast and without worry. He parked anywhere. He hit things, including pedestrians, was caught for speeding, had at least one auto incident in each calendar year. He hit a hay wagon in 1915.

Every day was a 24-hour flurry of activity. He dressed in a cacophony of plaids and colors, had a pair of yellow shoes. He was known in the sporting houses off the Fenway. He was increasingly known in the sporting houses across the American League. He hunted, fished, brought words to exclusive golf courses that simply weren't allowed. He had another sandwich, thank you very much. He developed a taste for beer.

Carrigan, who first fined him back in training camp, eventually came up with a plan to corral him on the road. Dutch Leonard was another late-night rambler, and the manager started ordering two adjoining hotel rooms at every stop. He put himself in one room with Leonard, coach Heinie Wagner in the next room with Ruth. That arrangement didn't end the wanderings (no word on whether Ruth used Heinie Wagner's toothbrush), but it did slow them down. Carrigan also tried to curb Ruth's spending. He drew Ruth's pay and attempted to ration out the money every day. This did not work as well.

"He had no idea whatsoever of money," Carrigan said. "You have to remember his background."

Carrigan had another plan for spring training in 1916. He invited the wives to come to Hot Springs. Helen made the trip. She was as much of a young, naive outsider with the other wives as the Babe was with their husbands. The couple did go out, however, with the Gardners one day to a carnival. The Babe paid the operator to stop the Ferris wheel while he and Helen were at the top, proceeding to rock the car back and forth and scare her witless. He loved carnivals, loved the midway at Revere Beach near Boston. Most kids did.

Sometime during the day the party passed the monkey cages. Ruth started jumping around in front of a cage, doing monkey impressions. One of the monkeys started to do exactly what Ruth was doing.

"Look, Babe," Helen said. "He knows you."

The next two seasons—1916 and 1917—were his grand moments on the mound. No pitcher in baseball, certainly no left-handed pitcher, was better. He could throw a fastball past anyone, including the feared Ty Cobb of the Tigers. He was 23–12 the first year, 24–13 the second year. In 1916 he had a league-leading 1.75 ERA and a record nine shutouts. In 1917 he pitched 35 complete games in 41 starts. He was durable and consistent.

The Federal League had folded after the 1915 season, creating a reverse stream of talent back to the major leagues in 1916, a situation that should have caused trouble for a young pitcher. Hadn't the talent vacuum created by the Federals been one of the reasons he'd jumped to the American League so fast in the first place? Shouldn't a tightening of talent make his job harder? Not really. He seemed to handle whatever came along.

"One night he and Helen were out riding when their car ran out of gas," Herb Pennock, a young patrician lefty from Kenneth Square, Pennsylvania, who'd joined the team in 1915 and oddly had become Ruth's best friend, said. "Babe had to walk five miles to get some. He didn't get to sleep until five in the morning. Then he pitched the first game of a doubleheader, won it, 1–0, and took the second with a homer. The next time Esther, my wife, saw Helen, she said, 'What do you feed that man?' "

His duels with Walter Johnson in 1916 were a memorable, season-long series of struggles. Johnson, the Washington Senators' 28-year-old star right-hander, had established himself as the benchmark for all pitchers. He was in the midst of a string of 10 seasons when he would win 20 or more games, on the way to 417 career wins, second only to Cy Young in baseball history. He was a tall (6-foot-2) and gentlemanly character who didn't smoke, drink, cuss, or throw at batters' heads. Cobb always claimed he crowded the plate against Johnson because he knew Johnson was too nice to brush him back. Not that it mattered. Johnson had exceptionally long arms and threw only fastballs from a sidearm motion that froze right-handed batters in the box. He was called both "the Big Train" and "Barney," after Barney Oldfield, the auto racer.

Matched against Ruth, the emotional, developing reprobate, Johnson easily was cast as the white hat against the black hat, goodness against perdition. The problem was, perdition had the much better team behind him. The two men faced each other five times during the '16 season:

April 17—Ruth was a 5–1 winner in a rain-shortened, six-inning affair. He gave up eight hits, struck out six. Johnson was whacked around for 11 hits.

June 1—Ruth was a 1–0 winner. He gave up only three hits. The winning run came in the eighth inning when speedy Mike McNally scored from second on an infield out.

August 15—Ruth was a 1–0 winner in 13 innings. Johnson gave up only five hits in the first 12 innings. Ruth gave up only one in the last seven.

September 9—Ruth was a 2–1 winner. He gave up four hits. Johnson gave up eight.

September 12—Three days after their last meeting, on two days' rest, goodness and perdition met for the last time of the year. It was the last home game of the season for the Senators, and Clark Griffith brought Johnson back because he wanted to give the fans a show. He tried to give Johnson an edge, having the shades on the windows at Griffith Stadium pulled up to create a glare every time the Red Sox took the field on defense. (The Red Sox protested and the practice stopped.) A drummer also played loudly every time Ruth was ready to pitch. (The Red Sox protested and the drummer was allowed to keep drumming.)

For a long time none of that mattered. Ruth cruised. He brought a 2–0 shutout into the ninth inning, but then loaded the bases, surrendered a game-tying, two-run double to John Henry, and was pulled from the game. The Red Sox scored a run in the top of the tenth, but Ernie Shore gave up two in the bottom to hand the Senators and Johnson the win. Ruth had no decision.

It was terrific athletic theater. Added to a win in his first year, Ruth was now 5–0 against the Train. The two men, between them, won 48 games during the year. Neither surrendered a single home run. In 1917 Ruth would stretch his string to 6–0 with a third 1–0 win, a two-hitter, but Johnson finally would prevail in the last month of the season, 6–2.

"That was one of the best ball games I have ever seen," American League president Ban Johnson exulted after one of the 1–0 thrillers. "It was a treat to be in the stands and watch two such masterful twirlers as Johnson and Ruth. Until the Red Sox bunched two hits and a sacrifice fly in the eighth, I thought the game would likely have to be called for darkness with neither team able to tally."

Ruth's two most memorable performances, other than his meetings with Johnson, came in different-sized packages. The first lasted 14 innings and was part of the 1916 World Series. The second lasted four pitches and was part of a 1917 perfect game.

In the second game of the 1916 Series against the Brooklyn Superbas, finally getting his first postseason start, Ruth surrendered an inside-the-park home run to Hi Miers in the first inning, a ball that was rifled between Speaker and Hooper and kept rolling in the Fenway Park outfield. After that, he simply shut down the visitors. Lefthander Sherry Smith, pitching the game of his life for the Superbas, surrendered a run in the third on a groundout by Ruth, then also settled down.

The game, played on a dark Boston day, went into extra innings, one after another, and the pitchers kept battling and the darkness grew increasingly darker. In the bottom of the fourteenth, after Dick Hoblitzel walked and was sacrificed to second, manager Carrigan made some inspired choices. He knew the game probably would not last another inning, due to the darkness, so he sent McNally in to run for Hoblitzel. He brought Del Gainer, a righty, in to bat for Gardner, a lefty. Gainer singled into the gloom in left. McNally ran home with the winning run. Carrigan was a genius. The Babe was a World Series winner.

"I told you a year ago I could take care of those National League bums," he told Carrigan, the Sox on their way to a second straight world championship. "You never gave me a chance."

The four-pitch appearance in a perfect game came on June 23, 1917. A number of things had changed from the glories of '16. Carrigan was gone, for starters, retired at age 34 to run a bank in Lewiston, Maine. Owner Joe Lannin was gone, replaced by Harry Frazee, a theatrical entrepreneur from New York. The precision also had gone from the Red Sox machine as it headed toward a second-place finish, eight and a half games behind the Chicago White Sox.

Ruth had turned petulant, even though he had a 12–4 record and the team was still only two games out. He grumbled loudly about errors behind him, about judgments against him by umpires. He had been involved in assorted loud discussions, arguments, both in his own clubhouse and on the field. He soon was involved in one here on June 23.

Facing leadoff batter Ray Morgan of the Senators at Fenway, he threw ball one and didn't like umpire Brick Owens's call. He threw ball two and then ball three and didn't like either of those calls. Grousing from the mound at Owens, he delivered ball four and really didn't like the call. As Morgan departed for first, Ruth continued to shout and Owens told him to keep quiet or he would be out of the game. Ruth then informed Owens he would punch him in the nose if Owens ejected him—and Owens did just that, ejected him. Ruth charged the umpire.

Catcher Pinch Thomas tried to stop him, and did in part, but Ruth still unloaded a punch that landed somewhere on the back of Owens's head. The umpire went to the ground. It all would have been racy but perishable stuff—the subsequent $100 fine and nine-day suspension from the league office soon forgotten—except for what replacement pitcher Ernie Shore did.

Morgan, after all of the hubbub, tried to steal second. Replacement catcher Sam Agnew, in the lineup since Thomas also had been ejected, threw out Morgan at second. Replacement pitcher Shore, working on only eight warm-up pitches and two days' rest, then proceeded to retire the next 26 Senators in a row. The feat was deemed a perfect game, one of baseball's rarest accomplishments.

For the next 74 years, until long after all the participants were departed, the perfection of Shore's performance would be celebrated. In 1991 the eight-man Committee for Statistical Accuracy would be formed to look at all the records that had been set in baseball's history. The committee would discard an asterisk typed next to one famous home run record and rule on the record-setting legitimacy of over 50 other events that had taken place. One of them was Ernie Shore's perfect game, which was changed to "a combined no-hitter" between Shore and George Herman Ruth.

It turned out to be the Babe's only no-hitter.

The off-season between 1917 and 1918 was spent mostly in New England. This was a change. With his first World Series check of $3,780.25 in 1915, Ruth had backed his father in the purchase of a bar on the corner of Lombard and Eutaw streets in Baltimore. He and Helen had spent that winter of 1915–16 in one of the two apartments above the bar, and he had run a small gymnasium behind the bar. They also had spent time there after the following season. He'd crashed a car in Baltimore in the winter of 1916–17, in fact, totaled it. Helen reportedly suffered "internal injuries."

This year's off-season car crash was in Boston, late on a November night, another total as he tangled with a trolley. Helen was not injured in this one because she was not in the car. Another woman, nameless, was. No other details given. Sportswriters and fans read between the lines and smiled.

Home, at any rate, was now a cottage in South Sudbury, Massachusetts, leased year round from a Sudbury man named Bill Joyce. It probably wasn't a bad idea to stay in the area. A backdrop for the entire season had been the war in Europe. The United States had entered the conflict on April 4, back in spring training, and no one had been affected by the first draft call in June. A second call in September, however, had sent manager Jack Barry and other unmarried members of the team to the enlistment office of the Naval Reserve. Who knew what would happen next? Would married men be called?

The Babe had found the cottage and Sudbury, a rural town 30 miles outside Boston, early in his Red Sox career. A number of players and local celebrities lived or stayed in the area. He liked Sudbury, and Sudbury, enthused at having a real-life baseball star in its midst, liked him. He had been given what Joyce called "a lifetime lease" on the cabin. He planned to use it.

No doubt there was some subterranean plotting here. Helen, stuck 30 miles from the big city, certainly gave the gentleman of the house a free pass for his in-town wanderings. The Babe also liked the place. It sat on the edge of Great Pond, perfect for whatever daydreams he might have glimpsed on a Currier and Ives calendar on a wall somewhere in the institutional cold at St. Mary's Industrial School.

He could fish and hunt and play farmer. The winter could be as much fun as the summer. He found the kids of the neighborhood and tried skiing: hit a first jump, flew through the air, crashed back to earth, ripped his pants, and walked home with his butt sticking out. He found hockey: couldn't skate, stuck in the goal, hurt his hip trying to make a save. Sent for Helen to bring him home. Told the kids to stop for hot chocolate at the house. He was a kid, and this was a place for kids. He brought out all the kids from a Roxbury orphanage, indulged them, sent them home with gloves and bats and balls.

The cabin, a sign that read IHATETOQUITIT painted above the door by a previous resident, offered the closest approximation to a true domestic situation he'd ever had. He held parties—maybe pushed a piano onto the ice, where it sank, maybe didn't—played whist, chopped down pine trees, took out his rifles and shot things that moved and things that didn't. Bullfrogs were favorite targets. His favorite fish was the pickerel. He also caught bass, but hated to clean them.

"Skinning a bass," he said, "is like taking the heart out of an elephant."

A reporter and cameraman made the journey out to this retreat in the woods in the middle of January, and the Babe and a friend picked them up in a sleigh at the train stop near the Wayside Inn. Helen cooked a fried chicken dinner, and Babe gleefully showed off the place and his toys.

. He had a few shortcomings as a modern man of nature. Fishing through a hole in the ice, for instance, he caught nothing. The photographer, who was cold, found another fisherman who had caught a pickerel. The fish was frozen solid, but when attached to the Babe's line and jiggled a bit, it still looked fearsome. Hunting . . . the Babe had a large collection of rifles and shotguns. Alas, his favorite gun was out of commission. The barrel had become jammed with ice and Babe had decided the best way to clean it out was to fire a round. The ice in the barrel was now gone, but the final six inches of the barrel also had been ripped apart by the explosion.

And then there was the stove. The Babe's idea for filling the Franklin stove in the middle of the living room was to chop down a tree when necessary. He wasn't big on chopping up a bunch of wood and letting it dry and age. This meant that the wood usually was green and often didn't burn right away.

"This wood doesn't heat very well," he said at the latest example of this, "but you'll bet I'll fix it."

He grabbed a can of kerosene to pour onto the fire. The reporter and photographer edged toward the door to be able to escape the blast. The Babe told them to relax.

"That's all right," he said. "I never had any trouble with the kerosene . . . only twice. Once I put it in through the door of the stove and the cover blew off a little. Another time we had a real explosion. The cover hit the roof and came down close to my foot. That, however, was when I poured gasoline in by mistake."

The Babe reported that he was in fine shape and ready for the new season. The reporter reported that Helen made some fine fried chicken and that the Babe was a lucky man. No piano was mentioned, but the reporter did spot a pump organ and "an automatic music box." He said the interior of the cabin was lit by Japanese lanterns and decorated with flags of all nations.

Almost all nations. There was no flag for Germany.

CHAPTER FIVE

A NEW CITY now lay less than 20 miles north of the Babe's IHATETO-QUITIT cottage in Sudbury. There had been no city when he left for spring training in 1917, simply 5,000 acres of woods and rolling Massachusetts farmland, no different from where he fished for pickerel and bass, but now there were 1,772 buildings and a population of over 10,000. From roughly the time he went into his one-third-inning meltdown in June, setting up Ernie Shore's perfect game, until the Chicago White Sox won the World Series over the New York Giants in six games on October 15, the land had been cleared and the city had been built. It was a staggering achievement, employing the largest construction force in U.S. history.

The name of the city was Camp Devens. The war was now serious.

Across the country the rush to mobilize for the European conflict had turned frenzied and profound. An immediate need had been created for a military force that didn't exist. Gen. John J. Pershing, looking at a standing army of 108,000, 17th-largest in the world, first asked for 1 million men, then nine days later revised his request, asking for 3 million. The draft call for April alone in 1918, not including the thousands of enlistments daily, was expected to reach 800,000 men between the ages of 21 and 30. They all needed places to lose weight, gain weight, learn how to salute, march, dress properly, and kill.

Thirty-two cantonments, camps, had been built in this absolute hurry, 16 to train newly added forces, 16 for the National Guard. Camp Devens, which would handle all recruits from New England, was one of the largest. A construction force of 10,000 men worked at such a speed that it built 10.4 buildings per day, a new building every 40 minutes. Twenty portable sawmills churned out 300 billion board feet of lumber in the project, enough to build a foot-wide path from San Francisco to Paris.

The entire country seemed to be running at the same electric pace. The War Industries Board under Bernard Baruch converted thousands of factories to the production of war essentials. Shipyards everywhere were busy around the clock. The stories about life in the trenches, about poison gas and artillery bombardments and unbelievable carnage, had been arriving from across the Atlantic since 1914. Now they had a greater urgency as more and more American names were listed among the casualties.

As a train carrying the Babe, some sportswriters, and assorted members of the Red Sox spring training party left South Station on March 9 and headed west toward Albany and St. Louis and ultimately Hot Springs through the start of a blizzard, the apparatus of war had begun to function. A group of soldiers from Camp Devens was on the train, going home for the weekend. The Babe passed out some of his cigars, talked, and fooled around. ("Pretty, huh?" one of the soldiers said as the train went through the Berkshire Mountains. "This is nothing," the Babe said. "The best scenery goes by when we're sleeping.") At each stop in the three-day trip, more soldiers, sailors, and air corps cadets would get on or get off. The camps were filling up everywhere. The lessons of combat were being taught.

"The first live grenades were sent hurtling through the air at the bombing field, 150 of the new American type, and they kicked up quite a fuss," Laurence L. Winship reported that week from Camp Devens in the *Boston Globe*.

Lieutenant Fox of Ordnance Bureau at Washington came on to witness the throwing of the first grenades on the first bombing field in America.

The first one was tossed out into No Man's Land by Lt. Colonel C. A. Romeyn of the 302nd Infantry. "Whing! Whang!" Six seconds after it left his hand, a deafening explosion announced that it worked. The bits of steel came whinging, whanging back over the heads of colonels and majors and other officers crouched behind cement barricades.

Straight up in the air and straight down and straight to the four corners of the winds, the jags and chunks of grenade scattered looking for something to hit. Some went 75 and 100 yards. The closeness of pieces which plunked into the ground near the fortified positions told officers of the reason for "heads down."

Spring training was for everyone this year.

Baseball was not immune from the effects of the buildup. The first announcement of a draft in September 1917 had sent unmarried players in both leagues scurrying to their local reserve units or into other military-related factory jobs to avoid the general call-up. Rosters had been altered for every team in the big leagues by these enlistments and defections. Would there, could there, even be a baseball season?

The Boston Marathon already had been canceled, a relay race between military units from Ashland to downtown Boston scheduled to take its place. The Indianapolis 500 and all auto races had been canceled. Horse racing had great problems shipping horses from track to track. Many intercollegiate sports, including Harvard and Yale football, already had been shut down. Baseball waited instead, to see what might come next.

The Red Sox had lost 13 players, including player-manager Jack Barry. The members of the reserves, including Barry, had hoped for special furloughs to allow them to play the season. The request was denied. Barry now was stationed at the Boston Navy Yard along with Ernie Shore, Herb Pennock, Chick Shorten, Mike McNally, Jimmy Walsh, and Del Gainer. They all would play for the navy yard in a benefit game on May 5 at Braves Field against a Camp Devens team headed by 1917 Red Sox utility infielder Hal "Childe Harold" Janvrin. With Whitey Witt from the A's and Rabbit Maranville and Arthur Rico from the Braves also in the lineup and 45,000 people in the stands, the navy yard would whip the visitors, 5–1.

The Red Sox of 1918 should have been blown apart by these losses, but Harry Frazee was one of the few owners in baseball to react positively to the situation. The American League was split into buyers and sellers. Frazee became one of the few buyers. His favorite seller was Connie Mack of the last-place A's. Fearing low attendance and financial disaster, Mack shipped pitcher Joe Bush, catcher Wally Schang, and outfielder Amos

Strunk to Frazee for three lesser players and $60,000 in December. In January the A's owner added first baseman Stuffy McInnis to the pile.

As camp opened in Hot Springs, right fielder Harry Hooper and shortstop Everett Scott were the only two remaining position players from the 1917 lineup, but the holes had been covered much better than could have been expected. Every team was struggling to find enough manpower, but the Red Sox were struggling less.

To replace Barry in the dugout, Frazee made an interesting choice, picking 51-year-old Ed Barrow. A large, combative man, who stood 6-foot-2 with a prominent chin, no-nonsense eyebrows, and a no-nonsense tongue to match, Barrow had worked in virtually every aspect of and around organized baseball except for actually playing the game. He had been both a circulation manager and a city editor at newspapers in Des Moines. He had been a business partner with concessionaire Harry M. Stevens in Pittsburgh. He had been the manager of the Detroit Tigers in 1903 and 1904, the manager of minor league teams in Indianapolis and Toronto. He also had been the president of three different minor leagues.

Frazee's idea was that Barrow not only would handle the team on the field but also would help with business matters off the field. Frazee was in New York much of the time, and Red Sox secretary John J. Lane, who had handled much of the day-to-day business work, was another employee who now was at the Boston Navy Yard. Barrow was available because he had just resigned as president of the International League after the owners voted to cut his salary from $7,500 to $2,500. Frazee called him "Simon," after Simon Legree, the pitiless slave owner in *Uncle Tom's Cabin*. The name pretty much summed up what Frazee thought should be Barrow's overall job description.

"He didn't know much about baseball, very little about the fine points," Harry Hooper said about the new manager. "But he was a disciplinarian. He was a very good disciplinarian."

Barrow, who would manage in the dugout in his business suit, had a list of problems to consider during training camp with his new team filled with new men. Not only did he have to fit the arrivals from Philadelphia into the lineup, but he had to find minor league retreads to fill other positions. No team in baseball had adequate depth, and players still were leaving every day to enlist. Nothing could be considered certain.

It was in this juggling atmosphere that another tangential problem developed. Barrow's best left-handed pitcher now wanted to play in the field. The thought had been floating around in the Babe's mind almost from the beginning of his time in Boston, but now gathered momentum as he saw openings appear. If many of the best players were gone, why couldn't he play first base? Why couldn't he play in the outfield? Why couldn't he play? He made his wishes known. Loudly.

Barrow, with his manpower difficulties, was able to humor the big man a bit. He let Ruth play first base in intrasquad scrimmages, then let him play first in the exhibition opener against the Dodgers. Ruth responded in the game with two home runs in two at-bats in an 11–1 win, the second blast landing in the Arkansas Alligator Farm. He also handled six chances in the field without error.

"That's ten bucks in balls you've cost me," owner Frazee shouted from the stands to his star pitcher after the second homer.

"I can't help it," the star pitcher replied. "They ought to make these fucken parks bigger."

The argument had begun.

Barrow was convinced that Ruth should stay a pitcher. Pitching was the soul of the game. Left-handed pitching was the hardest of all baseball talents to find. He let Ruth play a little more at first, a little in the outfield as the exhibition games rolled along, but let it be known that pitching was going to be Ruth's job when the season arrived. Ruth let it be known that he liked to hit.

Barrow hadn't met Ruth until less than a month earlier, when Ruth signed his contract at the Red Sox offices. The manager had a full look now. He saw the same loud and confident man-child everyone else saw, roaring through every day as if there never would be another. Hot Springs was a wide-open resort town with casinos, brothels, and a racetrack on the edge of town. The Babe, unleashed from his winter of domesticity in Sudbury, was a perpetual conventioneer on the prowl.

He found the casinos and the racetrack, Oaklawn Park, irresistible. He always had a tip on a horse, a scam that would make everyone wealthy. ("Bellboy" was the tip one day in the lobby of the Hotel Majestic. Leading. Broke down in the stretch. Finished last.) He was always moving, doing, heading to something next.

"He had no regard for money, none," Harry Hooper said. "The first year he was with the Red Sox, he lost more money in Hot Springs than he would make all year. That's a fact. Not that it was only him. John I. Taylor owned the team when I first came to Boston. His family owned the

Globe. He had to sell a pitcher once just to get out of Hot Springs. That's how much money he lost."

The Babe's pitching obviously wasn't affected by any of this as he took his regular turn for Barrow and did well in what was shaping up to be a solid rotation, with Ruth, Carl Mays, Joe Bush, and Dutch Leonard. His hitting, well, that wasn't affected either.

A pair of exhibition games a week apart against the Dodgers had been scheduled at Camp Pike, 53 miles outside Hot Springs. Camp Pike was another of the cantonments, another instant city created in the middle of an agrarian nowhere. One million board feet of lumber had arrived every day on trains 100 cars long from six sawmills when construction was at its height. The baseball field was built in 15 days in what used to be an apple orchard, 7,000 trees cut down, the land leveled, grass planted.

Heading toward the grand opening of the field on March 23, Ruth was the main entertainment as the Sox made the three-hour trip. He sang assorted songs to his confined teammates:

Molly, my Molly—my Molly, my dear,
If it wasn't for Molly, I wouldn't be here;
Write me a letter, send it by mail—
Shoot it to me at the old city jail.

The game was rained out, but not until batting practice had been held. Ruth was the entertainment here too, driving five shots over the new right-field fence. The soldiers in attendance went wild, and when the Red Sox and Dodgers returned seven days later for a final game in Arkansas before making the long trip north, the show was remembered. Ruth wasn't playing, but the soldiers chanted for him to appear.

Barrow relented, putting him on the mound in the fifth inning. In the eighth, after Sam Agnew had just homered to left, Ruth stepped to the plate and homered to right. The soldiers went wild again. In the bottom of the ninth, tie game, Ruth singled sharply over the center fielder's head, sending home George Whiteman from third for the 4–3 win.

The riddle of the spring became even more vexing as this part of the spring ended: what do you do when your best hitter is your best pitcher? Barrow would restrict the Babe to pitching on the exhibition grind homeward, but the "pitcher" had finished his time in Hot Springs with nine hits, including four homers, in 21 at-bats. The war was changing lives and situations everywhere. Had it changed the life and situation of the 23-year-old man now called "the Colossus" by sportswriter Burt Whitman of the *Boston Herald*?

The noise from the soldiers at Camp Pike was another argument in the affirmative. They liked, most of all, to see him hit.

Barrow knew his limitations. That made him smart right there. He knew that he wasn't any kind of a baseball strategist, so he hired someone else to do that part of the job. His first choice, Johnny Evers (of Tinker-to-Evers-to-Chance double-play fame), was a bit too intense, riding the players, wanting to win every inning of every game, driving everyone crazy. The second choice, veteran Heinie Wagner, good guy, also didn't work out. The job fell to 30-year-old Harry Hooper.

Hooper, as the season opened with the Babe pitching a 10–3 win over the Yankees at the Polo Grounds, was on the Babe's side. Hooper also believed that hitting every day—the way the Babe hit—was more important than pitching every fourth day. He loved the way the Babe swung at a baseball, free and easy, rhythm and power. Hooper had been interested since the first time he ever saw him swing, first year on the team.

"We played an exhibition in some small town out near Brockton," Hooper said. "Before the game, he took a bunch of balls and went with another guy out to the outfield, and the guy pitched and Babe just started swinging. I remember noticing how well he hit."

The Babe had a permanent red mark on his chest, something that looked like a woman's stretch mark, only it was on the chest. The mark was hard to miss in the locker room. Hooper asked him one day how he'd got it.

"Swung too hard," the Babe said.

Swung too hard? Hooper was on the Babe's side.

He campaigned often to have Ruth inserted into the lineup. He brought shortstop Everett Scott and Heinie Wagner and other teammates into the argument with Barrow. The Red Sox had edged to the front in the early stage of the pennant race, but had done it with pitching and speed. They needed hitting, especially left-handed hitting. Barrow's argument always was that he would be "the laughingstock of the league" if he switched his best pitcher into an everyday player. Hooper's comeback considered the economics of the situation. He had heard a rumor that

Barrow now had a $50,000 investment in the team. Did Barrow notice the way people clamored to see the Babe? Did he think they really wanted to see him pitch? More at-bats would equal larger crowds, which would equal more money.

The assault finally worked.

On May 4, the Babe pitched against the Yankees at the Polo Grounds and had a wild afternoon. Yankees manager Miller Huggins decided to attack him with bunts, and he handled 13 chances with two errors. At the plate, he drew revenge. In the seventh inning, after booming a tremendous foul ball and telling umpire Billy Evans, "I'll hit this [next] one right back and there'll be no doubt about it," he homered into the upper deck. The Yankees won, 4–3, but when the game ended, the Babe was sitting on second base after hitting a double.

On May 5, Sunday baseball still illegal in New York, the Red Sox played an exhibition in Clifton, New Jersey. They beat the Doherty Silver Sox, 3–1, and the important part of the day was that the Babe played the last four innings at first base. Dick Hoblitzel, a dentist and the regular first baseman, had injured a finger in the Yankees game. Ruth went hitless in two plate appearances but played well in the field, well enough that he made his major league debut as a position player the next day against the Yankees at first. Barrow had cracked.

A weird heat wave hit New York on May 6. In the 85-degree temperature, which broke a 112-year-old record, patrons were suddenly wearing straw hats. In the fourth inning, Stuffy McInnis on first, Ruth hit what was termed in one account "a saucy home run, high into the attic in the grandstand." Frazee was in the stands, sitting next to Yankees owner Col. Jake Ruppert, who turned and offered $150,000 for Ruth right there. It was a joke. Frazee laughed. Ruppert laughed. It was a joke to be remembered.

On May 7, the Red Sox had moved down to Washington. Walter Johnson was pitching. Ruth was again at first, this time batting cleanup. In the sixth inning, against the preeminent pitcher in baseball, he whacked a shot over the right-field fence that landed in someone's victory garden and scared a dog. The feat was so out of the ordinary that a sign said that a local tailor would give a suit of clothes to anyone who hit a ball over that fence. J. V. Fitzgerald of the *Washington Post* declared, "The tailor is going to have to use a lot of cloth to rig out the Babe." The Babe, once again, had three home runs in three games.

On May 8, he doubled. On May 9, pitching his regular turn, he went 5-for-5 with a triple, three doubles, and a single. He seemed to be involved in everything in the game, a 4–3 loss. He was even thrown out at third attempting to steal. He hit in ten straight games before he was stopped.

Harry Hooper, uh-huh, could spot a good hitter.

The war shuffled all the baseball cards again at the end of the month. A ruling called "work or fight" came down from the office of Secretary of War Newton Baker and Provost Marshal Gen. Enoch Crowder on May 23. It declared that all men of draft age must either be in the military or employed by some war-related industry by July 1. A fast reading said that July 1 would be the end of the baseball season. Eighty percent of the 330 players in the game were between 21 and 31 years old, the draft limits.

Store clerks, waiters, bartenders, elevator operators, many salesmen, and employees at places of amusement all were affected. Their employers quickly said that business would continue as usual, with older workers and women taking the vacated positions. (One Park Avenue hotel announced that it would hire "Negroes" to fill the void.) Baseball obviously did not have the same options. (Although the "Negro" option would have been interesting.) Baseball would die.

"Everything must be done to win this war," National League president John Tener said. "And if baseball is a sport as classified in this new order, and not a business in which there is a great investment of money, then baseball will not be behind other interests in contributing its part toward winning the war. If baseball is nonessential . . . there is a possibility that our ball parks will have to be closed and the season be brought to an end."

No mention of the players was made in the order, though they seemed to be covered in a section listing nonessential occupations that specified "Persons, including ushers and other attendants, engaged in and occupied in and in connection with, games, sports and amusements, excepting actual performers in legitimate concerts, operas or theatrical performances." Actors and opera singers were exempted; ballplayers were not.

The War Department said that a ruling on ballplayers couldn't be made until one of them was drafted and appealed the decision to his local board. The owners' hope was that the board in this test case would rule that a ballplayer was the same as an actor, exempt. Failing that, the owners hoped the War Department would give baseball an overall exemption to finish the season.

Ruth's draft status was class 4: married, head of household. That was why he hadn't been called already. He said little about the war and seemed to follow along with whatever the other players were doing. They joined the Massachusetts Home Guard, the backup to the activated National Guard. He joined too. They drilled in close order in a team competition set up by league president Ban Johnson, an attempt to give the game a patriotic shine. The Babe drilled too.

The ballplayers were in a predicament. The line between athletic hero and slacker had become a tightrope. A false move—look at boxer Jack Dempsey, criticized as a draft dodger—could drop a famous man into a swamp. Even the ballplayers who had gone into the service or to the shipyards were not exempt. Most of them were still playing baseball, only in different uniforms and for less money. Was it a contribution to the war effort to pitch for a shipyard? More and more fans were thinking that it was not.

The unsettled season was now even more unsettled. On each team, more players headed toward defense-related jobs or enlisted or were drafted. Dutch Leonard, having a good season for the Red Sox, soon left for the Fore River Shipyard in Quincy. Outfielder Fred Thomas enlisted. The rest of the players simply kept playing and waited for the next edict to roll out of Washington.

Ruth was not in the lineup when the work-or-fight ruling came down. He was sick. On May 19, a Sunday, a day off, he and Helen went to Revere Beach, the oldest public beach in the country, a Boston version of Coney Island. He had not been feeling well for the last week and now felt terrible. He had fever, chills, a 104-degree temperature. He had the flu.

In another two months that diagnosis would be a life-and-death proposition, another gift of the war, as the misnamed Spanish influenza came from the German trenches to the Allied trenches, back to the United States to become the most serious epidemic in the country's history. Before the end of the year, it would kill over 600,000 people in the United States, with Boston and Massachusetts hit hard. The flu for the U.S. troops would be more deadly than the war.

With the Babe—and this might have been the same strain of flu, simply not given a name yet—it simply was the flu. He appeared at Fenway the next day, Monday, his day to pitch, but Barrow looked at him and sent him straight to the trainer. The trainer treated him with silver nitrate, which at the time was used to coat a flu victim's throat. The trainer, alas, used too much silver nitrate. The Babe's larynx became swollen, a condition known as acute edema, and he started choking and collapsed. Barrow, hearing the commotion, grabbed him and took him to a nearby druggist, who administered an antidote to silver nitrate. The Babe then was rushed to Massachusetts General Hospital, where he stayed for the next week surrounded by flowers and comforted by Helen. Barrow fired the trainer.

On Decoration Day, 11 days after Ruth became ill, he pinch-hit at Fenway. Three days later he returned to the lineup in Detroit as a pitcher and . . . he hit a home run.

The next day, playing center field . . . he hit a home run.

The next day, center field again . . . he hit a home run.

The next day . . . he hit a home run.

Four home runs in four games broke his own record. The lasting effect of his illness would be a raspy voice from the irritation of the silver nitrate. He always would complain of that. The immediate effects of the illness seemed minimal.

The work-or-fight rule went into effect on July 1, and draft boards around the country slowly began to reclassify baseball players. Speculation in the *Globe* named Ruth and Amos Strunk as the two most vulnerable Red Sox. In Washington, 28-year-old catcher Eddie Ainsmith became the test, appealing his reclassification to the office of Secretary Baker. All of baseball awaited the decision, uncertainty everywhere, attendance down for a season that might end tomorrow.

Amid the uncertainty, the Babe was caught in a second uncertain bind. Barrow, with the defections and turmoil, wanted him to pitch. The Red Sox had dropped out of first place, and the Babe's home run barrage had quieted down after the four home runs. Barrow thought his star's pitching would help the team more now than his hitting. The Babe, alas, didn't want to pitch anymore.

He and Barrow went through a daily, contentious dance. The Babe claimed his wrist was hurt and he couldn't pitch. Barrow didn't believe him. Back and forth the argument went. The Babe, almost as if it were part of his case, started to hit again, whacking out homers number 10 and 11, the last one in the tenth inning against Walter Johnson over that same tailor's sign in right field in Washington on June 30. (No mention of another free suit.) He was now on a pace to do great things at the plate. Less than half the season had been completed, and he seemed a sure bet at least to break the American League home run record of 16 set by Socks Seybold in 1902. No one in 15 years had hit more than 12.

Barrow didn't seem to care. He still was looking for a pitcher. The day after Ruth's 11th home run, a Monday, the Red Sox had an off-day in Washington. Ruth went to Baltimore to visit his father and friends. He was late arriving back in Washington Tuesday afternoon, reaching the dugout only an hour before the concluding game of the series with the Senators. Barrow was not happy. Ruth was not happy.

"Say, isn't that Barrow there in the dugout?" asked a relocated friend from Sudbury who saw Ruth before the game.

"Yeah, that's the goddamned old shitpot," replied the Babe.

In the game, Ruth made an error and then struck out. Barrow made a comment about swinging at the first pitch, "a bum play." Ruth made a comment in return that involved punching Barrow in the nose. Barrow said that comment would cost $500. Ruth said that it wouldn't, because he had quit the team. He unbuttoned his uniform and wound up watching the last three innings with his friend from Sudbury in the stands.

By the next morning, the Red Sox were in Philadelphia for a series against the A's and Ruth was back in Baltimore, signing a contract to play with the Chester, Pennsylvania, shipyard. He, like other stars in the game, had been receiving offers from shipyards and other military-related companies (all with baseball teams) for the entire season. The news did not land well with Barrow and Harry Frazee. They sputtered about lawsuits and injunctions and the next day sent Heinie Wagner back to Baltimore to try to convince their man to return.

The convincing wasn't hard. Ruth already had talked with reporters at his father's bar and sounded ready to return. The anger had softened.

"I was mad as a March hare," he said, "and told Barrow then and there that I was through with him and his team. I know I was too mad to control myself, but suiting the action to the word, I did leave the team and came home. . . .

"I am all right and willing and ready to get back to playing. But I do not want to be fighting and fought with all the time."

He and Wagner showed up in Philadelphia at two o'clock in the morning of July 4. The Red Sox had a doubleheader with the A's at Shibe Park. Ruth did not play in the first game. Barrow would not speak to him or even acknowledge that he existed, and Ruth started taking his uniform off between games and declared that he was leaving again and for good. Hooper and other teammates convinced him to stay. They also convinced Barrow to talk with him.

The meeting went well. Ruth apologized. Barrow said there would be no fine. Ruth went back to center field for the second game, and the next day, July 5, he was back on the mound for the first time in a month. He beat the A's, 4–3, in ten innings. There was no mention of a sore wrist.

"I like to pitch," he said, "but my main objection is that pitching keeps you out of so many games. I like to be in there every day. If I had my choice, I'd play first base. I don't think a man can pitch in his regular turn, and play some other position and keep the pace year after year. I can do it this season all right. I'm young and strong and don't mind the work, but I wouldn't guarantee to do it for many seasons."

The fighting with Barrow ended, he went on a hitting spree. In the next week he had 12 hits in 30 at-bats, a figure that included five triples and four doubles. One of the triples was actually the longest home run ever seen at Fenway, two-thirds of the way up the bleachers, but good only for three bases under the rules because it came in the bottom of the ninth and a runner ahead of him scored to win the game. He also pitched a rain-shortened 4–0 shutout against the Browns. All was well.

The Red Sox moved back into first place and started to pull away, and Frazee gave Ruth a $1,000 bonus for playing two positions, money Ruth had wanted. The owner wrote in another $1,000 bonus if the team won the pennant, which would bring Ruth's salary to $9,000 for the season if the season was completed. The second qualifier, the second "if," was the catch.

On July 19, Secretary of War Baker made his decision on the Ainsmith case. The appeal was denied. Ainsmith had to go into the army, and, no, baseball was not exempt from work-or-fight. American League president Johnson immediately said the game would shut down in two days, on July 21.

The owners, headed by Frazee, immediately overruled Johnson and sent a 12-man committee to Washington to appeal for an extension until Labor Day, a chance to complete a truncated season. They also asked for a further extension for the two league champions to play a World Series in the first two weeks of September. On July 26, Baker's office agreed.

The season could be completed. For the first time in 1918, there was a semblance of baseball order.

Barrow politely asked Ruth to be a pitcher every fourth day for the remainder of the schedule. Ruth politely complied. His battles with the manager were done for now. He hit no more home runs in the final month, stuck forever on the 11 of June 30 that had seemed so promising, but he played almost every day, batted fourth, took the mound in regular rotation, and completed eight of nine games, winning seven of them.

The Red Sox clinched the pennant on August 30 and finished two and a half games ahead of the Cleveland Indians. The Babe missed three games in the finishing stretch.

His father had died.

The fog around his family, his roots, settled down one more time on August 25, 1918. A call from Baltimore on that Sunday morning told him that George H. Ruth, now 45 years old, had been killed in a fight outside the saloon his son had bought for him.

The fight, the death, was wrapped up in a second family situation the father had entered after the death of the Babe's mother. Married to Martha Sipes, his second wife, George became involved in a dispute between his two brothers-in-law. One brother-in-law was 30-year-old Benjamin Sipes, Martha's brother. The other was Oliver Beefelt, 35, married to Martha's sister.

Beefelt had left Martha's sister for a young girl he had met two years earlier when she was 15, a move that put him in assorted legal predicaments. On the night in question, he was drinking in Ruth's saloon. His estranged wife was upstairs in Ruth's apartment, where she was staying after a period of hospitalization.

Sipes came to the apartment to see his sister. She talked about Beefelt and the terrible things he had done to her, which sent Sipes downstairs to say a few words to Beefelt. No punches were thrown, but the words were heated. Sipes left, he said, to cool down.

He was standing in the street, he said, when Ruth came out of the bar and attacked him. Two punches sent him to the ground, and then Ruth kicked him. Sipes said he climbed to his feet and hit Ruth, who lost his balance on the curbstone and tumbled onto the street. Ruth's head hit the street hard, and his skull was fractured. That was the cause of death.

Sipes's story of self-defense, good enough to have a coroner's jury drop all charges, left several questions open. Why was Ruth attacking *him*? Why wasn't he swinging at Beefelt, the nemesis to family tranquillity? Was Ruth a friend of Beefelt's, but not of Sipes's? Was this simply a drinking situation, late at night, everybody too easy to argue and swing, a drunken row that turned tragic? Was there a longer history at work here, other factors and incidents involved? What? None of this ever was explained.

The Babe, if he knew, never told the story, not in all the words written about him. He never said anything substantial about how his father died and not much more about how his father lived. George Ruth left few more traces than the Babe's mother had six years earlier. His story was again part of the fog.

The Babe had been in Baltimore less than two months earlier when he was threatening to jump to the Chester shipyard. He was found at his father's bar, the same bar where the incident occurred. He supposedly stayed in the same apartment upstairs from the bar. Did he know any of the other parties involved in all this? Did he know them all? Did he—in the end—know his father? There had been obvious contact in later years. He had helped his father buy the bar, had helped work the bar. Wasn't that a sign they had come to some kind of an understanding? Why were there no tales of that, no words from a proud parent about a successful son, no words from the son about earlier life with the parent?

The man who took the boy on the Wilkens Avenue trolley went to the grave at Louden Park Cemetery in Baltimore on August 28. The boy, now 23 years old, who thought he was 24, stood at the graveside. A relative said it was the first time he "ever had seen George cry." What did the tears mean? Young George, Babe, the Colossus, the Home Run King never explained.

On Friday he was back in the lineup in left field, batting fourth, in a doubleheader against the Tigers. On Saturday the Red Sox clinched the pennant. He was back on the public record.

The 1918 World Series against the Chicago Cubs contained the same chaos that went through the regular season. The Red Sox were the win-

ners, four games to two. The Babe won two of the games. He won the
first as a surprise starter with a six-hit shutout, 1–0, and won the fourth
game 3–2, backed by his own two-run triple and despite needing relief
from Joe Bush in the ninth. Between the games, on the train back to
Boston, he had injured the middle finger of his left hand sparring with
teammate Walt Kinney. He pitched with a hand colored yellow from iodine and said later that the iodine, not the injured finger, hurt his grip on
the baseball.

"The Star-Spangled Banner," not yet the national anthem, was played
for the first time at a sporting event at the seventh inning in the first game
in Chicago, then repeated at each game after that. Carrier pigeons were
used for the first time at the sixth game at Fenway to transport inning-by-
inning scores to the troops at Camp Devens. Attendance was lower than
expected at all games, none of them a sellout.

Before the fifth game, the players threatened to strike, knowing that
the proposed winners' share of $2,000 and the losers' share of $1,400
were not going to be reached. In a comic opera sequence, with more than
20,000 fans already in the stands, American League president Ban Johnson hopelessly drunk, and the negotiations a mess, the players backed
down. They said they would play for the sake of the public and for all
the wounded soldiers and sailors who were in the stands. This decision
was announced to the crowd through a megaphone by former Boston
mayor John "Honey Fitz" Fitzgerald, who already had a grandson named
John Fitzgerald Kennedy. The winners' shares after the sixth game were
$1,102. The losers' shares were $724.

Ruth sat out the fifth game with his injured finger and played only the
last two innings of the sixth game as a defensive replacement when left
fielder George Whiteman was injured. He was not one of the leading
strikers—Hooper was at the head of that. The Babe mostly followed his
other, patterned pursuits. This was called "the Straw Hat Series" because
it was held a month earlier than usual, closer to summer, but the unofficial fashion rule was that straw hats shouldn't be worn after Labor Day.
Ruth took great pleasure in enforcing the rule, especially on the train ride,
by punching holes in offending straw hats. He also took great pleasure in
his usual pleasures.

One of the writers assigned to cover the Series was Gene Fowler, a talented young guy who had been called from Denver, the hometown of
famed columnist Damon Runyon, to replace Runyon for the *New York*

American. Runyon was being sent to Europe to write about the war. Arriving in Chicago the day before the first game, weighed down with the pressure of trying to fill in for Runyon, Fowler set out that night to find a friend, Harry Hochstadter.

After assorted misadventures, Fowler found his man in the hotel suite of a 300-pound wine agent named John "Doc" Krone. The room was filled with sportswriters and other freeloaders gathered around a galvanized steel tub filled with bottles of Doc Krone's product. When Hochstadter, who had been in the suite for a while, passed out, none other than the Babe helped him to a chair with an advisory to switch to beer.

The Babe also had been drinking. Fowler, who knew the big man was scheduled to pitch the Series opener, wondered if this activity would hurt a pitcher's performance the next afternoon. He asked—an exchange he described years later in his newspaper memoir *Skyline*.

"The hale young man gave me a bone-rattling slap on the back," Fowler wrote.

> "I'll pitch 'em all if they give me the word." The Babe then announced he was leaving us to keep an appointment with someone who wore skirts. On his way out he urged that Mr. Hochstadter be given a Christian burial.
>
> The Babe was young and strong: he managed to stay up all that night, and then shut out the Cubs, 1 to 0, the next day. At the close of the Series, which the Red Sox won, four out of six games, Ruth had established a pitching record of twenty nine and two-thirds consecutive scoreless innings for combined World Series play (against Brooklyn in 1916, and the Chicago Cubs in 1918).
>
> I was young and strong, too, but the all-night escapade at Doc Krone's left me somewhat less effective than the Babe the next afternoon.

The Babe wound up in Lebanon, Pennsylvania, on the books as an employee of Bethlehem Steel after the Series. He and Helen rented an apartment. Virtually every major league ballplayer made some kind of similar move. The prevailing wisdom now was that baseball was going to be shut down for a while, certainly for the 1919 season.

He took the long route to his new job, playing a couple of exhibitions in New Haven and Hartford, then left Lebanon to play another one in Baltimore, where he wrenched his knee. Singeing his hand in a kitchen accident and catching the flu again limited him to one game for the steel plant against a barnstorming group of his Red Sox teammates. It was a succession of nuisances but could have been much worse: he could have stayed in Boston.

The end of September and early October was when the Spanish influenza epidemic roared through the city. On October 2 alone, 202 people died in Boston from the disease. One of them was the wife of Edward F. Martin, the 34-year-old sportswriter who had covered the Babe's entire season for the *Boston Globe*. Martin himself died the next day, less than a month after typing out the details of the Red Sox World Series win.

Camp Devens was particularly hard hit. By October 20, about 14,000 men had been hospitalized at the camp with the Spanish influenza, and one out of 18 (773 men) had died. Dr. Victor Vaughan, Surgeon General of the Army, describing the soldiers in the hospital, said, "The faces wore a bluish cast, a cough brought up the blood-stained sputum. In the morning, the dead bodies are stacked up like cordwood."

The Babe, recovered from his own flu, told friends that he expected to be called to the service soon. This did not happen. Draft limits had been expanded to include men from age 18 to 45, more troops leaving every day, but in the second week of November startling news started to arrive from France. The Germans were meeting with the Allies in Gen. Ferdinand Foch's railway carriage headquarters in Compiègne. Terms of an armistice were being worked out, and, fast as that, amazing as that, on November 11 at 11 o'clock in the morning (the 11th hour of the 11th day of the 11th month of the year), the fighting ceased.

The war had claimed 7,996,888 men in uniform—civilian casualties were impossible to count. Over 21 million men had been wounded. The American death toll was 58,480 with 189,955 wounded. The end of hostilities brought people into the streets.

"A 100-foot line of sailors, containing one woman, and led by a drum major wielding an old broom, marched in lockstep, forming the most eccentric figures, in and out of the crowd," the *Globe* reported from what it called the largest celebration in Boston history. "A group of men wheeled a six-foot man in a child's perambulator with a sign, 'My Daddy's Coming Home.' A knot of marching sailors was led by a sign reading 'No liquor sold. Everybody sober.' A bunch of young Italians had pipes in their mouths and within the bowls burning candles, while they marched in the shelter of gay Japanese parasols."

Done.

With no need to be at the steel plant anymore, with the draft not a worry, the Babe could return with Helen to the IHATETOQUITIT cottage in Sudbury. The war that had rearranged borders and affected so many lives had affected his too. It had put him in the outfield.

CHAPTER SIX

A BETTER NEW YEAR than 1919 never had arrived. There had been better celebrations—November 11, less than two months earlier, had been much wilder across the country than anything that happened now in Times Square—but there never had been a year that began with as much promise, hope, expectation.

This was the year to get down to business. The troops were coming home every day, blinking at the miracle of their own continued existence, roaring to get started on whatever they really wanted to do. The shelves were filling up again, no more meatless or wheatless days by decree. No more heatless Thursdays. The logic of optimism was obvious: if we can win such a ghastly war with our efforts, then what can we do in other, easier areas? The message everywhere was that all things were possible, all goals obtainable.

"We must teach our feet again to trod on solid ground," Gov. Samuel W. McCall of Massachusetts declared in his New Year's address. That was the solemn approach.

"Discouraged boy, tired of waiting, ready to give up, with your heart down and the devil whispering to you, 'What's the use?' " *Boston Globe* columnist Frank Crane wrote in his New Year's column. "Listen! Don't you hear the clock? Up and at it once more! Slough off your disappointment as a dirty coat, roll up your sleeves—the world's your hickory nut, full of meat, and you're the boy to crack it." That was the giddy heart of the matter.

The Babe was as optimistic as everyone else. He was ready to get down to business too. Crack the hickory nut? Yes, indeed. He wanted more money.

"I'm going to ask for a figure in my contract that may knock Mr. Frazee silly," he announced. "But nevertheless I think I am deserving of everything I ask."

There was no doubt about his place in baseball now. He was the number-one attraction in the game. If there had been a Most Valuable Player Award in 1918, and there wasn't, he would have won it in a breeze. He was the best player on the best team, and if you listened, you would hear good young players compared now to Babe Ruth, not Ty Cobb, not anyone else. The best player deserved the best money, Ty Cobb money.

The Babe had made $7,500 in 1918. Now he wanted $15,000 a year.

He had picked up a business manager, Johnny Igoe, maybe the first business manager ever hired by a ballplayer, and had learned the first, halting dance steps of negotiation. Pretend that you have options: that was the ticket. Tell 'em you'll quit and be . . . a boxer. Tell 'em there are a lot of other things you can do. Tell 'em unless you get the $15,000, you won't be playing baseball. The Babe followed the program—"I always have wanted to box," he said quite seriously, discussing a $5,000 offer to fight Gunboat Smith—and more. He let it be known that he might be playing in the Delaware County League. He also suggested in a visit to New Bedford that he might invest in a franchise in a league that played roller polo, a sort of hockey on roller skates. He tried to sound resolute.

The weakness in his argument, of course, was that he wouldn't make anywhere near the same money in any of these other pursuits. He was a baseball player, and the reserve clause, the foundation of organized baseball's power over its employees, bound him for life to the Red Sox or to whomever they sent his rights. (The clause would be tested during the summer in congressional antitrust hearings, but upheld once again.) If he wanted to play baseball, he pretty much would have to do it for Harry Frazee.

Frazee knew the rules. He compared Ruth to the actors who always wanted big money from him.

"They swear they are through with the show, they'll leave it flat," the owner said, "But it would take at least two squads of marines to keep them out of the theater and off the stage."

The weakness in Frazee's argument was that he needed Ruth. He could threaten trades and say that he would refuse to pay exorbitant money, but Ruth was the centerpiece of his attraction. The preceding two years had been one worse than the other financially, and now, with the soldiers back and interest presumably returned to the game, he needed his star.

The two men engaged in this time-honored foxtrot of commerce through the end of January, all through February, and well into March. They met twice in Boston but solved nothing. The Babe and Helen spent substantial time with friends in Meredith, New Hampshire, where newspapers reported that he frolicked in the snow, bought out all the candy at the local general store, and told a bunch of rowdies to sit down and shut up at a community dance.

The lines hardened on March 18, when the Red Sox official party left Boston for spring training. Frazee had switched the site this year from Hot Springs to Tampa, Florida, so Ed Barrow, 11 players, and five sportswriters departed from South Station for New York, where they boarded a steamer, the *Arapahoe*, to sail to Jacksonville. They would then take another train to Tampa.

The Babe stayed in Sudbury. The season already had been shortened to 140 games, owing to the postwar chaos, everything starting late, and now training would start later than late for him. Frazee had noticed his condition, which included more than a couple of added pounds, and knew this would not be a good thing. He made the first move, asking the Babe to come down to New York the next day.

The Babe complied. The meeting in Frazee's office went surprisingly well. The Babe hadn't planned on signing, hadn't even brought extra clothes, but very soon he was shaking hands with the owner and calling Helen to pack a bag and have a friend put it on a train to New York. The final figure was three years for a total of $30,000. (The announced figure was three years for $27,000.) The Babe was on the midnight train to Florida. He had a $2,500 raise from his 1918 salary of $7,500.

"I don't expect that manager Barrow will ask me to play two or three positions this year, for I would rather play in one position," he said before leaving. "I enjoy being in the game every day, and there is nothing I like better than to get in there and take a hard swing at the ball when some of the boys are on the bases."

This was the second part of business that had to be handled. He knew where the meat of the hickory nut was located.

The Red Sox trained at Plant Field, which was built in the infield of a racetrack. The field, unused for three years, had been whipped back into shape to impress the new tenants. Next door was the Tampa Bay Hotel, where the team stayed, a sprawling resort with Moorish architecture. A large tent had been erected next to the hotel.

The Red Sox weren't the only attraction in the months of March and April. Evangelist Billy Sunday also was in town. The tent was his canvas cathedral.

"The hour is come for plain speech . . ." his loud and lively voice would suggest to the wayward souls of Hillsborough County, packed together in front of him every night for a month. "Everything the devil's in favor of, I'm against."

Fifty-six years old, the Rev. Sunday was a charismatic contortionist with both words and body, flipping around the stage, sliding up to the podium as if it were second base, shouting about how the devil threw spitballs at everyone in this wicked world. He was a dynamic speaker, now at the height of his popularity, and one of the major forces in the damnation of demon alcohol and the ratification of the Eighteenth Amendment, Prohibition, slightly more than a month earlier. It was estimated that he traveled over a mile, back and forth, as he delivered each sermon.

The beginnings of his success story sounded much like the Babe's story. He had been placed in an orphanage in Ames, Iowa, but escaped at age 14 and went to work on his own in an assortment of odd jobs across the Midwest. He also played baseball. Noticed by future Hall of Famer Cap Anson in Marshallton, Iowa, he was brought straight to the Chicago Cubs, never a day in the minor leagues. He was known as the fastest man in the National League. Flush with his success at a young age, he fell into a life of drinking, carousing, and following perfumed ladies into the night.

This was where the story changed. After eight years in the big leagues, he stumbled into the Pacific Garden Mission in Chicago one night and heard a preacher boom out the gospel of Jesus Christ. He claimed that his life changed in an instant. He quit baseball, turning down good money again and again, and evolved into this evangelist who shouted, "Whiskey and beer are all right in their place, but their place is hell."

Now he was not only in the same neighborhood but on the same ball field with the Babe. The Red Sox gave Sunday his own uniform, let him take batting practice and fielding practice with the team, let him umpire scrimmage games between "the Regulars" and "the Battering Babes." They even moved the starting times of their series of exhibition games with the New York Giants to 4:15 to accommodate Sunday, his staff, and the 6,000-plus worshipers who were arriving every night. The good folk could have baseball and salvation, all in the same trip.

The Babe and Sunday posed for assorted pictures together, young hedonist and old evangelist caught in the same moment, laughing at the same time. Did they talk? What did they say? They even shared the same physical condition at the outset, the Babe unable to go more than 100 yards when he tried to run a half mile on his first day in Tampa. The batting cage was a bit different. The evangelist was rusty, long away from the game. The Babe, despite breaking one of his two favorite bats, pounded the ball early.

In the dugout, Barrow still pondered the decision between pitching and hitting for his star. An off-season poll of managers in 1918 indicated that most of them thought the Babe should be a pitcher. The Babe, in the second half of his business plan, kept repeating that he wanted to hit. He said it in the most definitive way possible in the first exhibition on April 4 against the Giants.

The pitcher for the Giants was "Columbia George" Smith, the nickname handed to him because he had attended Columbia University. In the second inning, Columbia George served up a pitch that resulted in a home run that defied any lesson he ever learned in any physics class he ever took. The Babe swung his one unbroken bat, and the ball flew and flew and flew some more, over the fence in right and onto and across the racetrack. This was the longest home run he or anyone else ever had seen.

"Those who saw this homer were awestruck," Ed Barrow said years later. "And anyone who saw it still talks about it."

A knot of sportswriters, led by Mel Webb of the *Globe,* found a surveyor's tape and had right fielder Ross Youngs of the Giants show them where the ball ultimately had landed. They gauged that it had traveled 508 feet on the fly and rolled dead 579 feet from home plate. Even John McGraw, who always downplayed the value of Ruth's homers, was moved to react.

"I believe that's the longest ball I ever saw," he said.

Ruth and Barrow each signed the ball, and that night it was presented to Billy Sunday in the tent before he asked his listeners to "walk the sawdust trail" to give their hearts to the Lord.

The prime stop on the trip home for Ruth was Baltimore, where the Red Sox played back-to-back exhibitions against Jack Dunn's Orioles. This was his first hitting appearance before the home folk, the grown-up kids from St. Mary's, the Xaverian brothers, any doubters who didn't believe the stories they read about George from Boston, about Nigger Lips, now known as the Colossus and the Mauler and the Home Run King.

He did not disappoint. On April 18, he went 4-for-4 plus two walks in a 12–3 win. All four hits were home runs. On April 19, on his first two at-bats, he hit two more. Six home runs in six at-bats. If any last little bit of air was left in the question about whether he should hit or pitch, it was sent over the right-field fence and straight toward Baltimore Harbor.

"How do you teach someone to hit like that?" he was asked after the first barrage.

"You don't," he said, matter-of-fact. "It's a gift."

The fact was noted that not only did the Babe's friends get to see his work—"Today was my day to show them what I could do," he said, "and I did"—but a shivering Harry Frazee also was in attendance. He could see where all his money was going.

Frazee accompanied the team north, making a stop in Jersey City for a pair of exhibitions—no home runs for the Babe—and was in New York for opening day against the Yankees on April 23. The Polo Grounds, also named Brush Stadium, had been repainted for the new season. The stands were green, the hands of the center-field clock now a bright red, and the beer advertisements on the outfield walls had disappeared, replaced by nothing stronger than ginger ale. A crowd of 30,000, the largest opening day crowd in New York baseball history, appeared, giving an indication of how the "nonessential" sport of a year ago now had meaning. Men in military uniforms were everywhere.

It took the Babe one at-bat to deliver his message for the season. Hitting fourth, with the returned Jack Barry already on first, he scorched a line drive that bounced past the Yankees' new center fielder, Duffy Lewis, and rolled almost to the faraway fence. Barry jogged home, and the Babe rambled, one at-bat, one inside-the-park home run. The Red Sox cruised to a 10–0 win.

Three days of rainouts followed, sending the team to Washington for a three-game series before finally hitting Boston. This was where Barrow decided to deliver *his* message for the season. The Babe had slipped back into his late-night, all-night wanderings with the same ease with which he had regained his batting eye. Barrow thought that the first week of the season would be a good time to address this situation.

The Sox stayed at the Hotel Raleigh, and Barrow, as he sometimes did, took an after-midnight seat in the lobby to await the return of his players, notably the Babe. By 4:00 A.M., still waiting for the Home Run King, everyone else tucked into bed, the manager decided to tuck himself into bed. Angry, needing sleep, he asked the night porter the next evening to knock at his door when Ruth came in, no matter what the time might be. A few bucks, folded together, ensured compliance. The knock came at six in the morning.

"That fellow just came in," the porter reported.

Barrow put on his bathrobe and slippers and went to Ruth's room. He had assigned Dan Howley, a coach, to keep Ruth under control, but Howley obviously had fared no better than all other assigned roommates. Barrow knocked. He could hear voices and could see through the transom that a light was on. The voices stopped and the light went out as soon as Barrow knocked.

He turned the doorknob. The door opened.

Ruth was in bed, cover pulled up, smoking a pipe. Howley had bolted for the bathroom. Barrow asked Ruth if he always smoked a pipe in the middle of the night. Ruth said he did, that he found it relaxing. Barrow walked to the bed, pulled back the covers. Ruth was still in his clothes, even wearing his shoes. Barrow said he would see him at the ballpark.

The confrontation did not go well at the park. Barrow dressed down Ruth in front of the team. Ruth threatened to punch Barrow in the nose. Barrow, 25 years older but the same size as Ruth, offered to lock the door, just the two of them. Ruth wordlessly declined by leaving with the rest of the team to practice.

Barrow suspended Ruth, didn't let him play in the game, but that night on the train ride back to Boston the two men settled their differences. Ruth came to Barrow's compartment, not only contrite but willing to explain why he acted the way he did. The explanation went back to St. Mary's, back to his unsettled times at home. The conversation lasted for a while. Barrow was moved. The question was what he and his star would do next. Ruth had an idea.

"Manager," Ruth said, "if I leave a note in your box every night when I come in, and I tell you what time I got home, will you let me play?"

Barrow said yes, starting a routine that was followed on the road for the rest of the season. Ruth left his notes, starting with the salutation "Dear Manager" or "Dear Eddie," in the hotel mailbox every night. Barrow read them and threw them away. He said he never checked whether the notes were accurate or not. It was a good deal for both parties: Ruth was able to play; Barrow was able to go to bed.

The note writer, as it turned out, was the least of Barrow's problems as the season progressed. His defending world champions fell apart in a hurry. (Maybe he should have had everyone write a note.) Joe Bush had thrown his arm out in an exhibition game against the Giants and never recovered. Herb Pennock was slow coming back from the rust of war. Sam Jones was hurt for three weeks. Carl Mays jumped the team. The pitching staff was a yearlong mess. A six-game losing streak in the middle of a 21-game road trip left the champs nine and a half games out by May 27, and they never were in the fight, finishing in sixth place, twenty and a half games behind the Chicago White Sox.

The only show to watch during all of this was Ruth, who was climbing the statistical ladder, breaking past home run barriers on the way. It was quite a show: he was like a long-distance runner out ahead of the pack, running against a stopwatch. The rest of the race didn't matter. How far could he go? Fully tuned in to playing every day now, swinging hard every time at bat, he made the home run a new, loud art form.

The first marker put in front of him was Socks Seybold's American League record of 16, set in 1902. He tied that on July 29 with a ninth-inning shot into the Fenway bleachers off Dutch Leonard. A wire service report suggested, "American League pitchers appear at a loss to stop him, the big pitcher and outfielder having made scoring drives off balls knee high and over his head alike."

The next stop was the major league record of 24—the papers called it "the world record"—set by Buck Freeman of the Washington club in the National League in 1899. This was matched on September 8 with a bomb into the right-field pavilion at the Polo Grounds. Freeman, now an umpire in the American Association, was contacted in Toledo about the loss of his record.

"I was convinced several years ago that Ruth would at least equal my record, if not surpass it," Freeman said. "I never could hit like Ruth. I could not take the swing the big fellow does because I haven't the physique."

A final stop had been added too in the weeks leading up to number 24. Record books had been checked, and it was found that someone named Ned Williamson had hit 27 homers for the Chicago White Stockings in 1884. The fact was mentioned that baseball had been a much different game at that time—the batter, for instance, could request that the pitcher throw either a low ball or a high ball—and the right-field fence at Chicago's Congress Street Grounds was a ridiculously close 215 feet, but a record was a record. The Babe might as well break that one too.

He did that in fine dramatic fashion on September 20, a day that had been staged just for him, "Babe Ruth Day" at Fenway, with over 30,000 people in attendance. He returned to the mound for the occasion, pitching the first game of a doubleheader against the first-place White Sox, who were on their way to the pennant. He had pitched in a regular turn in different stretches during the season due to the injuries and Mays's defection, would finish with a 9–5 record and a 2.97 ERA, but this appearance was scheduled simply to be part of the day.

He struggled on the mound. When he was replaced in the sixth inning by Allan Russell, he moved to left field to finish the game. In the bottom of the ninth, one out, tie game, Ruth was fooled by a Lefty Williams curveball, but reached out with one hand on the bat and flicked it over the *left*-field wall and—the *Globe* reported—through an open window on Lansdowne Street. In one flick, he won the game, tied the weird record, and caused Lefty Williams to throw his glove in disgust into the outfield.

Between games, Ruth was honored with assorted gifts that included a diamond ring, a $600 certificate of deposit, cuff links, and a pair of baseball shoes, size 11. Helen, who stood with him and took each gift from him after each presentation, was given a traveling bag. In the second game, he probably should have broken the record with a shot that bounced into the bleachers (a home run under the rules at that time), but umpire Billy Evans ruled it a double.

The Massachusetts National Guard was at work for the day due to the bitter police strike taking place in Boston, and a sergeant from the Guard tried to help the Babe's case. He had a detail collect signed statements from people sitting in the bleachers, all of whom said the ball was a home run. He presented the statements to Evans.

"You are, as I understand it, supposed to protect the public and me," Evans told the sergeant. "It would be well for you to attend to your police duties and leave the umpiring to me."

"You can't talk to me that way," the sergeant replied.

A lieutenant intervened. The hit remained a double.

The Babe broke the record four days later. He hit a mammoth home run at the Polo Grounds in the ninth inning off the Yanks' Bob Shawkey, a shot that went over the roof of the stands and landed in a park called Manhattan Fields, the longest home run in Polo Grounds history. He finished with 29 homers, his final blast coming in the next-to-last game of the season at Washington.

He was the talk of baseball. He had hit a home run in every park in the American League, including the longest home runs ever seen in New York, Detroit, St. Louis, and Boston, not to mention Tampa, Florida. Fan mail had arrived in such piles that he now asked teammates and the Red Sox front office to handle it. He had opened the window to the future of the game while playing for a sad sixth-place team.

How sad? Harry Hooper, on the last western road trip, wrote an apology to Ed Barrow on stationery from the Hotel Winton in Cleveland. The season was a bust. "Having in view the many stories and rumors as to the cause of the present low standing of the Boston Am club: stories of dissension among the players and rumors of mismanagement; we the undersigned wish to correct an injustice to manager Ed Barrow," Hooper wrote.

We feel that he has treated his players royally, in a manner that could not be improved upon. The poor success was caused by a combination of bad breaks. The failure of some of the regulars to perform up to their past standards, weak pitching and continued bad luck on the field has upset the expectations of the management and the critics. The players are in harmony amongst themselves and with the manager, and stories to the contrary are not true. We are for him to the last.

The letter was signed by 21 members of the team. Ninth in the list, between Wally Schang and Everett Scott, was G. H. Ruth. He apologized, even though he had put together a unique and remarkable season. Maybe it was habit . . . another note for Ed Barrow's mailbox.

The Babe's business side jumped into action as soon as the season ended. Actually, it jumped in a day before the season ended. Barrow gave him permission to skip the final game in Washington and play in a lucrative exhibition game in Baltimore—the start of a string of lucrative exhibitions.

Every day he seemed to be in another town, hitting another home run against another stitched-together opponent. One day he was in Portland, Maine, going 3-for-5 with a homer, but also being struck out by "Bissonette, a former pitcher at Westbrook Seminary." The next day, all factories and stores closed at noon in Sanford, Maine, to see him hit a fifth-inning homer in a 4–3 win. Then there was a two-run homer in a 9–8 loss to the Comets in Lynn, Massachusetts. Then a homer in the sixth in Beverly, Massachusetts, to beat Marblehead. Then Troy, New York, where the next day's headline announced, "Babe Fails to Get Home Run," but he did go 3-for-4 with a triple. Then Rutland, Vermont . . . the longest ball ever hit in Rutland, Vermont.

His most interesting stop was in Attleboro, Massachusetts. A manufacturing town near the Rhode Island border, Attleboro for years had played an annual best-of-five series against rival North Attleboro. These were town teams playing for town pride—typical stuff. This year the stakes became a bit higher.

After Attleboro lost the first game, the millionaire owner of one local jewelry firm gave manager Dan O'Connell a bunch of cash and told him to "get some better ballplayers." O'Connell got the Babe and Carl Mays and fellow major leaguers Heinie Zimmerman and Dave Bancroft.

The North Attleboro team somehow heard about this, and a millionaire jewelry store owner in North Attleboro gave Frank Kelly even more cash to get even more ballplayers. He wound up with Walter Johnson, Grover Cleveland Alexander, Rogers Hornsby, Eddie Collins, Bob Shawkey, Harry Hooper, and Frankie Frisch.

The memories of who played in which game have become murky with the years, but by the time the deciding fifth game arrived, the event was being called "the Little World Series" and gamblers and prostitutes had arrived from as far away as Chicago. Attleboro won, 6–3, on a homer by Bobby Roth, the Babe did nothing special, and a party was held after the game that became grand local legend.

On October 24, the Babe and Helen and Johnny Igoe, the business manager, who also was a Boston druggist, boarded a train for Los Angeles. A number of exhibitions had been scheduled up and down California at $500 apiece, plus expenses, and the Babe was excited. He never had been past St. Louis, so this was an adventure. "Indefinite" was his stated time of return.

Before he departed, he placed a ticking package on Harry Frazee's front step. He turned in his two Red Sox uniforms at Fenway Park and said he probably was done with the team "unless Frazee comes through good." He explained that his idea of "good" was $20,000 a year.

"I will not play with the Red Sox unless I get $20,000," he said. "I feel I made a bad move last year when I signed a three-year contract to play for $30,000. The Boston club realized much on my value, and I think I am entitled to twice as much as my contract calls for."

To him, he was taking the first steps in the familiar dance. He would crack the hickory nut again. One step, two steps, he would stay in California for the entire winter. He would threaten to quit baseball for the movies. He would ponder a boxing career, training with Kid McCoy. He and Helen would live in a couple of $50-a-day bungalows and meet the celebrated figures of the celebrated town. He figured that the serious dancing wouldn't come until the spring.

"I have several propositions in hand, many of which will pay me over $10,000 a year," the Babe declared from the land of sun and palm trees.

Little did he know that Harry Frazee wasn't in the mood to dance this time. There would be a new set of partners by the time the Colossus returned.

CHAPTER SEVEN

THE OWNERS of the New York Yankees were known in the newspapers as "the two Colonels." It was a tidy phrase, but misleading. Though Col. Jake Ruppert and Col. Tillinghast L'Hommedieu Huston shared the title, the team, and sometimes overlapping portions of New York nightlife, they were two quite different men.

Col. Ruppert, age 53, was a member of the New York aristocracy, born into wealth, a member of all of the city's clubs of privilege, the head of the family brewing company, the owner of racehorses and show dogs, a former four-time congressman from the 15th District on the East Side, a lifelong millionaire bachelor who always explained his marital state with the saying "he travels fastest who travels alone." His rank had been handed to him in the silk-stocking Seventh Regiment of the New York National Guard.

Col. Huston, 54, whose name sounded far more regal, actually came from Cincinnati, the civil engineer son of a civil engineer. A captain in the Spanish-American War, he stayed in Cuba for ten years after the war ended and made a lot of money in a project to dredge and improve the harbors in Havana and other port cities. After moving to New York with that money and looking for investment and excitement, he reenlisted in the army in 1917 for the world war and was promoted to lieutenant colonel while building roads and railways under heavy shell fire behind the British lines in France.

Ruppert was a prince of fashion, groomed and immaculate, and spoke with a Germanic accent even though he had been raised in the family mansion at the corner of 93rd Street and Fifth Avenue. He now lived in a 12-room apartment on Fifth Avenue and had a country estate in Garrison, New York, that featured one of the largest privately owned art collections and libraries in the world plus a menagerie of exotic animals. He was a bit of an exotic animal himself: when the automobile first arrived in the city, he was one of the first drivers, a dashing figure in his linen duster and goggles. He directed a corps of servants that included a butler, maid, valet, cook, and laundress and owned a famous yacht named the *Albatross*. Huston, on the other hand, was rumpled and round, called people by their first names, had a big voice and a big laugh and a fondness for the product that came from Ruppert's brewery. He was married, with a son and two daughters, and owned a 30,000-acre farm in Georgia, where he had built a lavish—many said garish—mansion based on the Petit Trianon of Versailles.

The two men were thrown together in an arranged marriage. Each much rather would have bought the New York Giants, the glamour team of the city, the team of John McGraw and Christy Mathewson and championships. Ruppert, in fact, had tried and failed in attempts to buy the team in both 1903 and 1912. He often told the story about how he once practiced with the Giants in his teens and learned by taking only one of catcher Buck Ewing's bullet throws to second base, feeling the sting in his hand, wondering if any bones had been broken, that he would never be a major league baseball player. Huston, mad with his new money, mad with his new life, also had loved baseball as a boy and tried to buy into the game several times with his mad money, most recently with the Chicago Cubs in 1913. (Ruppert was offered the Cubs but declined, saying he wouldn't be interested in "anything so far from Broadway.")

When the Yankees, the very poor relations of New York sport, came up for sale at the end of the 1914 season, a friend in Cincinnati, Bill Fleischmann, casually suggested to Ruppert that he join with Huston to buy the team. Ruppert hadn't seen the team play more than four or five times, mostly to take a look at American League stars like Ty Cobb and Walter Johnson, but he was interested. He contacted Huston. The two men didn't know each other, didn't meet until they started talking about the deal, but both knew McGraw of the Giants and both loved baseball. This love—and money—brought them together.

On December 31, 1914, at the Hotel Wolcott, they bought the Yankees for $450,000. Ruppert brought a certified check and an attorney to handle his half of the transaction. Huston came alone and reached into his pocket for a large roll of money and counted out 225 thousand-dollar bills.

"For $450,000," Ruppert said later in the Germanic accent, "we got an orphan ball club without a home of its own, without players of outstanding ability, without prestige."

By December 1919, the partnership had survived five somewhat acrimonious seasons, the Colonels arguing with each other about almost everything, and the team had shown some progress. There were no championships, but the Yankees had finished a respectable third in 1919. The Colonels' money had allowed them to pry away a player here, a player there, from teams that had considerably fewer resources.

Two of their deals had been made with the Red Sox. At the end of the 1918 season, they had picked up pitchers Ernie Shore and Dutch Leonard and outfielder Duffy Lewis, all back from the war, for four players and $15,000. In the middle of the 1919 season, they had added pitcher Carl Mays for pitchers Allan Russell and Bob McGraw and $40,000.

The Mays deal was controversial. A troubled and disliked figure on the Red Sox, Mays became upset when his teammates made some errors behind him and put him in the hole, 4–0, in the second inning of a game against the White Sox in Chicago. When catcher Wally Schang, trying to throw out a runner trying to steal second, inadvertently hit Mays in the back of the head with the ball, that was the final perceived indignity. Mays finished the inning, batted in the bottom half, walked, didn't score, came back to the dugout, went straight to the clubhouse, and said he never would play for the Red Sox again. He went home.

Manager Ed Barrow prepared to suspend the pitcher, but Red Sox owner Harry Frazee told him to wait. Frazee said he could trade Mays to the Yankees. And he did.

It was an easy deal to make because he was a friend of Col. Huston's and friendly enough with Col. Ruppert. He was, after all, another New York guy, a resident of Park Avenue, another fast runner on the

Manhattan social map. Like Huston, Frazee was a self-made man, having started his theater career by working in the box office and as an usher at the local theater in Peoria, Illinois, when he was 16 years old. He was on the road a year later as an advance man for a touring production. He slowly graduated into producing his own shows around the country and finally landed on Broadway. He had toured the country promoting a performance involving boxers Jim Jeffries and Jim Corbett. He had been part of the promotion for the fight between Jack Johnson and Jess Willard in Havana.

He teamed with silent partners Hugh Ward and G. M. Anderson in 1917 to buy the Red Sox. The price was $400,000, half of that in a down payment, the rest in notes to Lannin that the partners thought could be repaid from gate receipts and profits from the team. Boston fans worried about the arrival of out-of-town owners, wondered if they would have the proper commitment to winning, but grew to appreciate Frazee's efforts. An attempt at purchasing Walter Johnson from the Washington Senators in the first weeks on the job gave him some instant credibility. His actions in quickly replacing the players who went to the war, leading to the 1918 pennant, further helped his image.

The Mays deal was a reminder of where he lived. It wound up binding him closer together with the Colonels of New York. They had been part of a three-team coalition (Charles Comiskey and the White Sox were the third partner) in assorted battles with American League president Ban Johnson. The Mays deal became a large battle. Johnson ruled the trade invalid and ordered Mays back to the Red Sox. The Colonels and Frazee resisted. Mays joined the Yankees and not only pitched but pitched well, finishing with a 9–3 record in the second half of the season. Johnson refused to distribute the money the Yankees had won for finishing third.

A round of injunctions and restraining orders was issued, everything winding up in court. Johnson in the process was forced to make the embarrassing admission that he not only was the league president but also owned a considerable interest in the Cleveland Indians. The Yankees and Red Sox won the battle, the trade was allowed to stand, and Johnson's power diminished as the third-place money was awarded, but the battle lines deepened. Frazee and the Colonels shared the same bunker.

That made a deal for Babe Ruth much easier to be arranged. The accepted version of how it happened when it happened was that the Colonels asked manager Miller Huggins what he needed to contend for a championship in 1920. Huggins replied, "Get me Babe Ruth." The Colonels then sent Huggins to Frazee to sound out the possibilities. The manager came back and said Ruth was available for $125,000, the largest price ever paid for a baseball player. The Colonels gulped—especially Ruppert—and made the deal.

Frazee's explanation was that he didn't want to deal with the "eccentricities" of his star player anymore. He said that Ruth's salary demands were far out of line, especially with two years to run on an existing contract, and that his behavior was a detriment to team morale. The club would be better off without him, a true team instead of ballplayers eclipsed by a petulant star. The money would free up possibilities to sign other, more team-oriented stars.

Missing in the story was the obvious friendship between the principals involved. Frazee eventually would be called "the Corporal" by at least one writer in New York. Another writer would say that Frazee, Ruppert, and Huston were "as close as three fingers on the same hand." Would Huggins have to act as an intermediary in this kind of relationship? Also missing, not public knowledge until ten months later, was the fact that a $300,000 personal loan from Ruppert to Frazee was a major part of the deal, with Fenway Park used as collateral by the Boston owner.

A much easier scenario can be imagined. Frazee and Huston were not only friends but Broadway drinking buddies, traveling the same glad round of restaurants and parties. Huston was the drinking patron of the New York sportswriters, buying rounds at the bar, always good for a colorful quote. He was called "the Iron Hat" in the papers, an inside nickname that referred not only to his ever-present derby hat but also to his construction background. Frazee, rapidly heading toward the same bulky size as Huston, was known as a heavy drinker.

"Harry Frazee never drew a sober breath in his life, but he was a hell of a producer," lyricist Irving Caesar, who helped write "Tea for Two" and other songs for Frazee's musical productions, once said. "He made more sense drunk than most men do sober."

Alcohol was the machine oil of the time in the baseball industry, despite the approach of Prohibition. Drinking was everywhere. Ban Johnson was an obvious drunk. Ruppert, as president of the United States Brewers Association, had argued against the coming law, claiming that beer was "a liquid food, a healthful beverage, and in no way injurious to the system." Frazee and Huston were definite believers in that philosophy.

Deals and decisions in the game routinely were made late at night after much consumption of liquid food. Would it be outlandish to consider
that was the case here? The idea that the consumption of liquid food by
friends, combined with conversation about personal problems and possible solutions (like a $300,000 loan), resulted in the trade of a notable,
home run–hitting consumer of liquid food would seem to have great logic.

The deal was completed in secrecy, the papers signed on December 26.
Nothing appeared in the newspapers until January 6. The timing was interesting too. Everything was completed in the midst of holiday parties,
the most active time on the social circuit.

The deal could be toasted legally before the new law on liquid food
took effect on January 16, 1920.

Part of the delay in announcing that the Babe was a Yankee was the stip-
ulation that the Colonels wanted to be sure that the Babe wanted to be a
Yankee. He was still on the West Coast with Helen, enjoying the sun and
churning out more palm tree quotes for the salary squabble he did not
know he already had won. The Colonels dispatched manager Huggins to
Los Angeles to inform the big man that the deal had been made and to
talk him into acceptance.

Huggins was one of the prime focuses of conflict between the
Colonels. Huston didn't like him, didn't want him as manager. Ruppert
had hired him in 1918 on the advice of Ban Johnson while Huston was in
France during the war. Huston had argued across the Atlantic Ocean for
Uncle Wilbert Robinson, who was "more his style in character and architecture," New York Times columnist John Kieran said. Ruppert nevertheless hired Huggins, whom he didn't really know, then stuck his heels in
deep and defended his decision.

Huggins was a small, frail man, roughly 5-foot-2 and 120 pounds, a
pipe smoker and a thinker. He had made himself a successful major league
second baseman with the Cincinnati Reds and St. Louis Cardinals
through ingenuity and industry. He scrunched down at the plate, offering
a tiny strike zone, and led the National League in walks four times. He
was a base stealer, a pest. Looking for an advantage, he made himself into
a switch-hitter. A natural right-hander, he concentrated in the off-season
on doing everything left-handed, from eating and drinking to opening
doors and chopping wood. He was a rarity in the game, an educated man

who had graduated from law school at the University of Cincinnati in 1902 before he started his baseball career.

From 1913 to 1917, prior to joining the Yankees, he had managed the underfinanced Cardinals well enough to attract AL president Johnson's notice and subsequently be introduced to Ruppert. He was 40 years old when he took the train west to see Ruth, convinced that the big man was the answer for his ball club. He told friends he thought Ruth could hit "at least" 35 home runs as an every-day player. Despite the fact that the slap-and-run game had been perfect for his small body and limited skills, Huggins was a converted believer in the long ball, a visionary.

When he reached Los Angeles, he set out to find Ruth. His research led him to Griffith Park, where the Babe was playing golf. This was on January 4, 1920. Not wanting to interrupt the Babe's golf, Huggins waited at the clubhouse. Ruth, when he arrived, was still upset with some transgressions suffered on the 18th hole. The meeting did not start well.

"I don't have any time," Ruth said. "I have somewhere to go."

Huggins said he should make time. There were some things that had to be discussed.

"Have I been traded?" Ruth asked.

Huggins indicated that, yes, a trade had been made but still had to be formalized. That was why he had come west. Ruth went into his salary demands. Huggins said they could be addressed when the contract was drawn up. He then began to talk about what he expected from Ruth in the manner of personal behavior. He tried to be fatherly, to help Ruth correct his wanton lifestyle. Ruth would have none of it.

He forever had a bias against small men. He tended to bully them, to make them the butt of many of his practical jokes. He paid small men no heed, as if physical size were the answer in all arguments, the small man's opinion worth nothing without the bulk to back it up. Huggins immediately was added to the small-man list.

The contract was signed the next day at the Hotel Rosslyn. Ruth received the $20,000 per year for two years he wanted, a $20,000 bonus making up the difference in his existing contract. The news was announced in New York and Boston and made headlines across the country. The largest amount ever paid for a baseball player had been $55,000 for Tris Speaker by the Cleveland Indians. The figure for Ruth more than doubled that.

Were the Colonels crazy? No one in New York thought so. "The two

Colonels—Ruppert and Huston—were praised on all sides for their aggressiveness and liberality in landing baseball's greatest attraction," the *Times* said. "If the club, strengthened by Ruth and by other players the owners have in mind does not carry off the flag, it will not be the fault of the owners." Was Frazee crazy? Opinion in Boston was divided. Red Sox fans universally—and often hysterically—thought Frazee had made a mistake. The 11 newspapers mostly took a more analytical view, especially the sportswriters, many siding with the owner.

"Ruth was 90 percent of our club last summer," Johnny Keenan, leader of the Royal Rooters, said from the fans' perspective. "It will be impossible to replace the strength Ruth gave the Sox. The Batterer is a wonderful player and the fact that he loves the game and plays with his all to win makes him a tremendous asset to a club. The Red Sox management will have an awful time filling the gap caused by his going. Surely the gate receipts will suffer."

"Stars generally are temperamental," the *Boston Herald* said as a voice of calm. "This goes for baseball and the stage. They often have to be handled with kid gloves. Frazee has carefully considered the Ruth angle and believes he has done the proper thing. Boston fans undoubtedly will be up in arms but they should reserve judgment until they see how it works out."

"It is believed that practically every man on the Boston team will be pleased at Ruth's sale to New York," columnist Paul Shannon wrote in the negative in the *Boston Post*. "Popular as Ruth was, on account of his big-heartedness, the men nevertheless realize that his faults overshadow his good qualities."

Frazee continued to campaign to his disgruntled electorate. His showmanship had to be put in reverse, unselling his prime attraction. He sounded like a politician discussing an opponent in a Democratic primary in South Boston.

"While Ruth, without question, is the greatest hitter the game has ever seen, he is likewise one of the most selfish and inconsiderate men that ever wore a uniform," Frazee said. "Had he possessed the right disposition, had he been willing to take orders and work for the good of the club like the other men on the team, I never would have dared let him go. Twice during the past two seasons Babe has jumped the club and revolted. He refused to obey orders of the manager."

The Babe blustered from the West Coast in response. He blustered that he now wanted a part of the purchase price. He blustered that Frazee was

a skinflint, so cheap that he'd charged Mrs. Babe Ruth for a ticket to Babe
Ruth Day at Fenway Park. He blustered that, okay, now he was glad to
be going to New York because he didn't want anything to do with H.
Harry Frazee.

"Frazee sold me because he was unwilling to meet my demands," Ruth
said, "and to alibi himself with the fans he is trying to throw the blame
on me."

In the middle of all the bluster, all the noise from everywhere, Miller
Huggins quietly made the most important announcement of all. He said
in California that the Babe's days as a pitcher were done. No man can
spread himself between pitching and playing the outfield. The Babe was
an every-day player now. He was a hitter.

Frazee's real reasons for selling Ruth would be debated for generations.
At the time the deal was made his statement to the newspapers was pretty
much accepted. Frazee's contention that Ruth, good as he might be, was
contentious, greedy, and a squeaky wheel had some truth to it. Perhaps,
from that view, it was possible the slugger presented as many negatives as
positives for the Red Sox in the future. The key argument was that this
was a baseball move that would be followed by other baseball moves to
strengthen the franchise. As news came out about the $300,000 loan,
however, and as other moves proved fruitless, as history unwound, and
Frazee dealt away other stars, the analysis became quite different.

Frazee was in a financial bind. That was the evening story. On November 1, he missed a $125,000 mortgage payment to Lannin. Forced to
choose between his two moneymaking businesses—baseball and the theater—he chose the theater, his first and biggest passion. The money from
the sale of Ruth, plus the money from the loan, was used to pay off Lannin and keep Frazee's theatrical interests viable, notably the staging of the
hit Broadway musical No, No, Nanette in later years, which proved to be
a tremendous hit and made him millions of dollars.

Frazee was cast in the easily constructed role of a villain, "the Man
Who Sold Babe Ruth," a Boston version of Judas Iscariot. For years, long
after all the characters in the drama were dead, Frazee would be seen as
the despicable cur with mustache and top hat, knocking on the front door
in the middle of a December night to foreclose on the widow woman and
her children. Babe Ruth for No, No, Nanette. This was Frazee's Folly.

Then, in the 1990s, a revisionist look appeared. Wait a minute, No,

No, Nanette didn't debut on Broadway until September 16, 1925. That was more than five years after the deal for Ruth. How could the two events be connected? Frazee's heirs, especially grandson Harry Frazee III, insisted that the owner had been unfairly maligned. He wasn't selling Ruth for personal gain. His finances were fine. The refusal to pay off Lannin was not a sign of financial weakness; it was a dispute, tied to payments Frazee thought Lannin should have made to the American League as part of a settlement with the now-defunct Federal League. Frazee simply was making shrewd business decisions, working mainly to thwart the efforts of American League president Ban Johnson, who wanted him out of Boston. He had been put in a box and was fighting his way out.

This all sounded very good, including the part about anti-Semitism at work because Frazee was perceived in Boston to be Jewish, even though he wasn't, except . . .

Except the final judgment wasn't true. *No, No, Nanette* was indeed part of the deal. Frazee did use the money to keep his theatrical interests afloat. The picture that had been handed down to generations of New England schoolchildren was essentially correct: Harry Frazee was the bad guy.

"In the spring of 1920, I was playing with the Boston Red Sox," Hall of Fame pitcher Waite Hoyt said in an interview for the Baseball Hall of Fame. "Before the season opened, we played an exhibition series with the New York Giants at the Polo Grounds. There was a notice posted on our bulletin board that we were invited to a theatrical performance, a light comedy, called *My Lady Friends*, that Harry Frazee was producing. There would be tickets at the box office.

"We went to the show, and it was quite amusing, very good. We enjoyed it a great deal. That show was put to music in 1924 and became *No, No, Nanette*. . . . If you trace it back, it was the sale of Babe Ruth that provided Harry Frazee with the $125,000 to produce that show."

The deal might not have been as straightforward as that—the Babe for the show—but the show and other theatrical ventures were involved. Frazee had a lot of things happening at the same time.

On October 23, 1919, he was quoted in the *Times*, under the headline "Red Sox Club Not on Market," saying he didn't want to sell because he considered "his star slugger Babe Ruth as the greatest attraction in the national game." Didn't that make him sound like he wanted to keep the Babe forever? On November 1, he defaulted on the $125,000 payment on the note to Lannin. On December 3, *My Lady Friends* opened in New York. On December 26, two days before he was quoted in the *Times* saying that he "would include any player in a deal with the exception of Harry Hooper," the deal for Ruth already had been made.

How had "the greatest attraction in the national game" become a liability in less than two months? Could Ruth's dance to renegotiate his contract have been that offensive? Frazee was from the world of the theater. He had worked in boxing. The contract dance with a temperamental star was a staple in both environments. He'd worked in baseball, had been through these dances with other players, had been through them with Ruth. Management always held the trump card at the end. Where could the player go?

In a 1951 memoir, *My Fifty Years in Baseball,* Ed Barrow, the Red Sox manager, recounted the dialogue when Frazee told him that Ruth was gone. He said he met the owner, who was sitting with actor Frank McIntyre, at six o'clock in the evening in the café at the Hotel Knickerbocker.

"Simon," Frazee said, "I am going to sell Ruth to the Yankees."

"I thought as much," Barrow said. "I could feel it in my bones. But you ought to know that you're making a mistake."

"Maybe I am," Frazee said, "but I can't help it. Lannin is after me to make good on my notes. And my shows aren't going so good. Ruppert and Huston will give me $100,000 for Ruth, and they've agreed to loan me $350,000. I can't turn that down. But don't worry. I'll get you some ballplayers too."

Three months later, on March 26, Frazee announced the purchase of the Harris Theater on West 42nd Street in New York. No details of the purchase were given, but the theater had been built 20 years earlier at the cost of $500,000 and certainly was worth more now. Frazee announced that he was renaming the Harris the Frazee. A hurry-up letter he sent to Ruppert in early April requested the transferral of funds for the loan. He said he needed the money "very badly to complete the balance of my negotiations."

An interesting footnote was that two days before he bought the Harris and renamed it the Frazee, the Yankees had announced they were moving their offices from 30 East 42nd Street to 226 West 42nd Street, where they had taken out a ten-year lease in the Cohen and Harris Theater Building on the same block of the same street as the Frazee. The Yankees now owned a mortgage on Fenway Park and Frazee was the Yankees' neighbor on 42nd Street, and everywhere, it seemed, he and the Colonels, the Red Sox and the Yankees, baseball and the theater, were entwined. The circumstantial evidence pointed directly to where Frazee's interests resided. In May 1923, news would come of Frazee's investment in the musical version of *My Lady Friends*. Nine weeks later, he would sell the Red Sox.

A second footnote was that he paid *No, No, Nanette* star Louise Groody $1,750 per week, which translates to $87,500 per year. He could have had four years of Babe Ruth—even at the Babe's extravagant asking price of $20,000—for one year of Louise Groody.

"The best part about Boston," Harry Frazee once said, "was the train ride back to New York."

The final Boston word on the deal came on the editorial page of the *Globe* on January 7, 1920. Under the title "The Athens of America," the paper decided that it was all right for even the most respected Brahmins and the smartest of the intelligentsia to shed a tear over the departure of a baseball player.

"The Red Sox without Babe Ruth will certainly be—different," the paper said.

> There is much to be said on both sides, and the fans gathered at the daily meetings of the Hot Stove League have already begun to do full justice to the sale of Boston's colossal fence buster.
>
> The Hub of the Universe, also known as the Athens of America, is undeniably "het up" on the prospects of next season. It is possible that unscholarly persons will rise and remark that the prevailing excitement concerning a man who merely made 29 home runs is unbecoming Boston's reputation as a center of learning. If any assertion of that sort is made, it will only indicate a lack of classical culture.
>
> Ancient Greece was both the intellectual and athletic center of the world. Much has been written about the simple chaplet of olive leaves as the only prize for winners of the Olympic games. That was all they were given at the stadium, but when they reached home they received substantial rewards—a jeweled casket filled with gold, a house and lot, no doubt a wife—possibly more than one—and the esteem of the highest circles of society.

The Stadium of Athens was laid out by Lycurgus, the orator. Praxiteles and Phidas, the sculptors, were not above making statues of great athletes. Pindar wrote odes to them.

Any Bostonian who feels sad on the subject of Mr. George H. Ruth may remember Athens and then give full vent to his grief in public.

The Babe was gone.

CHAPTER EIGHT

T HE MARRIAGE between the Babe and New York City had every chance to be perfect. He was built for the New York of 1920, and the New York of 1920 was built for him. He was a muscle man coming to a muscle city in a muscle time. The war was long done, everyone home, and the United States of America was second to no one, thank you very much. New York, New York, was the center of all that was fresh and new and without limit. Enormous buildings were beginning to grow out of the ground, fabulous concrete beanstalks that shut out the sun. Money was beginning to move, faster and faster, doubling and tripling, quadrupling itself, multiplying in the air. Engines were running everywhere. The streets were filled every day with more automobiles and more people of all description.

The Billy Sunday evangelists and their followers might have stuffed through the Eighteenth Amendment, but let those timid outlying souls live with it. The liquor never stopped flowing in New York City, where almost twice as many speakeasies soon replaced the bars that were closed. The night never stopped. Hemlines were being pulled up and stockings were being rolled down and women with short hair and high-fashion bobs were coming out to smoke cigarettes and dance. A faster, louder, outrageous syncopation was at work.

This was the beginning of what New York sportswriter Westbrook Pegler would call "the Era of Wonderful Nonsense" and Paul Gallico, another New York sportswriter, would say was a time when "we were like children who'd been let out of school." What was more nonsensical than standing and cheering the flight of a round, white, horsehide-covered ball with red stitching on the sides? Who, of all the 86,079,000 inhabitants of the country counted in the 1920 census, ever had charged any harder at the sound of the recess bell than the boy from the Baltimore orphanage?

"I began to like New York, the racy, adventurous feel of it at night and the satisfaction that the constant flicker of men and women and machines gives to the restless eye," narrator Nick Carraway says in *The Great Gatsby* by F. Scott Fitzgerald. "I liked to walk up Fifth Avenue and pick out romantic women from the crowd and imagine that in a few minutes I was going to enter into their lives, and no one would ever know or disapprove."

"Do we not stand, in this northern port, at the farthest post of history and look out on the newest horizons?" author Edmund Wilson asked. "Do we not get the latest news and explore the extreme possibilities? Do we not, between the office and the night-club, in the excitement of winning and spending, and slightly poisoned by the absorption of bad alcohol, succeed in experiencing sensations which humanity has never known?"

"New York is a home run town," Miller Huggins said.

If the Babe had stayed in Boston, no matter how many glorious feats he performed, no matter how many records and furniture store windows he broke with long drives over faraway fences, he would have been given a blue ribbon and a gold watch and celebrated as the owner of the prize turnips at the state fair. He would have been a good, great, interesting baseball player. To do the same things in New York not only would make him part of this giddy social upheaval; he would stand in front of the parade with marching boots and a big, 52-ounce baton and whistle. In a time of venial sin in a city of venial sin, the man of magnified venial sin would become the Sultan of Swat, the Caliph of Clout, the Wizard of Whack, the Rajah of Rap, the Wazir of Wham, the Mammoth of Maul, the Maharajah of Mash, the Bambino. The Bam. The Big Bam.

He had landed in the absolute right place.

He didn't arrive in the city until February 28, the day of the Yankees' departure for spring training to Jacksonville. A round of activities had kept

him in Boston, including a dinner at the Hotel Brunswick and a basketball game for the Shawmut Athletic Club, in which he scored eight points
in a 41–25 win.

He boomed into the club offices on 42nd Street, still tanned from California, animated, wearing a large leather coat and handing out cigars.
The Colonels, meeting with Miller Huggins, had their first good look at
their investment. He very much seemed to be the oversized character he
was supposed to be. In the course of conversation, Huston tried to preach
the virtues of moderation, much as Huggins had in California. It also
didn't work.

"Look at ya," the Babe said. "Too fat and too old to have any fun."

"That goes for him too," he added, pointing to Ruppert.

"As for that shrimp," the big man finalized, indicating Huggins, "he's
half-dead right now."

The grand experiment had begun. Ten minutes before the departure of
the *Florida Flyer* to Jacksonville, the big man appeared at the designated
track at Pennsylvania Station in his big leather coat. He was followed by
a porter pushing a cart loaded with suitcases and a new set of golf clubs
picked up in California. A gathering crowd of gawkers came next, merg-
ing into a crowd of the curious who already were waiting.

It was a comic yet majestic scene, due to be repeated every time he
took a train out of the city. He would turn to speak to the porter, or
change direction on a whim, and the crowd would turn with him, people
stepping on each other just to be closer, just to hear whatever he might
say, see whatever he might do.

After this fast, first snapshot, he was off, playing cards with his new
teammates for meal money and more before the train hit New Jersey. The
implications of all of this interest—new town, new team, new position,
new expectations—did not seem to faze him at all. He told reporters that
he expected to hit 50 home runs. He said, "Deal," and headed south with
the same expectations everyone else had.

On the first day in Jacksonville, practice was optional, since Huggins
hadn't arrived, so the big man played golf. Sixteen players showed up at
Southside Park to return to baseball, to get the muscles working again,
but the Babe toured 18 holes at the Florida Country Club. Newspapers
reported that he wore a silk shirt and white golf flannels and at one point
threw his golf club high in the air to intercept a golf ball in midflight.
Look! How many people could do that!

The Yankees team he joined had possibilities. The third-place finish of a year earlier had been put together by some veterans like shortstop Roger Peckinpaugh, third baseman Frank "Home Run" Baker, first baseman Wally Pipp, and outfielders Ping Bodie and Duffy Lewis. A new kid, outfielder Bob Meusel, taller even than Ruth, was supposed to be another big addition this year from Vernon in the Pacific Coast League. Another kid, infielder Aaron Ward, soon would prove vital when Baker, whose wife had died in the off-season, decided to stay home for a year to raise his two children.

The pace of the camp was casual. The Brooklyn Dodgers also trained in Jacksonville, on the other side of the city at Barrs Field, and practiced twice a day. Huggins, a manager who was not a disciplinarian and never had a curfew, worked his team only once every day. This left ample time for golf and hijinks, two areas pursued with great interest.

The Babe quickly established a man-of-mystery routine for hijinks that would continue for all of his time with the Yankees. Evening would come and he would disappear. Helen was back in Massachusetts, and he would cut through the lobby of the Hotel Burbridge, dapper and clean, flamboyantly fashionable, and step into a waiting car or a cab and be gone, off to whatever delights awaited. The other players were left to more modest frivolities around the hotel.

From the start, he lived a different life from all of them. The Yankees, who handed out $5 per day meal money, at one point had to change the policy to $5 credit at the hotel restaurant. The players were eating cheap hot dogs every day, saving the rest of the money for other things, then appearing at the ballpark weak and uninspired. The Babe lived on another economic and social level.

"He was a peculiar character," pitcher Waite Hoyt would say in future years. "If I may be so bold to say, so frank to say, Ruth reminded me of . . . we used to compare him to an Airedale dog or a sheep hound or something. He went around visiting girlfriends, and then he would come home. He would come and the family would, like a dog, pat him. He'd been out all night carousing, and then he would come home to a respectable family, and the family would pat the dog on the head, and the family would say what a nice dog Rover is."

Ping Bodie, nominally his roommate in Jacksonville, delivered the famous answer when asked what kind of guy the Babe was. Bodie said (the quote repeated various times in various ways), "I don't know. I don't room with Babe Ruth. I room with his suitcase."

A second ritual of the spring also was established: the Babe was a slow starter at the plate. Every year it would take a while before the internal mechanisms that measured speed and distance were matched to the external reactions of body mass and power. Every spring there would be a great speculation if maybe, just maybe, the big man's great trick had been lost or squandered through a winter of neglect. (His bats arrived late this time from Boston in Jacksonville. Was he having problems because he didn't have his favorite bats? It was a story.) Every spring, no matter what, the trick eventually would return.

The first big blast didn't come until March 19, 17 days after he arrived. The assembled sportswriters had been waiting for so long that when Ruth clocked a simple batting practice pitch from Mario DeVitalis over the center-field fence toward the St. John River, everyone in the press box became a little giddy. A couple of writers hustled out with a tape measure and figured the ball had traveled 478 feet. The fence was 428 feet, and the ball had traveled 50 feet more. Even though the Babe said it was the farthest he ever had hit a baseball except for the shot a year earlier in Tampa, even though it was the longest home run ever recorded in Jacksonville, those statements were not big enough. Exaggeration came into easy play.

"Ruth hit the ball over the centerfield fence at the Yankees' training yard in South Jacksonville," Damon Runyon wrote in the *New York American,* making fun of the shouting. "Yes, sir, clean, over, right over. My what a swat it was. My! My! My! My! My! My! My! My! My! My! My! My! My! My! My! My! My! My! Plumb over."

The Yankees advertised all exhibition games as an appearance of "Babe Ruth, the Home Run King," but he hit only one shot during a game in all of the time in Florida. That came on April 1 off Dodgers pitcher Al Mamaux in the first inning of a 6–2 win, and the *Times* gurgled that "no other man in baseball could have lifted a ball that far. The pellet cleared the center field fence."

More time was spent in discussion about the possibility of more home runs than was spent actually watching home runs. A change in the rules, outlawing trick pitches like the emery ball, the shine ball, and the spitball, had been made for the new season, giving the batter a projected advantage. No longer would he have to see the doctored balls, with their lopsided dynamics, spinning and dancing and dropping in ways that challenged conventional laws of physics. Huggins was one of the few baseball voices against the change ("When they prohibit a pitcher from using his noodle to develop freak deliveries they are killing the pitcher's initiative"), but it generally was thought his team would be the greatest beneficiary.

Another change had occurred with the baseball itself. Nobody knew the facts behind the change—that manufacturers now used a better grade of Australian wool and had developed new machines that wound the yarn tighter—but everyone knew that the ball seemed to fly better. Or said they knew. The "dead ball" era was done. Hit the new baseball, and it felt like solid against solid, bat against the kitchen table. Hit the old baseball and it felt like bat against living room sofa.

Ruth made some on-field headlines in the third week of March when he hurried into the stands to confront a smallish spectator who kept calling him "a big piece of cheese," then hurried out faster when the spectator pulled a knife, but mostly the stories of the spring relied heavily on invention and imagination. Some of the writers tried to promote an eating contest between Ruth, humorist Irwin S. Cobb, and outfielder Sam Vick, a noted trencherman, but that never took place. Runyon bought an alligator that he named Aloysius Dorgan and interviewed at length. Ping Bodie, whose real name was Francesco Pezzolo (he changed the name because it sounded too ethnic), jumped the team for a stretch in a salary dispute, then came back.

At the end of camp, the club went south for a three-game series with the Cincinnati Reds. The first two games were in Miami, the third at the Royal Poinciana Hotel in Palm Beach. The idea for that game was to put on a show for the rich and privileged guests, a little something to watch in the afternoon before another grand dinner. The makeshift field had been roped off on a cricket grounds normally used by Caribbean workers at the hotel. This caused certain irregularities, the most glaring of which was a palm tree situated in the middle of center field.

The Yankees' traveling party, freed from the dull perimeters of Jacksonville, had taken full advantage of Miami's nightlife. Some members even had found time for a quick trip to Bimini. The Reds, more than welcome hosts, held a dinner the night before the Palm Beach game on one of the Florida Keys, a raucous affair that involved a boat for transportation. Two sportswriters fell off the boat on the way home. Ping Bodie was carried off. The Babe returned under his own power, but with a fine liquid evening under his belt.

In the first inning of the game the next day, everyone squinting in the sunlight, the portable stands filled with high-society millionaires, a fly ball was hit to center field, where the Babe was playing. He went into a hung-over gallop and ran directly into the palm tree, which won the collision by a knockout.

This was the end of the game for the dazed Babe, who was fine except for the bells ringing in his head. The game was the end of spring training visits to Miami for the Yankees for the next 13 seasons. Col. Ruppert had seen enough of this kind of fun in the sun. He had insured the Babe for $135,000, but perhaps the policy did not cover bouts with palm trees in center field.

On the trip north the Yankees played an annual series of games with the Dodgers. In Winston-Salem, Ruth hit another instantly legendary blast. There was no center-field fence, and though Ruth's hit carried over a standing crowd—carried and carried—he was credited with only a ground-rule double. It might have been the longest double ever hit.

"Babe Ruth today hit a baseball 850 feet . . ." Runyon wrote, not to be outdone by other estimates of grandeur. "Babe hit the ball across a half-mile racetrack. We might have said he hit it around the racetrack, but we want to be conservative. . . . It was longer than a peace treaty; it carried longer than Al Mamaux' singing voice. If you don't think this is far, ask the top-floor tenants when Al is singing in a hotel lobby."

Attention New York: the circus was coming.

Ruth was 25 years old (thought he was 26) when he began his career in the biggest city in the land. He had little formal education, no parental ad-vice. The lessons of St. Mary's Industrial School for Boys, while useful in dealing with the necessities of daily life, had done nothing to prepare him for what he now faced in a cynical, high-voltage environment that chewed up dreamers every day and spit them back to Peoria.

The 25-year-old man who thought he was 26 never blinked. He quickly installed Helen and himself in an eight-room apartment suite in the Ansonia Hotel on Broadway, a 17-floor mock chateau designed by ar-chitect Stanford White that took up the entire block between 73rd and 74th Streets. He had a shave every day in the basement barbershop of the dignified Fred B. Mockel at the Ansonia, a ceramic mug with the name "Babe Ruth" on the front soon inserted among the mugs of bankers and philanthropists. He had a regular manicure, fingernails always perfect.

He found a personal tailor who could shape expensive tweeds over an irregular body. His shoes were from England, his cigars from Cuba. He bought a succession of automobiles whose common characteristics were that they looked wonderful and traveled fast. He charged into the nightlife, the day life, life itself, intimidated by nothing. He was the bourgeois royalty he was supposed to be, big and loud and unafraid.

He also hit home runs.

The difficulty of that task—so different from the on-command performance of a singer, actor, or juggler who could memorize, rehearse, and then simply walk onto a stage and do an act—was shown in the first couple of weeks. In the opening game of the season at Philadelphia, Ruth collected only two singles and dropped a fly ball in the eighth to allow the winning runs to the lowly Athletics. In the opener at home, he pulled a muscle in his right side and strained his right knee in batting practice, struck out in the first inning, then went to the bench for several days. The big opening day crowd mostly watched Frank Gleich in right field for the afternoon.

It wasn't until May 1, 11 games later, that the fun began. Playing against the Red Sox, who had sprinted out to lead the league with a 10–2 record despite losing their most famous star, the famous star unloaded in the sixth inning, a towering shot that was the third ball he ever had hit out of the Polo Grounds. The *Times*, working a May Day theme, said he had "sneaked a bomb into the field without anyone knowing it and hid it in his bat." The Yankees won, 6–0.

Number two came the next day, also against the Red Sox, a low bullet that hit far back in the grandstand, close to the bleachers, one of those balls that looked as if it were still rising. Fans in the crowd of 25,000 came down to dance on top of the dugout to welcome their man back from his trip around the bases. The Yankees won, 7–1. And away he went.

This was the advertised product. The adjectives rolled as the Sultan of Swat clocked 11 home runs for the month of May (a major league record for a month), then 13 for June (breaking his own record). He hit balls off facades and over fences that never had been reached. He hit three home runs in a day against the Senators in a doubleheader. In Chicago he hit a home run that coincided with a loud thunderclap.

One day he hit a towering fly ball that was speared by Oscar Vitt, an outfielder, who immediately showed the ball to the umpire. It had been knocked lopsided. On another day the man himself was knocked lop-sided, hit in the forehead by Chicago's Buck Weaver in the middle of an attempted double play. He came back the next day and kept hitting. He whacked his 29th at the Polo Grounds to tie his record on July 16, the ball hitting three feet from the top of the grandstand roof, no more than six feet from the end, where it would have gone onto the walkway to the subway, maybe purchased a token, and taken a ride all the way into Man-hattan.

There were still 61 games left when he broke the record with number 30 on July 20. How many homers could one man hit? Calculations and guesses were everywhere. Number 31 followed number 30 in the same July 20 doubleheader against the White Sox. He had 37 by the end of July.

The effect of all this was exhilarating, breathtaking. He and the Yan-kees broke attendance records in six American League parks. He hit homers in all eight parks. The attendance record at the Polo Grounds was broken once, twice, three times and would be broken again and again be-fore the season ended.

Pitcher Allan Russell of the Red Sox suffered a slight stroke and re-turned home to Baltimore unable to talk or use his right side. His doctor decided that the stroke had been caused by anxieties from facing the Babe. The pitcher had "overtaxed his strength and brain in the battle against the greatest hitter the world ever has known." A spectator at the Polo Grounds, Theodore Sturm of Bellrose, Long Island, died of a heart attack caused by the excitement. The fact was buried in the middle of another story about another home run, almost as if death by excitement was to be expected when confronted with the wonders of George Herman Ruth.

The Babe's Yankees teammates watched the barrage with the same sense of wonder as everyone else. They never had seen anything like it. The game they had learned was being changed in front of their faces. This was all revolutionary. A game was never finished. A home run could change the situation in a moment. Strikeouts, always a symbol of futility, didn't mean as much. Bases on balls—and the other teams were issuing them now to the Babe intentionally and semi-intentionally on a regular basis—were a disappointment more than a strategic advantage. The swing of the bat was more important. Let it rip.

How do you pitch to this guy? What do you do?

"Keep your fastball away from him," shortstop Roger Peckinpaugh suggested. "Make him hit slow stuff."

"Try to make him keep the ball in the ballpark," catcher Truck Hannah said.

"Throw the ball and duck," reserve outfielder Sam Vick advised. "The Babe could hit them high, low, fast or slow, good or bad, with both hands or one. I saw him go for a big swing on a left-hander, which turned out to be a curve low and outside. He reached across the plate with one hand, pulled the ball into the upper deck in right field. You can't stop that kind of hitting."

The collisions sounded different when the balls hit his bat, a click, like two billiard balls, solid against solid. The balls traveled different: higher, deeper, farther. He was a picture of fury and rhythm, all in one, as natural and free as anyone ever had seen.

· "In pitching, some players like Walter Johnson throw a light ball, some a heavy one that nearly knocks your hand off," Vick said. "Some throw a hard ball, but the ball won't carry, others throw balls that carry. It's the same with hitting. Babe's ball had that carrying quality. He could cowtail that bat, which was a long one, put every ounce of his 220 pounds in back of it and still hit. So when he got one in the air, there wasn't a park that would hold it."

By the middle of the season, people were sending him checks in the mail, just hoping that he would endorse them and his autograph would come back from the bank. The crowds outside the *New York Times* building in Times Square were larger and noisier watching the reports of the Yankees and A's than the crowds watching the reports from the Democratic convention in San Francisco. A woman in Lynn, Massachusetts, a headline said, did "A Babe Ruth on Her Husband" when she hit him in the head with a baseball bat.

The name was magic. Everything the big man did seemed important. Everything anyone else did seemed less important. The pennant race, even with the Yankees in the thick of it, seemed less important. The big man did his big things. Everyone else lived in his wake.

"My greatest moment during the season came one day with the bases loaded, the score tied, and Babe's turn to bat," Sam Vick said. "The height of ambition of the fans was to see such a setup. They were almost taking the top off the stand. There was a lull in the game, and Babe did not climb out of the dugout. He had hurt his wrist and couldn't go up to bat."

Vick and the rest of the players in the dugout looked at Huggins. The manager looked back, considering each possibility, staring at someone, then moving his eyes to the next player. Vick held his breath. Huggins looked at him, then looked away. Huggins looked again, looked away. This happened several times. The manager finally said, "Sam, get your bat."

"I began to breathe again, picked out my bat, and started to the plate," Vick said. "The announcer said, 'Vick, batting for Ruth.' When it dawned on the crowd what was happening, you could hear a pin drop. It seemed like five miles to the plate. The stillness was frightening, but on the way, down inside me, there was the reaction, 'That's what you think!'

"I then blacked out and don't remember anything until I slid into third base with a triple."

On another day, a doubleheader in Washington, Vick struck out seven times. The background was bad for hitters in Washington, and Walter Johnson pitched one of the games and was impossible to hit, and . . . seven strikeouts in seven appearances. The Yankees were shut out in both games. Vick was mournful as he walked back to the clubhouse.

He suddenly felt an arm around his shoulder.

"Don't mind that, boy," second baseman Del Pratt said. "When the Babe strikes out five times [and he had], they don't even see you."

On August 16, the Yankees played host to the Cleveland Indians at the Polo Grounds on a sticky, muggy day. It was an important series, the home team a half-game behind the visitors in the standings, both teams battling with the White Sox for the American League lead.

Carl Mays was on the mound. Mays, the subject of so much consternation a year earlier when he went from Boston to New York, was having another good season. He was 29 years old now and still seen as a dark and odd character.

The son of a Methodist minister in Kingfisher, Oklahoma, he didn't smoke, drink, or chase women into the night, which made him something of an outsider in baseball culture. He was distant to most of his teammates, disdainful of baseball players as a rule. He was known as a hard case once he crossed onto the field, a no-nonsense competitor, a hard thrower who demanded that hitters stay back from the plate.

As a boy, his arm was so strong and accurate that he hunted rabbits with rocks, although he admitted he once made a mistake and hit a calf in the forehead with one of his throws, killing the calf. A sore arm while pitching in the minor leagues in Portland, Oregon, had sent him to old-time legend Iron Man Joe McGinnity, who convinced him to throw with an underhanded, submarine motion. The switch was a success and had brought him to the big leagues.

Matched against Indians ace Stanley Coveleski on this day, Mays and Ruth and the Yanks had fallen behind, 3–0, after four innings. The first Indians batter in the fifth was 29-year-old Ray Chapman, a nimble short-stop who was the opposite of Mays in personality: a well-liked, gregari-ous character whose tenor voice could sing the songs of Irishman John McCormick to perfection. Chapman, off a Kentucky farm, had married well, his wife Katy the daughter of millionaire Cleveland businessman Martin Daly, one of the founders of Standard Oil. An office already had been established for the shortstop in Daly's company, his future assured.

In two previous appearances at the plate against Mays this day, Chap-man had bunted twice, once for a sacrifice, once for an out. He was an aggravating hitter with a stance that made him sort of hang over the plate, a challenge. Mays threw him a ball, then a strike. On the third pitch, com-ing from that submarine delivery, the only underhanded delivery in the league, Mays hit Ray Chapman square in the head.

The sound, *crack,* was as loud as if bat had hit ball. The ball rolled toward third base, and Mays in fact thought it was another bunt. He fielded the ball and threw to first. When he turned around, he saw Chap-man trying unsuccessfully to climb off the dirt. Some blood was coming from Chapman's ear.

After almost seven minutes, the Indians trainer and his teammates tried to walk Chapman to the clubhouse in center field, but he collapsed again on the way. His skull had been crushed. He was taken to nearby St. Lawrence Hospital in the Bronx, where doctors operated that night to take the pressure off his brain, but he died at 4:40 the next morning. He was the first and only major league player to die from being hit by a thrown baseball.

Mays, the loner, was now more alone than ever. The players on both the Red Sox and Tigers teams announced that they wouldn't play against him and wanted him banned for life. He protested that the pitch wasn't even a fastball, that it was a curve, that the ball was scuffed and took off. He also noted that Joe Bush of the Red Sox (ten) and Howard Ehmke of the Tigers (nine) had hit more batters than he (six) had. The league office quickly exonerated him, calling the death an accident (Chapman, it was thought, had lost sight of the ball because he never moved), but the controversy remained. When Mays made his first start, a 10–0 shutout of the Tigers a week later, every time he released a curveball that didn't seem as if it were going to break he shouted, "Watch out," from the mound.

The game back at the Polo Grounds had continued after Chapman left. The Babe was the first man up in the ninth, the Indians ahead, 4–0. He was 0-for-3 on the day against Coveleski, but singled sharply. The Yankees scored three times in the inning, but still lost, 4–3.

The game the next day was postponed.

The Babe became a movie star in the following weeks. Or at least he made a movie. He had signed in July to appear in *Headin' Home,* the story of a village simpleton's rise to baseball glory and the capture of the hand of the local fair maiden. (No typecasting here.) The deal was not unusual— sports stars were increasingly being brought into the growing movie business—but the timing was peculiar. The Babe made the movie almost immediately, in the middle of the season.

The studio was in Haverstraw, New York, 30 miles outside the city and on the other side of the Hudson River. For a succession of August days—often nights—Ruth took the ferry to New Jersey, drove to Haverstraw, played his role, and returned back on the ferry to the pennant race. He was supposed to receive $50,000 for his efforts. The producers, Kessel & Baumann, paid him $15,000 up front and gave him a second check for $35,000 to hold for a few weeks until they could put enough money in the bank. He folded the check and put it in his wallet and carried it everywhere. He was not averse to showing it in the locker room.

"Hey, I need some money," he would say, big joke, pulling out the check, which soon became worn-looking. "Could you cash this for me?"

During the production, there were days when he arrived at the ballpark and didn't even have time to wash off the makeup. He would make monster faces in the clubhouse, then go out to be the first man in baseball history to play right field with eyeliner and mascara. On the morning of August 22, he filmed all the live baseball scenes before a crowd of 2,000 at a local field in Haverstraw also known as the Polo Grounds. With a bat he supposedly had whittled from a tree trunk, he sent shots over the fence off constable Peter Reilly's house and into Frank Smith's front yard and onto a shed and into someone's kitchen. He then left the filming and played against the Detroit Tigers in the afternoon in the real Polo Grounds.

If he had any reservations, any worries that this moviemaking might hurt his home run making, he certainly didn't show them. He had developed an attitude to match his celebrity, his uninhibited behavior from Boston now wrapped in a true sense of privilege. The rules for everyone else didn't matter. He paid no attention to signs given on the baseball diamond, did whatever he wanted on each at-bat, and very soon no signs were given. He paid no attention to signs anywhere.

On the road he no longer had a roommate. He often didn't even stay in the same hotel with the rest of the team, choosing to rent his own suite somewhere else for $100 per day. On short trips he didn't travel with the team, riding in his own car with his own choice of company. Helen could come, friends could come, he could pick out coaches or players to take on the ride. On longer trips he had his own compartment on the train, freed from the upper-lower snores and grunts in the rest of the car, but most importantly from curious fans. He was living the same life as his teammates, but on an entirely different plane. If there was any resentment about any of this, he never heard it.

He continued to hold Miller Huggins, whom he routinely called "Little Boy" or "the Flea," in obvious disdain. He liked his teammates well enough but, except for a few regulars, remembered none of their names. He used his universal "hey, kid" with almost everyone. A pay phone that he never answered had been installed next to his locker for his personal calls. (Teammates answered, told female callers they were the Babe, and made dates for meetings at the Hotel Astor that were never kept.) The mail also never was answered. He had teammates and trainer Doc Moore sort through it for letters from women and checks. Doc Moore once totaled up $6,000 in checks from envelopes that simply had been discarded.

The life he chose to live seemed to be the life of Henry VIII or Louis XIV. He could be crude or rude or quite kind. His disposition at the moment told him what to do. There were no other constraints on a king.

"When we get to the Cooper Carlton, there'll be a stack of mail for me as big as my prick," he boasted one day to sportswriter Fred Lieb of the *New York Telegram* as they shared a cab to the hotel from the Chicago train station.

That was his basic unit of measurement. His favorite saying—he said it everywhere—was "I can knock the prick off any ball that was ever pitched." His language had little moderation. His libido was never far from his mind.

"A believer in reincarnation, I always felt that Ruth was a reincarnated African king or Arabic emir with a stable of wives and concubines," Lieb wrote years later in a book called *Baseball As I Have Known It.* "Or, perhaps, in an earlier life, he lived in ancient Babylon, where they worshipped Phallus. Babe was inherently a phallic worshipper. It cropped up regularly in his conversation. His phallus and home run bat were his most prized possessions, in that order."

The phrase that always had been used to describe him, "he's like a big kid," had been altered. He was now pretty much a big spoiled kid. Or a kid who was out of control.

In the last few days of making the movie, he was stung on the wrist by a wasp. Or maybe he was bitten by a tick. After the spot became infected, it was lanced and then stitched. He missed six games in the middle of the pennant race. The other players grumbled, but then he came back on Labor Day weekend at Fenway Park in Boston. This was the Yankees' last visit during the season. To honor the exploits of their transplanted star, the local Knights of Columbus presented him with a set of cuff links at the September 4 doubleheader, which was dubbed "Babe Ruth Day." The Babe returned the honor by belting home run number 45 into the right-field bleachers in the first game, then repeating with home run number 46 to the same spot in the second. Another record had been dredged up— Perry Werden of Minneapolis in the Western League had hit 44 home runs in another bandbox park in 1894 for the minor league record—so now Ruth had the record for all of organized baseball. The *New York Times* referred to him after this exhibition as "the Behemoth of Bangs."

Where would it all end?

The United News syndicate had struck a ghostwriting deal with him for a modest $1,000 in advance and $5 for a column every time he hit a home run. The ghost was Westbrook Pegler, who didn't like a lot of people and found the big man "on close acquaintance to be unbelievably mean, foulmouthed and violent," according to biographer Oliver Pilat (*Pegler: Angry Man of the Press*). Ruth contributed little to Pegler's reports beyond a telegram reading something like "Poled two out of the park today. High fastballs. Send check immediately."

Part of the deal also was a first-person autobiographical series. Again, the Babe was little help. Pegler, desperate, finally took a bunch of clippings to his apartment and with the help of another United News reporter inventively typed 80,000 words in two days in the Babe's "voice." The result was published in 16 installments that ran through the middle of the summer across the country. The life story read like juvenile fiction, and Pegler's sense of irony hung brightly through the words, put together in thoughts and sentence constructions that were far from the truth.

He can almost be seen smiling as he typed out the final two paragraphs of the series to young boys of the day under the name of one of America's most noted reprobates:

If you haven't started to smoke, don't begin now. If you have, keep it down, especially during the playing season. I smoke a lot of cigars and I wish I didn't, but I own a cigar factory, which I have to keep busy.

And here's another thing: get married. Pick a nice girl who understands you—she'll understand you a long time before you understand and appreciate her—and make a home run. Mrs. Ruth was only 16 when I married her and I was a youngster of 20. I wasn't any kind of a champion then except I was a champ picker and I certainly was good at that.

(The End.)

A rumor clattered across the country on September 10 that the Babe had suffered two broken legs and was near death. It started with messages received at W. E. Hutton and other Wall Street brokerage houses that Ruth had been involved in a terrible automobile accident and that not only had he been injured, but teammates Bob Meusel, Del Pratt, and Duffy Lewis also were in the car and injured. Later messages claimed that both Meusel and Pratt were dead.

Ruth had been involved in a previous celebrated accident in June when he flipped his big touring car in a ditch in Wawa, Pennsylvania, while traveling from Washington to New York after a series with the Senators. Helen, catcher Fred Hofmann, outfielder Frank Gleich, and third base coach Charlie O'Leary were with him. O'Leary was knocked unconscious, a cause for concern, but quickly awoke with the words, "Where the hell is my straw hat?" Everyone else was fine. The Babe and party spent the night in a farmhouse, and he told the mechanics who arrived from Media, Pennsylvania, the next morning to take the car and "sell it for whatever you can get. I'm through with it."

The accident obviously set nefarious minds to work. A quick rumor in Philadelphia, dispelled when the Babe played the next day at the Polo Grounds against the Detroit Tigers, had said that he was severely injured in Wawa and perhaps was dead. A group of gamblers now built a bigger, better rumor and distributed it across the country with great efficiency on the eve of an important three-game series with the Indians at League Park in Cleveland. The goal was to affect the odds, making Cleveland the favorite, which would open the possibility to place large New York bets and collect a very good return.

The *Los Angeles Times* reported that this was the biggest national rumor since the famous "Fake Armistice" story of November 7, 1918, which at first sent people into the streets in celebration of the end of the world war, then resulted in a number of riots when the news turned out to be false. The Babe rumor, while it did flash through poolrooms and boardrooms everywhere in the country, had a much quieter finish as baseball officials immediately denied it.

"It's a sure thing gamblers started this story," Col. Huston said. "I have no facts on which to base any charges, but one can understand the possibilities of gamblers getting unfair odds through just such tricks. This is something baseball authorities have no way of stopping. I want to say, however, that there has not been a suspicion of anything wrong, no matter what one may think about betting on baseball or anything else."

The incident was a public tug that brought the subterranean world of baseball betting into the newspapers. Betting had been a staple of the game since its conception and like almost everything else, especially everything else that was illicit, it was flourishing in the postwar boom.

The war, in fact, had helped baseball gambling. The racetracks had been cut back for the duration, and the bookies and gamblers had moved quickly into the ballparks. Bets could be made on games, innings, individual pitches, and at-bats without the patron having to leave his seat if he knew where to sit. Baseball pools, where the bettor picked the results of a number of games, were a staple of most machine shops and factories.

As the Yankees won two out of three in their series in Cleveland, to draw even with the White Sox in second place a half-game behind the Indians in the closest American League race in more than a decade, a much bigger gambling story than the rumor about the Babe was beginning to unfold. The Yankees won three straight in the next stop in Detroit, then lost three in Chicago to the White Sox to fall two games out of first. Then the details started to spill out from Chicago.

On September 21, New York Giants pitcher Rube Benton told a Cook County grand jury how the 1919 World Series between the White Sox and the Cincinnati Reds had been fixed. Ban Johnson and White Sox owner Charles Comiskey followed Benton to the stand and told about their suspicions from the first pitch of that Series, and then the parade began. By September 27, White Sox knuckleballer Eddie Cicotte and star outfielder Shoeless Joe Jackson had confessed and implicated six other teammates, including Buck Weaver, the Babe's barnstorming partner. Everything was true.

"I had bought a farm with a $4,000 mortgage on it," Cicotte said. "There isn't any mortgage on it now. I paid it off with the crooked money."

The news about the "Black Sox" scandal had every right to be devastating. If the games—the biggest games of all, in fact—were fixed, why should anyone pay attention? The core of baseball's believability was being challenged. The Babe himself said, upon hearing the news, "it was like hearing that my Church had sold out." The testimony detailed intentional errors, grooved fastballs, Cicotte's vow to throw the ball over the center-field fence if he had to for the money. (One of the early planning meetings for the fix, in fact, had been held at the Ansonia Hotel, the Babe's address, where the team stayed when it went to New York.) Nothing messier ever could be imagined. Wouldn't the public surely revolt?

The answer was no. Nothing happened. The eight players were suspended from baseball, the depleted White Sox went 0-for-3 in their last series, the Indians won the pennant, and the Yankees finished third. The people didn't care. They were hooked already on the melodrama in front of their eyes, not only caught up in the pennant race but also mesmerized by the home run show that went with it. Mesmerized by the Babe.

Fixed? How did you fix a 450-foot circuit clout by the Prince of Pounders, the Behemoth of Bash? The Babe just kept whacking through the headlines. On September 24, the scandal breaking everywhere, he blasted numbers 50 and 51 in a doubleheader split with the Senators. (Fifty home runs! Who ever thought it would be possible? The fact was noted that he "has hit as many home runs as Heinz has pickles . . . in fact, he is the greatest pickler the world has ever known.") A crowd of 25,000 was at the Polo Grounds for those meaningless two games, followed by a crowd of 30,000 the next day.

In the final series of the year in Philadelphia, he whacked numbers 52 and 53 against the A's in a single game. On the final day, September 29, the entire scandal out, first game of a doubleheader, he hit his 54th and final homer off Slim Hayes. His total gave him more homers than 14 of the other 15 big league teams. (The Philadelphia Phillies, with 64 homers as a team, played their games in tiny Baker Bowl.) He led the league in RBI with 137, and his .367 batting average placed him fourth. His slugging percentage was an unbelievable .847.

The Yankees had blown past all attendance records, becoming the first team to draw over a million fans at home with a final figure of 1,289,422. Major league baseball had attracted over nine million customers, easily a record. The Indians and the Brooklyn Robins in the World Series, after all of the headlines from Chicago, drew over 155,000 people as the Indians won in seven games. Scandal? What scandal?

The show was too exciting, too compelling, for a scandal to stop it. The Babe—though he probably would get too much credit for "saving baseball" from a crisis that never really developed—certainly was a huge part of that show.

He had finished the season accompanied by his own brass band. The fire that destroyed much of St. Mary's Industrial School for Boys in 1919 had left some huge bills to be paid. The Babe arranged for the 50-member school band to accompany the Yankees on the last western swing. He was an untiring host as he appeared at concerts in the different cities to solicit donations, posed for pictures in a sailor's cap and holding a tuba, ordered unlimited ice cream for the kids on the train.

Only six years removed from the institution, the boy called Nigger Lips was able to show these other boys what possibilities existed on the other side of the walls. With Brother Matthias along as one of the chaperons, the Babe had an opportunity to talk about old times. The band played in nine cities before returning to Baltimore for a large Knights of Columbus dinner at the Fifth Regiment Armory, followed by an exhibition game the next day between the Yankees and Orioles. Ruth, at the dinner, wrote out a check for $2,500. Nigger Lips had done pretty well.

THE BIG BAM   125

He went on a barnstorming trip with Hofmann, Schang, and Carl Mays as soon as the season ended. A sign of his popularity came in Rochester, New York. Franklin D. Roosevelt, the vice presidential candidate on an ill-fated Democratic ticket with James M. Cox against Warren G. Harding in the November elections, arrived at the Rochester train station and had to be escorted through a large crowd that spilled onto the streets. Roosevelt was heartened by the turnout until told that the people were there not to see him but to wait for the Babe's train to arrive.

After the barnstorming tour was completed, he and Helen embarked on a one-month trip to Cuba on October 27. He was the star attraction on a team put together by John McGraw, mostly members of the Giants plus Ruth. Havana, with its no-limit nightlife, had become an even more desirable destination since the advent of Prohibition. McGraw loved it. Ruth also soon loved it. He loved it too much. He gambled in Havana with Helen. He gambled without Helen when the team went on tour and Helen stayed back in the capital. He gambled.

"He came back to the room, and he'd made $900 gambling," one unnamed roommate reported from one of the stops on the tour. "He said he was going back down to clean out the casino. He went into his wallet and counted out six thousand-dollar bills. I told him to leave the $6,000 in the room and clean 'em out with the $900. He didn't do that. He came back in the morning and the wallet was empty. He'd lost $6,900."

It got worse. The team came home after its tour, finishing with a 9–8 record. Ruth, who'd hit only two homers in the games, mainly because they were played with a big wind blowing in, signed to play ten more exhibitions, and he and Helen stayed for a second month. This was not a good move. He soon was wiped out.

The amount he lost will never be known. In an article written for *American Weekly*, a woman who called herself "Mrs. Margaret Hill, Queen of the Underworld," detailed a complicated sting operation run on him by hustlers at the Plaza Hotel in Havana. Through fixed horse races, she said, Ruth was bilked of $130,000. That would seem like a lot of money, since he probably hadn't earned that much money in his career, but he apparently did lose whatever money he had made in Cuba. Helen luckily had saved enough of what he had given her for them to get home in time for Christmas.

"I am not a bit worried about the weight I have picked up," he told reporters on his return after they noticed that he had added as many as

40 pounds in Cuba. "I'm going back to the farm in Massachusetts and will put in six weeks or so of rugged outdoor life, chopping wood and the like. By the time I leave for Hot Springs, I should be fit to meet a grizzly."

He also had lost money on the movie he made. That $35,000 check he carried around the locker room? He finally went to cash it, and it bounced higher than a Wee Willie Keeler Baltimore chop through the infield. The company had gone bankrupt and was out of business. A second movie, an instructional film showing him batting, had been made without his consent and without remuneration to him. He had sued. The suit was denied, the court ruling that he was "a public figure."

The price of fame was getting expensive.

CHAPTER NINE

THE MAN the Behemoth of Bang needed to meet was looking to meet the Behemoth of Bang. His name was Christy Walsh, and he was a shrewd, 29-year-old entrepreneurial fireball from Los Angeles. He had been drawn to New York the same way oilmen were drawn to Texas: this was where the natural resources were located. This was where the Babe was.

The idea that buzzed loudest in a mind buzzing with ideas was that a ghostwriting syndicate for newspapers could be a growth industry. Walsh was convinced that if he matched the biggest names with the best writers and marketed the product across the country with energy and imagination, he would have a winner.

Walsh was a lawyer who placed his degree from St. Vincent's College on top of the dresser drawer about two minutes after he received it and took a job as a cartoonist. He had worked enough around the newspaper business to figure out what was attractive and what wasn't when slipped under the green eyeshades of the country's most powerful editors. He also knew how to sell. Wearing a double-breasted suit every day, and a Kelly green tie in support of the ongoing Irish struggle for independence, he was an engaging presence, a dapper charmer.

Walsh's one ghostwriting experience had been with Eddie Rickenbacker, the world war flying ace and automobile racer. Rickenbacker, who shot down 26 enemy planes over France, was the guest referee for the 1919 Indianapolis 500, the first race since the war ended. Walsh convinced him to lend his name to a ghostwritten account of the race, then sold the upcoming story to 37 newspapers. On the given day, Walsh typed like a madman with an account of Howard Wilcox's 88-mph victory in 5 hours, 40 minutes, and 42 seconds. Rickenbacker took a fast read and made a few changes. All of the papers used the story, 16 on the front page. Walsh and Rickenbacker split a profit of $874.

When he was fired from an advertising job at Maxwell-Chalmers Automobiles in Detroit, in part for printing an issue of the house organ on St. Patrick's Day that, instead of providing the usual news about horsepower and sales figures, issued a call for Irish independence with a lead article by republican leader Eamon de Valera, Walsh decided it was a sign telling him to go off on his own. He started with the idea of ghosting some show business names, like moviemaker D. W. Griffith, soprano Mary Garden, or Broadway songwriter Gene Buck, but soon switched to sports. This sent him to the Babe.

Why not work with the biggest emerging name of all? Walsh took out a $2,000 loan and journeyed to New York to meet his man. His man wanted nothing to do with him. Offers and strange people were coming at the Babe every day now, and he simply walked past all of them as if he were on the way to another train. The burns from Havana and the movies were still sore. The few times Walsh approached, there was a crowd around and the Babe waved him off and simply kept moving.

Walsh's answer was to stake out the Ansonia Hotel, where the Babe and Helen were staying after two months in Sudbury. He hoped he could catch his man coming or going. The problem was that the hotel had three doors on three different streets, and Walsh always seemed to be at the wrong one. Time became a factor, because now he learned the Babe was departing for Hot Springs the next day.

Wondering what to do, frustrated, Walsh sat in a neighborhood delicatessen that doubled as an illegal liquor store. The phone rang. He could hear the owner taking an order for "Mr. Ruth" for a case of beer. Walsh quickly had a suggestion about who could deliver that beer.

"Do you know who I am?" he asked as he helped the Babe put away the bottles in the kitchenette.

"Sure I know you," the Babe replied. "Ain't you been bringin' our beer for the past two weeks?"

Walsh laid out his offer. How much did the Babe get for each of those little stories when he hit a home run in 1920? Five bucks. How would $500 sound? Logic soon won the argument. On the next morning, Walsh hurried with a contract to Penn Station, where the Babe and Helen were supposed to leave.

The Babe was waiting. Walsh described the moment in a short memoir, *Adios to Ghosts*.

"The train leaves in 15 minutes and there he beams, belted camel-hair coat with cap to match, over-size cigar all aglow, and surrounded by the customary gallery of admirers," Walsh wrote.

> Mrs. Ruth stands nearby and gives me my first close-up of a mink coat; a luxurious, bulging wrap which probably set her man back a cool five thousand. While she obligingly diverts the autograph addicts, I spirit Babe through an iron gate, produce a badly wrinkled contract in the form of a short, informal letter and without question, he inscribes "George Herman Ruth" in the correct spot and I go in search of a ghost to do the writing.

The deal was a start for Walsh. He would build a syndicate that included the greatest names of American sport, from Knute Rockne to John McGraw to Ty Cobb to Doc Kearns, the manager of Jack Dempsey. He would sell their stories to countless papers across the country, his ghosts churning out the words, everyone making money. The deal was even better for the Babe. Walsh would turn out to be much more than the man behind the ghosts; he would become the man behind the Babe.

In short order, he became Ruth's friend, business manager, and booking agent. He was the voice of moderation that Helen never could be. He was the fiscal bodyguard against the hornswogglers and fast talkers, the friends of the "Queen of the Underworld" who wanted to take the Babe's money. He was the painter of a picture that all of America wanted to admire. A new concept that would be called "public relations" was emerging with people like Edward Bernays figuring out different ways to sell products and ideas, ways to create "image." Christy Walsh was a part of that.

He would become the first personal PR man in sport. No image would be created any better than the one around the Behemoth of Bang.

The foundation of that image—the sight of a white ball, with red stitching, flying through the air to previously uncharted destinations— soon was back in public view. The new year was no different from the old year.

A few columnists had written that the 54 home runs in 1920 were "a fluke," never to be matched again. The well-padded Bambino, still carrying some of that Havana weight, soon crumpled that opinion and swatted it into the nearest wastebasket. The Yankees had switched training sites to Shreveport, Louisiana, and he hit town, straight from Hot Springs, with the easy air of royalty.

A local dealer gave him a new green Essex roadster to use during his stay; a proclamation of the mayor, which referred to him as "His Majesty, Babe Ruth, the Sultan of Swat," allowed him to drive without a Louisiana driver's license; and local high school students presented a five-foot floral bat. He hit nine balls out of Gasser Park on his first day, hit a home run in a practice scrimmage the next, struck out three times on the third day, then walloped three homers and collected six hits against a visiting minor league team on the fourth.

Nothing had changed.

The bamming and whamming resumed as if it never had stopped. The extracurricular life, with its assault on the seven deadly sins from lust to gluttony and straight through to pride, resumed now that Helen was back at home. Teammates told a story of a car chase and a gun on a Louisiana night, Ruth saved at the last minute from the wrath of a local man. There was a story of the green Essex simply left in the middle of the road while the Babe rode off in the car of a local widow woman, and another of a woman with a knife on a train. A high school girl asked sportswriter Jimmy Sinnott of the *Mail* if he could fix her up with Ruth.

"Why would a nice girl like you want to get mixed up with a guy like him?" Sinnott asked.

"Oh," she said, "it would give me some standing in my class and sorority if I could tell them I had gone to bed with a national hero."

Beer consumption and food consumption were added up in daily, startling statistics. The long balls kept flying. The national hero was the attraction of attractions.

"In the Yankee-Dodger sette at Ponce del eon Park yesterday after-noon about 12,000 persons saw the mammoth slugger circle the bases," Fuzzy Woodruff of the *Atlanta Constitution* wrote as the Yankees and Dodgers stopped in his town on the way north. "They threw every kind of fit known to medical science when he slid into the plate with all the grace of a bear coming out of hibernation."

When he hit New York and the season started, he was 5-for-5 on opening day, had five home runs before the end of April, and went from there. Observations were made immediately that he was ahead of "his pace" for 54 in 1920. Attending a performance of Dunninger, the mental-ist, at the Hippodrome, Ruth was asked to write down how many homers he thought he would hit during the year. Ruth wrote, and after mentaliz-ing, Dunninger said the word "sixty." Ruth held up his blackboard. How did the guy know?

The Yankees of 1921 had undergone some off-season reconstruction. Again, the Red Sox had been involved. The biggest move was that Ed Bar-row, no fool, had sent himself to New York. The Yankees business man-ager, Harry Sparrow, had died, and Barrow took himself out of the Boston dugout and back into a front office. He was back with the Babe, resurrecting their tenuous relationship, but more importantly he was back in a situation where his owners had cash. He could make moves, the same way he could when Harry Frazee gave him freedom to spend with the Red Sox in 1918 and he wound up with a world championship. It is a base-ball fact that the presence of money makes baseball executives smarter.

(One Harry Sparrow story. In May 1919, anarchists had sent bombs to the residences and offices of many famous people in New York. The bombs all were enclosed in bags from Gimbel's Department Store. A friend shipped some lobsters from New Brunswick, Canada, to Sparrow. The wrapping had come apart in transit, so someone in the Yankees of-fice put the package in a Gimbel's bag on Sparrow's desk. The lobsters, alive, made a little clicking sound as they moved inside the bag. Sparrow discovered a clicking Gimbel's bag on his desk and just about fainted.)

Barrow's first move was a deal with his old boss. Frazee sent Waite Hoyt, Wally Schang, Harry Harper, and Mike McNally to the Yankees for Muddy Ruel, Del Pratt, Sammy Vick, and Hank Thormalen. It didn't seem like a bad deal for the Boston owner at the time, value for value, but again, it would be tilted wildly against him when the 21-year-old Hoyt, known as "the Brooklyn Schoolboy," 10–12 in his two seasons in Boston, almost immediately became a top-line pitcher in New York.

With Ruth whaling and with Hoyt added to Carl Mays and Bob Shawkey as the stars of a solid rotation, the Yankees sprinted to the front in the pennant race with the Cleveland Indians, a two-team affair that would stretch across the season. Not only was Ruth hitting homers, but his average consistently hung around the .400 mark. His name was everywhere.

The effects of Christy Walsh's whispers in his ear already were evident. The business manager had presented Ruth with a $1,000 check on the day he returned from spring training, and that had opened communication. Ruth suddenly was sending a telegram to child actor Jackie Coogan, ill in a New York hospital with bronchitis. He was posing with Georges Carpentier (George and Georges), the French boxer challenging Jack Dempsey. He was visiting St. Paul's Orphanage in Pittsburgh and talking to the national convention of Presbyterians at a banquet in St. Louis. He even had his own mascot in the dugout, three-year-old Little Ray Kelly. Hurtling down Riverside Drive one morning, the Babe had stopped at the sight of Little Ray, attired in a Yankees uniform, playing catch with his father. Three years old, the kid was good. The Babe recruited him on the spot to be his personal mascot at all home games. The arrangement would last for the next decade.

"Do any of the other players mind that the Babe has his own mascot?" Little Ray would be asked.

"Who would mind?" Kelly always would reply. "He's Babe Ruth!"

How famous was Babe Ruth? The newspapers reported that a kid who gave his name as George Kelly applied for an American passport in London. He had "an extensive repertoire of American slang," but his English had a French accent. The American consul was suspicious. What to do?

"Who is Babe Ruth?" he asked.

George Kelly did not know. Request denied. He couldn't possibly be American.

In the second week of June, Ruth's performance became a bit ridiculous. He hit seven home runs in five days. The culmination of the streak was back-to-back performances against the Tigers. On June 13, nobody else available, he voluntarily was the starting pitcher, back on the mound for one of two times during the year. He pitched five innings for the 13–8 win, striking out Ty Cobb. He hit two homers, the second into the center-field bleachers at the Polo Grounds, the first time that part of the park ever had been reached. On June 14, he hit two more in a 9–6 win. The second shot also went to the center-field bleachers, deeper than the one a day earlier. He now had 23 homers, well ahead of his "pace."

The *Los Angeles Times* was moved to write an editorial declaring him the nation's foremost hero. It said that in England the hero was an agreeable prince, in France a general, in Russia a "blood-stained Bolshevik," in Italy a leader of the Fascists, and in the United States a baseball player.

"True, he couldn't be elected president," the *L.A. Times* declared. "His popularity would defeat him; for to put him in the White House would be to take him out of baseball."

The Babe, heroic as he might have been, also continued to make his obligatory motor vehicle headlines. The fact that he now was driving a maroon 12-cylinder Packard that looked like a rocket ship and sounded like a fuel-burning calliope brought a certain interest from law authorities. The players called the car "the Ghost of Riverside Drive." He would pull up at the clubhouse, half the time missing a stolen radiator cap, steam and water shooting into the sky. He was as inconspicuous as a brass band.

Stopped for speeding in April—doing 27 mph up Broadway—he appeared contritely before Magistrate Fredrick House in traffic court, pleaded guilty, and was fined $25. Everybody laughed. Stopped again in June—this time doing 26 mph on Riverside Drive in the early hours of the morning—the reception was not as pleasant when he stood before Magistrate House again. The magistrate fined him $100 and sentenced him to a day in jail.

"Mr. Ruth, you were before me on April 27 on a similar charge," Magistrate House said. "I am sorry to see you back here, for I told you that you would have to answer as well as any other person. I find that anyone coming before me on April 27 and then again on June 8 is not showing proper respect for the law."

The day in jail began immediately. The Bambino was not prepared for this.

He was fingerprinted and found himself in a cell with three chauffeurs, all convicted on the same charge. They were even worse repeat offenders than the Babe and had been sentenced to five days in jail. A fourth chauffeur, Chester Williams, also sentenced to a single day, also was in the cell. He later reported on the activity. He said that a game of craps was started quickly by the other three chauffeurs. The Babe was not a participant. Neither was Chester Williams.

"They seen that I had some money on me when I was going to pay my fine, and they wanted me to shoot with them," Williams said. "They didn't have 50 cents between them, and they wanted me to go up against that with my roll of bills. I told them nothing doing. Then they abused me something terrible. They pinched me and kicked me and called me names. There were some roughs in the cell, I can tell you. Mr. Ruth was the only gentleman among them."

A single day in jail did not last 24 hours for any prisoner. Under court rules, the day ended at 4:00 P.M. Ruth was sentenced at 11:30, so actually he had to serve only four and a half hours. The Yankees were playing the Indians at 3:30 at the Polo Grounds, so his goal was to leave the Mulberry Street jail and hurry to the game.

The dice-rolling chauffeurs were taken to the Tombs at 1:30, and he and Williams were left alone. Ruth mostly stayed in a corner of the cell because he had spotted a photographer on a third-floor fire escape across the street, trying to get a picture that captured both baseball star and prison bars in the same frame. He and Williams could hear the photographer's boss giving instructions.

"Do you see anything?" the boss shouted from the street.

"I see a shadow," the photographer replied.

"Snap the shadow," the boss said.

Ruth was allowed to have his Yankees uniform and lunch brought to the jail. He ate the lunch and put on the uniform inside the cell. He then put on his street clothes over the uniform. He told Williams, "I'm going to run like hell to get to the game. Keeping you this late makes a speeder out of you." At 4:00, he started running. He was released, cut through 20 photographers, two movie cameras, and an estimated crowd of 1,000 on the street, jumped into the Packard, described by the Associated Press as "a maroon torpedo," started the engine, sent the crowd scampering, and hurried uptown.

Magistrate House remarked that the King of Home Runs was the second king he had put in jail for speeding in a week. He also had sentenced Frisco Rooney, the King of Jazz, the first famous dancer of the Jazz Age, to a day in jail. The theater where Frisco was appearing had protested that he would miss the matinee. Magistrate House said rules were rules. The Babe was lucky. His matinee started later.

Reporters tried to follow him to the Polo Grounds, but he lost them in Central Park. It was estimated that he covered nine miles in 19 minutes, which meant he had to be speeding again. He was on the field at 4:40 and walked to lead off the sixth inning. He then stole second, but died on the base paths. He batted again in the eighth, but grounded out. The Yanks scored twice in the ninth to win the game.

He then drove home.

Events like this caused the newest pitcher, the 21-year-old Hoyt, heading toward a 19–13 season, to stare at Ruth, to study him. Everybody on the Yankees—probably everybody who ever saw him—stared at Ruth sometimes, but Hoyt never would stop. He was fascinated with the big man. He felt a force, a strength emanating from Ruth, a predestination to greatness, that he never had felt from any other ballplayer, or any other person. He would struggle for a lifetime to put it all into words and was contemptuous of anyone else who tried, feeling that all attempts fell shallow and short.

"The first time I ever saw Babe Ruth was in the Red Sox clubhouse in July of 1919," he said years later. "I'd just come to the team. He's sitting there, and he didn't look like a monster nor anything, but he had black curly hair that dripped down over his forehead like there was spilled ink on his forehead, and he was utterly unbelievable."

Ed Barrow, who took the new pitcher around the room, made the introductions. The new kid . . . meet Babe. Babe . . . meet the new kid. Typical stuff.

"Pretty young to be in the big league, aren't you, kid?" the big man said, casually looking upward from his locker.

"Yep," Hoyt replied. "Same age you were when you came up, Babe."

Hoyt realized by the end of his sentence he was talking to the back of the black-ink head. The Babe had gone back to consider whatever world problems he was considering. There was only so much interest to be spent on some new arrival. The conversation was done. Hoyt, even years later, loved every millisecond of it. In the succeeding seasons, he would become both enemy and friend of Ruth. He never would become best friend—there never really was a best friend—but he would be around the table.

"There was nothing like Ruth ever existed in this game of baseball," he said. "I remember one time we were playing the White Sox in Boston in 1919, and he hit a home run off Lefty Williams over the left-field fence in the ninth inning and won the game. It was majestic. It soared. We watched

it and wondered, 'How can a guy hit a ball like that?' It was to the opposite field and off a left-handed pitcher, and it was an incredible feat. That
was the dead ball days, remember: the ball normally didn't carry. We were
playing a doubleheader, and that was the first game, and the White Sox did
not go into the clubhouse between games. They stood out there and sat on
our bench and talked about the magnificence of that home run."

The great hits fascinated Hoyt. The outrageous life fascinated Hoyt,
the don't-give-a-shit freedom of it, the nonstop, pell-mell charge into excess. How did a man drink so much and never get drunk? How could he
keep juggling, 24 hours a day, so many balls in the air, never dropping one
of them? The thread of humanity in the Babe fascinated Hoyt, his ability
to be mostly nice to people, especially ordinary people, even though they
arrived in long lines and constant bunches. The innate intelligence fascinated Hoyt, the supposedly dumb man doing a lot of not-so-dumb things.
How did he do it? Where did everything come from? The puzzle of Babe
Ruth never was dull, no matter how many times Hoyt picked up the
pieces and stared at them.

After games he would follow the crowd to the Babe's suite. No matter
what the town, the beer would be iced and the bottles would fill the bathtub. Take a beer. Watch. Watch everything.

"First of all, we'd all take showers after the ball game, so we didn't
ever use the bathtub because we'd all be clean after the game," Hoyt said.
"Ruth would order a couple of cases of beer, and he'd have the tub filled
with ice. This was before we went to the ballpark, and when we got back
the beer was iced and cold, and he'd take the position in a chair over in
the corner of the room, over on one side, and he was the King. Believe me,
there were some nights there'd be 100, 150 people pass through that
room. It's a wonder he could play ball."

Hoyt became the keeper of anecdotes, the one who remembered best.
This was only the beginning of the stories.

The idea that the Babe was superhuman—promoted in word, song, and
home run measurements everywhere now—was given a scientific impri-
matur in the first weeks of September. If the everyday observer couldn't
believe his eyes, ears, or the newspaper reports, a couple of psychologists
from Columbia University named Albert Johansen and Joseph Holmes
were ready to take the stand.

Hugh Fullerton, a sportswriter who had been at the forefront of exposing the Black Sox business, dragged the Babe to the psychologists' laboratory directly after a game in the Polo Grounds. The Big Bam was still in uniform, fresh from yet another home run, as he submitted to three hours of tests. No mention was made of compensation. The hand of Christy Walsh no doubt was involved.

"Tonight you go to college with me," Fullerton said he told the Babe. "You're going to take scientific tests which will reveal your secret."

"Who wants to know it?" the Babe replied.

"I want to know it. And so do several thousand fans. We want to know why it is that one man has achieved a unique batting skill like yours—just why *you* can slam the ball as nobody else in the world can."

Psychological testing, relatively new, had gained a measure of popular acceptance during the world war. The U.S. Army had used two well-known intelligence tests, the Alpha for men who could read, the Beta for men who couldn't, to help decide who was or wasn't officer material and what fields best suited each enlistee. Inflated claims of great success had been published. It seemed natural that the Babe should be tested.

He was first fitted with a pneumatic tube around his chest that was connected to a pressure device, handed a bat attached to wires that ran to a Hipp chronoscope, and then asked to swing. He was handed a rod and asked to place it inside a succession of holes as many times as possible in a designated amount of time. He was shown a sequence of dots and letters and shapes and asked to remember them. He was asked to tap a metal plate with an electric stylus as fast as possible.

In all of these activities, he was animated and absorbed. These were games, competition. He was interested. He also was very good at these games. Or so it seemed.

"The tests revealed the fact that Ruth is 90 per cent efficient compared with a human average of 60 per cent," the sportswriter Fullerton reported in his *Popular Science Monthly* article. "That his eyes are about 12 per cent faster than those of the average human being. That his ears function at least 10 per cent faster than those of the ordinary man. That his nerves are steadier than those of 499 out of 500 persons. That in attention and quickness of perception he rated one and a half times the human average. That in intelligence, as demonstrated by the quickness and accuracy of understanding, he is approximately 10 per cent above normal."

The headline on Fullerton's story was "Why Babe Ruth Is Greatest Home-Run Hitter." The *New York Times*, reporting the tests on Sunday, September 11, on the front page, had a headline that said, "Ruth Supernormal, So He Hits Home Runs." The results in the lab seemed to confirm the results in the Polo Grounds.

A Bowdoin College professor, Alfred H. Fuchs, would question a lot of the methodology in the *Journal of the History of the Behavioral Sciences* 77 years later. He would point out that the control group for the tests was mostly telephone and telegraph operators, not elite athletes. He would point out that the conclusions reached by Fullerton, not the two psychologists, tended to make them more dramatic. He would not debate the basic conclusion.

Was Babe Ruth good? Well, yes, he was. He was even good for psychology.

"The report that Ruth performed in superior fashion on psychological tests may have accomplished more at the time to validate psychological tests in the popular mind than the tests themselves did to demonstrate Ruth's demonstrated superiority in the batter's box," Fuchs wrote.

The two most interesting observations from the test were buried in Fullerton's text. First, it was determined that Ruth swung with the most power and could make the ball travel farthest when it was thrown to the low, outside corner of the plate. Second, he did not breathe during his entire swing. The psychologists said that if he kept breathing while he swung, he could generate more power. This was a frightening prospect.

Working without the pneumatic tube and the wires to his bat and the Hipp chronometer or whatever it was, the Babe was doing quite well outside the laboratory too. He banged out his 25th homer on July 15, the 138th of his career, which made him baseball's all-time leading home run hitter at the age of 26. He fell behind his 1920 "pace" in early August, but whacked two on August 8 to get back on track. In a sidelight, an exhibition game in Cincinnati, he whacked the first ball pitched to him over the center-field fence, which never had been done, then came back later in the game to knock a ball into the right-field bleachers, which also never had been done.

There was no more talk of a "fluke" about this home run business. F. C. Lane, in *Baseball* magazine, talked instead about the amazing change his favorite game was witnessing.

"Every owner of the 16 big league clubs is united with his manager in the prayer that somehow, somewhere, he can dig up a player who can remotely parallel Babe Ruth," Lane wrote. "Babe has not only smashed all records, he has smashed the long-accepted system of things in the batting world and on the ruins of that system, he has erected another system, or rather lack of system, whose dominant quality is brute force."

Ruth clouted the record-tying number 54 on September 9 in Philadelphia with—stop if you've heard this before—the longest home run in the history of Shibe Park. On September 16, "the Caliph of Crash," with the "whiz of an ashen club," smoked number 55 in the first game of a doubleheader romp over the St. Louis Browns. The day was filled with home runs, but Ruth's stood out like "an antelope in a field of ants" (all quotations courtesy of the *New York Times*).

To finish off the pennant race on September 26, he hit numbers 57 and 58 in an 8–7 victory over the Indians, a third and final win in a crucial four-game series. "The titanic figure of Babe Ruth stood out in the triumph as the Leviathan would stand out in a flock of harbor tugs" (again, the *Times*). He cranked number 59 on the final day of the season, falling one short of the number both he and Dunninger had predicted. He led the league in home runs, RBI, total bases, slugging percentage, and runs scored. He finished third in batting average at .378 behind Harry Heilmann's .394 and Ty Cobb's .389.

All of this set up the biggest sporting event in the history of New York City, the World Series between the New York Yankees and the National League champion New York Giants. Since this was the first Series in the Yankees' 19-year history, this was uncharted excitement. New against Old. Renter against Landlord. Ruth against McGraw. Brawn against Brains. The mind of any Leviathan in any flock of tugboats reeled at the many confrontations.

The Yankees, informed a year earlier by Giants management in the crush of Babe-o-mania that they should eventually look elsewhere for a permanent home, already had obtained land in the Bronx for a new stadium that would open in 1923. The Series would be their best-of-nine-games chance to make a lot of statements, to show that they were the team of the future, the look of the future. The newspapers had invented a nickname, "Murderers' Row," for their lineup. All of New York was paying attention.

"With the Yankees much depends on whether Ruth is in a pummeling mood," Grantland Rice wrote in the *New York Tribune*. "Some say the Yanks are banking too heavily on one man and this is no small talking point in favor of the Giants. If Ruth is poling 'em—great for the Yankees. But suppose he isn't?"

The interest was so high, the publicity so great, that as many as 10,000 seats at the Polo Grounds were empty. People had stayed home for fear they never could get seats. This did not mean they did not pay attention. A throng estimated at 15,000 gathered around the *New York Times* building to watch updates and stopped traffic on Broadway, and a crowd of 10,000 at Madison Square Garden paid to see a mechanical simulation, little pieces moved around the board. The speculation about how hard tickets would be to obtain, how much scalpers would charge, simply had scared people from going to the actual game.

The Babe, in the first game, was a buzz of activity. He walked, paced, shouted, swung at the first pitch he saw, and singled. He was so antsy that Huggins let him coach third base. The Yankees were 3–0 winners as Carl Mays's submarine ball befuddled the Giants and Mike McNally stole home. The Babe, noisy as he was, was quiet at the bat. The single was his only hit of the day.

He was "covering" the game and the Series for a string of newspapers in the fevered beginnings of the Christy Walsh ghost syndicate. McGraw also was "covering." Ring Lardner, sportswriter and humorist, was on the job as well, writing as himself. He noted the Babe's literary efforts:

> At the risk of advertising a rival author, I will say that the Babe is turn-ing out a daily article which appears in a whole lot of papers and if you don't read it you are missing practically all the inside stuff. Like for inst his write-up of the first game opened up with these words:
> "When I sent Mike McNally home in the fifth inning it was taking a big chance."
> The word "it" probably refers to McNally and the play spoke of is the one where Mike stole home and if Babe hadn't of been writing, we wouldn't of known that it was him that thought up the play.

McGraw decided in the second game the best way to handle Ruth simply was to walk him. The Babe walked three straight times. Frustrated with the third walk in the fifth inning, he immediately stole second, then stole third. The steal of third ultimately decided the Series.

While the Polo Grounds crowd cheered such a display of speed from a big man, Ruth was looking at a cut on his left elbow that he had sus-tained while sliding into the bag. The Yankees won the game, again by a 3–0 score, to take a 2–0 lead in the Series, but the cut quickly became in-fected. Ruth opened it again with another slide in the next game, a 13–5 loss. A day of rain intervened, but the cut did not heal. Ruth had the in-jury lanced, but the procedure did not help.

He played in the fourth game, heavily taped, and had a single and his first World Series home run in a 4–2 loss that evened the Series. He also played in the fifth game, a 3–1 Yankees win, and started the winning rally with a bunt that surprised everyone, scoring from first on Bob Meusel's double. It was obvious, though, that he was done. He had played with a tube hanging from the wound to drain the pus. He was so exhausted from running the bases that time had to be called so he could recover and go back to left field. His doctor soon ruled him out of the Series.

"To play while the arm is in its present condition would be to invite a spread of the infection," Dr. Edward King declared. "We have ordered Ruth that under no condition shall he attempt to play ball tomorrow."

Barred from coaching third, unable even to drive his car, Ruth was driven to the park and watched games six and seven in the stands. The Yankees lost both of them. During game six, Christy Walsh showed him a newspaper article by veteran sportswriter Joe Vila of the *New York Sun* that said Ruth's injury wasn't serious and such reports should be taken with "a grain of salt." Ruth, furious, found Vila and rolled up his sleeve and told him to "take a picture of that and put it in your newspaper." Vila declined.

Ruth did suit up for the eighth game in what turned out to be the final best-of-nine series in major league history, the wound wrapped in gauze, his left arm below the bandage blue with blood poisoning and swollen to twice its normal size. He pinch-hit in the ninth inning, but grounded out to first, and the Giants won the game, 1–0, and the Series, five games to three. Done.

"The last day of the World Series showed the awful effects of reform on murderers' row," Westbrook Pegler wrote for the United News syndicate.

They were murderers no longer. They were just ballplayers, playing strategy out of the manual, their old, slugging, slaughtering ways forgot.

They were trying to win on pitching alone, like a successful axe murderer turning to such subtle tools as the poisoned needle, Oriental incense or mental suggestion. They were pathetic.

The irony was that if the concluding games had been held only a week later, the lead murderer would have been fine, healed, able to play. He announced that he would play, in fact, embarking on a barnstorming exhibition that would last right up until November 1.

And then the fun began.

CHAPTER TEN

_____

THE PLAN was to do a barnstorming tour in two parts. The first part
was a succession of visits to cold, industrial hamlets around the
Northeast. The second part was a visit to Oklahoma, a warmer sequence
of oil and cow towns starting with a game in Oklahoma City. The fee for
all this would be as much as $30,000, more than George Herman Ruth
had gathered for laying out those 59 home runs and sending all of New
York City into a tizzy for the World Series.

The schedule began almost immediately. The man who had appeared
with the bandaged left arm in the ninth inning on October 13 would
be the leader of the "Babe Ruth All-Stars" in Buffalo two days later. He
said, "I heal quick. I always heal quick." Carl Mays, Wally Schang, Bob
Meusel, and reserve pitchers Bill Piercy and Tom Sheehan from the Yankees roster would accompany him, with the rest of the all-stars recruited
from the Buffalo area.

Barnstorming tours were a standard practice, a chance for the players
to make supplemental money, a chance for the outlying fans to put faces
and bodies with the names they had read about all year in the newspapers. Ruth obviously had done a tour every year since fame had arrived
at his locker. Today Utica, tomorrow Havana, no problem.

Now, as he prepared to leave for Buffalo the day after the Series, hangovers strewn around the Hotel Commodore with last night's dinner jackets after the Yankees' breakup party hosted by the Colonels, he was told he couldn't go. This tour would be illegal under section 8B of article 4 of the Major League Code. If there were any questions, he would have to deal with Judge Kenesaw Mountain Landis, the recently ordained commissioner of baseball.

"Law-abiding baseball men have no fear that the laws of the game will not be enforced," the Judge said ominously in perfect legalese. "The law of gravitation is still in force and what goes up must come down."

The rule stated that players from the two teams competing in the World Series could not play games elsewhere. Anyone from any team that finished lower in the standings was free to tour as much as possible, but the Series participants were banned. The intent of the rule was to keep the players on the two teams from restaging the Series on their own, town to town, cheapening the event that had just concluded and confusing fans about who was really the world's champion. With only six players from the Yankees on Ruth's All-Stars, one of them not even on the Series roster, there didn't seem to be much chance of confusion here, but Landis was firm on his decision that a rule was a rule.

Ruth was firm on his decision to play the games.

"We are going to play baseball until November 1," he said, "and Judge Landis is not going to stop us. . . . I am out to earn an honest dollar and at the same time give baseball fans an opportunity to see the big players in action."

This was a public confrontation of intriguing proportions. Ruth, the star of stars, had not been told no in a long time, not since his days with Brother Matthias and the Xaverians. Landis, like the Xaverians, was an expert in saying no.

A federal judge, he had been plucked by baseball's owners from the U.S. District Court of Northern Illinois early in the year after the Black Sox scandal hit in Chicago. He was an odd, foul-mouthed little man, an ego-driven, tobacco-chewing puritan with electric white hair shooting out of his head, a hanging judge with the wrath of God carved across his face. The best description of him was that he looked "like Whistler's Mother in slacks." His favorite phrase when he sentenced some seditionist, some violator of the Volstead Act, some miscreant, to the stiffest penalty possible was "Take that man up to Mabel's room."

His name itself had a touch of anger. Abraham Landis, his father, had been a surgeon in the Union Army attached to Gen. William Tecumseh Sherman's sweep through Georgia during the Civil War. Before reaching Atlanta, the army encountered resistance at Kennesaw Mountain. A Confederate bullet caught surgeon Landis in the leg, and he walked forever after with a pronounced limp. To commemorate the incident, he gave the name Kenesaw Mountain (misspelling it in the process) to his sixth child, even though the rest of the family objected.

The owners of baseball had noticed Kenesaw Mountain when his inactivity on a suit by the renegade Federal League caused the league to flounder and die, which was very good news for the owners of baseball. When they needed a strong figure, a czar, to replace the three-man National Commission and give the sport a cleaner-than-clean, gosh-darn-honest image after the scandal, they remembered him. The wrath of God face probably earned Landis the job by itself.

Taking on Ruth was not a bad strategy. The eight Black Sox players were still in court proceedings in Chicago. Landis already had banned them for life from organized baseball no matter what the outcome of the court case. (They were acquitted.) A move against Ruth was a consolidation of power. Nobody was "bigger than baseball." Nobody—translation here—was bigger than Landis.

The two Colonels were terrified about what he might do to Ruth. Would Landis ban him for an entire season? They tried to convince Ruth not to go. Huston even hurried to Grand Central Station for a final plea before the train left for Buffalo.

Ruth still went. Ruth played. He hit a home run as the All-Stars beat the Polish Nationals, not to be confused with the Giants, 4–2. Mays and Schang, after meeting with Landis at the Commodore, had decided to drop out. Meusel and the two young pitchers also played. The next day they played in Elmira.

"I see no reason why this rule should be invoked against us when [George] Sisler of St. Louis and others who shared in World Series money are playing exhibition games unmolested by Judge Landis," Ruth said. "I see no reason not to play, no matter what Judge Landis's views may be."

"What did Judge Landis say to you in your New York talk?" someone asked.

"He hung up on me twice when I tried to telephone to him," Ruth said. "I did not see him personally."

Huston, Ruth's bigger backer in the partnership of Colonels, now traveled to Scranton, Pennsylvania, to try again to make him quit. This time the big man listened. He had been working with an idea that Landis was going to fine him, probably take his $3,362 check for the World Series. Who cared? He would make that much in one exhibition. Huston explained that the big worry was a suspension. What would the Yankees do without their fabled home run slugger? He would be letting his teammates down.

Ruth said he hadn't considered that problem. He agreed to call off the rest of the tour. The weather had been cold, the crowds smaller than expected as cities had to scramble for alternative fields since their minor league teams were afraid to rile Landis. Okay, fine. The tour was done.

Huston also asked Ruth to go to Chicago to apologize to the commissioner. Ruth said he would. He then went hunting with Herb Pennock. He hadn't said exactly when he would go to see Landis. He never did. On October 27, he returned to New York for a press conference at the Palace Theater to announce that he had signed a contract with the Keith Theaters to do a vaudeville act starting November 14 for 20 weeks at $3,000 per week.

This was legal.

Landis didn't make his decision until December 5. He suspended Ruth, Meusel, and Piercy until May 20, 1922, approximately the first seven weeks of the season, and ruled they had to surrender all monies earned in the World Series. Sheehan, who was not on the World Series roster, was neither fined nor suspended.

Cols. Ruppert and Huston were relieved. The punishment was harsh, considering the fact that players in the past had been fined no more than $100 for consistently breaking this rule, but the Colonels had feared that Ruth was going to be suspended for the entire year. Ruth refused to comment.

"Lots of potatoes" was his most definitive remark, made to a waiter taking his order for steak à la Garusse when reporters found him sitting in a "delicate pink chaise lounge" in his Washington hotel room in the midst of his tour. He did say that he wasn't worried and that he wouldn't let the decision affect his vaudeville act.

The act, Ruth paired with veteran comic Wellington Cross, was not *Hamlet,* but critics were mostly kind, except for the man from the *New York World* who said Ruth had "a grace of carriage somewhere between John Barrymoreish and Elephantish." A one-armed aerialist, a roller-skating comedy duo, and Anita Diaz and her trained monkeys were some of the other acts. Ruth sang a couple of songs, one about feeling bad after striking out. He also did some routines with Cross, who acted as straight man. One involved a telegram from Kenesaw Mountain Landis himself.

"Is it serious?" Cross asked.

"I should say it is," Ruth replied. "Seventy-five cents, collect."

And so it went, across the country, $3,000 per week.

Ruth left the tour early in Milwaukee in February and went to Hot Springs for two weeks to soak in the tubs and the sun before heading to spring training. Under the suspension, he was allowed to train with the Yankees, play exhibitions, even practice before regular-season games. It was only the games themselves he had to miss for the seven weeks. He also was allowed to negotiate a new contract.

His last negotiation, well, renegotiation, which had landed him $10,000 per season for three years, had been the loud and noisy deal with Harry Frazee, who finally sent him from Boston to New York. This negotiation was a bit easier. Col. Huston journeyed to Hot Springs to do the business. He met with Ruth at the Eastman Hotel at eight o'clock at night—maybe in the tubs, maybe not—and the two men soon reached the same salary range. Huston had come up to $50,000 per year for three years, plus a two-year option. Ruth had come down to $52,000 per year, same number of years. He said he wanted $52,000 so he could say he made $1,000 per week. Huston and Ruth went back and forth.

"Let's flip for it," Ruth said.

Huston was not averse to the idea. (Might there have been drinking during these negotiations?) He said he had to call Col. Ruppert in New York to make sure a flip of the coin was all right. Ruth went back to his hotel, long-distance telephone connections being what they were, and at eleven o'clock Huston told him to come back. Ruppert had agreed to the procedure.

So somewhere around midnight the Colonel pulled out a half-dollar from his pocket and said, "Call it," and the Babe called, "Tails," and Huston flipped. The coin landed on the carpet and rolled underneath a rocking chair. Huston and the Babe went down on all fours. Tails it was. The Babe stood up as a man making $1,000 per week.

The figure was extravagant for baseball perhaps, probably the biggest contract any player or manager ever had signed, but it wasn't outrageous. Huston declared Ruth was getting "the salary of the president of a railroad." It would have been a smaller railroad. He wasn't close to joining the country's 67 millionaires. He did much better than the 5 million people who filed tax returns for 1921 of $4,000 or lower, which was over 70 percent of the taxpaying population, but he in no way approached the baseball stars of the future.

A conversion system from the American Institute of Economic Research translates the Babe's $52,000 into $564,737.43 in 2005 dollars. Only two members of the 2005 New York Yankees, outfielder Bubba Crosby at $322,950 and second baseman Andy Phillips at $317,000, made less than $564,737.43. Reserve second baseman Rey Sanchez made $600,000. The median salary for a member of the 2005 Yankees was $5,883,334; the highest-paid Yankee, third baseman Alex Rodriguez, made $26 million. To make the same amount in 1922 dollars as Alex Rodriguez, Ruth would have had to sign for $2,246,913.58. Baseball simply didn't pay that kind of money. Home Run Baker, second on the salary list after Ruth, made $16,000, the equivalent of $185,142.86.

Added to the contract was a clause, written just for Ruth, that he had to abstain from intoxicating liquors and not remain up later than one o'clock during the playing season. This mostly seemed to be an interesting technicality. Two weeks later he was with the team in New Orleans where a famous headline, "Yankees Training on Scotch," was written. He always liked New Orleans.

"Babe, somehow he'd get invited to those fine old southern homes, mansions, really, and somehow I'd get invited with him and be treated to a long, long, real old southern meal," one New York sportswriter said. "The host, coming from an old-time family down there, would put on an act. He'd have Negroes in hose, dressed just as they were at the end or before the Civil War. There would be a big show in the kitchen, waiters, all sorts of attendants, sometimes a small orchestra. So we'd sit there and get a sample of food that very, very few people really ever get a chance to eat.

"The Babe was a good trencherman. So he enjoyed this. We had opportunities down there to see that life that very few outsiders ever saw."

Judge Landis appeared in New Orleans for an exhibition game, bought a ball for $250 signed by Ruth as part of an auction for the Salvation Army, and rejected Ruth's plea for a commutation of sentence. The Babe was involved in an auto accident in New Orleans, was late for an exhibition with the Superbas, then pounded out a home run—the longest in the history of Heineman Park—in the sixth. All of the usual stuff.

The Yankees had rearranged their roster again during the winter, going back to Mr. Frazee and his discount store in Boston. They picked up shortstop Everett Scott and pitchers Sam Jones and Joe Bush for Roger Peckinpaugh, Jack Quinn, Rip Collins, and Bill Piercy, that barnstorming pitcher. They also picked up solid center fielder Whitey Witt for cash as part of another fire sale by A's owner Connie Mack. If anything, they looked stronger than they had a year earlier, only needing the return of Ruth and Meusel to fill out the lineup.

Opening day was in Washington with President Warren G. Harding throwing out the first ball. Ruth sat in the grandstand next to Huston and American League president Ban Johnson for the game, a 5–2 loss to the Senators. The big man was described as restless. His stretch in the slammer had now begun.

He broke up the waiting that followed with an occasional appearance in an exhibition—he clanged out a homer against Jack Dunn's Orioles on April 16—and sometimes showed up for morning practices before games and more often didn't. He also bought a house and had his tonsils removed.

The house was back in Sudbury, back in Massachusetts, actually a farm, the old Sylvester Perry place, built in 1737. It had 12 rooms and sat on 155 acres of tillable land, woodland, and water, which was Pratt's Pond. A barn, garage, and henhouse were in the back. The price, according to local rumor, was $12,000. Ruth appeared on April 29, driven from Boston by a chauffeur, to take charge. He named the estate "Home Plate Farm" and said it was going to be a working agricultural operation. He told a photographer to save the slides of the pictures he took so he could compare them to the place after all of the improvements were made. The move-in date, Ruth said, would be after the end of the season, although "the missus" would be up in a month to buy some new furniture.

"I thought the place was furnished," a reporter said.

"Oh, we'll buy some more," Ruth said.

The mention of "the missus" brought Helen back into the scene. The fog had descended heavy over her. No public mention had been made since she'd flown over the second game of the World Series in a blimp and dropped three good-luck baseballs down to the Polo Grounds in a fine Christy Walsh production. Did she go with the Babe on the barnstorming tour? The vaudeville tour? Fog. She was mentioned again when the Babe checked into St. Vincent's Hospital to have his tonsils removed on May 4. Helen also checked in to have an operation, but "the nature of her ailment was not revealed." This was one of a number of trips to the hospital for her, none of the ailments ever revealed.

She once told another ballplayer's wife that she had had four miscarriages. True? Not true? Not revealed. She also told the ballplayer's wife she had graduated from Smith College. Not true.

The Babe was discharged first and fully recovered in time for his big return on May 20, coming back as a man with more money, fewer tonsils, and a house that he didn't have when he left. The condition of Helen, still in the hospital, was not revealed. She didn't return home until the day before her husband returned to the field.

He was at the races that day. Jack Dunn ran into him at Jamaica Race Track in New York. Dunn's Orioles had been rained out of a game against the Newark Bears.

"How are you doing?" Dunn asked.

"Couldn't be better," the Babe said. "It's been a long suspension for me; it seemed like a thousand years."

"Any luck with the horses?"

"Pretty good day yesterday," the Babe said. "I cleaned up a little more than $18,000."

Dunn then watched the kid he pulled out of an orphanage proceed to bet $5,000 on the first race, $2,000 to win and $3,000 to place. He then bet $3,000 to win in the second.

The return to glory on May 20 was glorious until the game began. A crowd of 38,000, easily the largest of the season, packed the Polo Grounds. Ruth received a silver loving cup filled with dirt collected from the diamond at St. Mary's Industrial School for Boys by some fans from Baltimore, a floral horseshoe from the National Vaudeville Association, and a silver bat from Harry Weber, his vaudeville agent. He then, alas, also received a succession of dipping spitballs from Urban Shocker, one of the pitchers grandfathered into spitball legality, and went 0-for-4 in an 8–2 loss to the St. Louis Browns. Bob Meusel fared no better, also going hitless.

The day was a disappointment in the end.

"No scientist has ever figured out the purpose of tonsils in the human system," Heywood Broun suggested. "Maybe they have something to do with home runs."

The odd, shortened season began. The Yankees had been doing fine without their exiled stars, shooting out to first place, 22 and 11, two games in front of the Browns. Whitey Witt had been a hitting machine, hitting better than he ever had in his life. Now, "the Albino must move over for the Bambino," as one writer said. The great man was back, and he was making all this money, and the team was going well, and he had better do something spectacular.

He didn't.

The pressure to perform, coupled with the layoff, had him flailing at pitches. He was booed by the big crowd on that first day back for failing to catch up with Shocker's spitballs, and the boos increased as he struggled through his first five days with one home run and an .093 batting average. This was the first time in his career he had been booed daily, and it was obvious by his actions that he did not like it. He often tipped his cap in sarcasm to the booing fans.

In his sixth game back, he whacked a single in the second inning that he tried to stretch into a double. He was called out by umpire George Hildebrand. Reacting to the call, Ruth jumped up and threw dirt in Hildebrand's face. Reacting to the dirt, Hildebrand threw Ruth out of the game. The boos came from everywhere. Ruth gave the sarcastic tip of the cap, seemed to be in control, but when he reached the dugout, he could make out the words that were being shouted. He particularly could make out the words being shouted by two Pullman car conductors.

He leaped the fence and went into the stands to challenge one of them. The conductor bolted back a few rows and continued to shout. Ruth shouted back, restrained gently by a few fans. Someone shouted, "Hit the big stiff." The conductor continued to move backward. Ruth finally went back on the roof of the dugout, where he challenged anyone in the crowd who wanted to come down and fight. With no challengers, minus his cap, he jumped back onto the field. He picked up the cap, along with his glove, and started to walk to the clubhouse, which at the Polo Grounds was located beyond center field. The boos and the jeers followed him all the way.

"They can boo and hoot me all they want," he said when reporters found him back at the Ansonia. "That doesn't matter to me. But when a fan calls me insulting names from the grandstand and becomes abusive, I don't intend to stand for it. This fellow today, whoever he was, called me 'a low-down bum' and other names that got me mad, and when I went after him he ran."

The tone for the season somehow had been established. Luckily for

Ruth, Landis was not part of this judicial process and Babe was fined only $200 and given a warning by American League president Johnson, but he was off in a different, contentious situation that no one had predicted. The picture of the hero, hanging so well in the living rooms of America during the past two or three years, had been knocked askew during his seven weeks on the sidelines. Everything seemed off-kilter.

The missing seven weeks, 33 games, left Ruth with no chance to reach the standards that had made him famous. He was 11 home runs behind surprising outfielder Ken Williams of the surprising Browns in the home run chase before the chase even started. He had little chance to catch Williams and, more importantly, no chance to catch himself.

He had blustered during the seven weeks that he thought he still might hit 60 home runs, but two weeks of reality and opposition pitching convinced him that was impossible. He admitted the fact in Chicago on June 7. He said he still thought he had a chance to pass Williams and National League leader Rogers Hornsby, but this was hope more than certainty. He was caught in a hole, and people were yelling at him and didn't seem to understand.

The afternoon of June 12 at Sportsman's Park in St. Louis described Ruth's situation as well as anything. Williams hit his 15th homer, best in the majors, and the Browns won, 7–1, and Ruth . . . well, this was the way he was struggling.

The Browns pitched a rookie, a 21-year-old left-hander named Hub Pruett, fresh from the University of Missouri, who quickly had been nicknamed Shucks for his unflappable nature. As a kid, Shucks had idolized Christy Mathewson, the master of the "fadeaway." The pitch, later known as the screwball, was basically a curveball in reverse, thrown with an unnatural twist of the wrist and elbow. Mathewson was a right-hander, but Pruett figured the pitch would work for a left-hander too. Shucks, reaching the majors, had developed a pretty good screwball.

Every hitter in history, no matter how successful, comes across a pitcher and a pitch he cannot handle. Shucks was that pitcher for Ruth. He had faced the Bambino in relief in May, struck him out with the screwball and walked him, and now as a starter struck him out three times and walked him once. In July, meeting again, Pruett would strike him out three more times. In August, bases loaded, nobody out, Ruth at the plate, Shucks would come out of the bullpen and strike him out again. In the first 12 times he faced Ruth, that was nine strikeouts, two walks, and a tapper back to the pitcher for an out.

In September, Pruett already had developed a sore arm from throwing the pitch. He tried his one—and only—curveball against Ruth. Ruth deposited the ball into the right-field stands, crossed the plate, picked up a straw hat someone had thrown from the stands, and wore it with a smile back to the dugout. Everybody knew what the celebration meant.

"At the ballpark during the year we passed each other without speaking," Pruett, who finished with a career 29–48 record, said years later. "But every once in a while he would do something that would give me a kick. He would wink at me."

The three-strikeout game in June set the Yankees off on an eight-game losing streak, dropping them two and a half games behind the Browns. They were 13 and 16 since the return of Ruth and Meusel to the lineup. This was the great hero? He also drew a second suspension in the eighth successive loss for running in from left field to argue with umpire Bill Dineen over a play at second base. Dineen threw him out of the game, and that night Ban Johnson suspended him for three games because "my reports show that Ruth used vulgar and vicious language, calling Umpire Dineen one of the vilest names known." (The mind searches, of course, to figure out what that name would be.)

After batting practice the next day, Ruth approached the umpire again and made the situation worse. He told Dineen, "If you ever put me out of a game again, I'll fix you so you will never umpire again, even if they put me out of baseball for life." Dineen did not like this. Ruth also told him, "You're yellow," and challenged him to a fight. Dineen also did not like this. He took off his mask and started to go under the stands with Ruth, but was restrained by Cleveland Indians Tris Speaker and Steve O'Neill. Ban Johnson did not like any of this. He increased Ruth's suspension to five games and said he would suspend Ruth for the entire summer if necessary.

This at last brought the Bambino to contrition. He apologized to Dineen the next day in the umpires' locker room, swore off on more arguments, and sat on a table and tried to figure out what was happening. Why had the picture on the wall been knocked sideways? He couldn't understand.

"Some persons are saying that I welcome the suspensions because it gives me an alibi for not equaling the home run record of last year," he said. "This is ridiculous, as I realize that is impossible. Others claim I have a swelled head. My friends know different. I want to be in there every minute because I love to play baseball."

"It's no use," he continued on the field to a reporter, in between turns at the plate during batting practice. "They're all after me. If I'm not wanted in organized baseball, all they have to do is tell me and I will step down and out."

He stepped into the cage, hit a couple of balls out of Dunn Field, stepped back out, and continued. Why was he being singled out? Everyone had yelled at Dineen. He stepped back into the cage, hit another shot over the wall. Stepped out, said all the breaks seemed to be going against the Yankees, but things would improve. Stepped back in, hit a ball that was as long as any home run ever seen at Dunn Field. Stepped out.

"Tell my 'friends' about the four balls that have gone over the fence," he finished, heading back to the dugout.

The season was played out in this same discordant key. The Yankees won the pennant, of course, rallying, winning two out of three in a big series in St. Louis in the middle of September and then going on a six-game win streak to outlast the Browns by a game, and Ruth finished with 35 home runs, four behind Ken Williams and two behind Tilly Walker of the A's— not bad for four-fifths of a season—but nothing came easy. One brushfire, just about to be extinguished, seemed to ignite another.

This edition of the team—ten different players on the roster from the 1921 pennant winners—was filled with contentious veterans, devotees of the speakeasy and the racetrack in their off-hours, no-nonsense hardball players on the field. They didn't pay much attention to manager Miller Huggins, didn't pay much attention to anyone.

The Colonels went so far as to hire a private detective to follow the team around on the road and report back on what he learned. Using the name of Kelly, he quickly infiltrated the after-dark scene, became friends with the players by buying them shirts and neckties and whatever, and they brought him to a ham and cabbage dinner Ruth had arranged at a brewery in Joliet, Illinois. Somewhere in the night, Kelly posed everyone for a famous beer-filled photograph—smile!—which he brought back to the Colonels as exhibit A, the star right fielder directly in the middle.

Huggins confronted the players involved, one by one, in his hotel room in Washington. Ruth was the last visitor. Huggins asked Ruth why he always was moving, running, staying up late, finding himself in all of these situations.

"I didn't have a thing till I was 18 years old, not a bite," Ruth replied, as introspective as anything he ever said. "Now it's bustin' out all over."

He then went downstairs and told Whitey Witt in the lobby that if he ever found Kelly, he'd kill him.

No fines were given. No suspensions were levied. Kenesaw Mountain Landis did journey to Boston to talk to both the Yankees and Red Sox, gathered in the same room, about the perils of gambling, drink, bad friends, and staying up late.

"Seeing a glorious sunrise is all right if you get up in the morning to watch it," the wrath of God said, "but waiting up all night to see it is the rankest kind of folly, which has no place in the life of an athlete."

Yawn.

"Those of you who are innocent of this practice of betting on horse races need not reproach yourselves, nor consider my remarks as personal," the commissioner continued. "But there are some who are doing this thing, and to these I wish to say that they have not been unobserved and that the practice must cease or I will gather them in as surely as the sun rises in the morning."

Double yawn.

Fights were another feature of the season. Ruth had a fight with Wally Pipp, or rather Wally Pipp whacked Ruth in the dugout after Ruth criticized his fielding. Braggo Roth and Aaron Ward had a fight one day later. Al DeVormer, an eccentric backup catcher, had fights with Carl Mays and Fred Hofmann. Waite Hoyt wanted to fight Huggins. Ruth, oh, yes, was suspended again for using a vile and vicious word, maybe the same word, maybe not, this time to umpire Tom Connolly. The suspension was for three days, accompanied by another apology, a vow never to be thrown out of a game again. The format was familiar.

The result of all of this—or, perhaps, despite all of this—was that the Yankees had another date with the Giants in a second Subway Series. The format had been shortened to best-of-seven, a Judge Landis demand, but the matchups of old and new, brains and brawn, etc., were the same. The Giants had clinched their pennant early and appeared to be more rested. The Yankees, well, they had the Babe. The betting was evenly divided.

One difference this time was that the games were on radio, broadcast through an eastern network of an estimated five million people from WJZ in Newark, WGY in Schenectady, and WBZ in West Springfield, Massachusetts. Grantland Rice, the sportswriter, did the play-by-play to what the *New*

York Times called "an invisible audience." It was noted that the invisible audience could even hear the cheering in the background at the Polo Grounds.

Another difference this time was that the Giants killed the Yankees in four straight games. All of the sins of the season came back. The Yankees were pitiful. Miller Huggins forever thought Carl Mays and Joe Bush both threw games on purpose, a charge never verified. It was that kind of performance.

Bush did almost certainly groove a pitch to George Kelly in the final game. In the eighth inning, two outs, runners on second and third, Yanks ahead, 3–2, Huggins ordered the right-handed Bush to walk the left-handed Ross Youngs and pitch to right-handed George Kelly. Bush disagreed with the decision.

"What for, you stupid [vile and vicious name]?" he shouted at Huggins loud enough for the entire, packed stadium to hear.

He walked Youngs. He served a meatball to Kelly. Kelly rifled the meatball into center field. The Giants took the lead, added another run, and five minutes later were champions of the world.

Ruth was especially pitiful. McGraw instructed his pitchers to serve the Bambino a consistent diet of junk balls, low and inside. The Bambino was as helpless against this diet as he was against the screwballs of young Hub Pruett. He never saw one fastball in the strike zone. He finished with only a double and a single in 17 at-bats. The Giants didn't even bother to walk him, issuing only two bases on balls.

The frustration of it all hit Ruth at the end of the third game. The Giants had been riding him from the bench, bringing back that word "nigger" from St. Mary's Industrial School for Boys. They used the word as both noun and adjective, teaming it with (as Ban Johnson would say) every vile and vicious name imaginable, calling him a "so-and-so nigger" and also "a nigger so-and-so." Ruth had heard enough.

Taking Bob Meusel with him after the 3–0 loss, he went to the Giants' clubhouse. He first challenged reserve infielder Johnny Rawlings, the loudest voice on the bench. Then pitcher Jess Barnes became involved. Then Earl Smith, catcher.

"What'd he call you?" Smith asked.

"He called me a nigger," the Babe said.

"That's nothing," Smith said.

Ruth became aware that several sportswriters had been drawn to the confrontation. McGraw also had joined the scene and ordered him out of the clubhouse. The edge came off Ruth's anger. He joked with a couple of the Giants. He left with a request rather than a demand.

"Don't get me wrong," he said. "I don't mind being called a [submit vile and vicious name] or a [submit another vile and vicious name] or things like that. I expect that. Just lay off the personal stuff."

The strange season was done.

In the off-season, Christy Walsh wanted to repair the damage that was done. It didn't take an expert in this new public relations stuff to recognize that the Babe's image had taken a few good blows. He hadn't awed and amazed people, missing as many games as he did. He had come off as a combustible character, selfish, sometimes out of control, a bear that didn't react well when baited. The goal was to bring him back to the big, lovable galoot who had captured America's imagination in the first place.

Walsh knew that perception was more important than truth. He always told his ghostwriters not to strive to write the way their athlete talked, but to try to write the way the public thought the athlete talked. There was a difference. The character in the public mind was more important than the real character.

During the 1922 season, Ruth had two moments when he was an obvious big, lovable galoot. The first was when he bought the farm in Sudbury. The idea of him, the ultimate city kid, going off to raise chickens and turnips brought an immediate smile. The second moment was when he divulged that he was a father. He had a baby girl! Not only that, the baby girl was 16 months old!

The news came out of the fog of his marriage in strange circumstances. While the Babe was on the road in Cleveland on September 20, Helen showed up at the Polo Grounds for a Giants game with the baby and a nurse. Reporters inquired. Helen answered. She said the baby, named Dorothy, had been born very small, two and a half pounds, and had lived in an incubator, then with a nurse before recently coming home to the Ansonia Hotel. The Babe hadn't wanted news of the baby released until they knew she was completely healthy.

Contacted in Cleveland, the Babe admitted he was a father. He said the baby had been born on February 2 at Presbyterian Hospital in New York. Helen, alas, had said the baby was born on June 7 at St. Vincent's Hospital in New York. What was the deal?

"I guess she knows," Babe said.

"You know he's never good with names or dates," Helen said.

All this was confusing. Most guesses were that the baby had been adopted, but neither adoption records nor birth records ever were found anywhere. The truth—or another version of the truth—would not come out until more than 60 years later, when Dorothy would be told that she was in fact Ruth's natural daughter, born to a lover and taken from the lover to live with Helen and the Babe.

Whatever the case, he was now a dad, available for all of those dad photo opportunities. He was a big, lovable galoot of a dad.

Christy Walsh decided to focus on these domestic changes—the farm, the daughter—in rebuilding the Babe's image. He also devised what would become a staple of repaired public relations: the apology. When the Babe returned from a desultory barnstorming trip across the Midwest—the rules had been changed against Landis's protest to make this allowable now—he immediately telephoned the Yankees offices and described how the winter was going to be devoted to the simple life of chopping wood, hunting, hiking, and losing 25 pounds. He also said he had hit 20 homers in 17 games across Nebraska, Iowa, Minnesota, Colorado, and Oklahoma.

"Wait a minute," he said in this report from his new domesticity. "The baby's fallen out of the chair."

Walsh plotted out a far more public moment. He arranged a dinner on November 15 at the midtown Elks Club in New York. The theme was "Back to the Farm," a good-bye to Ruth before he left for Sudbury. Walsh invited the city's sportswriters, plus assorted politicians and Broadway notables. Attendance was good, a large papier-mâché cow stood atop the head table, and the show was memorable.

State Sen. James J. Walker, later to become the gadfly mayor of New York, then the embattled mayor of New York, was the star attraction. At the end of an evening of pleasant speeches extolling the Babe, he rose and cut the Babe to pieces. A man publicly known to stay up late and take a drink had advice for a man publicly known to stay up later and take more drinks.

"Babe Ruth is not only a great athlete, but also a great fool," Walker began. "His employer, Col. Jacob Ruppert, makes millions of gallons of beer, and Ruth is of the opinion that he can drink it faster than the Colonel and his large corps of brew masters can make it. Well . . . you can't! Nobody can."

The room became very quiet. The rest of the speech, as reported by Gene Fowler in his biography of Walker, *Beau James,* followed:

You are making a bigger salary than anyone ever received as a ballplayer. But the bigger the salary, the bigger the fool you have become.

Here sit some 40 sportswriters and big officials of baseball, our national sport. These men, your friends, know what you have done, even if you don't. They are sad and dejected. Why? I'll tell you. You have let them down!

But worst of all, worst of all, you have let down the kids of America. Everywhere in America, on every vacant lot where kids play baseball, and in the hospitals too, where crippled children dream of movement forever denied their thin and warped little bodies, they think of you, their hero; they look up to you, worship you. And then what happens? You carouse and abuse your great body and it is exactly as though Santa Claus himself suddenly were to take off his beard to reveal the features of a villain. The kids have seen their idol shattered and their dreams broken.

Fowler's report had the Babe sobbing by now. Other reports—sportswriter Fred Lieb's, for one—did not remember any sobbing. Walker, in Fowler's report, placed his hand on the Babe's shoulder.

"If we did not love you, Babe, and if I myself did not love you sincerely, I would not tell you these things," Walker said. "Will you not, for the kids of America, solemnly mend your ways? Will you not give back to those kids their great idol?"

Fowler had the Babe reply in tears.

"So help me, Jim, I will!" Ruth said. "I'll go back to my farm in Sudbury and get in shape."

He soon left with Walsh and this firm purpose to repent. The gathered sportswriters left with filled notebooks. They might have had some cynicism, some doubt about whether what they had seen was true, half-true, or completely staged, but words were words and these were good ones.

The writers too wanted the old Babe to return.

CHAPTER ELEVEN

NEW YORK had 18 daily newspapers when the Babe arrived in 1920. Though the competition for readers and distribution wasn't as deadly as it was in Chicago, where murders and sabotage were commonplace in the circulation wars in the first decade of the new century, the fight for the daily two cents from 5.6 million New Yorkers was serious and ferocious. The Babe was an answered prayer for everyone concerned.

The *Evening Journal*, a William Randolph Hearst paper, was the circulation leader at around 600,000. The *Times*, the *World*, and the *American* each averaged slightly over 300,000, while the *Sun* and the *Herald* each was around 200,000, followed by the rest of the pack. Sports occupied 10 to 15 percent of the average news hole in all of these papers, even in the *Times*, and the Sultan of Swat, the Colossus of Clout, filled that space better than any athlete who ever had come along.

Unlike, say, heavyweight champion Jack Dempsey, he was in public view for half of the days of the calendar year, 154 regular-season games plus spring training and whatever drama might emerge in the fall. He was out there, loud and noisy and big, big in everything he did on the field or off the field. He hit home runs, won championships, set records, ate lunch. There was no such thing as no news with the Babe. His strikeouts were as noteworthy as his home runs, his failures and pitfalls as memorable as his successes.

The Speed Graphic, the newspaper photographer's camera of choice, loved his broad face with its flat nose and tiny eyes, loved his absolutely unique look, features put together in a hurry, an out-of-focus bulldog, no veneer or sanding involved. This was a face that soon was instantly recognizable, seen again and again, more familiar in most households than the faces of a second cousin once removed or a Dutch uncle who always appeared for Sunday dinner. The Babe was an incorrigible, wondrous part of everyone's family. He posed in any kind of uniform, any kind of situation. He kissed dogs and cows and chimpanzees. He wore cowboy suits and patrolman blue, badge included. He posed with celebrities and bands of waifs whose eyes all glowed as if they were in the presence of a deity. He was the life of everybody's party.

The words that accompanied the pictures came from an open vault of superlatives. Laughing but earnest men in fedoras and off-the-rack suits, sportswriters, watched the sun rise and fall on his big head and were moved to grand statements. They typed the legend into place, adding layer upon layer of adjectives until often the man in the middle couldn't even be seen. He became a modern Vesuvius, a wonder of the world to be described daily. Everybody had a crack at him.

"No man has ever lived who hit a baseball as hard as Ruth," columnist Damon Runyon wrote in the *American* in a typical daily offering in September 1920. "In the olden days, soldiers were equipped with slings and slew their enemies with missiles thrown from these slings, but it is doubtful if they got as much force behind them as Ruth puts back of a batted ball. The weapon which was the nearest approach to Babe's deadly drive was the catapult."

The end of the war had brought a rush of writing talent into the city. Working for a newspaper was a glamorous occupation, and New York was the most glamorous, most vibrant city in the postwar world. The first two commercial radio stations, one in Pittsburgh and one in Detroit, had only started operation in 1920, so for the last few years the newspaper reporter and the columnist were the only voices that brought news, opinion, even entertainment, every day. Not only were these people stars, but some of them were shooting off toward greater accomplishments.

Runyon, who invented the nicknames "Bambino" and "Bam" and "the Big Bam" for Ruth at the *American*, already was shifting more and more toward his dialogue-filled tales of gangsters and Broadway lowlifes, but he still found his way to the ballpark. Grantland Rice at the *Herald* already was the preeminent sports columnist in the nation, a lyricist much more than an investigator, a few lines of doggerel starting each piece, Greek gods and portentous skies always in the background. Westbrook Pegler, increasingly acerbic and cynical in covering sports in New York for the United Press and then the *Chicago Tribune* syndicate, would evolve into an acerbic and cynical right-wing commentator about politics and life. John Kieran, the first sports columnist in *New York Times* history, had such a range of interests and knowledge that he eventually would become famous on a national radio show, *Information Please,* as a man who could answer all questions about anything.

The baseball beat writers, on the trail every day, sometimes switching to cover the Giants or Dodgers, sometimes not, were a strikingly literate and well-traveled group. Many of them had been in the war. Bozeman Bulger of the *Evening World*, a large and witty character from Birmingham, Alabama, with a fat southern drawl, had been a hero in the Argonne offensive. One-armed Bob Boyd of the *World*, an Australian, looked as if he had been a hero but, alas, had been a member of the Canadian air force and walked into a moving propeller before he ever left for combat. Richards Vidmer of the *Times*, such a sophisticated presence that author Katherine Brush wrote a best-selling novel about him called *The Young Man of Manhattan,* had survived a midair collision with a civilian plane near Hicksville, Long Island, during pilot training in the Signal Corps.

"How are the other fellows?" he asked after being pulled, badly injured, from the crashed fuselage.

"Oh, they're better off than you," he was told. "They're all dead."

Fred Lieb was at the *Telegram*, a statistics man, a baseball insider, who had grown up in Philadelphia. Ford Frick was at the *American*, a future commissioner of baseball from Fort Wayne, Indiana, who had learned to touch type at 15 because he knew he wanted to be a sportswriter. Dan Daniel, proud that he had been the first local sportswriter to use one of those new portable typewriters that everyone now used, was at the *Press*. Will Wedge, who took a note on absolutely everything that happened during a game and secretly wanted to be a poet, was at the *Sun*.

The list went on and on and would expand and contract through the years as affiliations changed, as papers were merged or killed, as assignments changed—Heywood Broun, Joe Williams, Tom Meany, Arthur

Robinson, John Drebinger, Jimmy Cannon, W. O. McGeehan, Bill Co-
rum, Bill Slocum, Frank Graham, people coming and going—but always
there would be a good-sized corps that followed the Yankees, followed
the Babe, typed out the words.

Everything was done in close quarters. The writers were thrown
together with each other, then thrown together with the players. The
clubhouse was not the meeting ground that it would become, stark-naked
athletes questioned daily about their views on hanging curveballs and
life, but incidental contact was perpetual. The writers rode with the players on the trains and in cabs, lived in the same hotels. The games were
played in the afternoon, so nights were open and often shared, ballplayers and writers in the same restaurants and speakeasies, seated at the same
card table.

A friendly atmosphere prevailed. The writers of the time grew to know
their subjects much better than future generations in the craft would.
They also reported much less than future generations would. Especially
about the Babe.

"Hell, I could have written a story every day on the Babe," Richards
Vidmer said. "But I never wrote about his personal life, not if it would
hurt him. Babe couldn't say no to certain things. Hot dogs was the least
of 'em. He couldn't say no to a hot dog, but there were other things that
were worse. Hell, sometimes, I thought it was one long line, a procession . . ."

The Babe was an ultimate test in writing and reporting. What to leave
in? What to leave out? His pleasure-dominated life constantly put him in
questionable situations. Was it news that he was drunk again late at
night? Was it news that he had been with one, two, three women who
were not his wife?

An unwritten, sometimes-spoken code existed not only with him but
with virtually everybody in public life. A boundary existed between the
public and the private. Unless a door was opened by a policeman or a
court proceeding, affairs of the heart and matters of the bedroom,
drunken vulgarities, and four-star orgies were not reported. This code
prevailed not only in sports but in politics, the arts, even show business.
If the president of the United States urinated into a fireplace at the White
House—as Richards Vidmer saw Warren Harding do—it didn't make the
newspaper.

Hints could be made, winks and nods, flaws in character sticking out
the sides of a feature story like lettuce in a fat BLT, but names seldom were

named, dates and places seldom included. A curtain of good taste pretty much came down in many areas once the game had ended. This was not a bad thing for the Babe.

An example: Vidmer would often play bridge in the Babe's hotel room on the long barnstorming trips back from spring training. The Yankees would play a 1:00 P.M. game in some southern town, the game finished by three, and everybody would go back to the hotel to await an 11:00 P.M. departure for the next town. The bridge games would take place, other ballplayers and Vidmer and the Babe, during that time.

The phone always would ring. Vidmer always would answer.

"Is Babe Ruth there?" a woman's voice would ask.

"No, he's not here right now," Vidmer would reply. "This is his secretary. Can I tell him who called?"

"This is Mildred. Tell him Mildred called."

"Mildred . . ."

Vidmer would look at the Babe. The Babe would shake his head, no, not here, not for Mildred.

"I'm sorry," Vidmer would say. "He's not here right now, but I'll tell him you called . . ."

Invariably, the Babe would have instant second thoughts. Invariably, he would sprint across the room and grab the phone.

"Hello, babe. Come on up."

"And she'd come up and interrupt the bridge game for ten minutes or so," Vidmer said. "They'd go in the other room. Pretty soon, they'd come out and the girl would leave. Babe would say, 'So long, kid,' or something like that. Then he'd sit down and we'd continue our bridge game. That's all. That was it. While he was absent, we'd sit and talk, wait for him."

This was not material for the paper. Should it have been? The curtain of good taste covered the situation. The curtain covered a lot of situations. The writers pounded away with their similes and allusions, constructed their grand rococo word sculptures, truly florid and inventive stuff. They worked within their limits.

Fred Lieb always told the story about the woman chasing Ruth with a knife through a Pullman car in Shreveport during spring training in 1921 as the train was almost ready to leave for New Orleans. Ruth was running as fast as he could, and the dark-haired, dark-eyed woman, said to be the wife of a Louisiana legislator, was five feet behind him. Ruth pounded through the car, jumped off the train, then jumped back on as it was leaving, the woman back on the platform.

Eleven writers, playing cards, watched the whole thing. None of them wrote a word.

"Well," Bill Slocum of the *Morning American* said as the card game continued, "if she had carved up the Babe, we really would have had a hell of a story."

The work of the writers would be derided in future journalism school classes, seen as the creation of a day-to-day hagiography, but there were subtleties that the public understood. The spaces between the lines of the nonstop words counted as much as the words themselves. The image came through. Was there any well-minded reader who did not suspect the crudities, the womanizing, the drinking? They were part of what made the Babe so intriguing. They were part of the big and blustery, oversized image that was created.

"So unique is Babe's record, so amazing his exploits, that the riches of the English language seem barren of words adequately to describe him," F. C. Lane wrote in *Baseball* magazine in October 1922, describing the daily exercise of writing about the new sensation.

Flaming adjectives lose their color when applied to the Babe. Overworked verbs falter in the narration of his record feats. While as for nouns that may serve as comparisons—the word painter who scans the verbal horizon for such things finds only a bleak and barren landscape. How are you going to find anyone when nobody like him has ever worn a baseball uniform? Babe is unique.

And yet Ruth is a theme which never grows threadbare. He is to the baseball scribbler as perennial a subject as spring to the budding poet, a sunset to the descriptive prose writer. Familiar from every angle there is yet something about him which is always new. No baseball player has ever been so thoroughly discussed. His most intimate acts and tastes and characteristics are subjected to the searching scrutiny of publicity.

The Babe sold papers. The papers sold him. It was a fine symbiotic relationship. For a man who liked company, the dance with the writers was hardly a chore. He remembered few of their names, didn't know which writer wrote for which paper, never read the papers in fact, but he remembered faces. A knock on his door, either at his home or in the hotel or on the train, often resulted in an invitation to share a libation and a story. Christy Walsh no doubt impressed upon him the need for publicity, but the Babe never really needed coaching. He inhaled and people watched. He exhaled and headlines were created. He breathed publicity naturally.

In an amendment to his 1924 income tax, he would file a request for a $9,000 deduction for money "expended for the purpose of establishing and maintaining good will to the extent of entertaining sports writers, press agents and other similarly situated in order to constantly keep himself before the public." This figure was larger than the salaries paid to most major league baseball players during a season and much larger than the salaries of average American workingmen. It also was approximately one-seventh of the Babe's own stated income for the year, $66,215.34.

He was not afraid of publicity.

A new contender in the newspaper war was the *Illustrated Daily News*, which began operation on June 26, 1919. The publisher, Capt. Joseph Medill Patterson, whose family also owned the *Chicago Tribune*, was on furlough in England during the war and was impressed by the *Daily Mirror*, a photo-filled London tabloid that had a rapidly growing circulation of 800,000. He decided he wanted to bring the same kind of publication to New York.

In the oft-told romantic version of the paper's creation, he and his cousin, Col. Robert McCormick, plotted out the operation next to a fumier, a large pile of collected manure, in the French countryside a few days before the second battle of the Marne. The war ended, and less than a year later the paper—the name soon shortened to the *Daily News*—was on the streets.

The early circulation figures bounced wildly, 35,000 one day, 75,000 the next. The *News* stayed near the bottom of the pile as Patterson refined his formula. Then it began to take off.

There never had been a paper like this in the United States. Pictures in prewar U.S. newspapers traditionally had been restricted to one-column headshots, austere faces set in a field of gray type. This had begun to change with the addition of rotogravure sections, but now the *News* rushed to the forefront. Pictures of people, animals, events—action pictures—were used throughout the paper to illustrate stories about love triangles and murders, politics, human interest, and celebrity. Two full pages of pictures were placed in the middle of each edition. Puzzles, comics, contests, and serial fiction were other parts of the tabloid mix, everything kept short and convenient to be read by the daily rider of the city's subways.

The first sports editor was Marshall Hunt, a 24-year-old native of Tacoma, Washington. The son of a newspaper editor, he had been a journalism student at the University of Washington when war was declared. Virtually the entire membership of his fraternity house, Phi Gamma Delta, immediately enlisted. He joined the U.S. Army Signal Corps and, when the opportunity presented itself, trained to become a pilot.

By the time his training was completed, the war was in its final months. He spent a pleasant year flying from airfield to airfield in France and developed an appreciation for wine in Bordeaux. Back in the States, he decided to forgo school and become not only a newspaperman but a newspaperman in New York. After finding a job at the *Newark Ledger* in New Jersey, the only spot open, he heard about Capt. Patterson's new enterprise. He became not only the first sports editor but the entire department.

"We had no wire service," Hunt said. "We practiced the greatest larceny in the world. I would wait until the late editions of the afternoon papers were delivered at my desk, and I would write three baseball stories almost simultaneously from the play-by-play accounts of the final editions. I did that for a long time. I really believed that Capt. Patterson thought we had a wire service doing all that. But it was a nip-and-tuck affair, three stories a day, stolen."

Luckily for Hunt, the importance of sports was established early at the paper. Patterson liked sports, and three months into production, managing editor Arthur Clarke decided to give the back page of the 20-page daily to the sports department. Unlike the random events covered in the rest of the paper, sports ran on a schedule. The moments of drama could be predicted, cameras focused and poised for the action. Sports were perfect for the *Daily News,* large shots from games involving any of the three New York major league teams run across the back with little labels attached to identify each of the participants in a given play. The reader's imagination was left to insert the proper colors and crowd noise.

Capt. Patterson soon allowed Hunt to expand the department, first with an office boy and then with writers to cover boxing and racing. Hunt liked the help but was frustrated with the boundaries of his work. He found that he had become an administrator, a copy editor, more than a writer. This wasn't why he had come to New York. He wanted to be out in the city, seeing people, doing things, being part of what he thought was a glamorous

Manhattan hum. His salvation came when Paul Gallico, a young movie critic and part-time short story writer from New York, was shifted to sports because Patterson disliked the negative tone of his reviews.

Hunt surrendered the job of sports editor and his column to Gallico and became a baseball writer. He convinced Patterson that he not only should cover the Yankees at home, which the *News* already did, but also should cover the team on the road. Only afternoon papers sent writers on the road at the time, the writers also hired as stringers for extra money to reconfigure their work for the morning papers. Hunt sensed there was an opening for the *News* here. He had a different strategy for covering baseball.

"I wasn't there to cover the Yankees or the games, you see," he said. "I was there to cover the Babe."

What was more important as the decade unrolled, as the Babe piled feat upon feat—how the runs were scored or where the great man went for dinner? The double that won the game or the raccoon coat the Babe wore when he left the clubhouse? He was the object of public fascination. He was the star, everyone else on both teams only bit players in his daily tragedy or comedy. He was the one who sold papers.

The back page of the *Daily News* was perfect for the Babe, and the Babe was perfect for the back page of the *Daily News*. Marshall Hunt was determined to keep him there.

"When the Babe came down from Boston, we knew a lot about him," Hunt said years later. "He'd been an amazing pitcher up there, a great hitter, really a good fielder . . . we knew the Babe. When we were in Boston, we always went down to the clubhouse. It's not like now. You were welcome. The players came over and shaked your hand, even though you had kidded them badly the day before.

"Patterson was always looking around for some outstanding people in tennis, football, baseball that we could latch on to and sort of cultivate and have exclusive stuff on the guy, just because we could go to his apartment at night, take him fishing, hunting, anything. So Babe arrived in New York, and we recognized him as someone we could do business with."

Hunt was one of those small, mischievous men with a twinkle in an eye that saw everything around him. He was always on the lookout for life. He appreciated a cocktail, a good meal, a late night. He was a respectable golfer, an avid fisherman. He was a perfect companion for the Babe.

There was no secret to the way he became close with his subject: he simply showed up. He went to the places where the other writers didn't, the nonbaseball places where the Babe was happy to see a familiar face. Dinners and vaudeville shows. Prizefights and hospitals. He was around and the Babe noticed, and after a while they would go to these places together.

The trap was sprung. The common bond was fun. Hunt became a figure in the background in pictures, a member of the foursome watching as the subject teed off. Christy Walsh was in the foreground in formal shots. Hunt was in the background in the informal ones. The Babe had become a *Daily News* man.

Hunt was his serial biographer.

"We got along fine," Hunt said. "I never had a cross word with the Big Baboon. He was no intellectual, you know, but he was an agreeable guy. He really liked baseball, and he liked people. And he tried to be agreeable."

"Marsh is okay, but someday I hope that little runt misses a train," the Babe said. "A guy has to have some privacy."

The job for Hunt was a joy. Not only was he out in the desired hum, he was at its epicenter. He was bright and well read, curious and funny, and when he walked the same red carpet as the Babe, he was able to notice all the things that the big man missed. The code was in place, Hunt so careful of the boundaries that he asked editor Phil Payne to send other reporters to the scene when scandal arose and tough questions had to be asked, but he still tried to present the outrageousness of his subject's life, the ceaseless, wonderful feast that was laid out, the unremitting excess. He was mesmerized by it.

The practice at the time was for the baseball clubs to pick up the expenses of the writers traveling with the club. The Yankees were no different. Hunt told Patterson that the *News* should pay his expenses. The Babe already was staying at a different hotel from the team on the road. With a carte blanche expense account, Hunt could join him. He could trail his man in all endeavors, not worrying about cost. Patterson agreed.

"No one ever questioned my expenses," Hunt said. "It was publish or perish. If you got the stories, no one bothered you."

The other writers mostly ended their coverage of the Babe at the end of the season, moving along to other sports, other subjects. Hunt would keep going. The Babe was a 12-month job. Hunt would move along to the barnstorming tours, to the vaudeville tours, to the off-season habitats of the great man. The stories were even better in the off-season. They mostly didn't have to be shared. They belonged only to the *Daily News*.

Example: Hunt showed up at the farm in Sudbury unannounced. He simply said, "I wonder what the Babe's doing?" and took a train from New York. He got off at a small station in Massachusetts in a blizzard, learned there was no such thing as a taxi, and found a man who would give him a ride to the farm in a hearse. He showed up at the Babe's door in a hearse! The Babe let him in.

"There was all of this snow piled up in the back of the house," Hunt said. "I thought it had been bulldozed into a pile. No. The Babe said he'd been trying to get his car, a big Packard, out of the backyard. He'd been driving the car back and forth, stuck, and built up the pile. He had burned out the clutch and was complaining about the cheap clutch. It wasn't the cheap clutch. He'd just killed it."

Hunt noticed a piano in the living room. The Babe said it had come with the farm. Hunt noticed some scratches on the top of the piano. The Babe said there was a reason. He had a cat that did a very good trick. Here . . . the Babe showed the trick.

He put the cat in a rocking chair. He waited for the cat to fall asleep, then brought out a shotgun and opened a window. He fired the shotgun out the window. The cat did one world-class leap from the rocking chair to the top of the piano, digging his claws into the finish as he landed. Wasn't that a good trick?

"I have no idea how many times he did it," Hunt said. "I don't know if the cat jumped every time. He did it this time, though. Jesus, what a trajectory."

Example: Hunt went bowling with the Babe. Off on a barnstorming tour, somewhere in the middle of America, killing time, he and the Babe found a dilapidated alley located on the second floor of a building on a steep hill.

"There were two lanes, both of which looked as though they had been used as a proving ground for Caterpillar tractors," Hunt recalled years later in the *Seattle Post-Intelligencer*. "The proprietor said we could bowl, but not until he found a pin boy. He departed on his errand, but not until he had propped open double doors at the head of the stairs.

"The Babe noticed that pins were standing up in one alley. He announced that he would take a practice roll, whereupon he picked up one of the three balls on the rails that appeared to be fairly round, but its surface suggested that perhaps an alligator had teethed on it."

The Babe rolled. He slipped in his follow-through. The misshapen ball veered across the misshapen alley, went into the gutter, then jumped out again and began rolling across the floor. It reached the open double doors, went down the stairs, *thumpeta-thumpeta,* hit the street, and kept going down the hill. Gravity made it move faster and faster.

Hunt and the Babe followed. They walked all the way to where the ball finally stopped. They estimated the distance at 1,050 feet. The Babe thought he might have established a world record for the longest rolling of a bowling ball. Hunt thought he had a pretty good story for the readers of the *Daily News*.

Example: Ice fishing in upstate New York. The Babe was cold; the fish weren't biting. It was time to go . . .

"We were preparing to leave when the Babe removed the backseat of his 12-cylinder Packard and lifted out a golf bag the diameter of a hot water tank," Hunt said. "He pulled out a driver and extracted a ball and a wooden peg. He hammered the peg into frozen ground, perched a ball on the tee, only to see it blown off. He replaced it, stood erect, wound up in his inimitable fashion.

"As he swung at the ball, as only the Babe could swing at it, I thought I heard, above the sound of the gale, a distinct whistle—which could have been caused only by the shaft of a golf club slicing the air with incredible speed. There was a loud smack, and the ball, lofted into a howling tail wind, left our vicinity as though fired from a mortar.

"We saw the ball strike the ice, far out on the lake. It bounded and bounded, then we lost sight of it. My feeling was that the Dunlop, given an aerodynamical assist by nature, didn't lose motion until it struck the opposite shore, perhaps a mile and one-half away."

In the coming years, Hunt would travel with his man to cathouses and communion breakfasts, to the big games at the World Series and the small games on crabgrass fields in Indiana with local standouts brought together for a day of glory in the shadow of an exalted presence. He would check out the Babe's women—"Always striving for accuracy, I must report that some of the Babe's paramours for a day would really appeal only to a man who was just stepping out of a prison after serving a 15-year sentence," he said—and ride fast with him through the night. He would put two live flounder from the local market in his bathtub in a hotel in Boston and invite writers and ballplayers to his room for a fishing tournament. He would put pinpricks in the bottom of all the cups in a dispenser on the train and watch as people tried to control the leaking water while they tried to drink.

Hunt would drag the Babe to the Boston Symphony. (The Babe fell asleep.) He would try to drag him to the ballet. (The Babe canceled at the last moment.) In the roaring time that evolved, Hunt was part of the roar. He went to the plays, the parties, ate everything with a discerning palate. He sat at the table and sent back dispatches to his readers.

"Action?" he would ask much later. "Did you ever see 500 persons, clad in garments permitting great freedom of movement, do the Charleston, the music provided by a 65-piece orchestra, every member giving his all?"

On February 14, 1923, he took the Babe to the almost-completed Yankee Stadium for the first time. Four inches of snow covered the field. The moment was arranged just for the readers of the *Daily News*.

"The writer had invited the home run champion to inspect the new home of the Yanks," Hunt wrote.

I had a curious desire to find out if the Babe could keep his eye on the ball after a quiet winter on his Massachusetts farm.

We sloshed out to a spot where Groundskeeper Phil Schenen will shortly pattern a nice new pitching mound. The Babe shed his fur-lined flogger and his imported skimmer and stepped nimbly to where the plate is to be. He was wearing a skillfully-tailored suit of blue serge.

Deponent never was a pitcher of any considerable parts. But the Babe stood there grinning broadly. After lengthy preparation, we launched a curve. It went wild. Poor control. But there was balm in two other sneaking curves and the Babe fanned wildly. Hence we say that we had something on the New England agricultural.

The fourth ball pitched hit the Babe's bat in some uncanny manner and the sphere went bounding over the snow. And so did every ball thrown from then on.

"Sorry you ain't pitching for the Browns," laughed the Babe.

The stadium opened on April 18, 1923. The circulation of the *New York Daily News* had shot past the 600,000 mark in slightly more than three years, passing the circulation of the *New York Journal*. The *News* was now the best-selling paper not only in New York but in the entire country.

CHAPTER TWELVE

THE NEW STADIUM was an amazement. It was a giant, three-decked wedding cake in the Bronx, a skyscraper in repose, covering the ten acres of land purchased from the Astor estate. The plan to enclose the field entirely had been altered to allow the structure to be built in 11 months and be ready for opening day. The bleachers now were on one level and open to the elements in center field, but that did not change the public reaction. The stadium was an instant hit.

"Once inside the grounds, the sweep of the big stand strikes the eye most forcibly," the *New York Times* decided at first glance. "It throws its arms out to each side, the grandstand ending away over where the bleachers begin. In the center of the vast pile of steel and concrete is the green spread of grass and diamond, and fewer ball fields are greener."

The nation was in the midst of a stadium-building boom. Harvard University had built the first prestressed concrete stadium in 1903, and Yale, in the ever-running battle of one-upsmanship with its rival, doubled the size of Harvard's effort with the 80,000-seat Yale Bowl in 1908, but the end of the war had started the true building explosion. Games had gained a new importance. Physical training in the cantonments had brought many ordinary men to sport, to athletics, forced them to take part and enjoy physical competition for the first time in their workaday lives. The interest continued.

Every university in the country seemed to be trying to raise funds to build a new stadium. Wisconsin, Illinois, Iowa, Cal-Berkeley, Stanford, the University of Pennsylvania, Syracuse, Ohio State . . . they all had new stadiums or stadiums under construction. In Los Angeles, the L.A. Coliseum was being built in an effort to attract the Olympics. In Chicago, a massive stadium, Soldier Field, was planned on the lake. The fact was pointed out in the *Times* that the Romans, the all-time lovers of sport, had constructed perhaps 10 to 15 larger stadiums and 100 smaller ones during their time of influence. The United States now not only had matched the Romans in stadiums, but had surpassed them in number and size. The Roman Colosseum, historians decided, held only 45,000 spectators. Bigger stadiums than that were being built every day.

Excluding the Indianapolis Motor Speedway, Yankee Stadium initially was expected to be the biggest. Some plans suggested that as many as 100,000 people ultimately might be accommodated. (This never happened.) The Stadium also was different from all of the other contenders because it was a baseball park, the first major league park built in eight years. Football games and prizefights were expected to help pay the bills, and a running track around the field opened the possibility of large track meets, but the Yankees were the owners, and the Stadium was their home, and baseball was the game.

The Osborn Engineering Company of Cleveland, which had designed Fenway Park and Braves Field in Boston, was listed as the architect. No individual architect ever was named. The politically connected White Construction Company was the builder after the obligatory dance with Tammany Hall delayed the start of the project for almost a year. When the politicians finally agreed, Cromwell Avenue and a section of East 158th Street were swallowed up by the plan.

Five hundred men fashioned 2,000 tons of structural steel, 1,000 tons of reinforcing steel, and 30,000 yards of concrete (made from 45,000 barrels of cement, 30,000 yards of gravel, and 15,000 yards of sand) into the final structure. Trucks brought 116,000 square feet of sod from Long Island to cover the field. Two million board feet of lumber were used for the bleachers.

The dimensions of the park favored power hitters down the lines, especially left-handed hitters, with a low and cozy right-field wall, but the park also featured a deep center-field expanse that helped pitchers with good control. The official capacity, which wouldn't be determined until an audit later in the season, was 62,000, but on opening day, April 18, 1923, Col. Ruppert released the attendance number of 74,200, which was quickly accepted. A later estimate was that 70,000 people, including standees, were inside on the cold, blustery day. Another estimated 25,000 were outside, shut out when all tickets were sold and the final gates in the bleachers were closed and padlocked a half-hour before game time.

Two entrepreneurs, 38-year-old Abraham Cohen of Brooklyn and 35-year-old Sebastian Calabrese of East 27th Street, were the first arrested Yankee Stadium ticket scalpers. Cohen was charged with trying to sell his $1.10 grandstand ticket for $1.25, Calabrese for asking $1.50. They faced fines of $500 and a possible year in jail.

The business of baseball had hit a new frontier. And there was no doubt about who had brought it there.

The Stadium was a grand monument to the drawing powers of the resident right fielder. (Did the Romans ever build a stadium simply to show off the talents of one gladiator? And if they did, did they—as the Yankees did—situate the playing surface so the late-afternoon sun always would be behind their star attraction, not shining in his eyes?) An argument could be made that Cols. Ruppert and Huston probably would have built a stadium at some point—they certainly had the capital to do so—but would it have been built as soon and as large? Ruth was the one who drew the large crowds to the Polo Grounds, invoking the jealousy of Giants owner Charles Stoneham, who asked the Yankees to leave. Ruth was the one who promised to bring the big crowds with him to whatever new park was built, no matter the size. Ruth was the one who at last had given the second-class Yankees first-class style and pizzazz.

Over 150 typists gathered at the grand opening, and it was Fred Lieb of the *World* who tapped out the words that stuck, immediately calling the Stadium "the House That Ruth Built." From the moment the big man walked onto the field and posed for pictures with Little Ray Kelly, now five, the place belonged to him. Any doubt about that fact ended when he was singled out during the pregame festivities. Gov. Al Smith threw out the first ball to catcher Wally Schang, and John Philip Sousa himself led the 7th Regiment Band in "The Star-Spangled Banner," and the Babe was presented with a carrying case that contained a large bat, presumably to give him an idea of what he was supposed to do in the new ballpark.

His much-ballyhooed return to the farm in Sudbury during the off-season had put him in the best physical condition he'd enjoyed since he was a pitcher with the Red Sox. He'd been spotted only three times in New York since the close of the 1922 season, all short visits, two of them for medical treatment on the finger he'd injured during the Series. An influenza attack at the end of his three weeks at the healing tubs of Hot Springs had ensured that his weight was as low as it ever had been in the big leagues, 202 pounds, when he reported late to training camp in New Orleans. He seemed primed for a return to the glories of 1920 and '21 except for one discomforting fact: he didn't hit well during much of the spring.

Huggins had cornered him on a train and warned that maybe 1922 hadn't been an aberration, that maybe he was done, finished. Ruth said nothing in reply. Questions were asked in the newspapers about whether his eyesight was beginning to fail at age 29 (actually 28). Westbrook Pegler, four days before the Stadium opened, had another thought. Maybe the good life wasn't so good for George Herman.

"They are beginning to wonder if too much probity isn't a dangerous thing," Pegler wrote for the *Tribune* syndicate.

> The Babe has been a model young fellow for all winter and spring, but daily his hitting gets more awful. They recollect wistfully that one time he landed in Detroit in the throes of passing personal reform and didn't get a hit in three days. They recollect that on the night of the third day, the Babe suspended the pious regime, went to a party, appeared at the ball park the next day with an undersized skull containing an oversized headache, and lashed out two of his best home runs.
>
> Of course no one is exhorting Babe Ruth to get down after the whip or any such thing as that. But still, if a man can hit better for having a mild little something the night before, why—why not?

On the day the story appeared, though, the subject of sudden worry went 5-for-6 against the Dodgers in a 15–2 exhibition win in Brooklyn. Never mind. The final calibrations had been made to give the first-day crowd what it wanted. The Babe knew what was expected.

"I'd give a year of my life to hit a home run today," he said before the game.

The moment came in the third inning. The opponent was the Red Sox, and their pitcher was veteran Howard Ehmke. The Babe had flied out to center in the first and came to the plate this time with the Yankees ahead, 1–0, and runners on first and second. There was no way to work around him.

Ehmke was one of those deliberate, slow-motion craftsmen who can be maddening to watch. He would hem, haw, adjust, and study before performing the one act he seemed to wish to do least in the entire world: release the baseball. His repertoire of pitches matched his demeanor, mostly running from slow to slower to slowest. He would have been perfect as one of John McGraw's Giants in the '22 Series, lulling the Yanks and the Babe to sleep.

A succession of slow breaking balls—strike, ball, foul tip, ball—left the count at 2–2 when Ehmke hemmed and hawed his fifth serving of grapefruit toward the plate and the Babe uncoiled. He hit a rocket that drew the assembled spectators out of their new seats to watch it travel well into the right-field bleachers, putting a first dent on some of that two million linear feet of lumber when a fan ducked out of its path. Hosanna. The largest crowd in baseball history delivered the largest ovation in baseball history.

Ruth happily tripped around the bases and tipped his cap twice before he went into the dugout. Christy Walsh had brought his friend and only nonsports client, historian and writer Hendrik Willem van Loon, to describe just this kind of moment for the Walsh syndicate.

"The fans were on their feet yelling and waving and throwing scorecards and half-consumed frankfurters," van Loon wrote, "bellowing unto high heaven that the Babe was the greatest man on earth, that the Babe was some kid, and that Babe could have their last and bottom dollar, together with the mortgage on their house, their wives and furniture."

The Yankees won the game, 4–1, Ruth's homer the difference. For the rest of his life, when asked about the home runs he had hit, he always would say this was his favorite. Theater never merged better with sport. He gave 'em exactly what they wanted when they wanted it.

In the second game ever played at the Stadium, he had a triple that traveled 480 feet in the air, then bounced 20 more feet toward the faraway center-field wall. In the third game, bottom of the ninth, bases loaded, he stroked another long shot over center fielder Shano Collins that was called a game-winning double when the first two runners scored for a 4–3 Yankees win but probably would have been the first inside-the-park homer if Ruth had been allowed to keep running. Four days later, with chain-smoking President Warren G. Harding in attendance, the Bambino unloaded a fifth-inning shot into the stands in right, deeper and higher than his opening-day blast.

He circled the bases, tipped his cap, bowed toward the presidential box, went into the dugout, then came back out and pinned a poppy on Harding's overcoat. Everybody smiled. Harding, alas, would be dead within four months of a heart attack in San Francisco. Ruth would be fighting for the batting title and the home run title and leading the Yanks to another pennant. He was back.

His personal life had not changed as much as the papers or he said it had. The addition of Dorothy to the mix in Sudbury had not stabilized his marriage with Helen. The pictures in the rotogravure sections looked great, but he simply now was an absent father as well as an absent husband. When he was on the road, he still was definitely single.

Temptation was not something he had to seek. Temptation would find him.

"If you weren't around in those times, I don't think you could appreciate what a figure the Babe was," Richards Vidmer said. "He was bigger than the president. One time, coming north, we stopped at a little town in Illinois, whistle stop. It was about ten o'clock at night, raining like hell. The train stopped to get water or something. It couldn't have been a town of more than 5,000 people, and by God, there were 4,000 of them down there standing in the rain, just wanting to see the Babe.

"Babe and I and two other guys were playing bridge. Babe was sitting next to the window. A woman with a little baby in her arms came up and started peering at the Babe. She was rather good-looking. Babe looked at her and went on playing bridge. Then he looked at her again and finally he leaned out and said, 'Better get away from here, lady. I'll put one on the other arm.' "

He and Helen had been married now for nine infidelity-filled years. Helen, it was suggested by friends, also had begun to look other places for companionship. Like her husband, she also had found the joy of drink.

The waitress was having more and more trouble in keeping pace with the baseball player, the potentate, the national fascination. The Babe felt at ease at the perpetual banquet table. The waitress shied away from it. The fog was all around her.

"As I remember her, she was not a bad-looking gal, but cerebrationally she was not an eight-cylinder, double-overhead cam job," Marshall Hunt said. "I think the Babe tried to make it work a few times, wanted it to work, but they were just going in different directions."

A messy bit of business was taken care of in the first weeks of the season. Four months earlier, on the night of the Jimmy Walker speech, as the Babe left the Elks Club, he was handed a summons. A pregnant 19-year-old woman from the Bronx named Dolores Dixon had hit him with a $50,000 paternity suit.

The details hadn't become public until March, when the suit was filed. Ms. Dixon, a telephone operator, alleged that she had been "automobiling" with Ruth four and five times per week during the previous summer and that he had assaulted her on a yacht in Freeport, Long Island. She said he called her "my little watch charm" because she was only five feet tall and "my little golf girl" because he would tell people he was playing golf when he actually was with her.

Ruth was at spring training with Helen and Dorothy in New Orleans when the news broke. He quickly called the charges "blackmail." Helen stood by him. This was when Hunt, pressured by his *Daily News* bosses to ask the tough questions, called back and asked for someone else to do the job.

"I asked the Babe about it, and you could tell he didn't like it," Hunt said. "He said he didn't know the girl, but the way he said it you knew he was lying. He knew that girl. I said, 'Okay, Babe. That's what you say. That's what I'll put in the paper.' I wouldn't press him."

The case fell apart in April when Ruth's lawyer, Hyman Bushel, produced a witness named Robert McChesney whom Bushel said would testify that all of this was a plot to extort money from the Babe. Before McChesney ever testified, Dixon dropped the suit on April 27, 1923, and faded into obscurity. The Babe had escaped, reputation enhanced or intact, depending on the observer's point of view.

In May, in Washington, a far more important meeting with a woman occurred. Her name was Claire Merritt Hodgson, and she was, in her own words, "a professional model and a three- and four-line actress." Appearing in the capital in a play called *Dew Drop Inn,* she went to the ball game with her roommate and the play's star, James Barton. A friend of the Babe's, Barton introduced the woman to the famous man during batting practice. A lifelong dance began quietly.

"The sum total of this first meeting was, I am sure, typical of any single woman's reactions to meeting a man," Hodgson remembered in 1951 in *The Babe and I,* a book she wrote with sportswriter Bill Slocum. "He is famous, so it's nice to say you met him; he is pleasant, he has a growling voice, a pleasant-enough smile, and he's married. I knew he was married for the same reason I recognized him on sight. I read the papers."

Hodgson was a Georgia girl who had her own action-packed tale to tell. Married at 14 to wealthy 33-year-old hotel owner Frank Hodgson, a mother at 16, she had left Hodgson and Georgia in 1920, heading to New York with her daughter and a maid to find her own kind of fame. Three years later, Hodgson had died and she was a widow, working as a model and bit-part actress. Her mother and two brothers had followed her to New York, and they all lived together in an apartment.

Ruth surprised her after the first meeting at the ballpark, sending Eddie Bennett, the hunchbacked batboy gnome, to the dressing room of the National Theater that night with a nicely written invitation to have dinner. Hodgson accepted, she said, on the condition that her girlfriend could come along. Ruth accepted her acceptance and told her to bring her girlfriend to his hotel suite the next night. Hodgson balked. His suite? He explained that he couldn't go to a restaurant because there would be too much attention. He promised that the room would be safe for single women, mainly because it would be filled as usual with people. She went.

The man she found, she said, was far different from the image the public had of him. The room indeed was full of people coming and going, a hullabaloo, and she sat with the Babe on the side. He had been drinking and talked about his insecurities. He wondered if the critics were right about 1922 and if he was indeed finished. He was afraid that 1923 wasn't going to be any better. He thought that people hated him, despite the attention and cheers. He said he pretty much hated himself.

"You drink too much," she said. "Drinking is not good for you."

"You sound like Miller Huggins," the Babe replied.

The melancholy evening wore on, and at the end he told her that she was the first "dame" who ever told him he drank too much. She didn't know how much she liked the word "dame," but decided she liked the man. She thought he was a big kid, lonely, out in the big sea with the sharks. She wondered if she ever would see him again.

He phoned the next morning, came to the show that night with catcher Benny Bengough. The relationship had begun. He was on the phone every other night from the road as he went off to St. Louis, Chicago, Cleveland, and Detroit and her show went to New Haven. When they both finally wound up back in New York, he asked for a date. She was soon "the other woman."

"I was not breaking up a home," she wrote. "It was broken."

She was strong and self-assured, forceful, as different from Helen as possible. She was very pretty, maybe beautiful. She would grow to be disliked by the writers. ("A gold digger," Marshall Hunt said. "I never knew why the Babe stayed with her.") Yankees teammates would tell other, unkind stories about her first meeting with the Babe, inferring she had known other ballplayers before she met him, notably Ty Cobb. It didn't matter. She had captured this man in ways no other woman would.

He had found much more than a lover. Claire Merritt Hodgson was soon confidante and mentor, someone to listen to him, someone to defend him. She would share a drink and a laugh, was a conspirator in keeping the affair secret. Her home on West 79th Street became his home, even if no pictures or traces of him were evident, part of the secrecy. He also inherited her daughter, Julia, her brothers, Eugene and Hubert, and her mother, Carrie, a clandestine family that was far closer to a family than any he'd ever had.

It was a dizzying accumulation of obligations. He now had a wife, a full-time mistress, a farm, an apartment, a mistress's apartment, an adopted daughter, an adopted family. The phone kept ringing and he kept answering, and he also had a whole other life as a bon vivant. He was seen at ringside for at least four major prizefights during the 1923 season. He talked with Boy Scouts in his spare time, telling them not to smoke. (He lit up a cigar as soon as he left.) A one-inch story in the *Times* reported that in Philadelphia, on a day off, as a favor to Rev. William Casey, rector of Ascension Parish, he played first base in a twilight benefit game for the Ascension Catholic Club. The Ascensions lost, 2–1, to the Lit Club, but he had a hit and scored a run and handled 15 put-outs. He was a busy man.

The only known photo of Ruth's mother. The baby in her lap is the Babe.

The recreation yard at St. Mary's Industrial School for Boys. Where it all began.

The 16-year-old baseball apprentice at St. Mary's. The athlete.

Can a team win with a left-handed catcher? The Red Sox, St. Mary's champs, could with this catcher (standing, left).

Providence, R.I., 1914. The journey
into the outside world has begun.

Boston. The pitcher becomes a hitter.
He can see what his future should be.

The best left-handed pitcher
in baseball. Fastballs and
a good curve.

The famed St. Mary's Industrial
School for Boys band always had
room for an alumni addition. The
Babe was always willing to pose.

Signed contract, 1918. (L–R) Red Sox manager Ed Barrow, the Babe, Harry Frazee, and new first baseman Stuffy McInnis finish business dealings prior to the World Championship season.

Cover boy. In October 1920, the erstwhile pitcher revealed "My Secrets of Batting." As the season unfolded, he showed that these were pretty good secrets.

BASEBALL
MAGAZINE

Oct.
20c.

BABE RUTH

Read what
RAY SCHALK
—— Says about him in
"Why Outguessing Ruth is
Baseball's Toughest Problem"

OVER 450,000 FANS READ THE BASEBALL MAGAZINE

WATCH FOR WORLD'S SERIES NUMBER OUT OCTOBER 2nd

The Babe and Miller Huggins. The big man and the little man were not always this close.

Col. Tillinghast L'Hommedieu Huston. He once flipped a coin to settle a contract dispute with the Babe.

Psychological tests in 1921 established that Babe Ruth was a pretty darn good baseball player. It was not a surprising conclusion.

Walter Johnson vs. the Babe. The Big Train had problems with the Big Bam, but gets him to foul this pitch.

The well-dressed fisherman.

The Sudbury farmer.
Maybe the log will be
shaped into a bat.

Injured (date unknown). Whenever
he was hurt on the field, the Babe
brought true drama to the situation.

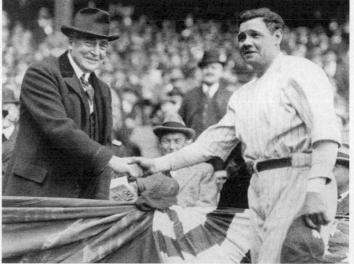

President Warren G.
Harding meets the
Babe, 1922. The
Babe, no doubt, had
something to say.

The swing was never subtle or tentative.

He always said he could hit .600 if he only tried for singles.

He didn't want to try for singles.

The famous face, a photographer's dream.

Celebrity. He drew a crowd no matter where he stood.

George Ruth and George Ruth. The Babe and his father at his father's Baltimore bar.

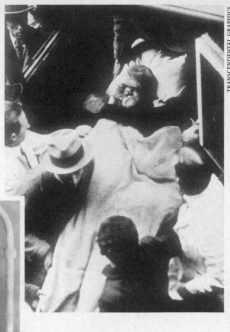

The Bellyache Heard Round the World. The Babe is taken from the ambulance in his famous 1925 distress.

The Bellyache Heard Round the World (recuperation). The true reason for his 1925 hospitalization has never been determined.

The transformation. The sins of 1925 brought about the transformation at Artie McGovern's Gym that saved the Babe's career.

Babe with Helen and daughter
Dorothy at the 1927 World Series.
This was solely for the cameras.
Babe and Helen had already split.

Helen's body is carried from
the funeral home in South
Boston, Massachusetts, 1929.

Football and fur. The Babe often went to other
sporting events, this time with (L–R) Julia,
mother-in-law Carrie Merritt, and Claire,
everyone dressed for the cold.

Adoption. (L–R) Claire, Dorothy, and Julia watch
as Babe signs papers to adopt both girls in 1929.

Artie McGovern rubs down bandleader Paul Whiteman (L). An unidentified attendant rubs down the Babe. John Philip Sousa himself prepares to ring the bell as the combatants get ready for fisticuffs at Artie McGovern's Gym.

Members of Murderers' Row. (L–R) Lou Gehrig, Tony Lazzeri, Mark Koenig, and Joe Dugan.

Waite Hoyt. He kept notes on the famous man's famous deeds.

Jumpin' Joe Dugan. A fellow traveler after dark.

The Iron Horse and the Big Bam. They were closest on the ball field, a 1–2 combination of unprecedented power.

The finish of The Called Shot in the 1932 World Series. After the commotion from Ruth's homer died down, Gehrig (no. 4) unloaded on the next pitch.

The House That Ruth Built, bakery version, was served on his 39th birthday in 1933. Actually, it was his 38th birthday.

The finish of the contract dance was always the contract picture. The Babe signs, Claire watches, Col. Jacob Ruppert smiles again.

Lou Gehrig (L) and the Babe played many barnstorming games in many towns. Some were in the West.

The Babe stands near the segregated section at an exhibition game on the trip north from spring training. Racial questions and insults dogged him throughout his career.

Connie Mack (R) had been thinking about signing Babe as manager on the trip to Japan, but by Hawaii had decided against the idea.

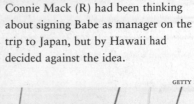

Program for the Japan trip by the all-Americans.

Aboard the *Empress of Japan*. Claire, Babe, and Julia begin their around-the-world trip in 1934.

The Babe in Paris. He was disappointed to find that American kids in France knew little about baseball.

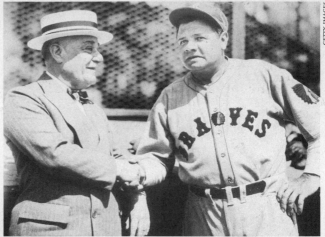

The uniform looks strange. The Colonel has gotten his wish, the Babe out of his hair. The Babe has not gotten his wish.

The Babe whispers information to one of his "ghostwriters." This was one of his lucrative sidelines, put together by manager Christy Walsh.

The Babe coaching third for the Brooklyn Dodgers, 1938. Riding the elephant.

Early immortals, 1939, Baseball Hall of Fame, Cooperstown, N.Y. (L–R) Back row: Honus Wagner, Grover Cleveland Alexander, Tris Speaker, Nap Lajoie, George Sisler, Walter Johnson. Front row: Eddie Collins, George Herman Ruth, Connie Mack, Cy Young.

Babe Ruth Day, April 27, 1947. The similarities to Lou Gehrig's farewell eight years earlier were in the Babe's mind.

Filming for *Pride of the Yankees*, 1942. The Babe lost weight in a hurry for the film, sending him to the hospital.

Final appearance (1). The occasion was the 25th anniversary of Yankee Stadium on June 13, 1948. The number 3 of the first man ever to hit a home run in the stadium was retired. Two months later he was dead.

Final appearance (2). This picture was taken by Nat Fein and won a Pulitzer Prize. It is one of the most famous photographs in American sport.

Mourners of all ages passed the Babe's coffin as he lay in state for two days at Yankee Stadium.

Oh, yes, and the Yankees were running away in the pennant race. And he was on the way to the best overall season of his career.

In the middle of that 1923 season, an interesting controversy developed. The Babe's favorite new bat was ruled illegal.

Slumping slightly, he had been convinced by retired Tigers outfielder Wahoo Sam Crawford to try a new bat called "the Betsy Bingle," which Crawford had invented and was trying to market. Selling for eight dollars, as opposed to two dollars for the normal bat, the Crawford bat was constructed of four pieces of lumber glued together instead of turned on a lathe from one piece of wood. The effect was supposed to make the bat stronger on all sides. The hitter no longer had to position the bat a certain way to take advantage of the strongest grain in the wood. The grain on this bat ran sideways.

Ruth started using the bat on July 2, and the slump was done. He had 27 hits, including six homers, in his next 65 at-bats. Superstition and performance merged. Ruth loved the Betsy Bingle. He was hitting close to .400 and had 28 home runs when American League president Ban Johnson declared the bat illegal on August 11.

"I can see no reason why Johnson should bar the Crawford model bat," Miller Huggins said, filing an appeal. "The rules simply state that the bat must be round, made entirely of hard wood and conform to certain dimensions.

"The new bat used by Ruth is made of hard wood and is perfectly round. The rules do not state that the bat be made out of one piece of wood. Ruth's bat is not a trick bat, but simply an improvement on the old style. A four-piece bat is much stronger than a one-piece affair and of course has more driving power."

Humorist Will Rogers dragged the situation into a column he wrote about new President Calvin Coolidge. At 2:47 on the morning of August 3, after the sudden death of Harding in San Francisco, the quiet man from New England had been sworn into office by his father, a notary public, in the kerosene-lit family living room in Plymouth Notch, Vermont. Worries were everywhere that Coolidge would be a do-nothing president, and Rogers had various suggestions about actions that Coolidge should take.

"Now they're trying to make Babe Ruth change the style of bat he uses," Rogers wrote. "Can you imagine a President standing idly by and not doing a thing?"

The league office offered an explanation eight days later. The problem with the bat was not with the four pieces of wood, but with the glue. The glue increased the velocity of the ball off the bat. If the glue were allowed, other substances, such as rubber, might also be inserted into bats. The appeal was denied. The Babe had been using a forerunner of the corked bat.

Never mind. On August 12, the first day back to a normal bat, against the Detroit Tigers, he went 3-for-4, including his 29th homer.

He finished with gaudy numbers and his first American League Most Valuable Player Award. (Instituted a year earlier, the first award was won by George Sisler of the St. Louis Browns.) Teams had decided to walk the Babe even more this season, to pitch to the number-four hitter, Meusel, surrendering a record 170 bases on balls. The Cleveland Indians intentionally walked him four times in one game. He had responded by becoming more selective, hitting .393, which would be the highest average of his career. His home run total suffered, though his 41 led the league, and he had 13 triples, 45 doubles, and 205 hits. He drove in 130 runs, and the Yankees won the pennant by 17 games over the Detroit Tigers.

The magic story of the season—and there always seemed to be at least one magic story in every season—had come in Chicago. The Yankees and White Sox were tied, 1–1, going into the fourteenth inning, and Mark Roth, the traveling secretary, was nervous. The team was scheduled to catch a train home, and now there was a good chance this wouldn't happen. Ruth, getting ready to go to the on-deck circle, noticed Roth's concern.

"What's the matter?" he asked.

"We're missing the train," Roth replied.

"Is that all?" Ruth replied, in best magic-story fashion. "Watch."

One pitch was thrown by Mike Cvengros, a strong-armed left-hander. One swing was taken by George Herman Ruth, another strong-armed left-hander. The tie was broken, the White Sox were retired quickly in the bottom of the inning, and the Yankees made the train.

"Why didn't you tell me about that before?" George Herman asked as the story went onto the pile.

The opposition for the World Series once again was the Giants. The matchup once again easily was cast as the brain matter of McGraw against the brawn matter of the Babe. Despite McGraw's triumphs in the last two Series, there was a sense that the results would be different this time. The Babe's season had convinced skeptics.

"Yes, sir, the Babe's grown up now," the *Washington Post* said. "This week McGraw's task of being 'acquainted' with a Ruth weakness will call for extra attention and a special code of wig wags inasmuch as the 1923 Ruth is not the adulation-drugged Sultan of Swat of 1922."

To enhance arguments on his side, the Babe hit a blast over the right-field bleachers at the Polo Grounds in a charity game on October 2 against the Baltimore Orioles. This was a strange event. He wore a Giants uniform and played with a team filled with Giants, and the manager on the bench was John McGraw. The proceeds went to John B. Day and Jim Mutrin, who were the owner and manager of the first baseball team ever to play in New York. It all had been scheduled long before the World Series matchup had been assured.

For good measure, Ruth returned to the Polo Grounds for practice the day before the Series started and belted a dozen over the right-field fence. He told reporters that after a year of playing in Yankee Stadium, right field looked awfully close at the Polo Grounds. Heck, pop flies became home runs.

"I'd have hit 80 home runs easily here," he said.

The Giants took a quick 2–1 Series lead on the home run heroics of well-traveled outfielder Casey Stengel (Casey was reprimanded by Judge Landis for thumbing his nose at the Yankees bench after homering in game one), but Ruth's two home runs in the second game, part of a 4–2 win, gave the American Leaguers confidence. They came back to take not only game four but three in a row. The final win, 6–4, featured a third Ruth homer and at last brought home the club's first World Championship.

Col. Ruppert, now the sole owner of the Yankees after buying out Col. Huston in the middle of the season, called this the happiest day of his life. His manager, Huggins, who vindicated Ruppert's faith in him, was presented with a diamond ring in appreciation for his services by none other than the Babe himself, who finished his brief speech with a request for "three cheers for Miller Huggins." Ruth completed a season that couldn't have been any better. He hit .368 in the Series with three home runs. Was this what Jimmy Walker wanted? Here it was.

The Yankees finally had stepped free of the all-powerful Giants and become the number-one baseball attraction in New York, a situation that would last all the way until 1958, when the son of Charles Stoneham, Horace, packed up the Giants and took them to San Francisco. Ruth and the long ball finally had stepped free from McGraw and all that inside baseball talk. The long ball was king.

"This World Series was generally recognized as a combat between the thinking power of John J. McGraw and the baseball agility of the Yankees," Pegler wrote. "Now that it is over and the Yankees have won, it is rumored that McGraw strained a tendon in his medulla oblongata in winning the first game of the Series."

The games, split between Yankee Stadium and the expanded Polo Grounds, broke all attendance records, totaling over 300,000 spectators and amassing the first million-dollar World Series gate. The Yankees received $6,140.46 per man, another record. The Giants received $4,112.88. The players went every which way after the Series with their new cash. The Babe, surprisingly, gave a bit of it to Harry Heilmann, an insurance salesman and the American League batting champion from the Tigers (.401), in payment for a $50,000 life insurance policy, then headed out on an immediate barnstorming trip through New York and Pennsylvania.

In Hazleton, Pennsylvania, the coal mine had to shut down work for the day because so many miners booked off to see the exhibition. In Scranton, the Babe was mobbed by kids, tripped in his escape, and the kids piled all over him. In Brooklyn, on the final stop of the tour at Dexter Park, he had to be rescued again. Kids mobbed him as a second game of a doubleheader with the Bushwicks was called due to darkness and a policeman on a horse had to intervene. The Babe grabbed the horse's tail and was pulled to safety.

He was a busy man.

CHAPTER THIRTEEN

Babe Ruth departed from Penn Station yesterday afternoon for Hot Springs, Ark. where he will boil out for three weeks before the regular training season. The Babe was accompanied only by Marshall Hunt, DAILY NEWS baseball scribe, who will give a humorous and interesting account of the doings of the Yankees' slugger.

"I guess I had a pretty good season last year," said Babe as he left, "but I intend to have a better one in 1924. First we must win another pennant and set a new record of four in a row. Then I hope to hit sixty home runs and pile up a batting average of .400. See you in April."

New York Daily News,
FEBRUARY 12, 1924

THE TRIP TO Hot Springs had become ritual. The Babe had been going there for ten years now, since his first training camp in 1915 with the Red Sox when he left most of his paycheck at the Oaklawn Park racetrack. The great pretense was conditioning, losing some weight to be ready for actual spring training, but there always was more fun than sweat.

The big man worked in spurts. He would play 54 holes of golf, run

three miles back to the Hotel Majestic, sweat through a hot mineral water bath, weigh himself, and announce to the nearby world that he had
lost seven pounds. Then he would be stiff and sore for the next three days,
eat well, and put the weight back onto his aching body. Maybe even add
weight.

Marshall Hunt loved watching the show.

"The Babe would go to Hot Springs for two or three or four weeks depending on how he felt or if Ed Barrow looked at him and said, 'My God,
you slob. Off to Hot Springs,' " Hunt said. "Barrow would call me, and
the Babe and I would take off and go down there and play a lot of golf
and take a lot of hikes.

"People would think I was the Babe's manager and ask me to intro-
duce them to him, and I usually did just that. You got an awful lot of Midwest businessmen and industrialists down there to boil out too."

Hot Springs was a mixture of the bawdy and the elegant, stuffed into
the scenic beauty of the Ozark Mountains. The tubs of Bathhouse Row
attracted visitors from around the country, the healing waters bringing a
relief for arthritis or rheumatism or other discomforts long before drugs
had been concocted to do the job. The horse races, the illicit casinos, the
women of leisure, the mixed cocktails gave the visitors something to do
when they were feeling better from their treatments.

This had been cowboy country, where Wyatt Earp and Bat Masterson
and the Younger brothers walked the land and came into town to order
up a little shot of something to take away the night chill. The last good
gunfight, between the police department and the sheriff's office, of all people, had occurred just before the turn of the century. The town now was
on the way to becoming gangster country. Owney Madden, the owner of
the Cotton Club and chief of New York crime, would retire to Hot
Springs. Al Capone himself would spend some time there.

Baseball long had been part of the action in the late winter. Cap Anson took his Chicago White Stockings to Hot Springs in 1886, one of the
first attempts at spring training, and when his team won the National
League pennant in 1887, other teams followed. In 1911 four teams
trained in Hot Springs, and many players arrived on their own to lose
weight and get in shape. Hot Springs was the hub of baseball training.

That era, alas, had ended. The Pirates and the Red Sox, the last two
teams in town, had severed their ties after 1923, joining the other clubs
that had opted for warmer sites in Florida or elsewhere. The more than

50 ballplayers in Hot Springs this year had mostly been sent by their teams for added conditioning before the start of the actual training camps. The Babe was the first of a group of Yankees, all financed by Col. Ruppert, to stop on the way to camp in New Orleans.

"We'd play golf every morning, then we'd get tired of the food in the hotel, and I'd hire a car, and then we'd go out in the country looking for farmhouses that said, 'Chicken Dinners,' " Hunt said. "What Babe really wanted was a good chicken dinner–and-daughter combination, and it worked out that way more often than you would think."

Hunt mostly sent nonsense, anything, back to the readers of the *Daily News*. He tracked the fluctuations of the Babe's weight as if it were a number on the New York Stock Exchange. He detailed golf matches, practical jokes, chicken dinners (without mentioning the daughter combination). It was movie star stuff, grease for all commercial wheels. It was what people wanted to read.

February 13:

Whereas one year ago the Massachusetts ball player, farmer, actor, author and versatile whatnot, talked with commendable candor on how he had squandered vast sums on thoroughbreds left at the barrier, on parasitic heels, as he terms a certain type of sponger, and how he had been bilked of various monies by the unscrupulous, this year Mr. Ruth pridefully tells an entirely different tale. . . .

"What," we asked, "shall we tell the people of New York about you?"

"You tell these people in plain language," Bambino replied forcefully, "that I have been working like a trooper all winter on my farm, that I never felt better in my baseball career, that I'm almost down to my playing weight right now, that I'll try very hard to be adjudged the most valuable player in the American League again this year and that if I don't sock sixty home runs, I'll buy Judge Landis a new white hat."

Stop the presses. Maybe the Babe said something about Landis's white hat in his actual quote. Maybe he didn't, but he did in the *News*. Hunt detailed how the Babe rented horses for everyone one morning, then slapped the butt of catcher Fred Hofmann's horse, sending the steed into excited motion and the backup catcher into a puddle on the street. Another tale told how the Babe spent $3.75 shooting mechanical squirrels at an arcade. No detail was too small to be detailed. Hunt spent an entire article describing a nest of corns being scraped from the great man's feet. The writer was skeptical about the results.

February 15:

> Mr. Ruth's purpose in coming to Hot Springs is to reduce. It cannot be denied that the pruning of calloused growths will result in a certain dimunation [*sic*] of weight, but we suspect the process will prove too slow and irksome to meet with the approbation either of Mr. Ruth himself or manager Miller Huggins. Continued paring from now until the opening of baseball season would not result in any substantial reduction, we are positive.

The Babe in the baths was the best scene. He would arrive in a robe "the dimensions of an ordinary circus tent," accompanied by an attendant. The attendant would draw a bath as hot as Ruth could stand. The Babe would swelter for a while, then be given a rubdown, then put in a steam contraption behind what looked like a shower curtain. The steam would continue until his face was bright red—"I still don't think he's done," someone like pitcher Joe Bush would say, calling for "more steam"—and then he would be hurried to a room like a sauna, where his body was wrapped in white cloth and he would lie for half an hour to sweat all liquid from his body. The process would be finished by a cold shower.

Except when he didn't take the shower.

Which was often.

Ready for the chicken dinners and the daughters, he would skip the shower, hurry into his clothes, and go out the door, still sweaty, into the cold. He invariably caught the flu. He caught it this year on February 29, Leap Year Day, and came down with a 103-degree temperature. The doctor at first feared pneumonia, but soon backed away from that diagnosis. Rest and fluids for the next seven to ten days did the job. A fat cigar in the Bam's fever-blistered lips was the first sign of a return to health. Solid food came next. The arrival of a new bat for the coming season indicated it was time to leave the Majestic, the less-than-sumptuous lodgings the Colonel favored for his men. The convalescent clearly had finished convalescing when he demonstrated the proper use of the bat.

March 7:

> Mr. Ruth assumed a stance as though he had a count of three and two on him when the bases were full with two out in the bottom of the ninth with the Yankees three runs behind. He gripped the bludgeon firmly and swung it far back. The muscles of his arms and shoulders were tense. He swung viciously, his lips tightly compressed, his features distorted. The heavy piece cut downward, severed from a bedpost a large brass ball and propelled it devastatingly against the bureau mirror, which collapsed into a thousand flashing daggers. The brass ball ricocheted among the globes of the chandelier. A twinkle of cascading glass climaxed the Bambino's superb act.
>
> "Well," he shouted gleefully, "it works."

Two days later, he left for New Orleans. The flu had brought him down to 220, his desired weight.

For Ruth, the 1924 season unfurled as a pleasant continuation of the previous year. He received his certificate—"his diploma," he called it—as the 1923 MVP on May 14, Babe Ruth Day at the Stadium, and went from there, leading the American League in both home runs (46) and batting average (.378). For the Yankees, the day was a step down. They hoisted their first World Championship flag in center field on Ruth Day, then lost, 11–1, to the St. Louis Browns.

They were trying to become the first team in AL history to win four consecutive pennants, but as the season progressed they never caught the right fire to move away from the pack. There always was the feeling, "We'll turn it on when we need it." The light switch, alas, never was pulled. The Washington Senators, already known as "first in peace, first in war, last in the American League," were the surprise winners under youthful manager Bucky Harris with a big month of September. The Yankees finished two and a half games back in second.

"We just sort of loafed and lazied along when we should have been doing our stuff," Ruth admitted. "I'm sure we were a better team than Washington, but Harris's Senators got playing together and his pitchers could be counted on nearly every time they went to the rubber and so they beat us."

The most interesting afternoon of the season came on June 13, Friday the 13th, in Detroit. The two clubs were on edge from a built-up pile of incidents, most recently a fight between Mike McNally and Tigers first baseman Lu Blue at the Stadium. All business was conducted at the far edges of baseball etiquette. The game was now in the top of the ninth at Navin Field, the Yanks with a 10–6 lead.

Ruth had been brushed back twice by Tigers pitcher Bert Cole during the day, once in the ninth, and was not happy about the fact. Watching from the dugout, he now thought he saw his nemesis, player-manager Ty Cobb, give a signal from center field for Cole to drill Bob Meusel with the next pitch. He shouted out that information to Meusel, and when the next pitch hit Meusel in the back, the Yankees outfielder threw his bat toward Cole and immediately followed it.

The benches emptied, Cobb ran straight in from center field, and Ruth, out of the dugout, ran straight for him. It was a confrontation straight from the fan imagination. What if the two best players in the game ever fought? Could the nastiness of Cobb overcome the size and strength of Ruth? Or vice versa? More words had been written about these two men than about any other baseball players who ever lived. Cobb was the personification of the wily, all-around player, the strategist and hustler, the schemer. Ruth was the slugger who had made all of that obsolete, taking away the headlines. The two men had never reached even a veneer of civility. Cobb hated everyone. Now they came straight at each other, both of them filled with anger and purpose.

"They were like two football linemen, charging at each other," Fred Lieb said. "They sort of collided. I can't remember if they got any punches in. They both bounced back."

They now were separated by chaos. Meusel had missed his punch at Cole, and players had pulled them apart. Fred Haney of the Tigers was looking to fight anyone with a New York hat. The umpires were involved. Ruth, yelling at Cobb about beanballs, was dragged away by Huggins and one of the umpires and a couple of teammates. The business appeared done until Meusel and Haney started arguing near the Tigers dugout and the players came back together, and now the 18,000 fans joined the fray.

Maybe 1,000 fans jumped onto the field. The police and security men tried to keep them back, and fans and police soon were fighting. Fans in the stands started ripping out the seats and throwing them onto the field. The Yankees were hastened back to their clubhouse.

"The whole field now, viewed from the lofty press box, was a surging mass of bobbing straw hats and swinging fists," the *New York Times* reported. "The bluecoats were getting the worst of it from some of the ringleaders of the rioting and they had to make menacing gestures with their clubs and threaten to pull their guns to hold onto a half dozen or so who they had put under arrest. As this scene of disorder was going on, Umpire Evans shouldered as near home plate as he could get and motioned that the game was called off."

The Yankees were declared 9–0 winners by forfeit. The next day, a crowd of 40,000 was so large—and Navin Field was missing so many seats—that people were allowed to stand on the field to watch. Policemen on horseback patrolled to make sure trouble did not erupt again. It did not. The Yankees won, 6–2. Ruth announced a $50 reward for anyone who would return his glove.

The remembered off-field moment for Ruth came in Philadelphia. Actually it started in Delaware. The Du Ponts had invited Herb Pennock to a high-society lawn party and asked him to bring some ballplayers with him, especially that Babe Ruth character. The Yankees had an off-day in Philadelphia, and Pennock received permission and Ruth agreed to go.

It was a pleasant affair, Ruth demonstrating how to hit with a stalk of celery, very nice, until the drinks began to add up and he spotted a waitress he greatly admired. As his admiration grew and his overtures grew louder, the whisper began that "we've got to get him outta here." He didn't want to go.

A Philadelphia fight promoter came to the rescue. He convinced Ruth that there was a much better party with many more women at an establishment he knew on Broad Street back in town. Ruth argued to stay, but finally he and a number of Yankees went with the promoter. They arrived at the establishment at 1:00 A.M.

At 5:00 A.M., the other Yankees decided it was time to head back to the hotel for at least a little sleep before meeting the A's that afternoon. They found the Sultan of Swat in a big chair, a girl sitting on each knee. The girls were pouring champagne on his head and giving him a shampoo. Everybody was singing.

"Anybody who doesn't like this life is crazy," Ruth said.

That afternoon Fred Merkle of the A's asked him before the game how he felt. Ruth said he felt fine. Merkle said, "You don't look fine." Ruth hit two home runs in a Yankees win. He felt fine.

The public reformation started by the Jimmy Walker speech of 1922 obviously was long gone, but who noticed? The great man had discovered the virtues of bicarbonate of soda—"Give me a bi, kid," he shouted to the clubhouse attendant a couple of times each day—and chewed the stuff, drank the stuff, coated his stomach, and kept moving. Third baseman Jumpin' Joe Dugan, picked up in another deal with the Frazee Red Sox House of Discount during the 1923 season, was another good late-night runner. Whitey Witt was a runner. The Yankees were filled with runners.

They called him "Bam," or "the Big Fellow," or "Jidge," a contraction of George. They never called him "Babe." That was the outside world's name for him. This was the inside. This was the core of the fun.

"Ruth was invited to a lot of elegant places because people were curious about him," Waite Hoyt said. "The Vanderbilts invited him once to some big brouhaha at their big stone mansion, which at the time was 57th Street—56th or 57th—and Fifth Avenue. It was huge, surrounded by an iron picket fence, and it had a fountain and a pool out in back. So Ruth, when he went out like that the night before, would like to tell where he had been."

"God, what a party," he reported after this one. "There were guys with green vests and plaid vests and tails on their coats, and they were serving champagne all over the place, and then I got a little high, and then everybody's diving in the pool and the fountain out back."

"Where was this?" Hoyt asked.

"Well, there was a dame named Mrs. Vanderbilt was the hostess and Mr. Vanderbilt was the hoster," the Babe said.

The one bump in all this fun was the second-place finish. Hoyt too remembered it as a season squandered. The Yankees always presumed they were going to win. They finished up on the road with a 23-game swing through the West, and Miller Huggins told them they were going to have to just about sweep the trip to beat Washington. They won 20 of the 23 games. The Senators did well enough to hold on and win the pennant by two games.

"The last game was in Philadelphia," Hoyt said. "Have you ever been to the North Philadelphia station? It's an elevated station, and after the game we're waiting by the tracks. Some of us are going to New York, and others are going other places now that the season was ended. It's October, of course, and the darkness had descended. I can never forget, standing on that platform, looking over the darkened city. Some of the lights had

come on, and it was a real desultory part of the city, and now it was raining, and I remember being despondent, crestfallen, still thinking we had
the best team except we were too cocky and too overconfident, believed
that we could win when we wanted to. And didn't."

The end of the season brought the most ambitious barnstorming tour yet
for the Babe. The hand of Christy Walsh was in this one, a coast-to-coast
extravaganza. Ruth "covered" the World Series, a surprising Senators win
over the Giants, for the Walsh syndicate, then took off with Bob Meusel
into the hinterlands. Helen was back in Sudbury, sometimes visiting family in Boston. Walsh, at the end of the tour, sent a capsule summary to
columnist Ed Hughes of the *New York Telegram and Mail* with a one-
paragraph cover letter:

> I enclose the box score of the Bambino's trip to the coast and return. The
> waiting public already has been advised by the press of New York that
> Mr. Ruth has returned, but there are quite a number of serious disclo-
> sures in the attached summary. Please do not think I'd be so vulgar as to
> desire any publicity for Mr. Ruth.
>
> Babe Ruth dropped into New York last Friday en route to his agri-
> cultural holdings at Sudbury, Mass. where broken fences, neglected cat-
> tle, plumbing and other rural items have suffered during his absence on
> the Pacific Coast.
>
> Interesting notes in connection with Mr. Ruth's sojourn are as follows—
>
>> He left New York October 11, the day after the World Series, ac-
>> companied by Bob Meusel and Christy Walsh.
>> Returned to New York December 6, accompanied by Walsh.
>> Meusel remained in Los Angeles.
>> The Babe covered 8,500 miles on the road trip.
>> He played in 15 cities in six states.
>> He got 17 home runs in 15 games.
>> He drew 125,000 people. The games were under auspices of a
>> leading newspaper in each city, with the backing of one of the
>> following organizations—Elks, Knights of Columbus or Ameri-
>> can Legion.
>> He made 22 speeches at breakfasts, luncheons, dinners and ban-

quets given in his honor. Seven speeches were given from Pullman platforms.

He rode 250 miles on a locomotive through Montana.

He autographed nearly 5,000 baseballs. He autographed 1,800
baseballs for the San Francisco Examiner alone—all of which
were sold for charity.

He headed four parades, accompanied by Mayors and city officials.
He wore his dinner coat 19 times and complained of so few opportunities. Two years ago he considered dinner coats things to
be avoided. He wore a silk hat once. (Under protest.) Someone
told him he looked good in it, so then he bought it.

He refereed a four-round bout in Hollywood, Calif. And was presented with a wrist watch by the American Legion. He appreci-
ates the watch, but fears other players will make unkind
remarks.

He batted 1,000 autographed baseballs to 10,000 Los Angeles
schoolboys and later nearly fell off the roof of the grandstand.

He beat Douglas Fairbanks in a game of "Doug." (Similar to tennis.) Fairbanks had previously beaten [Bill] Tilden.

The railroads refused to take his money for food. The hotels gave
him rooms for nothing.

He was Jack Dempsey's guest in Los Angeles.

He drove a golf ball 353 yards, breaking the course record at Ran-
cho Golf Club, Los Angeles.

He visited 18 hospitals and orphan asylums.

He posed for nearly 250 photos in every city. Total, 3,750.

He struck out twice with three men on base.

He failed to get a home run at Tacoma, Kansas City, Stockton, Los
Angeles or San Diego.

But he got 17 home runs at Altoona, Minneapolis, Spokane, Seattle, Portland, Dunsmuir [Calif.], San Francisco, Santa Barbara,
Oakland and Fullerton.

He always played on the opposite team to Bob Meusel. His team
won 15 games. Meusel won none.

He ate four buffalo steaks at one meal.

He talked over the radio at San Francisco for 12 minutes before he
knew he was being "framed."

He refused to wear a nightgown or pajamas at any time on the

trip—despite continued protests of Walsh and Meusel. He later
was presented with a big red flannel nightgown at a public
luncheon at the Biltmore, Los Angeles.

He established distance records at five ballparks. He was the first
lefthander to drive a ball over the left field fence at San Francisco. He was the first player that ever drove a ball over the
wall at Kansas City. He drove a ball to the top of a fir tree at
Dunsmuir [Calif.], a distance of 604 feet and 5 inches (measured by a surveyor).

He was made a life member of the Lions Club at Dunsmuir and
started a Christmas fund which has since reached $900. (Duns-
muir is a few miles from Mount Shasta. Population less than
5,000.)

The last game was in the smallest city—Brea, near Fullerton, Calif.
This is Walter Johnson's boyhood home. Johnson pitched. Ruth
also pitched—his first full nine-inning game in seven years.
Ruth beat Johnson, 9 to 1. Ruth got two home runs. Johnson's
team got but four hits and no runs until the ninth inning. Other
batters against Ruth's pitching were Ken Williams, Ernie Johnson, Jimmy Austin and Meusel and Johnson. Population,
3,500; attendance 15,000.

After the final game October 31, Ruth played at a Los Angeles theater.

He is about 10 pounds overweight, but otherwise in fine condition.
Stop the presses.

The return to Sudbury was short. He was at Home Plate Farm for less
than two months. Or at least everybody thought he was. The one public
sighting was at Madison Square Garden in the middle of January to
watch Jack Delaney knock out Tiger Flowers in two rounds. The rest of
the time Ruth kept a rare low profile.

The farm definitely had become more nuisance than nirvana. An adventure raising chickens had fallen apart when the chickens died. A second adventure, raising pit bulls, was disbanded when one of the dogs got
out of its pen and attacked and killed a neighbor's cow. Throw in a fal-
tering marriage to an overwhelmed woman, a lack of inclination toward
solitude, a mistress in the big city, and an ever-present buzz of Vanderbilts

and Du Ponts on the horizon, and the Currier and Ives picture of a New England winter had lost its charm.

The gas tank on his latest car probably showed best where his heart was.

"We used to sell a lot of gas to the Babe," Forrest Bradshaw, once the owner of a market and gas station in Sudbury, said years later. "The first time I waited on him he pulled his car up to the gas pump and told me to fill it up. I started to pump the gas (the hand crank in those days), and after I reached ten gallons, I asked him how much it would take. He said, 'You keep pumping and I'll tell you when to stop. It's nearly empty.' Well, I kept pumping and wondered where it all was going. I finally stopped at about 48 gallons. I looked under the car and there was no spillage, so I knew the gas was in the car somewhere."

A friend later solved the riddle. The Babe didn't like stopping on the ride to New York. He'd had a special 55-gallon gas tank installed. The small-town life had become the small-time life. He wanted different, bigger, better. He had acquired tastes.

"Babe would come into the market and order two slices of top-of-the-round steak cut about three inches thick," Bradshaw also remembered. "These were for him. He would order a pound, pound and a half of hamburg for his wife and the chauffeur."

And Helen?

"My wife thinks her hair was auburn," Bradshaw said. "She was small, as I recall, about five-feet-six, medium build, say about 130 pounds, not beautiful, possibly attractive. Serious and brooding. I think Catholic, Democrat, frugal, a girl that seemed to be lost. . . . What dealings I had with her were very pleasant. . . . She seemed to me that she was married to someone she had to live with and had to be at his beck and call. She was much smaller than he was. She acted more like a servant or slave than a wife. I don't know that Babe would have known how to treat a wife."

At any rate, Sudbury and Home Plate Farm were done early this year. Done forever, as it would turn out. On February 1, the Babe was back in New York at the Yankees' offices wearing a large overcoat and looking, well, large. The next day he was on the train again, headed to Hot Springs for his earliest visit ever.

The familiar pieces all were in place. The baths. The golf course. The chicken dinners. Then again, maybe not the chicken dinners. Mrs. Claire

Hodgson, the widow showgirl, also seemed to be in Hot Springs, Arkansas, for the baths. If there were searches for chicken dinners, they were only for chicken dinners. The other parts of the social calendar were occupied.

Marshall Hunt arrived two weeks after the Babe and Mrs. Hodgson arrived. If she was still around, she never was mentioned in the daily reports. The biggest news for Hunt was the strange end to the annual saga of the tubs: the Babe didn't catch the influenza bug this time. His favorite mode of weight reduction was missing.

February 27:

> Vast gloom unprettied the features of Herman Ruth today when he gave himself to serious contemplation of the distressing futility of many things and how increasingly tough it's becoming for an honest feller to get along in this wearying world.
>
> Herman Ruth left for the Yankees' training camp in St. Petersburgh, Fla. and he was 20 pounds overweight. It was the first time in many years the Bambino failed to reduce himself at Hot Springs to a normal playing tonnage. But it was the first year in five he did not suffer the ravages of influenza.

The first step toward the 1925 season was a fat step. The vast gloom on the Bambino's face was going to get much gloomier.

CHAPTER FOURTEEN

NOTHING WAS RIGHT in 1925 from the moment the Bambino hit the Yankees' new training site at St. Petersburg. Helen and Dorothy were there, and that was a crimp in his style. His weight wasn't good, and that was a crimp. The outfield fences in the partially refurbished Crescent Lake Field were not part of the refurbishment. There were no outfield fences. Home runs were hard to judge, and wait a minute, Ruth went to his position in the outfield and found an alligator already was there. No fences. That was a definite crimp.

"I ain't going out there anymore," he reported to Miller Huggins when he came back to the dugout. "There's an alligator out there."

Everything was a beat off, a succession of days when nothing good seemed to happen. A report came down from New York that Ruth was being sued by a bookmaker, Edward Callahan, over a $7,700 gambling debt. The debt ran back to May 25, 1924, and Ruth supposedly had promised to pay it off when he received his paycheck. This never happened. The lawsuit story led to another story that he was broke and "growing old and fat" and that "his best days are behind him."

Ed Barrow in New York quickly issued a statement that he could say "with authority that Ruth is far from broke," and maybe that was right and maybe it wasn't. Who knew? Ruth was in the middle of it all, questions like mosquitoes in the air. Maybe he was indeed broke for the moment—he often had to borrow money from teammates during spring training because he was low on cash and the paychecks for the new season didn't start until the season started—but was that anybody's business?

His efforts to lose weight suffered a setback when he broke a finger on his left hand making a catch and couldn't play for five days. His stomach was grumbling and he was chewing on the bicarbonate, and it was a relief when the Yankees packed up and started their slow zigzag northward with a series of exhibitions across the South against the Brooklyn Robins. Helen and Dorothy were on one train back to New York. The Babe was on another.

Freed from restraints, he started attacking the night again in each southern town. Healed from the broken finger, he started attacking the baseball, putting on a stop-after-stop show. He had said after the first comments were made about his weight when he hit Florida that his arms and shoulders were fine and they were what he used, anyway, hitting a baseball. So now he was hitting the baseball.

Then, when the tour reached Atlanta, he became sick. The flu that he'd missed in Hot Springs had arrived and laid him low. Or something laid him low. He played a shortened game in a cold rain in Atlanta and was shivering. A doctor was called and advised him to stay in town and rest, but he put on a couple of sweaters and boarded the morning train with the rest of the team to Chattanooga, the next stop. Still feeling terrible, he skipped batting practice in the afternoon, then took off his sweaters and clocked two home runs in the game. The teams moved along to Knoxville.

Here he hit a memorable home run, his seventh of the exhibition schedule, which moved his batting average to .456. He still felt terrible, but he hit a wrong-field blast that hit a tree filled with some African American kids, watching the game for free from a distance. The ball knocked off a branch, and the kids scampered out of the tree. The home run was memorable, but the reports of it were not pleasant.

This was the segregated South, where maybe certain things could be expected. The words, however, were written for the unsegregated North, where supposedly a different situation existed. Really? This was a window to the times. Intelligent, witty men wrote bad things.

The *New York Times* account, writer unnamed, was fine:

> The nice white ball left the bat as if it had been shot from a cannon mouth, cleared the left centre field wall by thirty feet and knocked a

limb off a dead tree from which a dozen boys were watching the game. Luckily it was not the limb on which they were sitting, but a smaller one some ten feet above their heads.

A description by Bozeman Bulger of the *New York Evening World*, writing a few years later in a long article in the *Saturday Evening Post* on Ruth, was not fine. He called this "Ruth's Funniest Home Run":

> Outside the park of Knoxville was a venerable oak tree . . . its great spreading limbs were crowded with little darkies perilously perched for a view of the hero. The picture from a distance was that of a tree full of blackbirds . . . even before the ball struck, darkies began dropping from the limbs. . . . The game was interrupted while the crowd roared with laughter. . . . "Boy, I'm tellin' you," exclaimed one of the Brooklyn players, a Southerner, "that tree fairly rained pickaninnies for the next half hour."

Marshall Hunt, Ruth's daily Boswell, alas, was worst of all in his next-day account in the *Daily News*:

> Lines of mahogany-hued humanity perched ape-like on the branches of a huge and stark elm tree outside of Caswell Park were imperiled this afternoon by your Herman Ruth, though not, assuredly, by any homicidal intent. Mr. Ruth declares with vehemence he bosoms no animosity against mahogany-hued humanity of any shade or proportions, temperament or previous conditions of servitude.
>
> Six senegambians, clinging to the branches of that tree almost were shaken to earth like ripe apples today when a virile, he-man, honest-to-goodness home run was made by your Herman, his third in two days. The ball cleared the left field fence by twenty feet in the fifth inning of a game with Brooklyn's Dodgers, struck the tree resoundingly and brittle branches beat the senegambians to the ground by only a fraction of a second.

This was 1925 humor. Nobody thought anything about it. Or at least nobody said anything. The next stop was Asheville, North Carolina.

The train left Knoxville early in the morning. Ruth still felt terrible. It was a trip of 100 curving miles through the Great Smoky Mountains. Ruth settled down to play cards, hearts, with catcher Steve O'Neill, Urban

Shocker, and trainer Doc Woods. Ruth felt like he was burning up. He asked Woods to take his temperature.

"You sure are running a fever," Woods decided. "I'll see what I can do for you when we get to the hotel."

The twists and turns of the train now upset Ruth's stomach. Everyone on the ride was a bit woozy. Ruth seemed to be getting incoherent. When the train reached Asheville, he tried to walk, but collapsed in the waiting room of the station. He grabbed a radiator, started to fall, but O'Neill and catcher John Levi grabbed him before he reached the ground. On the cab ride to the Battery Park Hotel, he was delirious.

"I want to go home," he said. "I'm sick. I'm going to take an airplane and go right to New York. I don't care if it drops."

At the hotel, Dr. Charles Jordan, an Asheville physician, was called. He diagnosed a dual condition of influenza and indigestion. It was decided in the morning that Ruth should take the 3:50 afternoon train back to New York. He was still weak, but did eat some breakfast and asked for more, which Dr. Jordan refused to give him. The good doctor had been doing some research into Ruth's lifestyle, talking with other Yankees, and had a cautionary message for the Sultan of Swat.

"All I can say," the doctor said, "is that unless somebody is appointed to act as guardian over him at the dining table, he won't be a baseball player very long."

Marshall Hunt noted that the doctor had made this diagnosis without ever seeing the patient in Hot Springs "at 11 o'clock at night, ordering sirloin steaks smothered with pork chops and devouring them in the same elapsed time and with the thoroughness it takes Henry Ford to fetch a flivver from the mines of Minnesota and relay the product to an Indiana farmer." The Babe was moaning again, hanging on to the shoulder of Yankees scout Paul Krichell when he walked through the hotel lobby on the way to the train.

Krichell, who would accompany Ruth back to the big city along with Bob Boyd, the one-armed sportswriter, went on a mission in the morning to buy some pajamas for the Bambino, who always boasted that he slept in the nude. Krichell was looking for size 48, but the best he could find in the town was size 42, color passionate pink. He said the plan was to slit the back on the tops and just throw away the bottoms. Better than nothing.

The news of the Babe's collapse, of course, already had made headlines because, as with any head of state, the reports of all his ailments made headlines. (Hunt, after all, had written that entire article about the Babe's corns.) This notoriety caused a problem when the 3:50 train out of Asheville missed a connection to the northbound train in Salisbury. When the northbound train arrived in Washington and reporters found no G. H. Ruth on board, a fast rumor started that he had died.

The rumor was spread by a Canadian news agency and picked up in England, where the London dailies, working on tight deadlines, produced front-page obituaries on the American baseball star. The *Evening News* said that "he was equally successful at batting, fielding and pitching, but his smashing hits were his specialties." It also said he was handicapped by the fact that "he was putting on fat."

While the English mourned a character they never had met or known, the character spent a relatively uneventful night in his lower berth on a later northbound train. He tried breakfast again in the morning, couldn't hold it down, and was still feverish and woozy as the train approached New York. The last stretch was called the Manhattan Transfer, the place where an electric engine was added to the train to bring it through the tunnel under the Hudson River and into the city.

The Babe, helped by Krichell, went to the washroom to freshen up for his public. Once there, Ruth realized he hadn't brought his comb, so Krichell went to find one. When the scout came back, the Babe was on the floor of the washroom, unconscious. He not only had fallen but had hit his head. Krichell, unable to rouse the slugger, notified the porter that he needed help, and the train arrived at Penn Station and a grand melodrama began.

Helen and a friend, Mrs. C. C. White, were waiting at the station . . .

Ed Barrow and a couple of Yankees officials were waiting . . .

The gathered writers and photographers from all of those New York newspapers were waiting . . .

Assorted fans and the ever-present New York curious were waiting . . .

The Babe was unconscious in his berth, where he had been carried.

Helen and Barrow, noticing that their man had not disembarked with the rest of the passengers, went onto the train, where they found him, still unconscious and in the midst of great activity. A doctor was called. A porter with a wheelchair arrived and was rejected. A stretcher and four men to carry the patient were called. Helen, "an attractive young woman in a blue coat with some vague kind of fur border and a diamond bat pin that looked as though it must weigh several ounces," began to cry softly. The four men with the stretcher arrived and wanted to slide the Babe through a window, but the window was too small. A man was sent for a screwdriver to unscrew the frame and make the window larger.

One odd moment seemed to follow another. The ambulance called from St. Vincent's Hospital—"where the Babe has a season's ticket," one writer said—broke down. Another ambulance had to be called. A train carrying the entire roster of the Boston Braves, on their way back to Boston, stopped at the next track. Pitcher Rube Marquard and manager Dave Bancroft came to the Babe's train, seeking information. They had heard that the Babe had died, were relieved that he hadn't, but were saddened that he was knocked out and in need of medical treatment.

The four men with the stretcher finally hoisted the great man through the expanded window. They carried him through a crowd, put him on a freight elevator. He awakened long enough to say, "Helen, I feel rotten." He then went into convulsions. He had one, two, three convulsions. A physician gave him an injection. He had another convulsion. He had to be held down.

Helen rode in the front seat of the ambulance, still crying every now and then, looking back at her husband. He had another convulsion. The ambulance did not travel fast. The driver explained that he didn't have a bell to warn the taxicabs that he was coming. The Babe had another convulsion, the largest, while being transferred from the ambulance to St. Vincent's. Seven men held him down.

Two hours later, all this had passed. He was sitting up in bed, talking and laughing.

"Ruth's condition is not serious," Dr. Edward King, the Yankees' team doctor, announced at last to reporters. "He is run down and has low blood pressure, and there is the indication of a slight attack of the flu. What he needs is rest. He should have been in bed a week ago."

"The Big Bam yesterday just about beat a long throw from Death, the outfielder in Life's game," Damon Runyon tapped out in a hurry for the *New York American*. "He slid in safe over the home plate of rest and medical attention."

W. O. McGeehan of the *New York Tribune* won the phrase-of-the-day contest with "The Bellyache Heard Round the World." The Babe, after all of this, was fine.

Or was he? The doctor said that the great man would be better in three or four days and might even be ready for the Yanks' opener on Tuesday at the Stadium, knowing the great man's recuperative powers. The three or four days passed, and the opener took place, and, alas, the recuperative powers did not seem to be working. He still ran a fever. His stomach still bothered him.

Here the fog rolled in. He had a medical problem, which never was adequately revealed. He had an operation on April 17, that much was certain, the scar on his abdomen being visible later to his teammates in the locker room. The nature of the operation was what was in doubt.

The hospital, Dr. King at the podium, talked about an abscess, an infected area, in the stomach that had to be treated. The hospital never deviated from this diagnosis, which led to the popular thought that piles of hot dogs and gallons of soda pop, all part of a general gluttony, had sent the Sultan to his knees. This served the public well, a cautionary tale for mothers to tell their indulgent children.

Baseball people always whispered a more titillating story involving gluttony of another kind. The Babe had syphilis. The Babe had gonorrhea. The Babe had any—maybe every—disease ever associated with carnal moments. Ed Barrow whispered this to at least one reporter. Claire Hodgson stopped short of naming diseases but years later talked about secrecy and "different mores" when the operation took place.

Possibly some other situation altogether could have been involved, some hernia or rupture or some need for a colostomy bag for a time, some kind of nether-region difficulties that no one wanted to detail for strangers. The net result, whatever the problem, was that the Babe stayed in St. Vincent's Hospital for a lot longer than expected. And Helen soon joined him.

On April 24, she was admitted for "a nervous condition from worrying about her husband" and put in a ward two floors above that of her husband. Again, the fog rolled in. Was that nervous condition helped along by the discovery that her husband had a sexually transmitted disease? Fog. Claire Hodgson also was on the fringe of this situation. She couldn't see her lover, the visitors' list being restricted to Helen, Dorothy, and Barrow, but were there phone calls? Hodgson had spent that time with the Babe in Hot Springs a few days before Helen and Dorothy had spent time with him in St. Petersburg. Had Helen found out about Claire? A doctor wasn't needed here to see that something was ready to burst.

The Babe made his first public appearance on May 2, when a group of sportswriters was allowed to visit. Propped up in his bed and wearing white pajamas, he said he felt "weak as a kitten," like "a featherweight," and said his problem was no more than his yearly battle with the flu. He said indigestion had no part in his sickness.

"That indigestion stuff is a lot of bunk!" he emphasized. "Every time anything happens to a fellow they say he's overeating. Why, I don't eat more than two-thirds of the club. I don't mean two-thirds put together. I mean man-to-man. I've had indigestion for ten years."

He didn't venture to Yankee Stadium for the first time until May 19, six weeks after he was stricken in Asheville. He got into a traveling gray Yankees uniform that sagged around his 6-foot-2 frame, down now maybe as low as 180 pounds, and took batting practice served up by his chauffeur, Thomas Harvey, who also wore a Yankees uniform. It was baby steps. He managed to hit only one ball into the stands, was exhausted, and returned to the hospital for the night.

This workout routine continued until his release on May 24. His return to the lineup didn't come until June 1 at the Stadium. It was an awkward moment. The other players were careful around him. They were convinced that his problem had been venereal disease and didn't want to use the same towel or touch where he had touched.

"The club had to have a male nurse in the dugout to make sure he didn't go against the doctor's instructions," pitcher Bob Shawkey told Ken Sobol years later. "You know, he wasn't allowed to shower with the other players or anything like that."

Walter Johnson was on the mound for the Senators, not exactly an easy way for Ruth to return, and he was 0-for-2 with a walk in six innings of a 5–2 Yankees loss. His test of stamina came after the walk in the fourth inning, when Bob Meusel tripled behind him. Ruth pounded around the bases and clearly gave out on the stretch from third to home, first slowing, then throwing himself at the plate as a big, rolling bundle, easily tagged out by catcher Muddy Ruel.

Westbrook Pegler wrote that Ruth was "out both ways" when he lay on the ground for a minute to catch his breath after the play ended. Pegler also said the Babe looked "weak and wan" and "had wasted away to a couple of carloads since he developed that national ache in his stuffing" and now resembled "a bag of oats on two toothpicks."

The writers were glad to have him back.

The Babe had played on only one bad club in his career, the 1919 Red Sox under Ed Barrow. He now was on his second. The Yankees had fallen apart in his absence. They were thirteen and a half games out of first place on June 1, the day he returned. Teams sometimes seem to get old overnight. This was one of them. Miller Huggins already was adjusting his lineup, talking about plans for "next year."

The addition of Ruth to this sinking ship was not a positive. Not for the team. Not for Huggins. Not for Ruth. Helen was still in St. Vincent's, wouldn't leave for a month after her husband left, and now the Sudbury farm was up for sale. Something had happened. The marriage unofficially was finished, and the Babe was liberated. A liberated Babe Ruth on a bad team with an undersized manager he didn't respect was a convergence of meteorological conditions that meant trouble. The storm soon began.

The admonitions of the many doctors and well-wishers were forgotten with a return to a semblance of health. Two weeks, three weeks, one month back, and the Home Run King was back in overdrive off the field. If anything, he was even more earnest in his pursuit of all pleasures. Even his teammates were stunned at the increase in his activity.

"The ballplayers sensed Ruth's tension, realized that something frightening was happening within that gigantic legend that Ruth had become," Waite Hoyt would write in a short 1948 book called *Babe Ruth As I Knew Him,* a frank account of life with the Babe. "His fabulous personal escapades were shaded with pathos, for the Babe no longer was sampling life. He was wolfing it down in immense, oversized doses. Although we all recognized his undiminished baseball genius, we knew we were witnessing the gradual disintegration of Ruth, the man."

He was not pleasant to be around . . . when he was around. He was just running, running, running. He and Hoyt weren't even talking. Ruth had been told something that Hoyt allegedly said, probably on the subject of Claire Hodgson, and promised the pitcher he would never talk to him again. He would, however, still shout at him and fight him.

A fly ball was hit to right field at the Stadium and dropped in front of Ruth for a base hit. Hoyt, pitching, thought Ruth had pulled up short on the ball, dogged it. Hoyt put his hands on his hips, looked at Ruth, and shook his head as if to say, "You should have caught the ball, you big baboon." Ruth noticed. Back on the bench at the end of the inning, he told Hoyt never to show him up again. Back in the clubhouse after the game, the argument started again.

Hoyt, knocked out of the game, already had showered and was naked in front of his locker. Ruth was in uniform. He called Hoyt a bunch of names and said he would punch the pitcher in the nose.

"Well, you're not tied," Hoyt said.

Ruth attacked, taking a kick with his spikes still on his feet. Punches were exchanged. Poor Miller Huggins jumped in the middle, took a couple of punches, but broke up the fight. That was life with the Babe.

Huggins had become more and more distressed with his star. The manager's history of confrontations with Ruth was not good. They argued all the time, back and forth, semi-comical stuff, but Huggins seldom was able to voice his real thoughts. Every time he was ready to say something, to truly read out the Caliph of Clout, the caliph would unload another couple of clouts. An oft-told story centered on the manager's long dissertation with traveling secretary Mark Roth one day about how this was it, the end, he was going to say something to Ruth the next time he saw him. A game was played, Ruth hit the big homer to win it, then he walked past Huggins and Roth.

RUTH: Hey, keed.
HUGGINS: Hey, Babe.

Ruth kept walking. Roth asked Huggins why he didn't say anything to the slugger. Huggins replied, "I just did."

This was different now. Huggins hired a private detective to trail Ruth in Chicago and St. Louis on a western road trip in the last half of August. The report from Chicago was not good. As expected, Ruth was out every night. Barrow later told Fred Lieb, the writer, that the detective reported that Ruth had been with six different women in one night in Chicago. Huggins waited.

St. Louis might have been Ruth's favorite town on the road. Things happened in St. Louis. Marshall Hunt told the tale of a layover in St. Louis, a few hours before catching the next train to Hot Springs. Ruth was met at the station by a bunch of fans and obliged them with autographs as he and Hunt made their way to a taxi stand. He was still signing, still surrounded, as he and Hunt got into the taxi. The driver asked where they were going.

"The House of Good Shepard," the Babe boomed.

Everyone in the crowd knew what that meant. The House of Good Shepard was the most famous whorehouse in the city. The people started chanting, "House of Good Shepard, House of Good Shepard," as the taxi took off, the Babe smiling and waving. He was greeted with equal hospitality at the establishment itself, where he was known to one and all. He and Hunt had a terrific dinner, the Babe availed himself of the product once, twice, "and I think he got a free one, one on the house," Hunt said. They were back at the station for the nine o'clock train. That was St. Louis.

"The House of Good Shepard," Hunt said, "served the best steaks in the world."

Huggins waited. By August 29, the Yankees had lost 10 of 14 games on the trip. Ruth was 12-for-49 in those games, four homers, a .245 batting average. He had stayed out all night in St. Louis and didn't arrive until an hour before game time. Huggins and Waite Hoyt, the starting pitcher for the day, were the only people in the clubhouse.

"Ruth had white flannel pants and a blue, sort of navy, jacket on," Hoyt said. "And a panama hat. Tan and white shoes, black and white, I forget which, and little Huggins was in there and said, 'Don't get dressed, Babe, don't put on your uniform.'"

"What are you talking about?" the Babe said.

"I'll tell you, Babe, I've talked it over, and I've come to the decision you're fined $5,000 for missing curfew last night and being late today," the manager said. "You're fined and suspended. The suspension runs the rest of the season."

Ruth, speechless at first, became very angry. He said he would talk to Kenesaw Mountain Landis about this. He would talk to Col. Ruppert. We'd see about this fine and suspension. Ruppert had handed back a $1,000 fine Huggins tried to impose on Ruth earlier in the season.

"No, I talked to Ruppert first," Huggins said. "Ruppert agreed that a suspension was the best thing to do."

Huggins told Ruth that Mark Roth had a ticket for him for a train back to New York that night. Ruth stormed out of the clubhouse. He was walking out of Sportsman's Park in his white flannel pants and blue, sort of navy, jacket and panama hat as Ray Gillespie, a young sportswriter for the *St. Louis Globe-Democrat*, was arriving.

"Where are you going?" Gillespie asked.

"I'm going to New York," the Babe said.

"You're not going to play?"

"No, I'm going to New York."

"How come?"

"You better ask Hug."

Gillespie went to the Yankees dugout and found Urban Shocker, whom he knew from the time Shocker played with the Browns. Shocker introduced him to Huggins as "a good guy." Huggins gave him the story. The Babe was fined $5,000 and suspended indefinitely for "insubordination."

Gillespie hurried to a telephone. The *Globe-Democrat*, like most newspapers, put out a great number of editions. This story could hit the streets within the hour. Except his bosses didn't believe him. The idea of a $5,000 fine was almost inconceivable. The managing editor finally came on the line. He told Gillespie to go back and check with Huggins again. Gillespie checked. He reported back that Huggins said all of the same things all over again. The managing editor grunted.

"Do you know what this means?" he asked.

"What?" Gillespie replied.

"It means if this story is incorrect, you're fired."

The *St. Louis Globe-Democrat* had the scoop.

The second Babe Ruth public melodrama of the season had begun. The fine and suspension opened the door to the Babe's entire life. The protection from sportswriters who felt that a player's life existed only on the field was gone. Claire Hodgson's name and picture were in the paper immediately, and reporters and photographers were camped outside her apartment house on West 79th Street. Helen was under siege at the apartment she and the Babe had rented at the Concourse Plaza on the Grand Concourse. Tabloid fun had begun for everyone.

"I know absolutely nothing about that matter," Helen told reporters when asked about the "New York widow." "And I don't care to talk on that subject for publication. However, I intend to discuss these matters with my husband when he returns."

"Early yesterday afternoon a limousine drove up to the curb before the apartment house," the *Daily News* reported from West 79th Street. "In the limousine were Eugene and Hubert Merritt, Mrs. Hodgson's brothers. A slim young woman, heavily veiled, but easily recognized as Mrs. Hodgson, slipped into the waiting car, the curtains were jerked down and the car whizzed away."

Unnamed sources appeared from everywhere to tell their name-filled stories. The stories were about how the Babe had changed with the advent of money, about how much he drank, about how he had been involved with a well-known shimmy dancer, about how Helen once had slapped the Babe in the face after he'd bet $1,000 on a race, drunk, at the dog track in St. Petersburg. There was more than one story that Helen had been preparing to file for a separation agreement.

The Babe missed the first wave of all of this. He didn't use the Yankees' ticket back to New York. He spent the night in St. Louis instead with friends, perhaps friends who were doing the Lord's work at the House of Good Shepard, and the next day went to Chicago to plead his case to Judge Landis. The Judge, alas, was on vacation at Burt Lake, Michigan, so the Babe pleaded his case with the press. The headline in the *Chicago Tribune*—"Babe Ruth, Mad, Denies Orgies; Here to Fight"— was a quick summation.

"Huggins is making me the goat for the rotten showing of the team," he told reporters. "He said that the fine and suspension resulted from misconduct off the ball field and drinking. He has been laying for a chance to get me and I gave it to him by staying out until 2:30 in the morning in St. Louis. As far as the drinking charge, he's a liar."

Ruth tore into Huggins's strategy, his management of the team. He said Huggins basically had blown the pennant a year earlier to the Senators. He admitted that he had disobeyed two of Huggins's orders during games in Chicago, but said he did so because the orders were bad baseball. Huggins, it seemed, could do nothing right. Ruth said he would never play for the Yankees again as long as Huggins was the manager.

"Can you imagine a fellow who hit .240 when he was playing ball trying to tell players who have .350 averages how to hit the ball?" Ruth asked.

Landis sent word he would see him—"There's a 5:30 train to Burt Lake"—but Ruth decided the next day to go back to New York to talk to Ruppert. He boarded the Twentieth Century Limited that afternoon, with "his pet portable Victrola and his huge suitcase that contained, among other things, nine pairs of white flannel pants, for which he has a failing," news reports said. The long overnight trip did wonders. The Babe Ruth anger died. This was his familiar pattern: anger in a flash, followed by acceptance and contrition.

"Ruth has the mind of a 15-year-old," American League president Ban Johnson said in the midst of this flap. It probably was the best appraisal of the man in all of the words spoken or written. The Xaverians had done their job. The 15-year-old boy at St. Mary's Industrial School argued against the whacks on the backside, then took them and was sorry and apologized. Sins gone. Slate clean. That was how he worked.

(After a year, maybe two, he offered Waite Hoyt a beer on a train trip back from St. Louis. The business was finished. They were friends again.)

Indeed, Father Edward Quinn, a New York priest who had been at St. Mary's when Ruth was there, met him at Grand Central Station when he arrived from Chicago. The scene was chaotic—a crowd estimated at 3,000 people had gathered to see him pass. At the front were the battalions of reporters and photographers. Getting into a cab with Father Quinn, Ruth said that maybe he would see them later at the Concourse Plaza. They naturally piled into cabs and followed his cab to the hotel, where another crowd awaited.

Helen now was under a nurse's care in her bedroom at the apartment. The stress had knocked her out again. She also had an infection on the ring finger of her left hand. Reports soon said she had sustained the injury while trying to rip off her wedding and engagement bands. When her finger swelled, the rings had to be sawed off.

Ruth went into the bedroom to see Helen, then talked with the reporters in the living room. The anger clearly was gone, replaced by an urgency to set things right. The photographers asked if he would pose for pictures with Helen, and he agreed.

"Sure," he said, "but first I want to say something. What really gets me sore is those stories about me and women, and the pictures. I can take the baseball stories, but can't you lay off the women stuff?"

He posed for the pictures, looking solemn next to his sick wife. She put her arms around him and began to cry. He began to cry. It was all too intimate to be public, but public it was. The photographers snapped. The brightness of their flashbulbs filled the room. Ruth walked to the window and stared below.

He then went to Col. Ruppert's office at 93rd Street and Avenue A to see about his future. Again, reporters followed. Ruppert was not alone in the office. Miller Huggins also was there, but left immediately. Ruth and Ruppert went behind closed doors. The owner told Ruth that the matter totally was in Huggins's hands. The decision about what to do next was up to Ruth.

He went almost immediately to the Stadium to see Huggins. Again, the reporters followed. They were there when the two antagonists met in the Yankees clubhouse.

"Hello, Miller," the Babe said.

"Hello," Huggins replied.

The presence of the reporters made everything awkward. The two men tried to move to a corner, but the pack followed. The search for privacy was impossible. Ruth finally broke the silence.

"Well," he said, "what do I do?"

"Babe," the manager said, "I can't see you today. I will call you on the phone when I want to see you."

"Can I put on a uniform to practice?"

"Well," the manager said, "I will let you know when I am ready to see you."

The battle was done. Huggins was the winner on all scorecards. The little man strung out the process for six more days, amiable but firm, the parent letting the child know that all was forgiven, but still there was a price to be paid for the transgression. Ruth, antsy, remained contrite. On Labor Day in Boston, Huggins finally relented and let him back into the lineup. It was a quiet return, 1-for-4 in a 5–1 loss to the Red Sox, but Ruth was the first man on the field by several minutes on the rainy afternoon and spent a long time in the batting cage, obviously happy to be back.

There were 29 games left in the season. He went on a 9-game hitting streak to start. He hit 10 home runs in the 29 games to finish the season with 25. He hit .345 in the 29 games to raise his final average to .290. He did nothing to incur Miller Huggins's displeasure.

The very public affair, finished now, had brought out thousands of words about the construction of heroes in America. Who was a hero? Who wasn't? What should a hero do? The easy approach was condemnation and sadness—"With the fall from glory of Babe Ruth, a million young Americans are bereft," the *New York Herald Tribune* said in an editorial. "Being a boy isn't as certain fun as it used to be"—but that was too easy. A million young Americans weren't bereft. They were intrigued, excited. They wanted to know more. And more.

The American hero was constructed differently from the classic heroes of the Greeks and Romans. Virtue never had been a necessity. The *New York World* had the right idea:

Babe Ruth has been fined $5,000 and indefinitely suspended. And are we, the great American public, virtuously shocked? Not at all. We long to look him up, pat him on the back and shake the brunoid paw. If it were anybody else who had provoked Mr. Huggins to such summary action, we would point a finger, shout "Fie, Fie!" and read a moral about a player's duty to his club and teammates. But not with Ruth. There is something about him, even when he is under the dark cloud of disgrace, which makes us find excuses and love him still. That is probably because we realize he has never grown up. He started life as a bad boy, and he is still a bad boy. And if now and then he pays the penalty that bad boys pay, he also reaps the reward that they reap. The whole world loves a bad boy. It ought to love Rollo, but actually it loves Huck Finn.

CHAPTER FIFTEEN

THE BABE SAT DOWN with Joe Winkworth of *Collier's* magazine a few weeks after the 1925 season ended. The bluster was gone. A contrite, apologetic character looked out the windows of the Grand Concourse apartment—the great stadium part of his view—and called himself "the sappiest of saps." This was a different kind of Sultan of Swat interview.

"I have been a Babe and a Boob," the Babe said. "And I am through—through with the pests and the good-time guys. Between them and a few crooks I have thrown away over a quarter million dollars."

The message of moderation finally had landed. He had heard it forever, packaged in different ways by Huggins and Barrow and Walsh, by Brother Matthias and Jimmy Walker, by Ban Johnson and Kenesaw Mountain Landis, by assorted sportswriters and worried friends, but never really paid attention. He always had nodded at the words, made his small promises to make amends, but then followed the first bright light that passed in the night.

George Herman Ruth, Sultan of Swat, was bulletproof and wonderful. That was the image he always had projected and pretty much fulfilled. Conventional advice might apply to conventional people, but conventional people couldn't do what he could. The 24-hour buffet line of life experiences had no effect on him, not even the dessert section or the cocktail bar at the end. Look at the performance. Look at the home runs, the money, the fame. Who could argue with that? He never had reason to listen.

He did now. His body talked to him in assorted ways. He was too heavy, too slow, too sore. He had become increasingly frail. His digestive system was an obvious mess. He even had to leave his annual ghost-reporting job at the World Series early because he felt ill, the effects of his operation still at work. The drop-off in his performance during the season of turbulence, combined with the Yankees' sad finish, was the ultimate indication that he was in trouble.

He soon would be 31 years old (and thought he would be 32), and he could hear the comments everywhere that he was on the downside, possibly finished. The money that had come and gone, without much thought used in the middle, suddenly mattered. Would the grand revenue stream somehow disappear? The time for accounting finally, reluctantly, had arrived.

He estimated he had roared through over $500,000 in gambling, bad business deals, and high living. He had owned nine different high-priced American cars. He once had worn 22 new silk shirts during three hot days in St. Louis, and then left them for the maid. The life of a Home Run King was not only expensive but complicated. He was sick of dealing with lawyers and private detectives, sick of the schemes that always seemed to surround him. He was sick of trouble.

"A fellow is defenseless unless he cuts out all good-timing," Ruth said. "And that's what I have done. I don't even say hello to anyone anymore unless I know him well. And parties are out because I have mapped out a comeback schedule for myself and I am going to live up to it absolutely."

There would be no barnstorming trip this year. There would be no trip to Hot Springs for the baths and the chicken dinners. Helen was gone, off in the fog, unseen, unheard, back in Boston with Dorothy. The farm in Sudbury was still up for sale. The Babe was alone for the first time in a long while. Okay, he had Christy, and he was involved with Claire, and his phone always rang, and he was in a crowd as soon as he walked out his front door, but this was as alone as he had been in his professional life.

The start of the comeback was a hunting trip to New Brunswick, Canada, with ballplayers Bob Shawkey, Muddy Ruel, Joe Bush, Eddie Collins, and Benny Bengough. Going into the woods, the Babe was so out of shape that he rode a packhorse while the other ballplayers all hiked 40 miles to their camp. The trip lasted three weeks, and when the Babe came back, he proudly reported that he had spurned the horse and hiked the 40 miles out of the woods. He then returned to New York and, after considering an early departure for St. Petersburg to work himself back into shape in the sun, made the decision that probably saved his career.

He showed up at Artie McGovern's door.

Artie McGovern ran an 11,640-square-foot gymnasium for rich people on the fourth floor of the Liggitt Building at 41 East 42nd Street at the corner of Madison Avenue. An enterprising former flyweight boxer who grew up in Hell's Kitchen at the turn of the century, he had developed theories of exercise and nutrition that now intrigued New York high society and made him a national authority on physical fitness. The McGovern Method of Physical Reconstruction, which cost $500 per year, featured only individualized instruction.

His list of clients included department store magnate Marshall Field, composer John Philip Sousa, financier John J. Raskob, architect Whitney Warren, golfers Gene Sarazen and Johnny Farrell, tennis player Vinnie Richards, lawyer and writer Arthur Train, bandleader Paul Whiteman, and dozens of other prominent New York names. His establishment was equipped with sunlamps, electric ray cabinets, massage rooms, handball courts, squash courts, rowing machines, sitz baths, and golf driving nets—all of the modern tools of exercise.

The biggest feature of Artie McGovern's gym, though, was Artie McGovern. A 35-year-old dynamo, he was a little man in a white sweater who worked 12-hour days filled with constant movement, pushing, prodding, extolling. To sign with his program was to hand your life to him and his staff. There were no excuses, no matter how busy you might be. Artie McGovern would send someone to your house to make sure you did the work. His wake-up calls were a symbol of status as much as good health. He delighted in making rich people sweat.

"Now I have about 20 boys out every morning," he said in an interview in *American* magazine. "In winter you will see them going into houses and apartments along Park and Fifth Avenues almost before it's light. They have keys—they just walk right into the bedrooms and yank the covers off the millionaires. The masseurs come along twenty minutes later.

"It's not as easy as you would think. It takes as much diplomacy as an ambassador to get some of them out of bed. You mustn't make them too mad, but you've got to get them up. You've got to give them orders. Some of those big fellows from Wall Street have got a new excuse every morning in the year. You just have to shove them out of bed and order them around if you want to get any results at all."

The McGovern philosophy of exercise centered on a concept he called "Vital Energy." Every human being was born with a finite amount of Vital Energy, enough to last a lifetime if used correctly. If used incorrectly, squandered, a person's Vital Energy could be gone in youth, his body left open to fatigue, disease, and ultimately death.

Artie believed that over-exercise was more harmful than no exercise. He thought that most college athletes over-exercised, using up their Vital Energy in great gulps. He railed against the weekend exerciser trying to cram fitness into two days. ("You'd be better off spending the weekend in bed!" he said.) The McGovern plan demanded daily work, half the exercises done on the back, half standing. Regularity was the key, not ferocity. Exercise should feel good.

"Your feelings will tell you when to quit," he said. "When there is no exhilaration, no fun in your game whatever it is; when you are holding on by your clenched teeth and your grit, it's time to stop. In fact, you've passed the time to stop by a dangerous margin."

The McGovern approach had been developed during an interesting rise to prominence. Artie estimated he'd had over 200 prizefights, professional and amateur, as a young man. His father, Happy Jack McGovern, was a full-time blacksmith and a part-time fighter, and Artie had grown up around the boxing game. John L. Sullivan's bar was across the street from the McGovern house. Billy Elmer's fight club was next door. Artie, 97 pounds, was in the ring by the time he was 15.

After a list of injuries that included a nose broken 18 times, front teeth knocked out, assorted broken ribs, and a partial loss of hearing, a fractured knuckle was both the end of his boxing career and the start of his new career. He had the knuckle rebroken and set at the Cornell Clinic. While that was taking place, the head of the clinic, Dr. William Hills Sheldon, suggested in conversation that Artie set up a small gymnasium to take care of the needs of the doctors at the hospital and some of their recuperating patients.

Artie, without other options, followed the advice. He had little formal education but knew how to train and exercise himself, and now he spent time at the hospital talking with doctors, further learning the mechanics of the body. The Great War gave him a laboratory full of customers to study as he worked as a volunteer with soldiers and sailors deemed unfit for service and with returning wounded and shell-shocked veterans. He developed his philosophy, and then his client list and his business expanded as he moved from smaller to larger locations.

His was another success story of the twenties. He now wrote articles for national publications. He was as famous as some of his clients. He had taken their Wall Street advice, investing well in the stock market and expanding still more, and he now owned a second home in the country. The rich people loved him. He not only had programs for them to follow, he had the charm and imagination to make the programs work.

"The strangest morning assignment I ever had was with Helen Clay Frick in 1919," Artie reported. "She was supposed to be the richest bachelor girl in the world. Her doctor had a theory that she should be made to do what she liked least. That was boxing; so I was sent up to the famous Frick mansion on Fifth Avenue to box with her. She put on gloves, but she had no interest in it. It was silly foolishness, she said."

The second morning, Artie appeared again with gloves. Again, there was no interest. Artie had a badly chapped lip, though, and in the sparring Miss Frick gave him a "little tap" and the lip began to bleed. Miss Frick was startled.

"What did that?" she asked.

"You did it," Artie said. "That was a terrible sock you gave me. Go easy."

A good wink was the only punctuation mark Artie needed for the story. Ms. Frick became a boxing fan and put on seven needed pounds. Artie moved along to the next hard case.

The Babe had found the right man.

"About the middle of December, 1925, Babe Ruth came into my gymnasium in New York City a physical wreck," Artie McGovern reported in *Collier's* magazine. "He weighed 254 pounds. His blood pressure was low and his pulse was high. He was as near to being a total loss as any patient I have ever had under my care. He had lived a life of excesses and was suffering the inevitable consequences. His stomach had gone back on him completely. His eyes had been affected. The slightest exertion left him short of breath. His muscles were soft and flabby."

The description might have been a bit overdramatic—a gruesome "before" to set against a wondrous "after" for potential customers—but there obviously was work to be done. Artie preached self-denial, a concept that obviously was new to the adult Babe. The adult Babe listened.

His new days began early with the Artie McGovern wake-up service. A set of exercises was done right in the bed, leg lifts and crunches and movements as simple as holding each end of the pillow and extending the arms out and bringing them back again and again. The exercises were followed by a brisk walk, which was followed by a massage, shower, and bath. All of this before breakfast.

Diet was important. Artie cut out red meat and sweets. No medicines were allowed because he wanted the Babe's body to do its own work. No snack foods. Breakfast featured poached eggs and one slice of toast. Lunch was a salad. The dinner entrée was lamb or chicken, served with two vegetables and another salad. No liquid was served with any meal because Artie wanted the Babe to chew his food regularly, not wash it down. Cold water was taken out of the diet because Artie felt it disturbed the stomach. Hot water, however, was served throughout the day—two glasses after most exercises and most meals—because Artie thought hot water cleansed the body. Constipation was another of Artie's great worries. The Babe was soon awash in hot water.

The exercises at the gym varied. Artie concentrated on muscles that weren't used for baseball. The baseball muscles were fine, being used regularly. Artie worked on strengthening the abdominal and hip muscles, feeling they weren't strong enough to support the weight that the Babe somehow could add simply by walking past a table of food. Artie wanted a better posture, a better silhouette. The other concentration was the legs. Artie wanted the Babe's thin legs also to help carry around that bulky torso.

In publicity pictures, the famous client was shown riding the stationary bike, rowing on the rowing machine, sitting in a sweatbox with a pained expression, sparring with Artie, both of them wearing huge boxing gloves. In the background, small weights and Indian clubs were hung on the gymnasium wall. A medicine ball was on the floor. The Babe presumably used all of the apparatus.

McGovern was surprised at how determined, how competitive Ruth soon became. Every day seemed to bring changes. The man who was introduced to handball and bushed after just one game now was playing five and six games in a row and asking for more. Artie would have to tell him to take a break.

"At the beginning the Babe was quite sluggish and went to his work in a dull way," Artie said. "Now he is more alert and keen—has more snap and pep; he kids and jokes with the boys, where as previously he had very little to say."

The Babe publicly laid out his goals for the 1926 season in the *New York Graphic* on January 2. They were listed as his New Year's resolutions:

1. To beat his world's record of 59 home runs made in 1921.
2. To observe strictly the training rules laid down by the Yankees.
3. To hold his temper.
4. To be obedient.
5. To be thrifty—no more extravagance.
6. To take part in every one of the 154 games on the schedule.
7. To watch his diet carefully.
8. To conserve his health.
9. To do his share in bringing another pennant to New York.

The newspapers were filled with questions about the great rehabilitation work that was taking place at McGovern's gym. Was this a publicity push for the Babe? Was this just another halfhearted, half-baked attempt to keep everyone quiet? Paul Gallico appeared at the gym to check on Ruth's conditioning. He also was surprised. He played handball with the Babe.

"Ruth plays a handball the way he does a fly ball against a concrete wall," Gallico wrote.

> Get the ball first and worry about the wall afterward. He is amazingly fast on his feet. Baseball fans realize that for a big man he is speedy, but not until you get him inside a small enclosed court do you realize how he carries those 220 pounds about. He gets his hands on shots he had no business making. I slammed one ball past him when he was at midcourt and he chased the thing back and by the time he got to the rear wall he was right with it. True, he slammed head first into the wall so

that the building shook, but what of it? He made the shot. And that seems to be all that counts when the Babe is playing.

A gag picture from the gym showed the famous client tooting on the saxophone. Paul Whiteman, a heavy man known as "the King of Jazz," was on one side, sticking his fingers in his ears and making a face. John Philip Sousa, in shorts and sleeveless T-shirt, looking as if he had been rousted out of bed in a daze by a house fire, was on the other side. There is no record of the conversation, but Artie McGovern did have stories about all three men.

"Paul Whiteman was a surprise," McGovern said. "Most people think he's just a fat man. They don't know he used to be an intercollegiate heavyweight boxing champ. Fast as lightning on his feet. He can beat Babe Ruth at handball.

"John Philip Sousa is a grand old man. In fine shape. When he came to me a couple of years ago, he couldn't lift his left hand to his head. He had conducted his band with his right hand, holding the left across his chest, for so many years the muscles of the left side lost their function. He had to take a slow, painful, patient set of exercises, but he went through with it."

The Babe was the story of the day. He wasn't with the program long at the gym—six weeks total—but the slide was stopped. He lost 44 pounds. His waistline was reduced by eight and three-quarters inches. (He now had a 40-inch waist.) His blood pressure went up from 107 to 128. His pulse rate went down from 92 to 78. In the six weeks, he stopped his body's sad decline and not only brought it back to what it once was but made it better. He was now the mature athlete hitting his prime.

The slide was done. Wait and see. He would spend time with Artie McGovern every winter for the rest of his playing career. He had discovered— or perhaps had been pushed by Ed Barrow or Christy Walsh or even Claire Hodgson to discover—a new approach to baseball training. To use a term that would not arrive until years later, he had a personal trainer.

Ballplayers of this time didn't go to gyms and work out under the direction of fitness specialists. They didn't work on specific muscle groups that might be a concern. Ballplayers mostly went home to their farms and planted their crops or raised their cattle. Ballplayers found off-season jobs. They needed the money. They needed the start toward second careers after their baseball lives were done. Ruth, because of his situation, because of the money he made, was one of the few ballplayers who could devote this extra time to preparing to play the game. It was the same situation the wealthy boxing champion traditionally enjoyed compared to the struggling challengers he would face. He was the full-time athlete, while the competition had to work a second job to survive. The champion had the advantage.

The caricature of the overweight fat man would remain, especially as Ruth grew older with an older man's body, the weight harder to lose with each succeeding year, but the truth was that he had rediscovered the athlete at his core, the secret of his performance. His appearances always deceived. He was a big man with an oddly shaped body, naturally thick in the middle, but with slender legs and small ankles and wrists that gave him so much whip, torque, when he swung a bat. He had the body of a Thoroughbred racehorse.

He would not exactly become a leader of temperance and fitness movements, but he also would never squander his abilities the way he had during the 1925 season. He would listen. In his own way, he would listen. He was not a fat pig.

"Babe Ruth has to be kidded into everything," Artie McGovern would say in later years. "If you suggest a thing, he's against it. If I told him to lay off sweets and pastry, he'd go out and eat a half-dozen pies à la mode. So I don't say anything. I look sad.

" 'What's the trouble Artie?' says the Babe.

" 'A good friend of mine died last night, Babe. Bill Brown. Diabetes.'

" 'What's diabetes?' says the Babe.

" 'Well, Bill Brown was a great big fellow. Always ate a lot of sweets and pastries. Gave him diabetes.'

"The Babe doesn't say anything, but he begins to go light on the pie à la mode."

Before he left for spring training, the new and improved Bambino showed up at the Yankees' office at 42nd Street for a day and asked assorted staffers to punch him in the stomach. He also appeared at the third annual New York baseball writers' dinner at the Hotel Commodore, an evening of sketches and laughs. He and Artie contributed to the fun when they became involved in a loud, comic argument about whether or not the Babe should have dessert and wound up sparring. One of the sketches also was devoted to the Babe. The title was "If the Babe Was the Manager." He was portrayed making out the lineup card in the hotel lobby at three in the morning after returning from a night on the town. After much debate about the perfect nine to face the Cleveland Indians, he was told that the opponent was the St. Louis Browns. It was funny stuff.

He arrived in St. Petersburg on the morning of February 5, wearing a now-unneeded camel's hair overcoat and muffler, Marshall Hunt in tow. A writer remarked that he looked very good and maybe had found the nearby Fountain of Youth.

"No," the Babe replied, "I found Art McGovern's gym."

"I used to eat ten meals a day," he added. "Every time I saw a frank-furter stand or a soda shop I had to stop. The trouble was I knew nothing about how to eat. A few months in the hospital and a few more in the gymnasium have taught me something."

His workout plan now was to play 36 holes of golf per day. He and Hunt went straight from the train to the Jungle Club to take care of the first 18 holes on the schedule. Hunt reported that the Babe's golf game needed some work. The big man—well, the not-as-big-as-he-was-before big man—shot an even 100.

"The orthodox construction of the modern golf course was a disastrous handicap to the Babe's style of play today," Hunt wrote. "Had the rough been directly in front of the tees and the fairway on both sides of the rough, Mr. Ruth assuredly would have had a much more satisfactory score. Yet, under a ripe Florida sun Ruth enjoyed a good workout, contracted a handsome case of sunburn and announced that his gross leakage through the hide was entirely gratifying."

For the next two weeks, golfing partners were amazed most at what Ruth had—or didn't have—for lunch between rounds. He would order a dish of ice cream. Or he would order tea and toast. End of order. This was the Babe? Where were the fat steaks and the Appalachian mounds of potatoes? He went deep-sea fishing on some days, once with a cigar-smoking Congregational minister. A minister? He returned for more golf.

When official workouts for the 1926 season began, he was tanned and healthy. He affected a new look with a rubber shirt that made him sweat more and a white eyeshade that soon had him compared to tennis player Helen Wills. He was more than friendly with Miller Huggins and filled with optimism. Everybody noticed the change that had arrived. The Babe was a professional athlete again—or perhaps for the first time—and ready for work.

CHAPTER SIXTEEN

H ELP HAD ARRIVED without much notice during the 1925 season. Who sees a pinch hitter in the eighth inning of a 5–3 loss to
the Washington Senators on June 1 when the King of Swat has returned
from his sickbed? As every eye watched and each pencil recorded the
slightest furrow in the brow of the wobbly Bambino, the fluctuations of
labored breath after labored breath, a 21-year-old rookie went to the
plate and hit for shortstop Pee Wee Wanninger. He flied gently to left, and
truth be told, even the Bam himself, pulled from the game in the sixth,
back in the clubhouse, missed the first of 2,130 games Ludwig Heinrich
Gehrig would play in succession for the New York Yankees.

Who knew?

He was a big kid, this Lou Gehrig, raw in the field, shy in personality.
He had been around the scene for a little bit, a local phenomenon signed
off the campus of Columbia University. He was young enough to have developed his approach to hitting in the glow of the Babe's heroics, one of
the first of a first generation of free-swinging imitators, kids who wanted
to hit the ball far as much as they wanted to hit it often.

In June 1923, shortly after scout Paul Krichell convinced him with a
$1,500 bonus to quit college, he went to the newly opened Yankee Sta-
dium for a first workout. The story—maybe true, maybe not—was that

he was told to grab a bat and the one he grabbed belonged to G. H. Ruth, which of course worked just fine. He spent that season and the next in Hartford, busting fences, loved by the local population, and was called up to the big club at the end of both years.

In the spring of '25, he had made the team, then mostly sat on the bench until Huggins decided to shuffle some cards in a losing hand. The day after Ruth returned and Gehrig pinch-hit, the little manager inserted Gehrig at first in favor of Wally Pipp, put Howard Shanks at second in favor of Aaron Ward, and Benny Bengough behind the plate instead of Wally Schang.

The first baseman was the one who stuck for the next 15 seasons.

Krichell had called Ed Barrow after seeing Gehrig for the first time— a game at Rutgers in New Brunswick where he hit two homers—and said he had found "the next Babe Ruth," but "next Babe Ruths" were being discovered everywhere. There seemed to be a "next Babe Ruth" in every town in America. There were young Babe Ruths, old Babe Ruths, female Babe Ruths, even animal Babe Ruths, dogs and cats and chickens that performed some feat of strength. John McGraw had tried out a guy from Texas named Moses Solomon, "the Jewish Babe Ruth," "the Rabbi of Swat," who lasted for only eight at-bats in 1923. The real Babe Ruth had been confronted with Cristobal Torriente during his misadventures in Havana. Torriente was known as "the Cuban Babe Ruth."

"What'd you think?" sportswriters asked the real Ruth.

"Them greasers are punk ballplayers," he replied. "Only a few of them are any good. The guy they calls after me because he made a few homers is as black as a ton and a half of coal in a dark cellar."

Gehrig was the closest thing that would come along. His swing was different from the Ruth swing, tighter, more compact, but he held the bat down at the bottom, next to the knob, and swung hard. His home runs went on a different course, straight and direct as opposed to Ruth's happy parabolas, but they landed in the same place.

Time would come when the two men would be compared in a thousand different areas, from the way they dressed to the way they spoke to the way they ate, drank, and made what each thought was merry, but that was the future. The new kid, the big kid, was good but not spectacular in his debut in 1925, with 20 homers and a .295 average, more than enough to keep his job. The legend would grow that Pipp had begged out with a headache, never to return, but this was not true. What did happen was that Pipp was beaned in batting practice a month later, suffered a fractured skull, played little the rest of the season, and was sold to the Cincinnati Reds in February for $7,500. Gehrig owned the job outright when he went to training camp in 1926.

"Lou Gehrig was sort of a model American young man," Waite Hoyt said. "He was sort of a Jack Armstrong, the all-American boy. . . . He was not very popular at first with the Yankees because, with his teammates, he was one of two or three guys who just lived in a world of their own. He was not a carouser or a nightclub guy or a fellow who sought out entertainment. He was shy, a family guy, in a sense, with his mother."

A look into the Yankee future had come toward the end of the 1925 season, lost this time in the attention paid to Ruth's recent return from tabloid exile and the inattention paid to a seventh-place ball club. On September 10, in the fourth inning at Shibe Park in Philadelphia, A's pitcher Dolly Gray surrendered a leadoff home run to Bob Meusel, a line shot to the center-field bleachers. Ruth, the next batter, pounded the ball over the right-field fence. Gray took hold of his third new baseball of the inning, delivered it to Gehrig, and watched it go over the right-field fence, farther and deeper than the first two shots. This was the first time since 1902 that three major league batters in a row had hit home runs.

The Babe now had a playmate.

The Yankees opened the 1926 season in Boston on April 14, a bone-cold, frozen day at Fenway Park with dignitaries shivering in their overcoats and 12,000 fans in the stands. This was the batting order:

Mark Koenig, shortstop
Earle Combs, center field
Lou Gehrig, first base
Babe Ruth, right field
Bob Meusel, left field
Tony Lazzeri, second base
Joe Dugan, third base
Pat Collins, catcher
Bob Shawkey, pitcher

Gehrig was far from the only change. Only Ruth, Meusel, and Joe Dugan, who had been picked up in the middle of the 1923 season, were left in the everyday lineup from the World Championship team of only three years earlier. First baseman Pipp, shortstop Everett Scott, center fielder Whitey Witt, and catcher Wally Schang all had been sent elsewhere. Second baseman Aaron Ward, whose hitting had been in steady decline and bottomed out at .246 a year earlier, was locked onto the bench.

The reformed Ruth—okay, the semireformed, kind of reformed Ruth—was now a senior man in the operation. It was the start of his seventh season in pinstripes, and only the fading Shawkey had been around longer. Meusel had arrived at the same time as Ruth, but everyone else had been brought aboard to fill out a team picture that had the face of the Sultan of Swat in the middle.

Koenig and Lazzeri were the biggest gambles. How many teams open a season with a rookie double-play combination? Koenig was a nervous, error-prone shortstop from San Francisco who had been obtained from St. Paul in the American Association in the middle of the '25 season. He had replaced the light-hitting Wanninger, who had replaced Scott. Koenig had played 25 games at the end of the year, showing an impressive arm that could compensate for his other shortcomings. Lazzeri, at second, hopefully was a star in the making.

He was a California version of "the next Babe Ruth," a slender, deceptive power hitter also from San Francisco. Five feet 11, maybe 160 pounds, he had put together amazing numbers at Salt Lake City in the Pacific Coast League in 1925, hitting a record 60 home runs, knocking in a record 222 runs, and scoring a record 202 runs. The numbers were suspect because the PCL schedule ran for 200 games and the ball flew in a tiny park at high elevation in Salt Lake, but they couldn't be ignored. His obvious strength came from working as a full-time boilermaker with his father from the time he was 15 years old.

Ed Barrow had paid $55,000 plus three players for Lazzeri. The 22-year-old kid never had seen a big league game, never had been east of the Mississippi River. Would he be overwhelmed? A further complication was that he was epileptic. Some teams had stayed away from him for that reason, wondering what the effects of the disease would be. Other teams had stayed away because he was Italian, a minority not in favor with the white, old-line managers of the game. Was there room for an Italian epileptic? Everybody knew his condition and watched.

"He'd be standing in front of the mirror, combing his hair," Koenig said years later, describing Lazzeri's epilepsy. "Suddenly the comb would fly out of his hand and hit the wall.

"One morning in Chicago he had a fit in the clubhouse. He fell onto the ground and started foaming. I didn't know what to do. I ran out the door without a stitch of clothing to get Hoyt, who was a mortician in the off-season. I figured he'd know something."

With Koenig, Lazzeri, and Gehrig in the lineup, three-fourths of the infield would be handled by virtual rookies. Third base also was a question. Dugan, a terrific fielder and a solid bat, was now 29 years old. He'd missed much of the '25 season after knee surgery. Could he come back? His lifestyle was closest to the Babe's. The same questions that surrounded the Babe surrounded him.

The catcher, Pat Collins, had also been picked up from St. Paul. He had major league experience with the Browns, but they had shuffled him back to the minors. He mostly won the Yankees' starting job by default. Huggins had slated defensive-minded, strong-throwing Benny Bengough from Buffalo for the spot, but Bengough showed up for spring training with a sore arm. He was strong-throwing Benny Bengough no more.

The outfield was more than solid with Ruth, Meusel, and fleet Earle Combs in center. A college graduate and farmer from Kentucky, Combs had arrived in 1923, missed most of '24 with a broken leg, and developed quietly in the midst of the chaos in '25. He was a throwback to the John McGraw School of Baseball, graceful, pesky, a perfect setup man for Ruth and Meusel and Gehrig at the plate, a perfect defensive standout between two large-sized outfielders. He didn't smoke, chew, spit, drink, or cuss. He read the Bible in his free time.

The pitching was familiar, with the hard-throwing Hoyt, veteran Sam Jones, and Herb Pennock, Ruth's friend, the master of three different curveballs, each one curvier than the last. The big pitching addition was Urban Shocker, picked up from the Browns in the deal involving Everett Scott. Shocker was another veteran, one of those grandfathered spitballers, very tough to hit. He also had a medical condition, a problem with a valve in his heart, so serious that he couldn't lie down; he had to sleep sitting or standing every night. He would sit up for the entire trip in the Pullman cars. How long could he last?

This was the basic team, pretty much built for the years ahead but playing in the present. The preseason prognosticators saw a lot of work here, hard and almost impossible work. The prognosticators did not prognosticate good things.

"The Yankees are dawdling through the gestures of spring training in St. Petersburg, paying the least possible attention to Miller Huggins, who reciprocates their disinterest and pays the least possible attention to them," Westbrook Pegler wrote. "They will start home a few weeks hence, about as well organized and disciplined as a panic."

"Despite reports to the contrary, the Yankees are not the worst ball club in the world," Ford Frick wrote in the *New York World* in March from St. Petersburg. "They look a bit better than the Boston Red Sox or the Cleveland Indians. Over a long schedule they probably would finish ahead of Saskatoon and Medicine Hat. But finishing ahead of Philadelphia, St. Louis, Detroit and other American League clubs is quite another question."

Frick, who went on to praise the revitalized Ruth as "the one largest asset in a field of probable liabilities," was joined in this thought by most other writers, even by Miller Huggins. The Yankees manager cautioned that the excitement around this team would come in two or three years.

Then the games began.

Sloppy at first, comical in two losses to the Boston Braves by 18–4 and 16–2 scores, the Yankees finished up their time in St. Petersburg by winning their final six exhibitions. They then went on the annual jaunt north, this time with the Brooklyn Robins, the forerunners to the Dodgers, and as the teams hit the now-familiar stops of the Babe's tour of sickness a year earlier, Knoxville and Asheville and all the rest, a powerhouse grew daily in front of small-town eyes. Just like that. Koenig could play, and Lazzeri, indeed, could hit, and Dugan had recovered, and Gehrig certainly could hit, and Meusel and Combs and . . . Ruth was back! Every day Robins manager Uncle Wilbert Robinson rolled out an array of pitchers, and every day this new lineup pinned their ears back. Twelve games were played on the trip, ending with a game at the Stadium. Twelve games, all twelve, were won by the Yanks, ending with a 14–7 romp at the Stadium.

"The 18 straight games the Yankees won during their exhibition campaign . . . have caused the experts to look a second time at the array Miller Huggins has assembled," Richards Vidmer wrote in the *Times*. "At first it did not seem the Yankees would be even on the outside looking in; now it is highly probable they will be well on the inside of the first division."

"The Yankees have the greatest hitting team that has ever been assembled under one tent," Wilbert Robinson said more forcefully at the end of his team's succession of shellackings.

The rebuilding process had taken exactly one spring.

In the chilly opener at Fenway, the reconfigured Bombers from the Bronx outlasted the Red Sox, 12–11. At the end of April, they put together an eight-game winning streak to sit easily in first place with a 13–3 record. At the end of May, they put together a 16-game winning streak for a 30–9 record. They cruised through the season, withstanding a little late charge by the Indians in September, and won the pennant by three games. They won 91 games, lost 63.

The Babe hit .372, had 47 home runs and 146 RBI, and caught a baseball dropped from an airplane that flew over Mitchell Field on Long Island. (It took seven attempts for the Babe to catch the ball. He was a dizzy, sweaty mess by the end.) Huggins told him to concentrate on catching baseballs hit by humans, not thrown out of airplanes. The king was back on his throne.

The new life, the new team, all seemed to fit together for the big man in the summer of 1926. He had settled in and settled down. Not a lot, understand. The "mind of a 15-year-old" that Ban Johnson mentioned was still there, but this was the 15-year-old who finally had figured out that if he stayed after school every day he was going to miss a lot of fun. The concept of consequences had arrived and been acknowledged. Give up a little to gain more. That finally made sense.

He moved back to the Ansonia, but spent more time at Claire's apartment on West 79th Street than he did in his suite. The farm was sold in the middle of the season, a worry off his list. Helen and Dorothy, both in Boston, would visit his hotel when the Yankees played at Fenway Park, but mostly were out of the everyday equation. He still chased women with a hound-dog sense of urgency—teammates talked about how he and a waitress had disappeared behind a sand dune in the first weeks at St. Petersburg—and still ate and drank prodigious amounts, and still stayed up later than just about anybody else, but the frenzy of it all was missing. He had developed a better, modified pace. He even seemed to dress better, leaving some of the more flamboyant outfits in the closet. The dissipation mostly had dissipated.

"After 1925, he was a good guy," Waite Hoyt said. "The ballplayers thought the world of him. He was well regarded by the ballplayers."

He still had the obligatory court appearances in 1926. There was a mix-up in Massachusetts about unpaid state taxes. (He claimed he was a New York resident, not a Sudbury resident.) There was a speeding ticket, doing 33 miles per hour again on Riverside Drive, settled with a $25 fine, no jail time, because he had been clean for two years. There was even the obligatory fistfight with a teammate, this time with the rookie Koenig. Ruth badgered the shortstop about some errors during an exhibition in Baltimore. Koenig had heard enough and jumped the big man with a flurry of punches back in the dugout. Ruth then held Koenig's arms back until other players intervened.

None of these things seemed to matter as much. They were symbolic of nothing, over, done. Normal. The most startling difference of the new life was Ruth's relationship with Huggins. The nicknames and the defiance were gone. The players who liked the little manager, who liked him very much, were the ones who listened to him. Ruth now listened to him.

"Huggins was sort of a fatherly guy," Waite Hoyt said. "He was sort of a baseball father and sort of a psychiatrist. He had a couch in his office, and I was on that couch more than I was on the field. I was always being lectured, because he always said to me, 'You should lead the league every year with your stuff, should lead the league, but you don't because you don't concentrate. You have friends in the stands and you're worrying whether your friends are there or not. You don't concentrate.' And it would go on for hours."

A moment came during the season when Huggins wanted to attack an umpire for some call. Ruth held him back. Hoyt loved that picture, remembered it for years. Ruth now worked with Huggins, and Huggins worked with Ruth. The father-psychiatrist had made his breakthrough.

Instead of hiring a private detective to follow the slugger when the Yankees visited Chicago this year, Barrow and Huggins found a more subtle approach. Ruth came to the lobby of the Del Prado Hotel one night, dressed and perfumed, ready for a taste of Windy City decadence, and found Brother Matthias from long-ago St. Mary's Industrial School sitting in a chair near the elevator.

An international Eucharistic Congress was being held in the city, and the Yankees had paid the bill to bring the good brother west. He invited Ruth to dinner, and what could the big man say? They ate, the brother gave counsel about life and responsibility, and they were back at the hotel by 11 o'clock. Goodnight, George. Goodnight, Brother. Who could run the streets after a night with Brother Matthias?

The net effect of everything—the better conditioning, the quieter life, all of it—was the wonderful season. In addition to the 47 homers, the .372 batting average, the Babe had 10 sacrifice bunts. He was part of team success. The nickname "Murderers' Row" had been given to the Yankees' lineup back in 1921, but never really stuck. It did now, and there was no doubt about who was the most efficient murderer.

The Bam was first in the major leagues in home runs (47) by an incredible margin: Al Simmons was second in the American League with 19, and Hack Wilson was at the top of the NL with 21. (Lazzeri had 18, Gehrig 16.) He had the same kind of margin in RBI, his 145 far ahead of George Burns from Cleveland (114) in the AL and Jim Bottomley's 120 in the NL. If his batting average had been five points higher, catching the .378 of Detroit's Heinie Manush, he would have been a Triple Crown winner for all of baseball. He would have been the easy MVP if rules at the time didn't state that a player could win the award only once. (Burns of the Indians was given the honor by default.)

As the Yankees went into the 1926 World Series against the St. Louis Cardinals, he was again the center of all attention. The sportswriters saw the Series as a matchup of the Cardinals' overall strength against the Yankees' hitting, which translated into the Babe. How would the Babe do? That would determine the outcome. The sportswriters made the Yankees favorites.

"We'll beat 'em," the big man said as he "elbowed his way through the crowd of small boys and men who met the Yankee Special" at Penn Station in one report. "There'll be nothing to it."

A newly formed organization, the National Broadcasting Company, which had purchased New York station WEAF during the season, broadcast the games on a 25-station radio network across the country and into Canada. This was the first true, easy-to-hear broadcast of the event. It was estimated that more than 15 million people would listen, an idea so staggering that the *Times* reported after the first game "in a fraction of a second the thrill of each exciting incident ran from coast to coast and probably from below the Mexican border to points around Hudson Bay."

The play-by-play announcer was 38-year-old Graham McNamee, whose excited portrayals of the action would set a standard for sports broadcasting. An out-of-work salesman and part-time baritone singer, he was on jury duty at federal court for $3 a day in 1923 when he walked into the nearby WEAF studios at 195 Broadway during his lunch break.

He was hired immediately for a job that required him to "open and close pianos for artistes, answer telephone calls, escort unaccompanied young ladies home after programs, sing operatic and religious selections and do some announcing." The "do some announcing" part became the most important.

He and partner Phil Carlin eventually did a six-hour show every afternoon—with an hour out for dinner—and they also covered the political conventions and sports events of the day. His voice became so familiar and accepted by America that recordings of it were analyzed in laboratories to pick up the cadence and frequencies to teach to young announcers.

The *Times* ran full-page summaries of his broadcast of every Series game. Sport as entertainment had never come close to reaching this kind of audience. The mind reeled at the thought of farmers in Iowa, ranchers in Texas sitting down and being part of each Series moment as it happened.

"We are just about to go on," McNamee told the country as the Series began. "The umpire is behind the plate now putting on his mask and adjusting his chest protector. The diamond and ground and everything look beautiful. The dark brown chocolate color of the base line and the beautiful ground is wonderful. Around the edges is a running track and still around that is an embankment of green. . . ."

The House That Ruth Built sat right there, perfect, in front of everyone. The white of the home uniforms and the gray of the visitors' could be seen in faraway living rooms. McNamee would describe the color of ladies' hats, the passing of advertising airplanes, the chill of the air or the warmth of the sun, the exhaustion felt at the seventh-inning stretch. Magic. Now he described the Babe, coming to the plate for the first time in the home half of the first inning:

> Babe Ruth at bat. He is taking his usual hand, a tremendous adulation from the New York crowd. Babe bats lefthanded with his right foot tremendously extended toward the plate. A slow ball, too low—ball one. Another ball, outside and low—two balls for the Babe. Ruth, one out and a man on first, Combs. Babe gets a tremendous slice at the ball, and he throws that entire body of his onto the right leg and pivots with it. Again, a little low, over the pan, but a little for three balls, no strikes on Babe Ruth.
>
> The Babe is quieter at the plate than he usually is. He usually is

rather nervous and moves around quite a bit, you know, but today he is very quiet. Four balls. The Babe has been passed. (Yelling and shouting.)

The Series that America heard evolved into a classic. The teams split the first two games, then went to St. Louis, where the Cardinals won the third. In the fourth game, Ruth exploded. He hit home runs in his first two at-bats, walked in the next, then hit his third homer in the sixth as the Yankees took a 10–5 win to tie the best-of-seven Series at two home games apiece.

Three home runs in a game was not only a Series record but seemed to border on the unbelievable. Each shot was longer than the last, the final one bouncing in the center-field bleachers and skipping out of Sportsman's Park. Newspapers around the country the next day printed large pictures of the park with dotted lines and arrows following the path of the three balls. One newspaper even printed a large picture of Yankee Stadium and dotted lines to show where the balls would have gone if hit in New York. The man who described the final blast probably had the emotion right.

"Oh, what a shot!" McNamee screamed. "Directly over second. The boys are all over him over there. One of the boys is riding on Ruth's back. Oh, what a shot! Directly over second base, far into the bleachers out in center field, and almost on a line and then that dumbbell, where is he, who told me not to talk about Ruth! Oh boy! Not that I love Ruth, but oh how I love to see a shot like that! Wow . . . that is a mile and a half from here. You know what I mean."

The Yankees won the fifth game in St. Louis, 3–2, in ten innings, which brought the Series back to New York with the home team only one win away from the World Championship. Alas, Grover Cleveland Alexander, the veteran Cardinals pitcher who was one of the few men in baseball known to not only drink more than Ruth but feel the effects less, masterfully shut down the Yanks, 10–2, to set up a winner-take-all seventh game at the Stadium.

On a cold, wet October day, wind gusting everywhere, Waite Hoyt went to the mound against Jesse Haines. Ruth put the Yankees ahead, 1–0, with a shot in the third, his fourth homer in the Series, and made a spectacular running, diving catch on the warning track against Bob O'Farrell. The Cardinals came back in the fourth with three unearned runs off Hoyt. It was one of those maddening rallies filled with a botched double-play ball by Koenig, a dropped ball in left by Meusel, and a pop fly by the Cards' Tommy Thevenow that scored the final two runs.

"With a two-strikes-no-balls count, I threw him a curveball that was a foot outside the plate," Hoyt said. "I was criticized for that later on, for allowing Thevenow to hit the ball with a count of two strikes and no balls. But the ball was a bad ball. It was a curveball, and it was about a foot off the plate, outside. Thevenow reached out, and he popped the ball over the head of Lazzeri.

"The ball never reached the outfield. It hit the mud and twisted around, and Lazzeri couldn't find it, and the runs scored while he looked."

The Yankees scored a run to come within 3–2 and then loaded the bases with two outs in the seventh. St. Louis manager Rogers Hornsby pulled Haines and brought Alexander out of the bullpen, a move that surprised everyone, especially Alexander. Forty years old, hungover after celebrating his game six win, maybe even still half-drunk, he came to the mound to face Lazzeri.

"Are you all right?" Hornsby asked as he gave Alexander the ball.

"I'm okay," Alexander mumbled in reply. "But no warm-up pitches. I don't want to give anything away."

The first pitch, no warm-ups, was a called strike. On the second, Lazzeri swung and lifted a long fly to left that everyone thought was a grand-slam homer until a gust of wind sent it just foul. On the third pitch, Lazzeri expected another fastball. Alexander, known as Alexander the Great, threw a slow curve that was so low, according to the *New York Times*, that "a Singer midget couldn't have hit it." Lazzeri swung for strike three, the end of the rally.

Alexander retired the Yankees one-two-three in the eighth, then took care of the first two batters in the ninth. This set up a confrontation with Ruth. Working carefully, Alexander took the count to 3–2, then walked the Bam. Bob Meusel came to the plate, swung at a pitch, and Ruth tried to steal second.

And was thrown out. Easily.

It was—and probably still is—the weirdest end to a World Series. Ruth explained later that he had a hunch. The decision to steal was his decision. He didn't think the Yankees would collect two hits in a row to bring him home. He tried to put himself in position to come home with one hit. It simply didn't work out.

"Ruth is walked again for the fourth time today," Graham McNamee told the country. "One strike on Bob Meusel. Going down to second!!! The game is over! Babe tried to steal second and is put out, catcher to second!"

The Series was done.

There was surprisingly little debate about Ruth's bold decision. Miller Huggins defended his man.

"We needed an unexpected move," the manager said. "Had Ruth made the steal, it would have been declared the smartest piece of baseball in the history of World Series play."

The enduring Big Bam story from the World Series thus was not the attempted steal of second. It wasn't even the three-home-run game or the four home runs in the Series or the .300 batting average or even the ten records he set. It was the story of Johnny Sylvester, the 11-year-old boy from Essex Falls, New Jersey, pulled from death's grasp at the last moment by the heroics of a big lug half a continent away. Fact and myth and good PR, the new science, merged with marketing and America's great love for pathos to create perfection. Johnny Sylvester and the Babe. This was the best story of them all.

"(SPECIAL TO THE NEW YORK TIMES) ESSEX FALLS, N.J., OCT 7.—John Dale Sylvester, 11 years old, to whom physicians allotted thirty minutes of life when he was struck with blood poisoning last week, was pronounced well on the road to recovery this afternoon, after he had contentedly listened to radio returns of the Yankees' defeat of the Cardinals."

The story started small and grew out of control, like the tales of the rescue of the cocker spaniel that fell in the well, the Boy Scout who stops a robbery, the old-timer who regains his hearing after he falls off the ladder. Somewhere a push came along to convert the mundane into a national fascination. One step led to another.

The first step: Johnny, kicked by a horse, sustained some sort of injury and was confined to his bed. The injury was to the head or spine, according to the newspaper a man read. (Readers of the *Times* were told it was blood poisoning.) The severity of the injury also varied, from simple inconvenience to—as the *Times* said—30 minutes from the Grim Reaper.

Johnny loved baseball, loved Babe Ruth. His well-connected father, Horace C. Sylvester Jr., vice president of the National City Bank of New York, trying to cheer up the lad in any way possible, sent a wire to friends in St. Louis asking if they could obtain autographed baseballs from both the Yankees and Cardinals. The baseballs arrived by air mail, apparently accompanied by a note from the Babe that said he would hit a home run for Johnny. The great man then, of course, hit three in one game.

Eureka! Johnny's condition improved. Doctors were "baffled" by how this had happened. Must have been the baseballs. Must have been a miracle. Must have been the Babe.

The second step: someone alerted the press. The hand of Christy Walsh, though never matched publicly for fingerprints, would lead any list of suspects.

The third step: madness. Tabloid chaos.

"Did Babe Ruth knock a homer?" asked Johnny in one typical account. "His father displayed the evening newspaper. 'Babe Ruth Hits Three Homers' was the big black type at the top of the first page. Johnny sighed and went to sleep, a baseball in each hand. When he woke up, the nurse took his temperature. It had gone down two degrees."

Eureka.

Stories about the Babe and kids were sports page favorites. Walsh loved them. Writers loved them. People loved them. The basic thread always was that the Caliph of Clout, the Rajah of Rap, the Behemoth of Bangs loved kids and kids loved him because he was one of them. He was pictured often with kids. He appeared at events for kids. He sold a bunch of products to kids. There was a tale, once a year, maybe twice, maybe more, about some kind thing he did for some kid. The runaway from Kansas always went home to start life anew. The tyke in the wheelchair had a signed baseball and a new, bright outlook.

The messages always were sweet and uplifting, almost Sunday school homilies. St. Francis of Assisi didn't love birds as much as the Babe loved kids. A layer of truth always existed—there was a kid and there was an interaction with the Babe—but the words always seemed like they were spread too thick and deep and too absolutely perfect.

"For every picture you see of the Babe in a hospital, he visits fifty without publicity," *New York Sun* sportswriter Bill Slocum, one of Ruth's ghosts, once wrote. "I know. I get him there. Every road trip it'll happen three or four times. . . . I'll be going to bed around 11 and I'll meet the Babe. . . . He'll say, 'Bill, I promised some guy I'd go out to a hospital tomorrow morning. Saint Something-or-Other hospital. Find out which one it is. I'll meet you at eight o'clock here in the lobby.'"

Was that the way it really was?

Fred Lieb, in his memoir *Baseball As I Have Known It*, gave a different Slocum opinion. He said Slocum always thought the Babe's love for kids was "a sham and a put-on." Lieb wrote the tale of Slocum, angry with Ruth, telling him this face-to-face. Lieb quoted Slocum: "You're smart enough to know that your visits to sick and maimed kids square you with the club and the public for some of the rotten things you've done and all the trouble you've caused Miller Huggins." Lieb then said, though, that he did believe that Ruth cared for kids.

Truth no doubt lived at an address in the middle. Kids loved Ruth. That was fact. He was a perpetual department store Santa. They followed him, mobbed him, reinvented him in their minds at home every night while they stared at his picture. He, in turn, did his job quite well. He made the stops, delivered the appropriate "ho-ho-ho's."

Though negative anecdotes seeped out in later years—he spit on this kid, kicked this other one, etc.—he certainly did not hate children. He listened with some animation to their words. He signed the autographs. He went to a lot of hospitals, orphanages, and Boy Scout jamborees. Put in the proper situation, he was good with his juvenile public. He simply wasn't as good as the newspapers made him out to be. No human being could be that good.

Christy Walsh or maybe a reporter—and it had to be someone, because the newspapers had been alerted and sent photographers—convinced him to visit young Johnny Sylvester two days after the Series ended. Ruth was playing an exhibition that day anyway at Bradley Beach, New Jersey, against the Brooklyn Royal Colored Giants and was supposed to be honored at a reception there before the game. The stop made sense, even if he would be late for the reception.

He walked into Johnny's room and flashbulbs popped, and he asked how Johnny was doing and made small talk, and the reporters scribbled and the wheels of commerce moved. ("Nice looking brother you have there," the Babe said. "That's my sister," Johnny replied.) The scene was a postcard to the public, due to be reproduced in many saccharine variations for years.

"Supposing that while you were sick a baseball came from Babe Ruth himself because his name was on it and he promised to hit a home run for you in the World Series, a private home run and all, and then he hit *three* of them," Paul Gallico wrote in the *Daily News* the next day.

I say just supposing. That's all dreams are anyway—supposing. And then supposing one day mother came in all excited and said, "Johnny there's someone here to see you," and in walked Babe Ruth right out of the newspapers except he didn't have his baseball suit on and he came over to your bed and held out his hand to shake and said, "Hello, Johnny; how do you feel now?" What would you do? What would you say? What would the fellows say? Not just someone dressed up like Ruth, mind you, but Babe Ruth himself, and he'd left a baseball game and a lot of people with silk hats and medals and things waiting for him while he called on you because he heard you were sick and needed him. . . . Life has no greater beauty to offer than that our dreams shall, at some time or other, acquire even a faint tinge of reality.

Two sportswriters, John Drebinger and Frank Graham, years later told about a meeting on an elevator between Ruth and a stranger, a man who shook Ruth's hand, introduced himself as Johnny Sylvester's uncle, and thanked the slugger for being such a help. The man left and Ruth said, "Now who the hell is Johnny Sylvester?" It didn't matter. He always was bad with names. The story was the story.

Votive candles now flickered again under the picture of the man who a year ago had been seen as an overweight, overpaid, out-of-shape adulterer. The new science of public relations seemed to work quite well.

CHAPTER SEVENTEEN

MARSHALL HUNT put together his ultimate "Babe and Me" exclusive in the first two months of 1927. The Babe was in Hollywood making a movie called *The Babe Comes Home*, and he secured for Hunt a low-paying but heavily privileged role as "a technical adviser." Hunt convinced the *Daily News* that he should do a series on the whole thing, an easy bit of salesmanship, and headed west. He arrived two days into production while the crew was filming at a small amusement park at Venice Beach.

"Stop the camera!" the Babe shouted in mock horror when Hunt appeared. "This guy is everywhere!"

Unlike the Babe's first venture into the movies, when the check ultimately bounced, this was a big-time operation for First National Pictures, the leading studio of the day. The director was Tim Wilde, who had directed many of Harold Lloyd's comedies. The co-star was Anna Q. Nilsson, a bona-fide leading lady.

A native of Ystad, Sweden, she was the first of many Scandinavian beauties to capture Hollywood with their startling good looks. She had arrived in the town in 1910, 22 years old, and found immediate work as a model. The modeling led to movies, and she cranked them out, 84 films between 1911 and 1917 alone, her Swedish accent no problem in the age of silent film.

An accident while riding a horse in 1925, however, threatened her career. Thrown by the horse, she landed against a stone wall and was paralyzed for a year. She returned to Sweden, where she worked her way back through physical therapy to a point where she could walk and move again. *The Babe Comes Home* was part of her comeback.

It was generally known that she was not happy with the casting. The Babe was a late selection for an unnamed script that had been written. The original plan was for an actor to play the role of the slugger. Then someone had the idea to recruit the Babe himself and tweak the story. Anna Q. didn't want to be paired with a baseball player, even if he was the most famous baseball player of all. There was little relationship between the star and co-star. The movie was made in parts, and Anna Q. and the Babe had only a few scenes together.

The plot was boy meets girl, sports version. Babe played a character named Babe Dugan, star slugger of the Los Angeles Angels. Nilsson played Vernie, the washerwoman who had to clean all of Babe Dugan's dirty, tobacco-stained uniforms. By chance they meet, fall in love on a roller coaster, and soon plan to be married. Vernie has only one request: Babe has to stop chewing tobacco. He complies but, alas, finds that his hitting suffers when his routine changes. He is headed to bat in the big moment of the big game, of course, struggling, when he looks into the stands and sees Vernie, who, of course, takes pity and throws him a plug of chewing tobacco. Ta-da. Representatives of the American tobacco industry presumably would stand and cheer along with Vernie as he resumes masticating and spitting and blasts the ball out of the park.

Marshall Hunt started typing.

"The scene is Wrigley Field, a baseball enclosure in these remote precincts, and the time is the present," Hunt wrote. "George Herman Ruth, an athlete of considerable fame, a director, his five assistants, a general supervisor and his assistants, a guardian of the script and her assistant, a chief electrician and minor electricians, a corps of property men (the property consisting of two baseballs and a dozen uniforms), a score or more of ex pugilists, pretzel molders, barbers, tightrope walkers and second story men posing as ballplayers, all are discovered in the act of creating a moving picture in which Mr. Ruth and Anna Q. Nilsson will be featured. The picture is yet an infant without a name."

For the next 20 days, the stories continued. Hunt took great delight in describing the former boxers cast as baseball players, the director's sketchy knowledge of baseball, the Babe's ham-handed walk through moviemaking. This was the perfect out-of-context way to have fun and present the ungainliness, the humanity, of the character of George Herman Ruth.

No moment was too small to overlook. The Babe is wearing makeup! He tries a number 6, the same foundation used by stars like Ramon Navarro and John Gilbert, but finds it is too white, too light. Number 5 is the ticket, a ruddier, sunburned look. The Babe is looking at rushes! That har-har-har is from the big man himself. He thinks he is hilarious. The rain arrives! The filming is done indoors. The Babe wins the game and has to kiss the girl! He kisses the girl! Hunt covered it all with great enthusiasm.

"Does Mr. Ruth express his love with fawning looks, with sickly grins, with puppy-like grimaces?" Hunt wrote about the Babe's big love scene. "He does not! There is nothing Westphalian about the wooing of the Babe. His features register tender affection as he first embraces the flaxen button cruncher. And in the final fadeout, there is warmth, intensity of passion burning in the optics of a man who would do murder to an umpire during the summer. And when lips meet lips, the connubial seal, there is a sizzling sound—hot lips! Hot dog! Alacazam!"

The circulation of the *Daily News* had rocketed past one million in the first weeks of 1926 and would approach 1,250,000 by the end of 1927. It had doubled the circulation of its nearest competitor, the *New York Journal*, and captured the attention of the common man. An advertising campaign started in 1923 called "Tell It to Sweeney" focused on what the paper thought was its audience: the working-class families of the big city, the first and second generations of immigrants. Don't tell the story to the Stuyvesants and the bluebloods, tell it to Sweeney. The bluebloods had the *New York Times* and the other papers. Sweeney had the *News*.

Sweeney loved all the pictures. Sweeney loved the stories of crime and political shenanigans. Sweeney loved the comics. Sweeney loved the movies and sports. Sweeney loved the Babe. The *News*—through Hunt— was more than happy to present the Babe.

"The Babe Breaks Pet Bat in Hollywood" (headline): "You will recall that for years the Bambino treasured a pet bat," Hunt wrote. "He guarded it zealously. No other player ever used it. The bat was one with which he knocked three home runs in one World Series game. That bat enabled him to break a dozen records in the last series between the Yankees and Cards.

"But yesterday, while rehearsing a home run blow, he connected with a ball with such power that the club was split from end to end. A piteous expression wrinkled the features of the Babe. His head dropped. He trudged disconsolately to a chair. Smelling salts were applied. . . .

"Whee! The Bam's a Director Now" (headline): "The outfielders go to their positions and orders are megaphoned to them by Mr. Wilde," Hunt wrote. "But Babe shakes his head. He takes the megaphone. The Bambino: 'You, you left field and you, center field guy, move to the right! There's a left handed batter at the plate in this shot. What're you doing so far to the left? Move, you boilermakers, move to the right! What league do you think we're in? A right hander's league?'

"Mr. Wilde nods his approval. The Bambino has become a director!"

The amount of space devoted in the slim subway tabloid to these softer-than-soft news offerings was amazing. They were a tribute to the Babe's commercial popularity, a window open to the giddy possibilities that danced in workingmen's heads. Wouldn't it be great to live like that! Sometimes too the stories showed some not-so-giddy realities.

In his 13th installment, for example, Hunt described a particular scene in the movie. Again, he danced lightly, looking for the laugh. The story was headlined "Babe Gets in Shape with an Ethiopian."

"The scenario requires that the Bambino throw baseballs at a target in an amusement park which releases a trap and causes an Ethiopian to be precipitated into a pool of water," Hunt wrote. "Each time the gentleman of color drops from his perch in a wire cage into the water the Babe is presented with a doll by the barker.

"The generous hero of the photoplay, accompanied by the pure and wholesome laundry maiden he is wooing, causes the Ethiopian to cool his ears in the pool twelve times and he is presented with twelve dolls which, with a gesture of magnificent generosity, he distributes among a group of children who gaze in open-mouthed astonishment at his accuracy in flopping the Ethiopian into the water."

Hunt not only presented the picture but offered an extension of it:

"What a great benefit would the caged Ethiopian prove to pitchers in training camps!" he wrote. "Throwing a curve or fastball to a catcher whom they will face all summer becomes monotonous. The catcher's glove is not stationary. The catcher can hop or leap to receive the ball. There is no great thrill, nothing to improve accuracy to a marked degree.

"The installation of an Ethiopian at a training camp would serve to stimulate the pitchers. A certain kick is derived from hitting the smallish target and watching the gentleman of color plunge into the pool."

And finally:

"The supply of Ethiopians in Florida is practically inexhaustible and the cost of the accuracy developing mechanism would be negligible considering the effectiveness it is almost certain to produce."

Sweeney probably was not a black man.

Artie McGovern had arrived early in the proceedings, leaving his gym in New York to personally handle the off-season health of his most notable client. Hunt thought that Ed Barrow had sent the trainer west, but Ruth certainly had the right of consent or refusal and obviously had consented. The bouncy McGovern, as he stated in a letter to *New York Post* sportswriter Walter Trumbull, was more than happy with what he found.

"When I left the East to come out here, take the Babe in hand, and try to duplicate the job of last year, I thought the publicity concerning Ruth's being in good physical condition due to golf, tennis and other sports was the bunk," Artie wrote. "But when I caught up with the big fellow, I received a very pleasant surprise. He really is in good physical condition. Most of those in the East figured as I did that a 14-week vaudeville tour was likely to put the rollers under anybody. The truth was that most of Ruth's tour was in this part of the country and he has availed himself of every opportunity to get out on the golf course, not for the sake of exercise, but because he loves the game.

"When I checked the Babe's weight and measurements I found him to be 10 pounds lighter than he was at this time a year ago. In other words, he is down to 231 pounds and his best weight is around 220 or 222, so there is not a great deal of work for me to do beyond a general systemic toning up and a concentration on the abdominal muscles. This will be easy in conjunction with the vast amount of exercise he is getting on the picture. The studio has constructed for Ruth a handball court and exercise room, supplying all that is necessary for us to work with."

Hunt was enthralled by the exercise regimen. He noted that Ruth was out on Hollywood Boulevard by 6:30 in the morning, running distances from three to five miles as passing motorists and housewives stared. What a sight! Maybe "Tom Mix could be seen on a horse once in a while in Hollywood and Doug [Fairbanks] and Mary [Pickford] might be seen in the comforts of a limousine and there's no telling where Lon Chaney might be seen, but here was a hero on his own hoof!" The Babe would return to the Hollywood Plaza, where Artie would give him a rubdown.

Exercise would run through the movie workday. Many of the scenes required physical activity from the Babe. He was always running, throwing, swinging a bat, sliding into home, again and again. Every noon would be an exercise show in itself.

"The professor [McGovern] would appear with boxing gloves, a medicine ball, a hand ball, a rope, a training table, tennis racquets, a grim determination and a small motor truck," Hunt wrote. "Lunch for the Babe between 12 to 1? No! For ten minutes the professor and the Babe would box for all that was in them. McGovern would instruct the Bambino to stand upright while the professor would slam 50 virile blows to the tummy of the Babe. Ruth did not flinch. A hard midriff there, brethren!

"Tennis. Five minutes of rope skipping. Passing of the medicine ball. Exercises on the training table placed in the middle of the tennis courts on the company lot. A great show this, too, with hundreds of movie extras and stars and officials to look on in rapt approval.

"And to top off the exhibition, Prof. McGovern would mount the back end of the truck and command the Bambino to follow the truck wherever it might go. It usually went two miles; the professor standing on the rear and shouting to the driver to increase speed and daring Babe to pass the truck."

At night, Artie sometimes would have the Babe run sprints in the corridors of the Plaza. Sometimes Artie would spar with him in the corridors, lively sessions complete with whoops and hollers. Other residents of the hotel complained. Management was not amused.

The result of all this work was that the Babe was in even better shape now than he had been at the start of the 1926 turnaround season. He had been following the McGovern plan for over 14 months. What other player in all of baseball was doing the things he was doing, sustained workouts under an expert in physical fitness? The image of the overweight hedonist continued—the *News* ran a cartoon to illustrate Hunt's story that showed a black janitor saying, "Great Day. Ah thought its was a elephunt!!!" as a stocky Ruth ran past—but the image was wrong. The Babe was as ready as anyone in his game for the 1927 season.

McGovern reported a favorite Hollywood moment. The producers of

the film wanted to fill tiny Wrigley Field with fans for one day of shooting, so they placed an ad in the paper saying that the Babe would give a
home run exhibition for an hour before the filming. The ad worked, and
the stands were filled when the Babe came to the plate. The boxer-
ballplayers were sent to the field to shag. A pitcher was stationed at the
mound and instructed to throw only fat and straight strikes. The show
began.

"For one hour the Babe stood at the plate banging balls over the
fence," McGovern said. "The pitcher started with 12 dozen balls and
when they called a halt there were only 19 left, which means that the balance were scattered around the surrounding real estate."

Yes, the Babe was ready. He had done what he was told to do.

"The poor Babe," Marshall Hunt said, remembering the California trip.
"He saw all this stuff around—the most beautiful women in the world—
and he couldn't have any of it. Artie put him to bed at nine o'clock in the
midst of all of this unless he had to work over at the studio. Broke the
poor Babe's heart. He never was in the midst of so much and got so little,
you see.

"The phone rang all the time, and finally Artie got permission from Ed
Barrow to tell the operator to lie like hell, so Babe was under wraps for
six or seven weeks."

Hunt was not in training and could take advantage of the situation.
He rolled around the town in the chauffeur-driven limousine the studio
had at his disposal 24 hours per day. He went to other motion picture lots
and watched other movies being made. He ate at the best restaurants,
played golf, met interesting people, roared through the Raymond Chandler streets and boulevards of Los Angeles that soon would become
world-famous as the city and the movie industry grew. Even more than in
New York, there was the feeling here of growth, expansion, possibility.

Hunt wound up one night at the home of Christy Walsh's father in the
Hollywood hills. The view from the living room was the great spill of
lights of the city. It was like looking down from a cloud. The cloud had
plush leather couches and good food and drink. What could be more
beautiful? The days went past, he said, "a mile a minute."

One night he stayed in his room at the hotel to read. A knock came at
the door. The Babe and Artie had someplace to go. Alas, the Babe had

promised to sign 250 baseballs for some charity, but now didn't have time. Could Marshall sign them? He went to the Babe's room and signed the Babe's name 250 times, leaving the balls on the bed. The Babe was grateful, especially because Hunt had become quite proficient at copying his name, but in the morning he had some second thoughts. What kind of havoc could someone wreak if he were a good forger?

"Don't get too good with that signature, kid," the Babe advised Hunt over breakfast.

The few bits of solid news from the motion picture capital involved finances. Walsh convinced the Babe at last to invest in some annuities, and an announcement was made on February 7, the Babe's supposed 33rd birthday, that he had "fined himself" $1,000 per each year of his life and invested the money. It was another visible sign of his reluctant maturity (the Babe would later try to take out some of the money and be distressed that he couldn't get at it), and another sign of great financial times. Even the Babe was investing!

A more substantial story concerned the Babe's contract. How much did he want? How much would he get? He had played for $52,000 a year for the past five years, and when the Yankees sent a contract for the same figure for 1927 to the Plaza, he quickly sent it back unsigned. Ty Cobb recently had signed for a reported $75,000 with the Philadelphia A's (a figure later determined to be $60,000), and conjecture soon whirred in New York about how much the Babe would want and how hard it would be for Col. Ruppert to sign him.

The Babe said nothing as he finished work on the movie. The last week featured 3:00 A.M. bedtimes and 7:00 A.M. Artie McGovern wake-up calls, everything in a rush because the star had to be finished by noon on February 26 to make his train back to the East Coast. Everyone associated with the production agreed that the Babe had worked hard. Ethel Shannon, an actress in the film, called the Babe "a second Roscoe Arbuckle." She said Anna Q. had been upset because the Babe was too funny. Director Wilde said Ruth had added "at least six belly laughs" to the finished product. It was movie talk, typical overpraise as part of the promotion, but the Babe loved it. He talked about a possible movie career.

On February 25, the day before he left, he finally sent a letter to the Colonel with his demands. He gave a copy to Hunt, who printed it in the *News*. Ruth wanted $100,000 per season for two years, plus an extra

$7,750 to pay his back fines. He called the Yankees' offer of $52,000 "an insult" and said the team more than made his salary back in just the exhibition games it forced him to play during the year. He lamented that he was caught, alas, in the contractual bind that was part of baseball.

"If I were in any other business I would probably receive a new contract at higher salary without request," the Babe wrote in part. "Or rival employers would bid for my services. Baseball law forces me to work for the New York club or remain idle, but it does not prevent a man from being paid for his value as 'a business getter' as well as for his mechanical services."

"My demands are not ex . . . , ex . . . what's the word?" Babe said to Hunt.

"Exorbitant?" Hunt suggested.

"Yeah, that's the word," Babe said.

The train ride back to New York on the Union Pacific had all the grandeur of any trip taken by a head of any important state. The studio put together a suitable bon voyage celebration at the station, and the Sultan posed for the appropriate pictures and repaired to the drawing room for the long trip back to his kingdom of Swat. Marshall Hunt recorded the glory of it all.

"Tonight the gargantuan Bambino is on his way to New York, not the Bambino of several years ago who was on the direct route to the poor-house," he wrote. "A new Bambino, who saluted the milling crowd, a businessman, a gentleman of opulence off to confer with Col. Jacob Ruppert about the greatest contract ever associated with baseball!"

Since the end of the '26 season—actually, since the end of the '25 season, when he went hunting with Shawkey and then showed up at Artie McGovern's door—the Babe had been in perpetual motion. His life was a public exhibition. Virtually no day passed when his whereabouts were not reported in some newspaper somewhere.

He went from that final out in the '26 Series, that ill-fated attempted stolen base, directly into a two-week barnstorming tour with Gehrig in the Northeast. He went from the barnstorming tour directly into his 12-week vaudeville tour on the Pantages circuit for $100,000, the largest sum to date ever paid for a headliner.

He'd been to cities across the country and up and down the West

Coast, following the usual routines, endorsing different autos and Victrolas from Seattle to San Diego, visiting the local newspapers to put on an eyeshade to "edit" the next edition, standing on the stage and doing his routine. He'd "practiced" with the East-West football squads in San Francisco. He'd been arrested on a bogus child-labor charge for giving baseballs to kids onstage in Long Beach. He'd hunted and fished and played golf everywhere. Golf was a constant.

When he was asked about all the golf he played, he replied, "You see, divot-digging and slicing the white-washed walnuts keeps the avoirdupois down." At least that was what the reporter said he said.

At his arrival in L.A. on January 2 for his week of vaudeville shows, three shows daily, four on Sunday, he was greeted by Mayor George Cryer, football coaches Pop Warner of Stanford and Howard Jones of Southern Cal, president Harry Williams of Pacific Coast Light, and the local heads of the Shriners, Elks, and Knights of Columbus. A fan in the crowd yelled, "See you in Tijuana, Babe," and he replied, "Like hell you will." At least that was what the reporter said he said. He was right. All through the weeks of vaudeville, then through the weeks of filming, the big man never did travel below the border.

One of the other travelers on the train back to New York was Capt. Joseph Medill Patterson himself, the publisher of the *Daily News*. Patterson had been in L.A. on business, and Hunt bumped into him walking toward the dining car. The Captain wanted to know what Hunt had been doing in L.A. Suppressing an urge to tell his boss to read the paper (the stories had been there every day for three weeks), he said that he had been covering the Babe and now was traveling home with him.

"Babe Ruth is on the train?" Patterson said. "I've always wanted to meet him."

"It could be arranged," Hunt said.

"When would that be?"

"Right now if you like."

The Captain told Hunt to bring the Babe to his drawing room. He said he was a bit tired, so the visit couldn't last long. He would give Hunt a sign that the time was finished, and Hunt would guide the visitor out of the room. This was fine except the Babe came to the room and the conversation began and then would not end. Hunt kept waiting for a sign that never came. After various subjects had been visited, including the Captain's baseball career and the problems of running a newspaper, Hunt finally said *he* was tired and had to go to bed.

"They just hit it off together," he said. "The Babe had reached a point where he could talk with anybody."

Hunt reported the Babe's progress across the country. In Salt Lake City, the great man sparred for six rounds at the train station with Artie, to the delight of fans. In North Platte, Nebraska, he predicted the Yankees would be an even better team with the development of Koenig and Lazzeri. He said the A's would be the team to beat. In Chicago, where a crowd gathered at the station, someone asked if he really thought he would get $100,000 a year for two years, plus the $7,750.

"I hope to tell you," the Babe replied.

His arrival at Grand Central Station on the morning of March 2 was another event. Marshall Hunt described the scene.

"The Twentieth Century coming to an aristocratic stop," he wrote. "A flurrying, hastening group in the station platform gloom. Photographers, reporters, porters, that flurry; the photographer to photograph the epochal home coming, the reporters to ask questions answered by the Babe a hundred times before.

"The Babe grew impatient. His departure was sudden. A great limousine—and Babe was off to visit Mrs. Ruth in St. Vincent's Hospital. A brief visit. (Helen had gone into the hospital again for nervous exhaustion.) Mrs. Ruth was recovering rapidly. An order for a great bunch of flowers.

"O, there is tenderness in the heart of the Bambino, the gargantuan figure who is rude to umpires now and then. A streak up 3rd Ave. and the Babe had been hustled to the Ruppert brewery at 91st Street."

The negotiations with the Colonel and Ed Barrow at the brewery, despite all the speculation, took less than an hour and a half, and most of that time was spent simply chatting. The parties agreed to a three-year deal at $70,000 per year. The Colonel told reporters that he was satisfied. The Babe said he also was satisfied. Done. He also told reporters he had invested $15,000 with Artie McGovern to open a string of gymnasiums on both the East and West Coasts. He used himself as a prime example of what the gyms could do. "If you're a heavyweight and want to be a welter, come see us," the Babe said.

The newspapers had great fun with the large new numbers in the contract. It was estimated the Babe would make $4.33 a minute if he played all 154 games and each game lasted one hour and 45 minutes. If he kept at the 48-home-run pace of '26, he would earn $1,458.33 per home run. Every day he would earn $454.54, enough for a trip to Europe . . . every week, $3,304.53, enough for a new auto . . . every month, $11,666.66, enough for a new home . . . every year, $70,000, enough to support 20 large families.

The Babe Comes Home would open during the 1927 season. It was far from a hit, though it received some favorable reviews. The Babe liked it and later said that he saw it ten times in various cities. Another movie, made on the Warner Bros. lot at roughly the same time, opened in October 1927 with larger implications. It featured that other famous onetime St. Mary's Industrial School resident, Al Jolson, and was called *The Jazz Singer*. A sound-synchronization system called Vitaphone allowed the actors to talk for the first time. Jolson delivered the famous first line of movie history: "Wait a minute. Wait a minute. You ain't heard nothing yet." Within two years, the silent movie era was finished, and with it the careers of many of the actors who worked with the Babe, including Anna Q. Nilsson.

The Babe's career was another story. Three nights after he returned from Hollywood he was on a train from Penn Station to St. Petersburg and the start of spring training. He was off to the greatest season that any baseball team ever would have.

CHAPTER EIGHTEEN

G RAHAM MCNAMEE was on the air again. The same excited voice
that described the strikeout of Tony Lazzeri by Alexander the Great
and the failed stolen base attempt by the Babe to end the 1926 World Series was heard around the country on June 13, 1927. The location of the
microphone was different this time.

The first-place Yankees were playing the Cleveland Indians at the Stadium, but McNamee was at Pier A on the New York docks. The noise was
even louder than it had been at the Series. Boat whistles and the sound of
airplanes were added to the cheers, the roar of the people. Pandemonium,
it seemed, made a fine radio background.

"This is an exquisite parade of boats," McNamee shouted. "There must
be 150 or 200 of them coming up here to show Col. Charles Lindbergh
what a New York welcome consists of. . . . The fireboats are sending up
mountains of water high into the air. . . . I cannot hear my own voice. . . .

"This is the greatest thing in the history of the world to be given any
one man. . . . The sky is full of airplanes. . . . Lindbergh is on deck. . . .
He is without uniform. . . . He is standing on the deck of the approaching
Malcolm. . . . There she docks. . . . The din is something terrific. Every
steamer is blowing. . . . In every window in lower New York people are
shouting."

The Babe had competition for the fickle hearts of America. They had been given, at least for the moment, to the boyish, 25-year-old son of a former congressman from Minnesota who sat down in the wicker seat of his tiny airplane on May 20 at Roosevelt Field on Long Island, took off into the morning mist, and didn't leave that seat for 33 hours, 30 minutes, and 30 seconds, when he landed at the field at Le Bourget, outside Paris, France.

No one-man endeavor by any human being, dead or alive, ever had been celebrated with more enthusiasm than the solo flight of Charles A. Lindbergh across the Atlantic Ocean. He had defied death and common sense to win a $25,000 prize established by hotel impresario Raymond Orteig. Unknown when he took off, the aviator was bigger than kings and presidents, actors and great thinkers, bigger than Babe Ruth, when he landed.

"Colonel Lindbergh, New York City is yours," the Babe's old adviser on conduct, Jimmy Walker, now the mayor, said at City Hall. "I don't give it to you; you won it."

The snowstorm of ticker tape was so dense in the parade through the city streets that Lindbergh's open car had to be bailed out as it moved. He wondered if New York would have to print new phone books to replace the ones that had been torn apart. An estimated four million people cheered as he passed, beginning a succession of dinners, awards, medals, proclamations, and scrutiny that never would be matched. Eighteen hundred tons of confetti were cleaned from the New York streets. The Armistice in 1918 had been only 155 tons.

Lindbergh was the Babe times two or three or four or maybe ten. The apparatus of fame developed in the rise of G. Herman Ruth and Jack Dempsey and Red Grange and swimmer Gertrude Ederle and other sports stars of the decade had been tuned and tested, waiting for the quiet and brave airman. It whirred into action. The offers that had come to the Babe—for books and movies and vaudeville tours, for endorsements and charity appearances—now came to Lindbergh with bigger numbers, more zeroes on the end.

This was the apogee in the age of new heroes. They were delivered to the front door now, these heroes, consumed like breakfast cereal. They weren't long-ago characters of mythology or simple words on paper; their voices could be heard on the radio, their pictures could be seen in the paper, in the news shorts at the theater. They were personal, exciting friends of every family. In 1927 A.D., America chewed up heroes, swallowed them whole. This was a time for large and outrageous deeds. In a time of soaring possibility, everything seemed connected and wonderful. What would man do next? Look at Lindbergh.

Money was being made, fortunes doubled and tripled at the clicking of a telegraph key from Wall Street. The Model T was being replaced by the Model A, and Henry Ford had 50,000 orders. A seven-mile tunnel had been opened through the Rockies. A seaway on the St. Lawrence River was planned. Laurel had met Hardy, and Mae West had a show on Broadway simply called *Sex*. No boundaries were impenetrable.

What next?

"Here is another band and then we have the Colonel, this darn nice boy, Lindbergh," Graham McNamee reported, now moved to the Welt-Mignon Studios in Manhattan. "The police escort is passing. . . . Lindbergh is in the back of the automobile, bareheaded. . . . The crowd is going wild [cheers and whistles are heard] . . . Lindbergh has passed and approaches Central Park."

Three days later, the final stages of the New York celebration were held. After attending a dinner staged by William Randolph Hearst the previous night, where Charlie Chaplin was another guest, Lindbergh had flown to Washington to pick up his plane, the *Spirit of St. Louis*. He flew back to New York and on little sleep was taken in the morning on a 22-mile parade route through almost a million people in Brooklyn. He then went to Roosevelt Field for a ceremony at the site where all of the excitement had begun. He was supposed to go next to Yankee Stadium, where the Bronx Bombers were playing the Browns.

The plan was that he would arrive at 3:30 for the start of the game. One of the sweet moments surrounding his flight had happened at the Stadium when a crowd of 23,000, gathered for the light heavyweight title fight on May 20 between Jack Sharkey and Jim Malone, had observed a moment of silent prayer for the young man alone in the night over the Atlantic. A crowd of 15,000 now awaited his arrival.

He was late.

In a move that had no precedent, the umpires delayed the start of the game for 25 minutes. The Babe, waiting along with everyone else, predicted that he had a gift for Lindbergh.

"I feel a homer coming," he said. "My left ear itches. That's a sure sign."

At 3:55, no Lindbergh, the umpires could wait no longer and started the game. In the bottom of the first inning, the Babe also could wait no longer. Down two strikes to Browns pitcher Tom Zachary, a 31-year-old veteran left-hander, he started to check his swing, then unloaded late to send the ball halfway up the bleachers in left-center field. It was his 22nd home run of the year.

"I held back as long as I could, but it had to come," the Babe said. "When you get one of those things in your system, it's bound to come out."

Lou Gehrig, next at the plate, also must have had an itch in his ear. He too unloaded, a bit late, the ball traveling almost to the same place. It was his 15th of the year. Col. Lindbergh, alas, missed both blasts. His motorcade didn't reach the Stadium until 5:30, and then he decided they should skip the visit and get back to the Hotel Brevoort, where he picked up his $25,000 prize. That was followed by a dinner at the Hotel Roosevelt, where Charles A. Schwab was the featured speaker. The meeting between America's heroes never took place.

"I had been saving that homer for Lindbergh," the Babe told reporters, "and then he doesn't show up. I guess he thinks this is a twilight league."

Two days later, back in St. Louis, the aviator went to Sportsman's Park. With 40,000 people in the stands, he walked in procession with Kenesaw Mountain Landis and National League president John Heydler to the flagpole in center field, where he raised the St. Louis Cardinals' 1926 World Championship banner.

So what could the Babe do? How could he recapture at least a piece of his audience? A two-paragraph filler in the *Washington Post* the morning after Lindbergh departed New York contained a possibility. The headline was "Babe Ruth Is Ahead of 1921 Homer Pace." Deadlines had caused the writer of the article to miss Ruth's latest home run, but the numbers were suitably prescient.

"Ruth's 21 circuit drives for 53 games give him an average of .389 per game," the article said. "Thus by playing at this average in the remaining 101 games, his total home runs will be 60, or one better than the 59 four-baggers credited to him in 1921."

Take on the impossible. Yes. Of course. The idea of hitting 60 home runs had changed for both the Babe and the public in the five seasons since he hit the 59 in '21. In the first couple of springs after he set that record, the Caliph had predicted that 60 clouts would arrive almost momentarily, a simple matter of time. In the last couple of springs, he had been much more reserved. He hadn't hit 50 again, much less come close to 60. He wondered openly if he had made a mistake in putting a mark so high on the wall so early in his career.

The quest for 60 or more home runs, somewhat like flying across the Atlantic or climbing some impossible mountain like Everest or crossing any frontier of physical performance, needed a combination of good health, proper circumstance, and luck. A situation had to arise, with conditions just right and the pieces all in their proper places.

A situation like the one where the Babe now found himself.

In the third month of the season, with more than three months to go, the Yankees already had won the American League pennant. The young and uncertain lineup that had surprised everyone a year earlier now was tested and true and had acquired a tobacco-chewing swagger. No lineup in baseball history ever had been as fearsome, top to bottom, presenting a stress that wore opposing pitchers down with each passing inning. "Five o'clock lightning" was the term the writers had found for the late-inning destruction that awaited the poor souls working on the mound. The Yankees had sprinted to an eleven-and-a-half-game lead by the Fourth of July, and no one was going to stop them. The Yankees knew this. Everyone else knew this.

At the third spot in the batting order, Ruth couldn't have resided in a better place to hit home runs. Combs had become the ideal leadoff man, always on base, taking away the pitchers' big windups, putting each hurler into the stretch position. Koenig was a perfect second man, almost as pesky and proficient as Combs. When Ruth came to the plate, more often than not, trouble already had begun. And just as important, trouble waited behind him.

In spring training, Huggins had adjusted his lineup. A year earlier, Gehrig had batted number three, Ruth number four, and Bob Meusel number five. During the season, the manager had changed the order to Ruth third, Meusel fourth, and Gehrig fifth. Now, for 1927, it became Ruth third, Gehrig fourth, and Meusel fifth. Gehrig had moved into position to protect Ruth, a backup force to be feared. Walk Ruth? A pitcher knew then he would have to face Gehrig with a man on first.

The nice boy from Columbia had matured as a player. He still lived with his mother and father in an apartment on Eighth Avenue, still went home most nights after games in New York, still was nervous in the presence of women, but he had become almost as fearsome at the plate as the Babe. In the closing weeks of June, he went on a home run spree. He edged closer and closer to Ruth—he took a big jump on June 23 when he became the first man ever to hit three homers in a game at Fenway Park—and tied the big man on June 29 at 24.

The Babe now had a rabbit.

"[Gehrig] is traveling fast enough to give point to the words of Ruth the other night, when he said that Columbia Lou is the only man that would beat the Babe's record of 59," James Harrison of the *Times* wrote after the three-homer game. "That's the Babe's prediction and he's going to stick to it, and the way Gehrig smacked them today it looked as if G. Herman is the seventh son of a seventh son."

Never before had Ruth had competition in the home run race. When he was healthy or not suspended, the field always belonged only to him. Now, not only did he have a challenge, but it came from the man directly behind him in the lineup, from the quiet figure under the next showerhead after the game. This was a deluxe and unexpected plot development for the public: a two-man marathon of strength and endurance that would play for the rest of the summer without the distractions of a pennant race.

The day after the student caught the master, the student pounded out number 25 in the second inning to claim the lead. In the fourth, the master struck back with his own 25th, a shot to the right-field bleachers at Fenway. On July 2, now in Washington, the student whacked number 26 to forge ahead again. On July 3, the master came back, hitting the longest home run ever seen at Griffith Stadium. Tied again.

And so it went. One edged ahead, the other climbed back. They were never separated by more than two home runs, a number that could be made up on one doubleheader day. They were characters on a big Parcheesi board, moving back and forth—captivating stuff. A fan had better than a 50 percent chance to go to a Yankees game and see one or the other of the two strong men hit a home run. Maybe both.

Christy Walsh quickly moved onto the scene and signed Gehrig to his burgeoning group of ghosted clients. The promoter tried to frame a public picture of buddies and friends, Gehrig and Ruth, a couple of the Three

Musketeers off on a home run lark. Although it might have worked when sent across the country, it fell flat with people who knew the situation. These really weren't buddies or great friends. Off the field, they lived far different lives, as different as different could be. An attempt to give Gehrig a sports-page nickname, "Buster," to match against "Babe" went nowhere. Gehrig wasn't a Buster. And Babe unquestionably was a Babe.

"Can Falstaff be playmates with Volstead?" one headline asked. That was the true matchup.

"They were on the bench recently," Rud Rennie wrote in the *New York Herald,* describing the two men. "Ruth squirting tobacco juice and advising the other team's catcher, who had just missed a foul ball, to look on the ground for it; Gehrig at the other end explaining to a friend how he speared eels at night. A group of photographers approached the dugout and said they wanted a picture of Lou and the Babe. They asked Lou. 'It's all right with me,' said Lou, 'if it's all right with the Babe.' "

The deference always did exist. The master always was the master. Gehrig, good as he was, always looked at Ruth with a certain wonder, studying him to see how a star should act. The baseball was easy for Gehrig, but the rest of this star stuff seemed incredibly hard.

The competition went straight into September. The two men were tied at 44 homers apiece as they reported for a doubleheader in Boston against the God-awful Red Sox. In the fifth inning of the first game, Tony Welzer on the mound for the Sox, Gehrig unloaded a shot into the right-field bleachers to take the lead at 45 in what now was called everywhere "the Great American Home Run Derby." In the sixth, Ruth came back at him. With two men on base, Welzer tried a change of pace on the Bam. The Bam was waiting for it. He ran up on the ball and—in the *Times*—"dealt the sphere a fearful blow," sending it into the center-field bleachers, a shot instantly considered the longest homer in Fenway history. The two men were tied at 45.

In the next inning, poor Welzer still on the mound, Ruth connected again. This was a tall fly ball that sneaked into the stands close to the right-field foul pole. Ruth 46, Gehrig 45. Finally, in the seventh inning of the nightcap, Ruth broke up Charlie Russell's shutout with another fly ball down the right-field line that snuck into the stands. Gehrig, the next batter, followed with a shot to left-center, longer and harder hit than Ruth's homer, that stayed in the park for a triple.

And yet somehow, just like that, the chase was done.

Gehrig, like any good rabbit, now peeled off to the side. He would hit only two home runs for the rest of the season, ceding the stage to the well-paid leading man. He had done his job as a credible Volstead, but now Falstaff had all the speaking lines. The battle became a chase between the big man and his younger self, wholly as fascinating as the battle against his teammate. The Babe was seven games behind his 1921 pace at the end of his work on September 6. He had 22 games remaining in which to hit 13 home runs.

This seemed almost impossible. Then again, he hit two more the next day at Fenway, numbers 48 and 49, to close out the Yankees' road schedule. Maybe it wasn't impossible. All of the action for the rest of the year would be at the Stadium. John Kieran of the *Times* was moved to poetry by the chase.

With vim and verve he has walloped the curve from Texas to Duluth,
Which is no small task, and I beg to ask: Was there ever a guy like Ruth?

As each succeeding series passed, the big man whacked away at the numbers, getting one home run against the Browns, two against the Indians, two more against the White Sox, two against the Tigers, but then he stalled with only one against the A's. When he hit the final three-game series of the season against the Senators, he needed three home runs in three days to reach 60. Two, of course, would tie the record.

On September 29, he took care of business quickly. In the first inning, down two strikes in the count, he caught Hod Lisenbee trying to sneak a curve past him for strike three and neatly deposited number 58 into the right-field bleachers. In the fifth, with the bases loaded, Senators manager Bucky Harris brought in a 25-year-old kid up from the New Haven Pilots named Paul Hopkins to face Ruth. This was Hopkins's first appearance in a major league uniform, and the first batter he ever faced. When he looked toward the Yankees' dugout to see who was coming, he thought, "Oh, my." He also thought he could get Ruth out because he was 25 years old and he thought he could get anyone out.

The rookie threw a succession of curveballs at the Bam and saw two of them turned into monstrous foul balls, one down either line. With the count at three and two, he threw what he thought was the best curveball of them all.

"Real slow and over the outside of the plate," Hopkins recalled for *Sports Illustrated* almost 70 years later. "It was so slow that Ruth started to swing and then hesitated. He hitched on it and brought the bat back. And then he swung, breaking his wrists as he came through it. What a great eye he had! He hit it at the right second. Put everything behind it. I can still hear the crack of the bat. I can still see the swing."

Recounting the narrative in the next morning's *Daily News,* Marshall Hunt wrote, "There was a moment of hushed expectancy as the count became three and two on the captain of the home run industry. There was that ominous sound of a heavy instrument, swung with vast force, meeting a pitched ball from the right arm of Master Hopkins. There was a shriek as the white pellet whistled its course into the right field bleachers, and as the mammoth character legged his way around the bases, pursuing his three comrades, there came a symphony of rejoicing from the clients such as these sagging ears have not heard in many a year."

The 60th almost followed on Ruth's final at-bat of the day. He clocked another shot to right that was caught by rookie outfielder Red Barnes against the fence. Earlier in the game, he had tripled, the ball caroming off a railing and back into the field. He conceivably could have hit numbers 58, 59, 60, and 61 in the same afternoon.

The Washington pitcher the next day was Tom Zachary, a hard thrower. Zachary was a Quaker and had served in a noncombatant division in the Red Cross during the war. He was one of the few players who had pitched under an assumed name in the big leagues, appearing in two games for the A's in 1918 under the name Zach Walton in an attempt to keep his college eligibility. He might have wished he had appeared in this game as Zach Walton.

In the eighth inning, the game tied at 2–2, and with Koenig on third, he faced Ruth for the fourth time of the afternoon. Ruth had walked once and singled twice, driving home the Yankees' two runs. Zachary's first pitch was a called strike. The second was high, a ball. The third was over the plate, a fastball. Ruth pulled it directly into the right-field stands, halfway to the top. Number 60 was done. Zachary threw his glove to the mound and complained to the umpire that the ball was foul. His words were blotted out by the noise from a small but exultant midweek crowd of 10,000. Number 60 was done.

"While the crowd cheered and the Yankee players roared their greetings, the Babe made his triumphant, almost regal, tour of the paths," the *Times* reported.

> He jogged around slowly, touched each bag firmly and carefully and when he imbedded his spikes in the rubber disk to record officially Homer 60, hats were tossed into the air, papers were torn up and tossed liberally and the spirit of celebration permeated the place.
>
> The Babe's stroll out to his position was signal for a handkerchief salute in which all the bleacherites to the last man participated. Jovial Babe entered into the carnival spirit and punctuated his kingly strides with a succession of snappy military salutes.

He had hit 17 home runs in the month of September, a record for any month. The 60th was his third home run of the season off poor Zachary, but he had hit four off both Rube Walberg of the A's and Milt Gaston of the Browns. He had hit home runs in every park in the eight-team league, at least six homers against every team. He had 11 against his old friends the Red Sox, eight at Fenway Park. For all the talk about how Yankee Stadium had been designed for him, he had hit 32 of his shots on the road, 28 at home. He had pulled 39 of them into the right-field stands and hit only four to left. He had one inside-the-park homer, number 27, a shot to the flagpole in center field in Detroit.

His three bats had become characters in the drama and in the press were named Black Betsy, Big Bertha, and Beautiful Bella. They were black, blond, and red. He used Black Betsy to hit number 59, Beautiful Bella for 60. The weight of the bats varied with the press accounts, some of which declared each weighed 52 ounces. Ruth actually never used a bat heavier than 42 ounces, and as his career progressed, he went to lighter and lighter bats.

Ruth, in the clubhouse, said, "Sixty! Let's see some son of a bitch try to top that one!" but there was no grand celebration. The Yankees had one more game left with the Senators the next day, and the feeling was that he would hit one, two, or three more to close the show. He didn't. Gehrig hit a final home run to close with 47, and the Yankees recorded their 110th win against 42 losses to capture the pennant by 19 games, but Ruth went hitless in three appearances. Sixty was the new number on the wall. The record of records. This was his flight across the Atlantic.

"A child of destiny is George Herman," Paul Gallico wrote in the *Daily News*.

> He moves in his orbit like a planet. He sneaked up inevitably on his own home run record. One moment we found him engaged in a home run race with young Gehrig, in which he seemed to be getting the worst of it, and in the next he had passed the fifty mark with enough games left to accomplish his lifetime ambition.
>
> I even recall writing pieces about these two and saying how Gehrig would soon break Ruth's cherished record, and feeling kind of sorry for this old man having this youngster come along and steal all his thunder, and now look at the old has-been.

The World Series seemed to be nothing more than a curtain call for the Yankees and Ruth after what they had done during the season. It was finished in four straight games, the opposing Pittsburgh Pirates overwhelmed from the first batting practice when the Yankees lineup, especially Ruth, hit baseballs to strange places around and outside Forbes Field. Ruth had the only two home runs in the Series and was a factor in all four wins. He set nine Series records, all of them career records, most simply extensions of his previous records.

The Christy Walsh syndicate was at its best for the event, one Pittsburgh paper running ghostwritten articles by the Babe, Miller Huggins, Lou Gehrig, Waite Hoyt, Paul Waner, Rogers Hornsby, Honus Wagner, and Pirates manager Donie Bush. Another paper, at the risk of being overwhelmed, replied with articles by Pirates pitcher Vic Aldridge and boasted that Aldridge actually was writing the words himself. Lee Meadows, ten-year-old son of the Pirates pitcher of the same name, also was part of a ghostwriting enterprise. As an eight-year-old, he had "written" articles when the Pirates were in the Series two years earlier.

"Has his writing improved in two years?" someone asked the boy's ghost.

"Whenever I point out some play in the ball game and ask for some significant impressions," the ghost replied, "young Master Meadows would say, 'I wish I had some peanuts,' or, 'Why don't you buy me a hot dog?' "

Walsh had Ruth and Gehrig on the barnstorming road immediately to capitalize on the Series interest. They were scheduled the very next day to play a doubleheader in the Bronx but were rained out. Then they were off (okay, only as far as Brooklyn for the first stop) for 21 games, 9 states, 20 cities. They wouldn't stop until they hit the West Coast, "the Batterin' Babes" in blue uniforms, "the Larrupin' Lous" in white.

An afternoon in Asbury Park, New Jersey, early in the tour was typical. The entire Asbury Park police force was called out to control a crowd of over 7,000. The game against the Brooklyn Royal Colored Giants was an hour late in getting started as the Babe waited at the Berkeley Carteret Hotel until a certified check was delivered from the promoter; then it was played in chaos.

Small boys wandered the field at will, walking out to Ruth to request his autograph or running to grab loose baseballs. Deal Lake was at the edge of the field, no fences in the way, and baseballs, fair and foul, found their way to the water. Ruth played the entire game with a fountain pen in hand or pocket to accommodate the autograph seekers. He carried boys off the field. He tried to steal one time, but the ball escaped from the catcher and was grabbed by a boy who was faster than the catcher. Gone. When Gehrig hit a homer in the eighth into Deal Lake, that was the disappearance of the 36th and final baseball. End of game.

On the tour, 13 of the 21 games ended before the ninth inning owing to some occurrence. Ruth, for the record, had 20 home runs. Gehrig had 16. They played, Christy Walsh claimed, to a combined audience of 220,000 people.

Back together in New York, the two sluggers went to the Army–Notre Dame game at the Stadium, guests of Knute Rockne, another Walsh client. During the winter, Ruth went to North Carolina to hunt birds, visited Herb Pennock's house in Pennsylvania to hunt foxes, wearing the red coat and everything, spent a bunch of time with Claire and little or none with Helen, and settled into workouts with Artie McGovern after the first of the year. Artie boasted that his man was "five to ten years younger" than when he had first met him.

The world was just lovely.

An odd interview awaited the Home Run King when he reached St. Petersburg on February 26, 1928—traveling with Gehrig and three rookies on the Florida Express from Penn Station—to begin his toils anew. Carl

Sandburg, America's foremost poet, was at the Mason Hotel. While he waited, he told Westbrook Pegler he once had been a ballplayer until he stepped on a broken bottle, badly slashing his foot and ending his career. He didn't have much use for baseball now. He said he planned to ask Ruth a series of questions about current events, about world matters, about life.

Pegler smelled the obvious setup. He asked Sandburg what the point of those questions would be.

"I didn't exactly get the answer," Pegler reported. "It was something about moron hero worship and dusting off an idol."

The meeting took place on a sunny Florida day. The poet, a tall and slender man, too young to have developed his trademark white hair, delivered his sequence of spinning, curving questions. The Babe, the boy from St. Mary's Industrial School, was predictably handcuffed. The results were published in the *Chicago Daily News* under the byline "By Carl Sandburg, Noted American Poet."

SANDBURG: If some boys asked you what books to read, what would you tell them?

RUTH: I never get that. They never ask me that question. They ask me how to play ball.

SANDBURG: If you were to name two or three books you like a lot, what would they be?

RUTH: I don't know. I like books with excitement, dramatic murders.

SANDBURG: At least a million hot ball fans in the country, admirers of yours, believe in the Bible and Shakespeare as the two greatest books ever written, and some of them would like to know if there are any special parts of these books that are favorites of yours.

RUTH: A ballplayer doesn't have time to read. And it isn't good for the eyes. A ballplayer lasts only as long as his legs and eyes. He can't take any chances on his eyes.

(Pause.)

RUTH: If somebody reads a book to me I get more out of it. I memorize nearly all of it. When I read it myself I forget it.

SANDBURG: You have met President Coolidge, haven't you?

RUTH: Oh, yes.

SANDBURG: If some boys asked you for a model of a man to follow through life, would you tell them that President Coolidge was pretty good?

RUTH: Well, I always liked President Harding.

SANDBURG: If some boys asked you which of all the Presidents of the United States was the best model to follow is there any one you would tell them?

RUTH: President Wilson was always a great friend of mine.

SANDBURG: Is there any one character in history you are particularly interested in, such as Lincoln, Washington, Napoleon?

RUTH: I've never seen any of them.

SANDBURG: Some people say brunettes have always been more dangerous women than blondes. How do you look at it?

RUTH: It depends on the personality.

SANDBURG: What's your favorite flower?

RUTH: I don't care about flowers.

SANDBURG: What's your favorite horse?

RUTH: Oh, I quit that. I quit playing the horses a long time ago.

SANDBURG: There's a lawyer, Clarence Darrow, staying at the hotel there that some people call the Babe Ruth of lawyers.

RUTH: Yes, I met him yesterday. We were talking.

SANDBURG: Have you followed any of Clarence Darrow's big cases when the newspapers were printing so much about them?

(Pause.)

RUTH: I just bought a piece of property this morning—$32,000 it was— $200 a front foot. We're thinking about forming what they call a corporation, capital $165,000.

Sandburg thanked the Babe at the end. He said he hoped, as a ballplayer, Ruth's legs and eyes wouldn't give out for many years. That was his dry, final, easy shot.

"Can you imagine the gall of the fellow?" Pegler asked in the *Chicago Tribune*.

The interview certainly did what Sandburg wanted it to do, finding the many holes in the Bambino's education, but Sandburg's air of intellectual superiority left the reader looking for a companion piece: what would happen if the Noted American Poet went over to the ballpark and tried to hit Lefty Grove, say, for half an hour? The Babe was the Babe. He had never pretended to be anything else. That was the beauty of him.

America didn't care if Huckleberry Finn didn't know anything about flowers. He'd hit 60 home runs.

CHAPTER NINETEEN

T HE BABE WROTE a book in 1928. (Take that, Carl Sandburg.)
Okay, maybe he didn't actually write the book. Maybe Ford Frick of
the *New York Evening World* wrote it, but it was titled *Babe Ruth's Own
Book of Baseball*, and the listed author was George Herman Ruth, and it
was quite good.

Frick/Ruth told a lot of stories, made some observations, used some
words that one of the two collaborators probably didn't know. The subjects ran from hunting to bunting, the different pieces of George Herman's
life. One of the best little vignettes was a description of the world champions in transit, Murderers' Row on the train:

> In one section, a card game is in session, Meusel and Bengough, [Dutch]
> Ruether, Koenig and Lazzeri are playing "black jack." They have
> their coats off, their collars discarded and their shirts open at the neck.
> They're kidding and laughing over the game. . . . Down the car a bit,
> Hoyt sits reading a book. Further on, the fussy foursome is busy at bridge.
> That's Gehrig, [Don] Miller, [Mike] Gazella and myself.
>
> Shocker is reading the newspapers and his berth is messed up with a
> dozen sports pages, torn from as many different papers. Now and then
> he makes some discovery and pauses to discuss baseball with Pennock,

who is writing letters across the aisle. . . . Through the open door of the drawing room, you can see Huggins, smoking his pipe and talking with [Charlie] O'Leary and [Art] Fletcher, his assistants.

This was the life of the world champions.

The train was their portable fraternity house, membership open to an exclusive few men who knew absolutely what to do with a well-thrown baseball. They clattered through the small towns of their individual pasts, zip, a bell ringing, a barrier dropped across all roads. They stayed in the best hotels, ate in the best restaurants. Dressed in suits that became better with each jump in pay, they traveled the seven-city circuit of 77 road games on a 154-game schedule, plus exhibitions, plus spring training, plus the World Series itself, preceded by press clippings, notable if not famous, caught in a sophisticated environment most of them never even had known existed. They sang songs and won ball games and learned which fork went with which course at dinner. Waite Hoyt had said it first: "It's great to be young and a Yankee." Well, that was right.

It was magic.

"You'd have players come up to New York from the sorriest little towns," Marshall Hunt said. "I mean they were born on a farm, probably the whole income $125 a year. Then they got to playing on a Sunday school team, then a town team, and then they got into a small league, and of course, when they hit, there the scouts would be looking at them, and if they were good, they'd wind up here. . . . It always fascinated me that this fellow that came from that horrible side hill farm with that smelly outhouse, very little to eat, some kind of pork, corn, and pretty soon he's getting $22,000 a year and wearing Brooks Brothers clothing and conducting himself real well.

"All the time these players would be with the Yankees or any other major league club they would be quite credible fellows. You could take them anywhere. They read the papers a little bit. They didn't crucify the king's English. . . . I mean, this rise—I don't think you see it or have it brought to your attention as much in the steel industry, even in the movies, as you do in baseball."

Trips would start and end in big-city palaces of transportation, heels of shined shoes clacking across the marble floors of Grand Central or Pennsylvania Station toward an overnight to Boston, the *Orange Blossom Special* to Florida, a long jaunt all the way to St. Louis. Action was everywhere. People. Bustle. Style. An estimated 47 million travelers would move through Grand Central in 1928, everybody going or coming, busy. The idea of airplanes as commercial carriers was only beginning to dawn. The long automobile or bus trip was a bouncing, punishing aggravation. The train was the way to travel. Seven cities to visit in the American League.

"To go from New York to Philadelphia, driving a car, you started by taking the ferry to Hoboken or someplace," Hunt said. "Then you'd drive over cobblestones for stretches. Then you'd get behind a hay wagon. Couldn't move. It would take a good five hours to reach Philadelphia. You'd be hard-pressed, driving from New York to Boston or Washington, to make that trip in a day."

The Yankees and the writers who followed them would travel in two, sometimes three Pullman cars attached to the end of a regularly scheduled train. They would rattle along, take their meals in the dining car with the rest of the travelers, look out the windows, talk, play cards, talk, sleep, talk some more for as much as an entire 24-hour day. The trip to St. Louis would start around five o'clock in the afternoon in New York, with dinner at sunset while crossing the Hudson River, and finish at five o'clock in the afternoon the next day on the banks of the Mississippi.

There was time to get to know each other.

Marshall Hunt, say, would be sitting in the dining car. Earle Combs would come along for lunch.

"Anyone sitting here?"

"No, sit down, Earle."

America would slide past the window. Hunt always would look at the men working in the fields, red necks bright in the sun, and feel comfortable and secure with his newspaper and his cup of coffee on the white linen tablecloth. Wouldn't you rather be here than there? America would open up conversation.

"Now, look at that," Earle Combs might say. "There's a very prosperous farm, and that farmer's out there working with a mismatched team. He can do better than that. We do better than that in Kentucky."

More farms. More.

"That's good ground, though," Earle Combs might say. "Much better than Kentucky. Too many hills in Kentucky. Can't get enough bushels from an acre of land."

"Did you farm, Earle?"

"Barefooted. I pushed one of those plows."

"I suppose you're pretty lucky, Earle."

"Luck? I'd like to think I had something to do with it."

The hotels at the ends of the trips were filled with businessmen, with well-to-do families on vacation, with bellboys and room service and maids to make your bed with clean linens every day. The Buckminster in Boston. The Aldine in Philadelphia. The Raleigh in Washington. The Book Cadillac in Detroit. The Hollenden House in Cleveland. The Cooper-Carleton in Chicago. Now there was a place, the Cooper-Carleton over on Lake Shore Drive, because management didn't want the players too close to the Loop and the after-dark temptations. The Cooper-Carlstein. That's what the players called it. Filled with Jewish people. Kosher kitchen. Part of the education.

In St. Louis, the hotel was the Chase, across from Forest Park. On hot nights, after that 24-hour trip, players would just sit out on the lawn. Talk baseball. Some other subjects might intrude, but baseball was 90 percent of a night's conversation. If the heat was too much, some of the players and some of the writers would take their blankets to the lawn and sleep under the stars.

With the 3:30 starting time and most games completed in two hours or less, both the nights and the mornings were open for exploration. A man could think, walk, read, watch a movie, name his poison. All choices were laid in front of him.

"They had these black-and-tan clubs in Chicago," Marshall Hunt said. "These great Negro tap dancers. Great singers. Great food. We were there one night, a guy pulled a gun and started shooting at another guy. Ford Frick was really amazed by it all. He was kind of a rube. He kept saying, 'What if we got hit?' I told him, 'They weren't shooting at you.' I don't think he ever got over it."

Magic.

"Here's one that might surprise you," Hunt said. "I took Babe to an art gallery one time, some show that was going on. I remember he came out and said, 'Goddamn it. How do those bastards do it?' Something he saw had got to him, touched him. You wouldn't think that."

The Babe traveled a bit differently from the rest of the players. He was the only one with a drawing room on the train. The rest of the players were in berths, uppers and lowers designated by seniority. The manager and the traveling secretary each had a drawing room. The two coaches shared one. The Babe had one to himself.

It was a move of necessity more than privilege. Out in the cars, he was a lure for travelers seeking an autograph, a moment. He could play his portable Victrola in the drawing room. He could play his ukelele. (Mercifully, he left his saxophone home most times.) He could entertain in his satin smoking jacket and slippers.

That didn't mean he stayed away from the noise in the rest of the Yankees' Pullman car. He would play cards, and he played a lot of bridge with Gehrig as his partner. They were predictable partners who played the way they lived, Gehrig reserved, Ruth flamboyant. He would nip into a quart of Seagram's 7, become more flamboyant as the nips and the game progressed, bid on anything. Gehrig would become disgusted. Everett Scott, when he played with the Yankees, had made good money off the Babe in poker. Anyone who knew cards and had time would make good money off the Babe. He needed action and more action, pushing the bets. Money streamed from the Babe.

"One night in Cleveland I invited Herb Pennock, Bob Meusel, and Mark Koenig to dinner," Joe Dugan said. "We used to exchange dinners, you know. I was broke as usual, though, and needed to borrow some money. Ruth was standing in the lobby of the Hollenden House. I went by him—he had the big polo coat on—and I said, 'Jidge, your pal is empty.' He reached in, handed me a bill. Just handed it to me, you see."

The group had dinner. Dugan grabbed the check. He handed the waiter Ruth's bill. The waiter asked Dugan if he was a wise guy. Dugan said he wasn't, why ask? The waiter said a restaurant of this size never could cash a $500 bill. They had to wake up the owner to come down and cash the bill.

"Anyway, payday, I went up to Ruth and counted out five hundred-dollar bills," Dugan said. " 'What's this for?' Ruth says. I said, 'Remember that night in Cleveland you gave me a bill?' 'Oh, I thought I lost it. Thanks, kid.' "

Ruth had become the most experienced traveler on the team. Adding the barnstorming trips and the vaudeville trips and any number of other trips to the Yankees' trips, he easily was on the road for more than half the year. He had connections everywhere. In every city, he would be met by a woman, by a man, by somebody. Who were these people? Even in the small cities in the South, places the Yankees never had visited, somebody would be waiting. How had it been arranged? He was not a planner, not someone to make a call. Did the people call him?

Mark Roth, the traveling secretary, always thought that railroad telegraphers were involved, that Ruth had the best communications network in the country. He knew where to find a bootlegger. He knew where to find a woman, a bunch of women. The fact that he left large quantities of money behind him did not hurt. These people liked to play with him for the same reason the cardplayers liked to play with him.

"Whenever we left St. Louis we left out of what they call Brandon Avenue, this suburban station," Waite Hoyt said. "It wasn't even a station, it was a crossing, really, and we'd wait there for the train to come from downtown. Ruth knew some people, and he always, when we left like that, he'd have a few gallons of home brew delivered to the train plus about 15 or 20 racks of spare ribs.

"We'd get on the train, and since we had our own car and nobody used the ladies' room, Ruth would take over the ladies' room and set up shop and for 50 cents you could have all the beer and all the spare ribs you could eat."

The Babe would have the suite at the hotel, another difference, this one at his own expense, the bathtub filled with beer and the room filled with people. Or he would be gone, off by himself to see the local people, whoever they were. The House of Good Shepard! There were few contemplative moments. Maybe none. Except in the morning.

"Ruth and Joe Dugan always were making bets," Waite Hoyt said. "I roomed with Dugan, and Ruth would come down in the morning, and they'd call these two friends back in New York, handicappers, Claude Kyle and Maddie Glennin. It's strange I remember those names. They'd call up these handicappers from the road, ask who they liked, and make their bets, and they were ahead of the game. Except when they went home, they'd forget to call Claude Kyle and Maddie Glennin. And then they wouldn't do well.

"I wasn't a bettor, and I used to hate when they made bets from the room."

The eating and drinking stories sometimes were overstated with the Babe—he'd usually have a normal breakfast, bacon and eggs, a large orange juice, and he wasn't drinking alcohol every hour of every day—but he had his moments. John Drebinger, who traveled sometimes for the *Times*, once saw him chug a Coca-Cola bottle filled with whiskey in one gulp. Marshall Hunt saw him do some damage to some hot dogs.

"We'd just gotten on the train, everybody had eaten," Hunt said. "The Babe gave the porter $5 to buy as many hot dogs as he could. The porter came back with this basket filled with hot dogs. Babe offered them around, but nobody was hungry. He stacked the hot dogs on the windowsill of the train. He was just sitting there, watching a card game, eating hot dogs. Pretty soon they were all gone. I bet he ate 18 hot dogs. All by himself."

Richards Vidmer, another *Times* writer, returned pretty late to his room one night. He found a stack of messages from the Babe, asking him to come to room 436 as soon as possible. Vidmer was worried. He called room 436.

"Where the hell have you been?" the Babe asked.

"I've been out," Vidmer replied.

"Come on up. I've been waiting for you."

Vidmer went to room 436. The Babe poured him a drink. Vidmer asked what the heck this was all about. He was tired.

"Well, Goddamn it, last night we killed a bottle of scotch between us and I had two home runs today," the Babe said. "I don't want to break the spell."

There were no clocks for the Home Run King on the road. The rules for everyone else simply did not apply. He was part of the Yankees' traveling show—nailing Lazzeri's shoes to the locker-room floor, making impossible bids to drive Gehrig crazy, selling spare ribs from the ladies' room—but he also had his own traveling show, fueled by a different level of money and fame.

"I must have that thing that Elinor Glyn calls 'it' out in Hollywood," the Babe said one day.

The description of "it," as written by Ms. Glyn, author of steamy contemporary love stories, was a strong, overriding sexuality, visible to anyone who watches the owner pass. Ms. Glyn said actress Clara Bow, "the 'it' girl," was the only one who had "it" in all of Hollywood. Maybe the Babe was the only one who had "it" in baseball. Maybe not. He certainly wanted to find out.

"Nobody with the Yankee club seems to know much about the Babe's unofficial activities," Westbrook Pegler wrote. "He runs alone and where he runs or what he does are matters of no interest whatsoever so long as he shows up at the yard no later than 1:30 P.M.—and hits home runs."

For the first four months of the 1928 season, the road trips of the Yankees were a time of joy and wonder. As the first of what would be many teams compared to the 1927 Yankees, this team looked even better. It had opened up an eleven-and-a-half-game lead on the second-place Philadelphia Athletics by July 24 and appeared to be a cinch for another runaway pennant. The Babe, as the first of many hitters to be compared to the Home Run King of 1927, also looked better. On July 24, he hit a rocket to a previously unexplored section of the center-field bleachers at Fenway Park for his 40th home run of the season. He was 28 games and 10 home runs ahead of his pace to 60 in 1927. The *Times* predicted he would break his record "barring sickness, injury and the other misfortunes to which human flesh is heir."

Question: is a slump a misfortune to which human flesh is heir? That was what happened next.

The Babe slumped. The Yankees slumped. The A's, a mixture of young talent added to Ty Cobb and Tris Speaker, who were playing out their last seasons, started rolling. The Yanks started falling. The two teams continued in their opposite directions until they collided at the Stadium on September 9 in a doubleheader. The A's, one day earlier, finally had taken a half-game lead for first.

Interest in the games was overwhelming. The Yankees had renovated the park prior to the season, expanding capacity to 72,000, and the doubleheader brought a further expansion. The largest crowd in baseball history, 85,265, stuffed the Stadium, people sitting, standing, crawling everywhere. Policemen worked two blocks away to force crowds off fire escapes on apartment houses for fear the walls would collapse. Traffic jams and parking were problems, the interest was so great.

In the midst of all this attention, the old 1927-style Yankees returned. They won the first game, 5–0, on a shutout by stellar rookie George Pipgras. They won the second, 7–3, on an eighth-inning grand slam by Bob Meusel. They now led by a game and a half, all work done in one day.

"We broke their hearts today," the Babe said. "And we gave that greatest crowd in baseball history some real baseball."

His 49th homer the next day capped a 5–3 win that put the Yanks ahead by two and a half, a lead the A's never could overcome. The pennant wasn't clinched until two and a half weeks later in Detroit. Two tales about Ruth grew out of that series. Maybe one or even both were true.

The first was that coming into the series he still was in his slump. He had tried everything to start hitting again, even abstinence from liquor as a final resort. Nothing had worked. Finally, first night in Detroit, he decided the opposite of abstinence was necessary. He chased the night, came out the next day in the sunshine at Navin Field, and hit two home runs in a double-header sweep of the Tigers that put the Yankees on the verge of clinching.

The next day, as they clinched with an 11–6 win, the second tale evolved. Ruth rented four or five adjoining rooms in the Book Cadillac, bought a piano because there was none available at the hotel, and threw a victory party. He was said to have stood on a chair sometime in the pro-ceedings and announced, "Any girl who doesn't want to fuck can leave now." True? Not true?

Circumstantial evidence would suggest that something happened. The next day the defending world champions lost, 19–10, to the Tigers. Ruth, Gehrig, and Meusel were the only regulars in the lineup. Hangovers per-haps filled the bench.

The St. Louis Cardinals somehow were five-to-three favorites over this merry band of travelers in the World Series. The leagues, remember, were virtually autonomous universes, one man's Poland against another man's Lithuania, and the only time teams seriously played against each other was in the World Series. The last time the Yankees had seen the Cards was in 1926, and remember, the Cards had prevailed in that final game when the Babe tried to steal second. The prognosticators fixed on that picture.

The Yankees also had some injury problems. Herb Pennock's arm was hurt, and he could not pitch. Earle Combs had injured a wrist in batting practice and would not play. Tony Lazzeri had a shoulder that needed an operation, and every throw pained him. Mark Koenig had an injured foot. Lou Gehrig had been beaned in the final game of the season, and there was doubt about his condition. Even the Babe had been moving slowly on a gimpy knee for the last four weeks of the season.

The injuries were a final factor.

"To me, the St. Louis Cardinals should make short work of the New York Yankees," Walter Johnson, the now-retired pitching great, predicted through his ghost. "The Yankees don't look good. They haven't looked good for a while."

(Ghost note of the Series: Eddie Bennett, the Yankees' hunchbacked batboy-mascot, had a ghost. Eddie and his ghost picked the Yankees.)

The Series opened at the Stadium. The Colonel and Ed Barrow were hoping for some more mammoth crowds like the one for the doubleheader against the A's, but that didn't materialize. Interest in these games was mild at the box office, perhaps because this was the third Series in a row at the Stadium. Neither of the first two games drew more than 65,000.

In the first one, Waite Hoyt tidily shut down the visitors, 3–1, on a three-hitter. In the second game, Alexander the Great, the nemesis of 1926, finally received the full Murderers' Row treatment as the Murderers pounded out a 9–3 win. Gehrig hit a giant home run, and Ruth was all over the place, and young rookie George Pipgras pitched well enough to keep the Cardinals quiet.

The games now shifted to St. Louis. In 1926 one of the features of the Series had been a race between the trains carrying the two teams from site to site. The *Cardinals' Special*, riding the Pennsylvania Railroad's 1,051 miles, covered the distance in 21 hours and 20 minutes, the fastest time ever recorded. The train was two hours and 40 minutes faster than a normal St. Louis–to–New York run. The Yankees, handicapped by taking a longer route on the *New York Central,* finished second. Alas, there was no rematch here. The two teams whisked across the country in the normal 24 hours.

In the third game, at Sportsman's Park, Gehrig hit two homers, and Tom Zachary, the man who surrendered number 60, now a Yankee, pitched a 7–3 win. Ruth broke the game open with a thumping slide into home in the sixth inning, causing catcher Jimmy Wilson to drop the ball. Huggins cautioned his players against "making whoopee" with a 3–0 series lead, and they had an extra rainout day to follow his advice. Then, in the fourth game, fill in your own cliché for excellence, the Prince of Pounders took control. He had the best World Series game of his career.

"If there is any lingering doubt, if anywhere in this broad land there were misguided souls who believed that Babe Ruth was not the greatest living ballplayer, they should have seen him today," James Harrison said in the *Times*. "They should have seen him, hooted and hissed, come to the plate three times, twice against Wee Willie Sherdel and once against the great Pete Alexander, and send three mighty drives whistling over that right field pavilion."

Three home runs were only the beginning. This was one of those games in which he was a protagonist in some hearty drama, involved in whatever happened. He was in left field, Meusel in the sun in right field, and was involved in a constant dialogue with the fans behind him. They kept telling him how useless he was; he kept telling them he was going to hit two home runs, just for spite. He lost a ball in the sun for an error, which gave the fans some ammunition, then hit the two home runs for his own ammunition. Then he hit the third home run, to match his feat in 1926 as the only man ever to hit three homers in one Series game.

The second of the blasts, hit in the seventh inning, was a drama in itself. Sherdel, burned already by Ruth's homer in the fourth, quickly whipped two strikes past him this time. The second strike was called, and Ruth turned around to argue with umpire Charlie Pfirman. While Ruth was turned, catcher Wilson whipped the ball back to Sherdel, who in turn whipped it back to Wilson, straight across the plate. The crowd cheered for strike three.

Ruth objected immediately in colorful and emphatic words. He said this was a quick pitch, which was illegal. Pfirman agreed. Sherdel never had set himself, simply had thrown the ball back in an absolute hurry. This was legal in the National League, but not legal in the American. The two leagues had agreed prior to the first game that the quick pitch would be illegal in the Series.

Sherdel protested. Catcher Wilson protested. Manager Bill McKechnie came out of the dugout to protest. The entire Cardinals team, in fact, gathered around Pfirman in protest. Ruth stood at the side, making fun of all of them, the longtime truant suddenly on the right side of the law.

Pfirman held firm. Sherdel was forced to throw another pitch, a curveball, and the result on this day was totally predictable. The ball cleared the pavilion and was last seen heading toward Grand Boulevard.

Ruth loved this home run. He waved his hand at the crowd. He waved directly toward his friends in the left-field stands. He waved again as he turned third base, headed for home. The shot had tied the game, 2–2. Gehrig then came to the plate and hammered Sherdel's second pitch down the line for another homer. The Yankees wound up scoring four times to take a 5–2 lead on the way to a 7–3 win.

The third homer by Ruth was in the eighth off the fading Alex the Great, who had been brought into the game in relief. The Bam finished off his day by making a spectacular running catch of a high fly ball from the bat of Cardinals shortstop Frankie Frisch for the final out of the game. He galloped at full speed on a diagonal across the foul line and speared the ball as he hit the fence, fighting off fans in the process.

He held the ball high in the air as he ran across the field in triumph. He was still holding it in the clubhouse, still excited, still babbling.

"There's the ball that says it's all over," he shouted to no one and to everyone. "There it is, right where I grabbed it out of the air. What a catch! Boy, maybe I wasn't glad to get my hands on *that* ball."

"Hooray," someone shouted. "Ruth for President!"

"Ruth for Sheriff!" someone else shouted. "Vote for Ruth."

"I told my friends out there in the bleachers I'd hit two homers in this game," Ruth babbled. "Wow! And I hit three. And what'd I hit? All hooks."

Someone started to sing "The Sidewalks of New York," and soon the whole team, everyone in the room, was singing. They sang the entire song, the parts about the "ginnie playing the organ" and "Me and Maggie O'Rourke" and "East Side" and "West Side, all around the town" and the tots singing "Ring-a-Rosie" and "London Bridge Is Falling Down." The final line—"On the sidewalks of New Yorrrrrrrrrk"—was held longest and loudest by the man still holding the baseball.

Was there any doubt about the best team in the game? This same group now had won three pennants and two World Series in a row. Won? They had annihilated the National League, four games and out, for two straight years. Was there any doubt about the best player in the game? The man still holding the baseball had hit .625 for the Series. It was a record.

"Gee," Waite Hoyt, who was the winning pitcher, said, "it's great to have a fellow like Ruth in there with you and not against you."

The final train trip of the year was a cross-country alcoholic hayride. Ruth had his mysterious St. Louis sources deliver a clothes basket full of ribs and ample amounts of what one paper called "amber-colored liquid that foams when poured." Other, heartier spirits magically appeared. The players sang, cavorted, and floated home.

"The hustlingest, fightingest world champions that ever rapped home runs over right field walls are on their way back to Baghdad-on-the-Subway," Jack Kofoed of the *New York Post* reported with a headline, "Eastbound on the Yankee Special." "This train is just one large package of exuberance."

The leader of all exuberance was the Bam. He had picked up a Mexican hairless dog somewhere along with the ribs, beer, and whatever else. He carried the dog, which shared space with a few bottles of ginger ale on a silver tray, through the cars on the train. An ice bucket was under Ruth's other arm.

A conga line was formed, and the party danced through the aisles of the entire train, Ruth at the front. He left mayhem in his wake, going back to his favorite trick of smashing all straw hats. Another favorite trick, a specialty, was grabbing hold of a person's shirt from behind, yanking in a certain way, and ripping the shirt off the person's body. This was a trick that seemed to be learned easily, and soon everybody was doing it to everybody else, and soon the train was filled with shirtless bodies. The Babe was soon down to his silk underwear.

An attempt was made to stuff Miller Huggins into some overhead compartment, but failed. (He was not hung off the back of the train, as legend has it.) A successful attempt was made to rip the silk brocade nightshirt of Col. Jake Ruppert. Ruth was the perpetrator.

"Don't you do it, Root," the Colonel said, discovered in his drawing room. "This is custom-made silk."

"Aw, I only want a piece of it," Ruth said.

"Mr. Root, you are suspended!"

Riiiiip.

The train stopped at assorted towns and cities during the night. Assorted Yankees, many wearing their suit jackets but no shirts, came out to wave. Ruth, in an undershirt, spoke and directed cheers with a spare rib. In Mattoon, Illinois, he started to lead a cheer for the defeated Cardinals, then said, "No, they quit, the hell with 'em."

It should be mentioned here that during this season the Bam had become political for the first time. He had never voted in his life, but encouraged by Christy Walsh and other friends in New York, he had become a backer of New York Gov. Al Smith, who was running for president. Ruth had made headlines across the country by refusing to pose with President Herbert Hoover at a game in Washington in September ("I'm an Al Smith man"), and later he apologized.

In Terre Haute, Indiana, before a crowd estimated at 2,000, people just waiting to see the new world champions pass, he added Al Smith to his list of people to cheer for. And three cheers for the next president of the United States . . . silence. The Babe left with the words, "The hell with you," returning to the fun.

It was quite a ride. Miller Huggins awoke in the morning and couldn't find his false teeth. Ruth couldn't find his dog.

"Where the heck is my dog?" he shouted.

"Doc Woods has it in his stateroom, giving it a dose of bicarbonate," Joe Dugan said. "Your dog couldn't stand the pace last night. It has a hangover."

There were crowds in Buffalo, Syracuse, Rochester, and Albany as the train from St. Louis continued to move closer to New York. At each stop there were cries first for Ruth, then for Gehrig. Each would come out for a wave and a few words. A kid in Rochester asked how Ruth had hit those three homers.

"I just took a good sock at 'em, boys," the Bam explained.

The train reached Grand Central Station an hour and 15 minutes late at 9:05 P.M. Only a few hundred fans were waiting, but when word circulated that the Yankees had arrived, a crowd estimated at 3,000 soon mobbed the runway up to the station. Ruth was surrounded by six policemen as he made his way through the cheers. He then led a bunch of his teammates across the street to the Hotel Biltmore to see Al Smith. The governor was getting dressed to take his own train trip to campaign in the South. He was glad to see Ruth, whom he called "the boss of the youth of America."

"Are you all through for the season now?" Smith asked.

"All except for a little barnstorming," Ruth replied.

"That's what I'm going to do too," Smith said. "Only instead of hitting the ball, I've got to hit the other candidate."

Waite Hoyt always remembered that the Babe talked on a radio broadcast from the room too, but that almost certainly took place on another day. Ruth spoke a number of times for Smith, even went to a convention in Louisville to speak for him. Whenever and wherever it was, the broadcast Hoyt remembered included Gehrig and Tony Lazzeri. Ruth introduced Gehrig, who said a few words for Al, then Ruth introduced Lazzeri.

"Here's Tony Lazzeri, great second baseman, world champions, blah-blah," the Bam said in introduction. "Tell us, Tony, who are the wops going to vote for?"

Tony presumably said the wops would vote for Al.

CHAPTER TWENTY

A SEQUENCE of different typefaces led the reader of the *Boston Post* down the front page and into a tragic story on the morning of January 12, 1929, a Saturday. This was the *Post* style, a one-column progression of tight headlines that virtually told the story before the reader reached the story. Except this time it didn't.

BURNED TO
DEATH, HER
BED AFIRE

Woman Is Victim as
Home Blazes with
Husband Away

WIFE OF PROMINENT
WATERTOWN DENTIST

Flames Go Through
Ceiling to Reach
the Bedroom

The two paragraphs on the front page described how Mrs. Helen Kinder, 31, wife of Dr. Edward Kinder, prominent dentist, had burned to death in her bedroom at 47 Quincy Street in the Boston suburb of Watertown. Her husband was attending a night of boxing matches at the Boston Garden, and she was alone. The fire started downstairs in the living room, probably from faulty wiring.

A woman, passing along Waverly Avenue, saw the flames coming from the Quincy Street home at around ten o'clock and pulled the corner alarm. The story was continued in the fourth column of page 6. That was where the picture was.

The picture of Helen Kinder.

Who was Helen Woodford.

Who was Helen Ruth.

Poor Helen. Even in death there were complications. She smiled from the printed page the same way she had smiled on opening day and other stiff-upper-lip occasions, the stylish little hat on her head, the diamond brooch the Babe had bought attached to her sweater, and if one of her sisters in South Boston or a bunch of other people hadn't spotted the picture and disregarded the caption that said "Helen Kinder," the onetime waitress from Landers Coffee Shop who married the young baseball player from Baltimore would have been buried under the wrong name in a West Roxbury cemetery, invisible to the end.

The true identification of her remains by her sisters wasn't made until Sunday morning, two hours before she was due to be interred, but by that time a rush of activity had occurred. The Boston newspapers had gotten hold of the story on Saturday night after calls from readers and were blanketing the Watertown neighborhood. Dr. Kinder, wanted for questioning, had gone into hiding. Members of Helen's family were asking questions and making charges. Helen wasn't married to this Dr. Kinder! What had happened here? The word "murder" was mentioned more than once, quickly denied, then mentioned again. The word "drugs" was mentioned. The quiet life of the quiet wife of the famous man was laid out for tabloid autopsy. The burial, of course, was put on hold, and confusion was everywhere, bound to grow larger before it ceased—because the Babe arrived at Back Bay station at seven o'clock on Sunday morning on the overnight train from New York.

He looked terrible, dressed in black, rumpled from the ride, cigar ashes on his suit jacket, grief obvious on his famous face. He had learned about Helen's death at nine o'clock on Saturday night at Joe Dugan's house. One story said there was a call, another said a telegram, a third said an unnamed emissary from Dr. Kinder had appeared, carrying Helen's diamond brooch, singed from the fire. The news, however it arrived, had sent the Babe to the train station.

He was met now in Boston by Arthur Crowley, a friend, the son of Boston police commissioner Michael Crowley. Crowley shook the big man's hand, and they hugged.

"Arthur," the Babe said, "isn't it a tough break to get?"

He wanted to whip into action, wanted to go to Watertown, wanted to go to see his daughter Dorothy—Dorothy! Where was she? She was at the Academy of the Assumption, a boarding school in Wellesley—wanted to do something. Crowley urged him to check into the Hotel Brunswick, his usual suite waiting for him, room 574, and clean up and quiet down.

Crowley ordered him breakfast at the hotel, a double portion of ham and eggs, but Ruth could touch nothing. He drank only coffee. He paced. At 8:45, he and Crowley left the hotel and went to the nine o'clock Mass at St. Cecilia's. The Babe prayed the rosary in a monotone, fingering the large brown beads as the Mass progressed. Once he let out a large sob, startling the people around him.

What the hell had happened?

Helen and Kinder had been living as man and wife in Watertown for at least a year and a half. He was the same age as Helen, and they had grown up together in South Boston. He had served in the war and was cited for bravery in France for crawling into no-man's-land and treating three fallen American soldiers under heavy gunfire. He had returned to dental school at Tufts University. His father said that Kinder and Helen had been legally married in Montreal, a statement that proved to be wrong.

Helen, though, was known in the Watertown neighborhood as "Helen Kinder" and Dorothy was known as "Dorothy Kinder." Neighbors suspected that Helen had money because she dressed well, owned a new car, and bought the 50-cent magazines at the local newsstand rather than the 10-cent or 15-cent magazines. One neighbor knew that Helen really was the Babe's wife because she had seen a picture in the paper of Helen with the Babe at a ball game. The neighbor had never mentioned this to Helen.

The couple seemed to stay up and go out late, but otherwise seemed unremarkable. They had few guests, no parties. No one remembered seeing the Babe in the neighborhood, but one man did remember Kinder saying that he was friends with the slugger and that a family Doberman, in fact, had been given to him by the Babe.

Kinder, when he finally showed up at the Watertown police station, said he had been almost incoherent when he returned from the fights and found out Helen was dead. That accounted for the fact that he had said Helen was his wife. No, she was not his wife. He said he was "helping her out." He had no comment for the press.

The Woodford family in South Boston had a lot to say. Helen had four brothers and three sisters. One of the brothers, Thomas Woodford, who was a Boston policeman, brought up the subject of murder. He didn't like the string of circumstances around his sister's death: the fact that Kinder conveniently was at the boxing matches, the fact that the house was relatively new and shouldn't have had any wiring problems, the fact that Helen never had mentioned a relationship with Kinder.

"I want the truth," Tom Woodford said, "and I'm going to get it, no matter who it happens to hit."

A sister, 19-year-old Nora Woodford, said Helen certainly wasn't Kinder's wife. Nora said she had traveled to New York with Helen and Dorothy only three weeks earlier in December. They all stayed at the Commodore Hotel. She said Helen wanted her along as a witness, because they went to Christy Walsh's office to meet with Walsh and the Babe. The subject was divorce.

The Babe, she said, wanted to marry another woman and "give her child a legal name." Helen, she said, agreed to a quiet divorce in Reno, but only if the Babe would give her $100,000 to take care of her and Dorothy and pay expenses to Reno. The Babe said, "I'm not going to give you another cent," and negotiations fell apart. Christy Walsh tried to be a voice of reason for both parties, but failed.

"And there's one other thing that I want to add and that is that the Babe threatened Helen with a gun while they were at the Sudbury farm about three years ago," Nora Woodford said. "He chased her all over the farm and said that he would shoot her. I don't know what the trouble was about at that time. The maid knows all about it and could tell you the whole story."

The district attorney, confronted with all of these accusations, ordered a second autopsy of Helen's body, this time by a medical examiner who had equipment to analyze the contents of her stomach for traces of poison.

A second fire inspector was called to reexamine the house to make sure that an overloaded socket caused the fire. A local hospital, in other news, confirmed that Helen had been a patient for nervous exhaustion three months earlier and had been advised to enter a sanitarium. Instead, she had checked herself out of the hospital and gone home. A second Woodford brother said Helen had told him in the past year that "she knew a doctor who could get her opium tablets." Ruth Olson, a neighbor, said Helen had been in poor health for the past year and a half.

"Mrs. Ruth faded away to a shadow in the year and a half I was her neighbor," Olson said. "She was a healthy, robust woman when I first moved into the house next door to her. But after her last illness, when she was in the hospital, she weighed only 100 pounds."

One of the many mysteries was the relationship of the Babe and Helen to daughter Dorothy. Various reports had Dorothy born in Boston, Brooklyn, or New York City. She was Helen's natural daughter. She was not Helen's natural daughter. No resolution ever was made. No records of adoption ever were found. Members of the Woodford family declared that they would adopt her, that the Babe was not home enough to be a fit parent. The Babe's attorneys said she would live with him.

In New York, reporters staked out Claire Hodgson's apartment on West 79th. She and her family had disappeared on Sunday night, and their whereabouts were unknown. The newspapers in both Boston and New York were riding the story hard.

The headline in the *New York Daily News* was "Mrs. Babe Ruth Dies in Love Nest Fire."

The Babe invited 20 reporters to his suite at the Brunswick Hotel on Monday. It was a cramped, embarrassing moment in room 574. Just a look at the troubled Ruth made the reporters pause. None of them wanted to intrude on his sorrow, so everybody sat and respectfully waited for the big man to compose himself. This really didn't happen.

"I'm in a hell of a fix, boys . . ." he said.

He clenched and unclenched his hands. He clenched harder until his knuckles turned white.

"All I want to say is that it was a great shock to me . . ."

He started to sob. He tried to speak again, but couldn't. He pulled out a handkerchief. His face contorted. He sobbed again.

"Please let my wife alone," he said. "Let her stay dead."

He cried a little more.

"That's all I've got to say."

The reporters filed out of the room. How could they push him? In the midst of all the charges and accusations and false reports, the Home Run King was a character of sad dignity in this situation. He had no bad words for anybody. Maybe it was years in front of a crowd that made him act the way he did, maybe it was good advice, maybe it was simple good-heartedness at his core, but he walked through the days of mourning, putting one foot in front of the other, with nothing but unadulterated grief. Maybe it was guilt.

The check marks in researching the tale quickly arrived. The second medical examiner announced that there was no evidence of foul play. There was no poison, no alcohol, no drug in Helen's body. She had died from smoke inhalation and the burns she received. The fire inspector again ruled that the fire had sprung from an overloaded connection and faulty wiring. The investigation was done. Death by natural causes.

The many voices in the situation suddenly went silent. The members of the Woodford family made no more claims, telling reporters they accepted the decisions. They said they would not fight for custody of Dorothy. Kinder and his father backed away from the scene with no more comment. The lawyers, hired by everyone in the matter, had nothing more to say. If there had been a financial settlement by Ruth with all parties, which seemed to be the case, it was never discussed. The silence simply came, and Helen could finally be buried.

Ruth paid for all the arrangements. Helen was buried out of the Woodford family home at 420 West Fourth Street in South Boston on Thursday morning, January 17, 1929. At midnight the night before the burial, Ruth arrived at the house to pay his respects. A crowd, estimated as high as 5,000 people, held back by 25 Boston patrolmen, was waiting as his car turned off F Street and came down West Fourth. Flashbulbs lit up the night as he walked up the stairs to the house.

The parlor was filled with flowers, mostly from the Babe. He had received dozens of telegrams of condolence, including messages from Miller Huggins and Lou Gehrig. He moved across the room and knelt next to the body of his wife, which lay in the $1,000 bronze casket he had purchased. It was an open casket; her death was mainly due to smoke inhalation. He stared at her for a full five minutes, looked directly into her eyes. And then he began to wail.

"Oh . . . oh . . . oh . . . oh . . ."

He was sweating, crying, holding on to his rosary beads. The room became quiet. Everyone simply watched.

"Oh . . . oh . . . oh . . . Helen . . ."

When he tried to stand, he collapsed. Arthur Crowley and his father and assorted men grabbed him. They virtually carried him from the parlor, down the stairs, and into the car. His attorney, John Feeney, told him that it was all right to leave. Everything had been arranged for the funeral in the morning.

"What funeral?" the Babe asked.

He was not in much better shape in the morning when he returned to the house for a short, 15-minute service, followed by the cortege to Calvary Cemetery and the 10-minute burial service. The day was cold, and snow was falling as Helen was laid to rest. The Babe stood with his sad face in a group of sad faces. He looked as if he would collapse again at any moment. Photographers took his picture. He was 34 years old, and he had been married to Helen Woodford for 15 tumultuous years.

Now it was done.

"The boys in Boston all said Helen was with the doctor for the drugs," Marshall Hunt said years later. "She was hooked on the stuff. He could give her the prescriptions."

The return to New York was quiet. The newspapers said the Babe returned with Dorothy, his daughter, but that was not the case. She was still in her room at Academy of the Assumption in Wellesley, nine years old and miserable. No one had told her that Helen had died.

Dorothy recalled many years later in her book *My Dad, the Babe* that she had been placed in the school when Helen moved into the new house with Kinder. Helen had explained that the school was wonderful and there was no need for Dorothy to worry, she would see Helen and the doctor every weekend. This was a lie. She said she hadn't seen either of them for six months. She also hadn't seen her father. The other girls would go home for weekends, and she would be left alone in the dorm wondering what had happened to her parents.

The mystery soon deepened.

"One cold night in the middle of January, a week after Helen's death, two nuns woke me up and told me to get dressed and pack all my belongings," Dorothy said in her book. "I had no idea what was going on, but

I did what I was told. The next thing I knew I was boarding a train bound for New York with two nuns who kept saying, 'Trust in God. Everything will be all right.' When I heard that, I knew I was in trouble."

She wound up at the New York Foundling Hospital on East 68th Street. The next morning the mother superior told her that she was going to live with a nice woman named Miss Dooley until her father came for her. Miss Dooley lived in a brownstone in Brooklyn. Her first message to Dorothy was that Dorothy's name had been changed. It was now "Marie Harrington."

What was the deal? For five months, she lived under this new name. Miss Dooley even wrote it on all of her clothes, all of her possessions. The nine-year-old girl despaired. She hated the new name, hated her situation. Would she ever see her father again?

Back in Boston, unknown to her, she had become one of the richest nine-year-olds in the country when Helen's will was read. The will gave five dollars to the Babe, five dollars to her mother, and five dollars to each of her brothers and sisters. Everything else, a figure later determined as $34,224, went to her "ward."

On a spring day in 1929, Miss Dooley took Dorothy back to the New York Foundling Hospital, and there was her father. He looked the same as she had remembered, a teddy bear of a man with a big smile. He was alive! He had come for her! She ran to him and hugged him. That was when she noticed that he was accompanied by a woman with brown hair.

He introduced the woman. He told Dorothy to meet her new mother. That was when she met Claire Hodgson.

The Babe and Claire were married on April 17, 1929, three months and six days after Helen died. They had spent most of those three months and six days apart. He was in spring training in St. Petersburg, had left for Florida early, two weeks after returning from Boston, just to get away from the attention. She was in New York. The phone bill between the two places, she said, was $1,600.

The decision to marry was mutual. They both had worried about the timing, so close to Helen's death, but they consulted with Father William Hughes, a friend from St. Gregory's Church on West 91st Street. He said he saw nothing wrong with getting married immediately. He offered to perform the wedding.

An attempt was made at secrecy, but after their late visit to the marriage license office at the 8:00 P.M. closing on Monday, all the ears of the press were perked. An announcement by Christy Walsh on Tuesday said that the marriage would take place on Wednesday at 6:30 in the morning at St. Gregory's. Walsh, ever the publicist, said that the couple had wanted the wedding to be secret, but "as an appreciation of the consideration that has always been shown him by newspaper writers and photographers," Ruth had authorized him to release the news.

The Babe and Claire then showed up an hour early the next day and were married before most of the press arrived. (Walsh was left to handle the disgruntled journalists.) Two friends, Mr. and Mrs. George Lovell, were the best man and maid of honor. Claire's mother and brothers and Walsh were in attendance, but the rest of the crowd was composed of people going to an early Mass. No ballplayers were at the wedding.

Westbrook Pegler said there was a reason for this.

"The Babe has been drawing away from ballplayers socially these past few years and finding his companionship outside the business," Pegler wrote. "He always had trouble associating with ballplayers. He likes to gad about at night and has the physique to stand up under a brisk social program, but less durable ballplayers who tried to go along with him found themselves asleep on double plays or snoring under fly balls. So they yawned their way out of the league and the Babe was blamed for leading them into evil ways."

The bridal breakfast was held at an 11-room apartment on West 88th Street that was the couple's new home. They would live there with Claire's mother, two brothers, daughter Julia, and, eventually, Dorothy. The Babe proudly showed off the apartment to visitors. He called one room "the billiard room," although no table had been installed. His gift for Claire on their wedding day was a $7,000 diamond bracelet.

"Nice workmanship," someone said.

"The workmanship cost more than the stones," Babe said.

He gave his bride a second gift a day later. Opening day, scheduled for Tuesday, was rained out, then shifted to Wednesday, rained out again, and finally played on Thursday. The opponent was the Red Sox, and the pitcher was Red Ruffing. In the first inning, on a three-and-two count, the Babe swung hard but late and lifted a long fly ball to left that ducked into the stands for a home run. The showbiz audacity of the hit was wonderful. He turned third base on his home run trot and looked at

Claire in her box behind the dugout, tipped his cap, and blew her a little kiss.

Claire stood and cheered. She said she was going to attend every game and the Yankees were going to win another pennant.

This marriage brought a change in the Babe's well-documented modus operandi. The cartoons of the time about marriage often showed the little woman of the house holding a rolling pin while she waited for the late arrival of her man from some transgression. The rolling pin was used to bop the man over the head. Claire now held the rolling pin.

She had done this with some success during her six-year relationship with the Babe, operating as a force behind his subtle moderation since the bad season in 1925. Now, with the title, not to mention the checkbook, she was able to implement a range of reforms. The Babe would spend less, sleep more, eat better, settle for beer instead of harder spirits, dress with suitable panache, and signal before all left-hand turns. For the first time, really, since he had left the Xaverian brothers, someone else would have firm control of his daily life.

"I don't think I am disclosing any secrets when I state that a bride can do an awful lot with her husband of a few months that a wife of ten years can't do," Claire wrote in her memoir. "I was persistent, but persuasive."

The Babe was now on an allowance. If he wanted money, Claire wrote him a $50 check. If he wanted more money, she wrote him another $50 check. Sometimes $50 checks flew through the day like autumn leaves, but there was no more walking around with uncashed checks for $35,000, no more mistaken grabs into the pocket to hand a teammate a random $500 bill. There would be so many endorsed $50 checks that Claire would routinely send them to people requesting the Babe's autograph.

She called herself "an All American wet blanket." She established a ten o'clock curfew both in her own home ("I'm sorry, you have to leave now") and at all events ("I'm sorry, we have to leave now"). She substituted a club sandwich for the big steak the Babe liked to eat before bed. She served only beer in the house during the season. She banned the daily racing form. She cut certain high-living friends from the roster.

When Col. Ruppert invited her to travel with the team on the first road trip of 1929 to Boston, she blanched a bit at the destination but accepted, and soon she was making most road trips, traveling in the drawing-room car with the Babe, the only woman in this roving band of men. She answered the phone in the hotel rooms, was amazed at the number of women who called, and told them that the Playboy of the Western World was out of commission.

"The Babe brought out the beast in a lot of ladies the world over, and I enjoyed very much setting them straight on their problem," Claire wrote. "The Babe was always amused by my reports and rarely failed to point out that this was further evidence that I was the luckiest of women to have snared so obviously desirable a man."

The Babe, for his part, seemed to enjoy the routine. There were still days spent with the boys, some trips that Claire didn't take, some time to operate, but he had the home base that he'd never had before. There was a genuine family with Claire's mother and two brothers and two kids on the scene, all of it legitimate and real. Claire opened all the windows for him so he wouldn't throw out his back. She cut his toenails so he wouldn't stick himself with the scissors. She worried that he would catch a cold.

No one ever had worried that he would catch a cold.

The new season started magnificently, the Yankees of 1929 looking very much like the Yankees of 1928 and 1927 as they bolted off to 13 wins in the first 17 games. But that was an illusion. The surging A's of a year ago were still surging. Led by their own back-to-back sluggers, Jimmie Foxx and Al Simmons, with Lefty Grove and George Earnshaw on the mound, they took over first place on May 13, soon went on an 11-game winning streak, and pretty much had won the pennant before summer even arrived.

The Babe was not part of the problem. With Claire in the stands and newfound virtue in his heart, the well-rested wage earner went back to his job of placing baseballs in strange locations. Early in June, though, he developed a severe chest cold (Claire was right to worry) and wound up at St. Vincent's Hospital for a night. An erroneous report out of Boston said that he had suffered a heart attack, and that report magnified quickly to yet another rumor that he was dead, but he simply had a cold. He needed liquids and rest.

His life since the death of Helen in January had been a merry-go-round of activity, and it was decided that a lot of rest, rather than a little, was the proper answer. He announced that he and Claire were going to an undisclosed location near a lake for a week or ten days.

"No, boys, I can't smoke," he told reporters when they came to his new apartment and he welcomed them in a rose-colored bathrobe. "Doctors' orders. But you can light up. I can't chew or take snuff either. Pretty bad."

He said Dr. Edward King, the Yankees' physician, had outlined a plan for when he returned. He would, if possible, stay out of the ever-present exhibition games the team played on off-days. He also would play only one game of any doubleheader. That would give him more rest during the season.

"It's tough, you know, with all those people around you on the field, charging you after the game," he said about the exhibitions. "Then, after autographing heaven knows how many balls, they mob you, meaning well enough, of course. I am always afraid of spiking some of them, and I generally wind up spiking myself when I have fifty people on top of me.

"What can a man do? Just lie there until they get up. The small-town cops don't help you. They stand by and grin."

The Babe and Claire went for a week to a cottage on Chesapeake Bay. This might have been his quietest stretch in a decade. Three weeks after he left the lineup, he came back in time to hit a pair of homers in a five-game series at the Stadium against the A's. The teams split back-to-back doubleheaders, each twin bill attracting over 70,000 fans, and the A's took the final, single game to leave town with an eight-and-a-half-game lead and total control.

The Babe went back to his long-ball production. Despite missing 17 days and falling nine home runs behind Gehrig, he again would lead the league with 46 and hit .345. He reached a milestone on August 11 in Cleveland when he smacked Indians starter Willis Hudlin's first pitch in the second inning far and wide over the right-field fence at League Park for his 500th home run. It was a startling figure, more than twice as many home runs as anyone in the majors ever had hit. The clout also was the Babe's sixth home run in the past six games.

The ball ricocheted off a Lexington Avenue doorstep and rolled to the feet of Jake Geiser, 46, who was walking to catch a bus home to New

Philadelphia. Geiser was found, brought to the Yankees dugout, and presented with two baseballs and an autographed $20 bill by the Bambino, in exchange for the ball in his possession.

On September 6, Ruth hit one of the longest home runs of his life. The Yankees played an exhibition against inmates at Sing Sing Prison in Ossining, New York, and the Babe, good resolutions about no more exhibitions forgotten, was part of the traveling squad. In the second inning, he hit the first of three home runs on the day, a rocket that soared over the 40-foot stone wall and seemed to carry forever, the inmates in the crowd probably wishing that he could hit them out too. Local legend said that the ball came to rest 620 feet from home plate, but later research indicated the spot was 100 feet closer.

The Babe tried out the electric chair for size, autographed baseballs, and chatted with inmates. He talked for a while with an older man, now blind, and later asked one of the guards what the man had done to land in Sing Sing. The guard said the man had killed his wife and had been on Death Row until his sentence was reduced to life in prison.

"Gosh," the Babe said.

On September 20, a sad conclusion to a long year began. Miller Huggins entered the hospital. The little manager had felt lousy for most of the season and had promised to whip himself into shape when the campaign ended. An aggravating carbuncle on his face near his eye and unremitting headaches finally sent him to St. Vincent's Hospital.

Waite Hoyt, knocked out in the fifth inning, had come into the clubhouse a day earlier and found Huggins with his face under some kind of a heat lamp, trying to find relief from the carbuncle. The treatment, it turned out, was absolutely wrong. This wasn't a normal growth, it was the symptom of a skin disease called erysipelas, also known as St. Anthony's fire. Instead of drawing the carbuncle to a head, the heat helped the disease germinate and spread. His body was filled with poison.

Two days after he entered the hospital, Huggins's temperature was 105 degrees. He was receiving blood transfusions, and his condition was listed as "grave." Five days after he entered the hospital, the little man was dead. He was 50 years old.

"Huggins was the best manager I ever played for," Hoyt said. "I played for Connie Mack, John McGraw, Bill Terry, Bucky Harris, and Pie Traynor and quite a number of managers. Huggins had an unenviable job in managing Ruth and a group of fairly temperamental ballplayers, but he did it great.

"The discipline on the Yankee bench was impeccable. You sat there as if you were in third grade in school, and you did nothing but talk baseball or talk about the game that was being played, and every once in a while, why Hug would call down to someone on the bench and say, 'What's the count on the batter?' And you'd better know."

"He didn't have physical size, so he had to use other things to control players," Marshall Hunt said. "He'd made some good investments, that was his hobby, so he'd made some money. He'd tell a player, 'I'm all set. Financially, I don't care about anything. So I can make a decision and not worry. I don't care if I'm fired. I'm all set, and Colonel Ruppert is all set, and so we don't have to put up with this. Do you understand?' "

The Yankees were playing in Boston when Huggins died. Men walking through the stands with megaphones announced the news to the 7,000 spectators at Fenway Park. The game was halted at the end of the fifth inning, the flag in center field lowered to half-staff.

"It is one of the things you can't talk about much," the Babe said about Huggins's death. "You know what I thought of Miller Huggins, and you know what I owe him. It is one of the keenest losses I have ever felt. I, as well as the rest of the boys, cannot realize yet that we won't have him with us again on the bench."

The funeral was held at the Little Church Around the Corner on East 29th Street. Ruth, Gehrig, Lazzeri, Combs, Pennock, and Shawkey were pallbearers along with coaches Art Fletcher and Charlie O'Leary. The burial was in Cincinnati. Marshall Hunt was part of the group that accompanied the body.

"Babe Ruth took five years off my brother's life," Huggins's sister, Mildred, told one reporter.

Huggins's death seemed like a milestone. There is a time in most lives approaching middle age when the scorecard starts to fill up, when the eyes notice a list of departed figures from a circle that had seemed immune, bulletproof against normal attrition. One person dies, and maybe there is an explanation; two, an accident; three, a strange disease. But when four or five die, the eyes notice and the brain starts considering the limitations of mortality.

The Babe was 35 now, and that kind of time had arrived. Huggins was dead, and Helen was dead, and come to think of it, some other people from his life had died in the past year or so. Harry Frazee for one. The man who sold the Babe to the Yankees had died in June.

The cause was Bright's disease, a problem of the kidneys often linked to excessive alcohol consumption. Frazee was 48, supposedly had beaten the disease, had taken a trip to Europe, and was back with more show-business plans. He suffered a fast relapse in New York, and Jimmy Walker, the mayor and a friend, hastened to be with him at his Park Avenue bedside at the end.

Jack Dunn had died too. The man who had signed the Babe off the back field at St. Mary's School and brought him to professional baseball had a heart attack while riding a horse during field trials with his dogs in Maryland. Fell off the horse and was dead when he hit the ground, maybe before he ever fell. He was 56 years old.

Joe Lannin, the Red Sox owner who had purchased Babe's contract from Dunn, the man who had sold the Red Sox to Frazee, had died. He had either fallen or jumped from a ninth-floor window at the Hotel Granada in Brooklyn. He was worth $8 million when he died and was the owner of Roosevelt Field in Long Island. That meant he had been the owner of the spots where both Charles Lindbergh and the Babe took off.

Finally, Urban Shocker had died a year ago in September 1928. The heart problem that had dogged the troubled spitballer while he pitched in 1927 and ended his career in 1928 had ended his life. He had argued with a nurse only 40 minutes before his death because he wanted to hear the big doubleheader between the Yankees and the A's on the radio and she thought it would be too stressful. He was 38 years old.

There might have been other names too, names not associated with the Babe in public but people he encountered in the quiet parts of his life—a familiar waiter, a business guy, a golfing companion—who joined the list. Even if there weren't, it was obvious that a darker time had come along, that the free ride of a young and constantly impetuous spirit had come to an end.

In a lot of ways the party was done. There would be no pennant to hang from the center-field flagpole when the new decade opened in April at the Stadium. The roster would shift again, with friends traded or released, replaced by kids with names that couldn't be remembered. The end of his career was a lot closer now than the beginning was. The Babe still felt good, certainly still could hit the baseball, but there had been a change of seasons, a change of approach.

Life had become harder, hadn't it?

This was 1929. Twenty-three days after the end of the baseball season, everybody in America would begin to feel that way.

CHAPTER TWENTY-ONE

J OHN JAKOB RASKOB, the noted financier and capitalist, called "the creator of General Motors," sometimes moved in the same circles as the Babe. He was an Artie McGovern guy, one of the Wall Street bigwigs who received a wake-up call to come to McGovern's gym for conditioning. He also was, while it lasted, the head of the Babe-endorsed Al Smith campaign for president that failed in 1928 when Smith lost to Herbert Hoover. Raskob was the ultimate New York mover, shaker, doer.

In the August 1929 issue of *Good Housekeeping* magazine, he was the focus of an article that soon became infamous. The title was "Everybody Ought to Be Rich." Raskob, interviewed by Samuel Crowther, advocated vigorous investment in the stock market by even the smallest investor. He pointed out that $10,000 invested ten years earlier in General Motors would now be worth $1.5 million. He forecast similar growth in the future.

"No man can become rich merely by saving," he advised. "Putting aside a sum each week or month in a sock at no interest or in a savings bank at ordinary interest will not provide enough for old age unless life in the meantime be rigorously skimmed down to the level of mere existence."

The words hung in the air two months later as the last happy whistle of the canary before the mine shaft exploded. Over a five-day stretch from October 24 to October 29, the final day forever known as "Black Tuesday," the stock market crashed. The descent to what would be known as the Great Depression had begun.

Mere existence soon would become a desirable state.

"October 29, 1929, yeah, a frenzy," industrialist Arthur A. Robertson said in *Hard Times: An Oral History of the Great Depression* by Studs Terkel.

> I must have gotten calls from a dozen and a half friends who were desperate. In each case, there was no sense in loaning them money they would give the broker. Tomorrow they'd be worse off than they were yesterday. Suicides, left and right, made a terrific impression on me, of course. People I knew. One day you saw prices at a hundred, the next day at $20, at $15.
>
> On Wall Street, the people walked around like zombies. . . . One of my friends said to me, "If things keep going as they are, we'll all have to go begging." I asked, "Who from?"

The national good times had stopped. The great unemployment and the shuttered businesses and the breadlines and the shantytowns in public parks did not appear, just like that, next day, but the reverberations from the implosion of the market had begun and would continue for an entire decade. The breadlines, shantytowns, and all the rest would soon arrive, and the great optimism, the do-anything confidence of the Jazz Age twenties, would be replaced by the pessimism and gloom of the thirties, the struggle for . . . mere existence.

Though the Babe basically was untouched by the Wall Street Crash—his money in annuities, his job secure for the moment—he would be in the midst of what would follow. As he grew older, heavier, slower with each year, he would present a convenient reference in the troubled today to the giddy, all-powerful yesterday. This would be inevitable, wouldn't it? He was a picture from yesterday, a picture of the twenties, aging in front of public eyes. His good time and the country's good time seemed forever entwined in the past tense.

Except now, none of this mattered . . .

"If the Yankees reject my request for an increase [in salary], I will remain idle, which at my age means retirement from baseball," the Babe wrote in a letter that was mimeographed and sent to every New York sports editor in the shadow of the Crash. "I mean organized baseball. A few years ago I could not take this attitude. I would be obliged to sign at any terms for the same reason that 95 percent of all players have to sign— bread and butter. Every holdout in baseball had to sign because he had no money in the bank.

"Well, there is enough bread and butter in our home, even if I never touch another baseball in my life."

Except this was 1930. This was just the start. Who knew what would happen next? Who knew the Great Depression had started? In March 1930, John Jakob Raskob sat in the Manhattan office of architect William Frederick Lamb. During meetings, Raskob liked to take notes with those oversized fat yellow pencils that children use in first grade, easy to grip, capable of drawing fat first letters. He stood one of those pencils on its unsharpened end on architect Lamb's desk and said, "Bill, how high can you make it so that it won't fall down?" Fifteen months later, the Empire State Building was open for business.

In March 1930, after Babe Ruth asked for a raise, he got it. Who knew?

The first meeting in the contract dance was held at Col. Ruppert's office at the brewery on January 7, 1930, ten years to the day after Ruth had been purchased from the Red Sox. The only participants were Ruth, Ruppert, and Ed Barrow. The Yankees opened with $70,000 for one season, the same figure Ruth had earned for the last three years. He laughed. Ruppert and Barrow moved the number to $75,000, the same salary as the president of the United States, for each of the next two seasons. Ruth laughed again. His figure was $85,000 per year for the next three years. Ruppert and Barrow laughed.

Five days later, the Babe and Claire left early for Florida. All of the numbers sat on Ruppert's desk as the standoff began.

The Babe took delight in the Florida sun. He played golf with Al Smith. He was a judge at a heavyweight fight, giving the decision to Big Jeff Carroll over Bert Finch, a St. Petersburg fireman. He went quail hunting with teammates Benny Bengough and George Pipgras and shot a rattlesnake dead in the head when it poised to strike. He sent his mimeographed letter to the sports editors, not the Yankees, in the first week of February.

"No comment," Barrow said when asked about it. He was not happy with the Babe's new strategy.

The situation rolled along, straight into the opening of training camp on March 3. The Babe showed up, participated in workouts. The Colonel showed up on March 7, the eve of the first exhibition against the Boston Braves, and offered $80,000 per year for two years. The Babe said he would give up the third year, but wanted $85,000 per year. The Colonel said he had made his final offer.

Dan Daniel, baseball writer for the *New York Telegram*, now became involved. Or at least that was Daniel's story. He had a tendency to put himself into most stories, so they often were viewed as a bit too . . . elaborate. He swore that this was true.

He said that he and Ford Frick from the *World* ran into Ruth after Ruth had turned down the offer in the meeting with Ruppert. They questioned the big man about why he was going to play the next day against the Braves. Wasn't he worried about injuries? He'd be a fool to play. The Babe agreed with their thinking. He said he would either sign in the morning or turn in his uniform.

Daniel went back to his hotel room and typed long and hard, telling this story about Ruth's edict, that he was either going to sign or hand in his uniform. In the morning, Daniel had a congratulatory phone call from his editor for the scoop. No other paper had it.

Daniel became worried. Why hadn't Frick written it? Had Ruth changed his mind? Did Frick know that? Ruth had. Frick, who was also Ruth's ghostwriter, knew.

Daniel, in a panic, went to find Ruth. The slugger said it was a nice day and he wasn't worried, really, about getting hurt and was going to play without a contract. Daniel, thinking that his editor might take back those congratulations in a hurry, had to do something. He urged Ruth to sign for the $80,000 per year for two years.

"What's the matter with you?" Daniel said he said. "Did you know that yesterday in Union Square there was a riot? A lot of people were rioting for bread."

"What'd you say?" Ruth said.

"A lot of people were rioting for bread," Daniel said. "They're broke. There's a depression. And you're holding out for $85,000 a year while they're starving. It's making a very bad impression, and it's hurting baseball."

"Nobody told me."

Ruth agreed to sign. Daniel called Ruppert. Two years at $80,000 per year. The Babe and Claire showed up at Ruppert's suite at the Princess

Martha Hotel at noon, and he played that afternoon in the 12–9 exhibition win over the Braves. There was only one addendum. Ruth wanted the $5,000 fine levied on him in 1925 to be returned. The fine always had bothered him.

"If Huggins had lived, you would not be getting this," Ruppert said. "But Miller is dead and he won't know."

That was Daniel's story. It was as good as any.

Three weeks later, American humorist Will Rogers signed a one-year contract for $72,000 to deliver 14 radio talks during the coming year on the National Broadcasting System. Each talk would last from 12 to 15 minutes, which newspaper mathematicians soon figured meant that Rogers would receive $350 per minute for his services.

"Compared with Will Rogers," one mathematician said, "Babe Ruth is a piker."

Not everyone was jumping out of windows as the hard times hit.

In the next two seasons, the Yankees and the Colonel received good value for their two $80,000 payouts. The Babe led the league in home runs both years, with 49 in 1930 and 46 in 1931, a tie with Gehrig. He hit .359 in 1930, .373 in 1931. He continued an amazing stretch, leading the league in slugging average for the 13th season in the last 14, having missed only in the troubled 1925 campaign. Even with the formidable Gehrig behind him, he led the league in walks in both 1930 and 1931.

More importantly, from an $80,000-per-year perspective, he kept the Yankees alive at the gate. The A's ran off into the horizon in the standings—finishing eight games in front of the Senators and sixteen in front of the Yankees in 1930, thirteen and a half in front of the second-place New Yorkers in 1931—but 1,169,230 people still went to the Stadium in 1930, and 912,437 in 1931. These were very good numbers in a market that would grow more bleak as the economy faltered. (The A's, despite their success, drew pitiful crowds in Philadelphia. The Yankees wouldn't have another 1,000,000-fan season until 1946.)

The Big Bam was still baseball's best attraction. The team still played an average of 33 exhibitions every year, along with the regular schedule, and he still was the reason small-town fans came to the box office. A chance to see the Sultan of Swat still was considered the chance of a lifetime, even more so now that he was edging slowly toward the exit.

His range as an outfielder obviously was diminishing—his legs were a problem, and the geometry of a large man shifted toward his waistline as he became older—but he still could hit. In May 1930, in back-to-back doubleheaders at Philadelphia's Shibe Park, he hit six home runs in two days. The A's and Yankees then went to the Stadium for yet another doubleheader—who made up this schedule?—and he hit two more. This made eight home runs in six games. Against the best team in the league.

"The only one who will beat Babe Ruth out of the home run leadership is Father Time," John Kieran wrote in the *Times*. "The old gentleman with the scythe may cut him down at any time, but as long as he can stumble up to the plate and have his share of swings he will have more than his share of home runs when they come to check up on the totals."

His pace toward 60 home runs in 1927 always offered illusionary hope because he had hit so many in September, but it was well noted that he was far ahead of the pace in 1930 with 31 by July 2. He ripped the nail off the ring finger of his left hand on the outfield screen making a catch at the Stadium that day, however, and missed more than a week while it healed. He manufactured home runs at a slower pace after that to reach 49 as the Yankees fell far behind the A's.

This was not a happy Yankees team. Former pitcher Bob Shawkey was now the manager, having replaced the deceased Miller Huggins. The first choice had been coach Art Fletcher, but he declined. Shawkey, also a coach in 1929, was a Huggins recommendation from the grave, a candidate Huggins had endorsed to Ruppert before he died.

Thirty-nine years old, retired for only two years from the active roster, Shawkey was caught in the uneasy situation of the former player back as the boss of veterans who had been his friends. He was still "Sailor Bob," "Bob the Gob," former yeoman petty officer in the war on the USS *Arkansas*, the right-hander who always wore a red-sleeved sweatshirt when he pitched. The transition was hard for everyone.

"Shawkey and I didn't get along too well," Waite Hoyt said. "We used to have an apartment together before he married, and he was married about four times, and between marriages he and I and Fred Hofmann had an apartment over on Riverside Drive, and I knew him pretty well and Bob was a pretty good guy, but we just didn't get along. He lived in a different world than I did.

"So we had an argument down in San Antonio during spring training, and that, of course, caused a breach between us, and in May of 1930 he traded Mark Koenig and myself to the Detroit Tigers."

Ruth was friendly enough with Shawkey, had gone on hunting trips and golfed with him, but Ruth had wanted another choice for manager: himself. After Fletcher declined, Ruth (with Claire in back of him no doubt) pushed his own candidacy with Ruppert and Barrow. Why shouldn't he be the manager? Any number of stars—Cobb, Hornsby, Speaker, now Walter Johnson—had become managers. That was a natural progression. Shouldn't he follow it?

Ruppert and Barrow told him that they didn't want a player-manager and that he was more valuable as a player. It was a convenient excuse, but only pushed the confrontation off to the side. When the Yankees bosses decided toward the end of the 1930 season that Shawkey had been a mistake, they had Ruth back in front of the door. They tried the same arguments, but this time Ruth argued back. Player-managers had been part of baseball history. Player-managers had won pennants.

"How can you manage a team," Ruppert finally asked, the heart of the matter, "when you can't manage yourself?"

Ruth replied that he had changed.

He took the selection in October of Joe McCarthy as the new manager as almost an insult. McCarthy, 44, had just been fired by the Chicago Cubs. As a player, he never had reached the big leagues. He was known as a disciplinarian, an enforcer of rules, the opposite of Miller Huggins. The new manager of the Yankees had about a thousand things wrong with him in the mind of Babe Ruth. The worst was that he wasn't Babe Ruth.

Ruth played for McCarthy, played well, but didn't like it. McCarthy made some quick changes to set a tone—no more card playing in the clubhouse, compulsory breakfast at 8:30 in the hotel dining room on the road, little tweaks to establish a businesslike atmosphere. No more shaving in the clubhouse! A man should come to this job the way he came to any job: clean-shaven and ready to work. The changes didn't affect Ruth much—he always was clean-shaven when he came to work, was exempt from the breakfast rule owing to the commotion he would make, and rarely played cards in the clubhouse—but they were symbolic nuisances. Hadn't Yankee teams won some pennants and World Series championships with a card table in the clubhouse? With a razor in the shower room? Without a good breakfast on the road?

McCarthy was smart enough to leave Ruth alone, to simply let him play. He did respect Ruth's stature and obviously wanted his offensive production. Ruth was smart enough to leave McCarthy alone. The grand collisions that would have happened ten years earlier, the Babe flouting all authority if a stronger disciplinarian than Huggins had been in charge, did not happen. Ruth played, hit his 600th homer in the middle of the 1931 season, did his job for the man he didn't like, and went about his own business. It was an efficient situation, a truce, but lacked a certain joy.

When the season was done, the Babe went to Hollywood to make some short instructional films about baseball. While he was there, he gave an interview that described a life that had grown tired in many respects. The comments quickly were called "Babe Ruth's Ten Can'ts."

"I can't go to movies. It might hurt my eyes," he said.

"I can't dance. They tell me it's bad for my legs.

I can't attend a night club. They'd say I was drinking and carousing.

I can't read a book on a train. It's too hard on my eyes and I spend most of my life on trains.

I can't gamble. I love to bet on horses—on anything, but if I was seen with gamblers or in gambling houses it would start gossip.

I can't travel on airplanes. It's against the rules of my contract and my insurance policies.

I can't shake hands promiscuously. It's dangerous.

I can't go swimming. I'm told I would expose myself to colds.

I can't speed my sixteen-cylinder automobile. If I was hurt while speeding, my wages would be stopped.

I can't enjoy golf. I'm followed by autograph seekers.

Hang it all, I can't do anything. Not just yet. But wait. In two years I'll be through with baseball, then I'll break loose—wide open. Not for long, but for a while."

There was exaggeration here for sure. He still could do—and did—many of these things, but the sparks of discovery and defiance were long gone. The long-ago wonder of the boy from St. Mary's Industrial School was long gone.

His personal life was as settled as it had ever been. On October 30, 1930, after he had "covered" the World Series for the Christy Walsh syndicate, the Babe and Claire signed the papers at Surrogate's Court in New York to adopt jointly both Claire's 12-year-old daughter Julia and Dorothy, now nine. This officially made him father as well as husband. He not only was a family man but had papers to prove it.

He slipped into the role without much difficulty, but it wasn't a difficult role. He wasn't home that much, so Claire and her mother and her two brothers had more to do with the two girls than he did. When he was home, he sat in his big chair, the only overstuffed chair in the house, smoked his cigar, looked out the window at the Hudson River, and listened to *Gangbusters, The Shadow*, and *The Lone Ranger* on the radio. He was the father as caricature. He was gone by 7:30 in the morning, never home before 7:30 at night.

"He loved to come home and throw his huge raccoon coat at me and see if I could catch it—which was almost impossible, since the coat weighed more than I did," Dorothy wrote in *My Dad, the Babe*. "I would always wind up on the floor underneath the coat while my father laughed and laughed."

Julia, Claire's daughter, loved when the Babe would wake her at five in the morning on the days he was going hunting. He would make breakfast for the two of them, his special breakfast of browned bread with a fried egg in the middle of it, topped by a slice of fried bologna. They would eat alone, then he would go hunting and she would go back to bed.

The complexities of domestic life were left to Claire. Dorothy always felt that she was the forgotten figure in the house. She painted a picture of an alliance between Claire and Julia that worked against her. Julia had the better room. Julia had the better clothes. Julia went to private school, Dorothy went to public. The Babe was the titular head, but Claire pretty much ran the show.

A look at the Babe at home for photographers and sportswriters came in the first month of the 1931 season. He had been injured in the first week of the season in Boston when he tried to score from third on a Lazzeri fly ball to right. Beaten by the throw, he went into a football collision with Sox catcher Charlie Berry, who indeed once had been a football player at Lafayette. Ruth dislodged Berry from the ball and touched the plate with his hand, but he also dislodged some blood vessels in his left thigh. This caused him to collapse in the field in the bottom of the inning, his left leg paralyzed, when he tried to chase a fly ball. He was carried to the dugout, spent five days in a Boston hospital, and now was finishing his recuperation at home.

He lay on a pale green divan in his green bathrobe and pajamas, a color-coordinated patient. He ordered up cigars for everyone, Artie McGovern passing around a humidor, and smoked and posed for pictures with Claire and said he thought he might be back in 48 hours if things kept going well. Claire, on the side, said he didn't have a chance. He hadn't even walked yet with a cane.

"Two weeks," she said. "That's what the doctor said. He's going to take two weeks."

Claire, who was right in her prognosis, ran his life and he did not argue. The role of the henpecked husband fit an older man. He had an explanation for why he sometimes didn't do the things he used to do—his wife wouldn't like it. He worked under Claire's rules much happier than he did under Joe McCarthy's rules. He had a partner. An irony was that Jumpin' Joe Dugan and Waite Hoyt both were in the midst of divorces brought about by the Murderers' Row fun times and here he was, the family man.

Claire also had become part of all business discussions about the Babe. All deals went through Claire. She asked the questions that he never had asked. He was much more financially solvent.

"It took three varied skills to make the Babe wealthy," Claire said in her book. "First and foremost there had to be a demand for Babe's services. Babe more than provided that. Somebody had to handle the offers and see that Babe got a fair price. Christy Walsh handled that. I handled the Babe."

Christy Walsh was still involved but now spent more time with his other clients. The biggest probably was Knute Rockne, the Notre Dame football coach. Walsh worked the same program with Rockne that he had worked with the Babe: the ghostwritten articles, the publicity appearances, the constant spread of the name, leading to business opportunities. Rockne wound up at the Mayo Clinic once, exhausted from the schedule.

On the night of March 30, 1931, Walsh had dinner in Chicago with Rockne and Alfred Fuller, a local hotel man. The agent had arranged a movie deal for Rockne in Hollywood, and at the end of dinner Walsh and Fuller put Rockne in a cab to the train station to catch an overnight to Kansas City, where he would take a morning mail flight to Los Angeles.

"Hope you have a soft landing," Fuller said in good-bye.

"You mean a happy landing," Rockne replied.

At 11 o'clock the next morning, the plane carrying Rockne and seven other passengers crashed shortly after takeoff in a field in Bazaar, Kansas.

All eight people were killed. It instantly became the most famous crash in American aviation history.

Christy Walsh's wife, Madaline, fainted when she heard the news in Los Angeles. She had expected her husband to be one of the passengers.

In 1932 Ruth took a $5,000 pay cut. Salaries were being reduced everywhere. People were being asked to work one week a month for free in many industries. Banks were failing. Even a leader in home runs, second in the American League in batting average, was affected by the new national austerity. Baseball owners across the board had promised to cut over $1 million in salary for the new season. The best place to start was at the top.

Ruth at first asked for two more seasons at the same $80,000 he had made the past two seasons. The Colonel offered $70,000 for one season. He said no player should make $80,000 in these troubled times. Ruth did not agree.

"What about the depression?" a sportswriter asked Ruth.

"I didn't see much of a depression with the Yankees," Ruth replied.

This was a gentlemanly dispute as befit the times. The compromise for one year at $75,000 plus 25 percent of net proceeds from exhibition games (part of his previous contract) came again in St. Petersburg at the Rolyat Hotel, where the Babe and Claire were staying. He and Ruppert signed the contract in front of a wishing well, then Claire and both of them tossed coins into the water. The Babe asked for a Yankee pennant. Claire asked for two more years of Yankees contracts. The Colonel asked for the money in the wishing well. Ruth tossed in an extra silver half-dollar to that end.

"There goes some of this year's contract," he announced.

The season that followed again was solid, with 41 home runs and a .341 batting average, but for the first time in his American League career the Babe was not the acknowledged King/Sultan/Maharajah of Swat. Jimmy Foxx of the A's took the honors this time. He was the one who was matched against the 1927 homer pace in the newspapers and gave it a good run, finishing with 58. (He came to the final weekend needing four home runs in three games to reach 60.) Foxx even took away the slugging average title.

Although the drop-off in the Babe's numbers wasn't great, the symbolic shift of coming in second in both categories was huge. The inventor now saw someone use his invention better than he did. He never would lead the league again. Even on the Yankees, Gehrig had become the subtle constant, the true star. He hit four home runs on June 2, 1932, in a game against the A's at Shibe Park, something the Babe never had done.

The game was a fight now. Claire talked about putting an electric pad on her man's knees every night to keep him going. He left games early, replaced by Sammy Byrd or Myril Hoag for pinch-running or for defensive purposes in late innings. He missed a few games in June when he pulled a muscle in the back of his leg while chasing a fly ball. In September he had a mystery ailment. He and Claire left the team in Detroit on September 7 with the permission of Joe McCarthy and hurried back to Dr. King in New York because the Babe had shooting pains in his side and thought he had appendicitis.

The doctor never announced what Ruth's problem was. There was no operation, but he missed ten days and was packed in ice for much of the time. When he returned to the Stadium for his first workout on September 17, he was so weak that he didn't hit one ball into the stands during batting practice. He said, after the ice, he had to get thawed out.

He was in a hurry, of course, because the silver half-dollar in the wishing well in St. Petersburg had worked. The Yankees had had an extraordinary season. Ten days later, they would open up the World Series against the Chicago Cubs. If McCarthy's methods hadn't found favor with the Babe, they had with other parts of the roster. With Lefty Gomez and Red Ruffing as a one-two combination on the mound, backed by solid defense and the familiar bats of Ruth and Gehrig, Combs and Lazzeri, plus heavy-swinging catcher Bill Dickey, the Yankees had pulled away from the A's this time, winning the pennant by thirteen and a half games.

The Babe would have his tenth World Series. Healthy again by the time the games arrived, he also would have his most remembered moment, a combination of timing, excellence, folklore, and fun. That would be "the Called Shot," a story that should be told from the beginning.

On July 6, 1932, a 21-year-old woman named Violet Valle went to the room at the Hotel Carlos at 3834 Sheffield Avenue in Chicago where 24-year-old Cubs shortstop Billy Jurges lived. Ms. Valle, a jilted lover, was upset with Jurges and had a 25-caliber revolver to prove it. Her plan was to kill Jurges and then kill herself.

"To me, life without Billy isn't worth living," she wrote in a good-bye note she left for her brother. "But why should I leave this earth alone? I'm going to take Billy with me."

Her execution of the plan, once she was admitted by the shortstop into his room, was a bit slow. Jurges was able to wrestle her for the gun. He was shot twice, once in the ribs and once in the hand, and she was shot once, but neither of the combatants was seriously injured. They both were taken to the hospital.

Jurges, the gentleman, refused to press charges. Violet, passions subsided, signed a 22-week vaudeville contract for shows that billed her as "Violet (What I Did for Love) Valle—The Most Talked-About Woman in Chicago." The story had a reasonably happy ending for everyone concerned except for the Cubs, who needed a shortstop to replace Jurges while his injuries healed.

They settled on Mark Koenig, the shortstop on the 1927 Murderers' Row Yankees, who had been released by the Tigers in the spring and now was playing for the minor league San Francisco Seals. Koenig, who had thought his big league days were done, hurried to Chicago, hit like a madman, never left the lineup, even when Jurges returned, and finished with a .356 batting average as the Cubs outlasted the Pittsburgh Pirates and won the National League pennant.

In voting for World Series shares, dividing up the money that would be won in the next week, a perilous moment in many teams' intrapersonal relationships, the Cubs, alas, disregarded his fine effort and voted him only a half-share as they prepared to face the Yankees. (It was, after all, the Depression.) The Yankees, most of whom knew Koenig, of course, took this as great catcalling ammunition for the Series, a chance to tell the Cubs many times how cheap they were.

The chief catcaller was Ruth. He was no great friend of Koenig's—indeed, they'd had a locker-room fight in 1929 when Koenig made a deprecating remark about Claire shortly after Ruth's marriage—but Ruth always had an active mouth on the bench. He riddled the Cubs with comments about Koenig and cheapness during the first two games of the Series in New York. The Cubs riddled him back with questions about his parentage, his increasing weight, his racial features, his sexual preferences, and whatever else they could invent. The "nigger" word from long ago surfaced. It was all familiar baseball stuff for the time, but with an exaggerated edge.

The Yankees won the first two games at the Stadium and traveled to a packed Wrigley Field to try to take care of the rest of business. Newspaper accounts of the back-and-forth bench jockeying had stirred the local public. The Yankees had been subjected to insults as they made their way to the Edgewater Hotel, especially Ruth, who was walking to the hotel with Claire. The back-and-forth resumed as soon as the third game started, with a crowd of over 51,000 in the stands.

Ruth had one hole card in all arguments on this afternoon. A terrific wind was blowing out toward right field. In batting practice, both he and Gehrig had hammered a bunch of shots over the wooden temporary stands. He couldn't have asked for better conditions.

"The Babe is on fire," Gehrig said after batting practice. "He ought to hit one today. Maybe a couple."

The first one came in the first inning off Cubs starter Charlie Root, with two men on base, to give the Yankees a 3–0 lead. In the third inning, Root won the battle, getting Ruth to fly deep to right-center. All of this time, the back-and-forth with the Cubs dugout continued. Ruth also had established communications with the fans in right. They hooted at him when he was too slow to reach a soft line drive by Jurges in the fourth and Jurges wound up on second base. (Koenig had injured a wrist in the first game of the Series.) Ruth hooted back, tipping his cap. His entire day was a happy, malevolent dialogue with somebody. Two lemons had been thrown at him when he went to the plate in the first inning.

All of which was prelude to his at-bat in the fifth. Root was still on the mound. The score was tied, 4–4. Nobody was on base. Ruth came to the plate, and another lemon rolled his way. While the umpire disposed of the lemon, Ruth did more gesturing with the fans. He then settled in to face Root.

The first pitch was a called strike. The players in the Cubs dugout were yelling, particularly pitcher Guy Bush, a native of Aberdeen, Mississippi, who was standing on the top step. Ruth looked toward Bush and the dugout and put up one finger, as if to say, "That's just one strike." Root then delivered two balls, followed by a second called strike. More yelling. Bush was out of the dugout, onto the grass, and yelling. Ruth held up two fingers this time as if to say, "That just two strikes." He then pointed. Where he pointed is a question, but legend has it that he pointed to dead center field.

Cubs catcher Gabby Hartnett later said that Ruth said, "It only takes one to hit." Gehrig, in the on-deck circle, said Ruth said to Root, "I'm going to knock the next one down your goddamned throat." A pair of 16mm home movies discovered more than half a century later seemed to indicate that Ruth might have pointed at the Cubs bench and at Bush rather than dead center field (maybe Ruth wanted to knock the ball down Bush's goddamned throat?), but both films were taken from angles that left room for doubt.

Whatever happened, the next part was not debatable. Root threw a slow curve. Ruth slammed the baseball up and into the big, carrying wind, and the ball left the park somewhere between the scoreboard and the edge of the right-field bleachers, one of the longest and prettiest home runs in Wrigley history. He circled the bases as happy as he ever had been, saying, "Lucky, lucky, lucky," and imparted wisdom to each of the Chicago infielders as he passed and raised four fingers at the Cubs bench as he rounded third and laughed and laughed all the way home. Four fingers. Four bases. Four games.

When all the celebrating calmed down, Root took a fresh baseball and served it to Gehrig, who swung on the first pitch and hit a homer deep, deep to right, and the Yankees were off to a 7–5 win. The next day they won again, 13–6, to close out the Series in four games. Gehrig was the undeniable star of the show with three home runs and a .529 batting average, but it was the Ruth home run—"the Called Shot"—that was remembered.

"It was a privilege to be present because it is not likely that the scene will ever be repeated in all its elements," Westbrook Pegler wrote for the next morning's *Tribune Syndicate*. "Many a hitter may make two home runs or possibly three in World Series play yet to come, but not the way Babe Ruth hit these two. Nor will you ever see an artist call his shot before hitting one of the longest drives ever made on the grounds, in a World Series game, laughing and mocking the enemy with two strikes gone."

Did he call his shot? Didn't he? Though not mentioned in most immediate deadline accounts of the game, the moment would be gilded two and three and four days later, embellished, built into Johnny Sylvester death-watch proportions. Then, years later, it would be debunked, seen as pure fable. Proof would be requested and questions asked of participants and bystanders, everything taken as seriously as if this were the examination of a final miracle needed from the Vatican for sainthood.

The moment became quite overblown.

"He shouted to his enemies," Paul Gallico wrote two days later in the *Daily News*. "He pointed like a duelist to the spot where he expected to send his rapier home and then he sent it there. His second home run in the face of the razzing he was taking from the Cubs camp was a stroke of genius. He went so far out on his limb with his gestures and his repartee and his comportment at the plate that if he had missed he never would have been able to live it down. But the point is he didn't miss."

Did it happen exactly that way? Probably not. Did it happen? The Babe always was predicting home runs. He had that itchy feeling that he was going to hit a home run for Lindbergh. He told Mark Roth, the traveling secretary, that he'd end the game so the team could make the train. He once told Ford Frick's father, at an exhibition in Fort Wayne, Indiana, "You look like you want to get home for supper," and hit a home run. In 1930 he hit three home runs against the Philadelphia A's, then came to the plate the fourth time, batted right-handed for two strikes, then stepped across the plate and swung with a fury to strike out on the next pitch. What if he had connected? Where would that have gone down in the lore?

He called shots all the time. He loved to create situations. It was for other people to determine what they meant. Did he call a shot here? That probably never will be answered to every nitpicker's satisfaction. He definitely created a situation. He challenged his entire environment, whipped up all parties, then made them shut up. The specifics might be hazy, but the general story was not wrong.

Ruth himself gave different versions through the years of what happened that day, which did nothing to help historians. He said more than once that he absolutely pointed at the flagpole to indicate where he was going to hit the ball. He also said more than once that "only a damn fool" would do something like that. Rather than make the moment into the mythical event that it became, he seemed inclined to have fun with it.

His best description probably came at a cocktail party held by sportswriter Grantland Rice in the spring of 1933. This was a dignified affair. The wife of Walter Lippmann, the famous political columnist, asked Ruth what happened with that famous home run in the 1932 Series. Rice printed the Home Run King's answer in his 1955 autobiography, *The Tumult and the Shouting*, leaving blanks for words that can be quite easily filled in now.

"It's like this," the Babe said, dressed in white and waving his cigar. "The Cubs had fucked my old teammate Mark Koenig by cutting him for only a measly fucken half share of the Series money.

"Well, I'm riding the fuck out of the Cubs, telling 'em they're the cheapest pack of fucken crumbums in the world. We've won the first two and now we're in Chicago for the third game. Root is the Cubs' pitcher. I pack one into the stands in the first inning, but in the fifth it's tied, 4-to-4, when I'm up with nobody on. The Chicago fans are giving me hell.

"Root's still in there. He breezes the first two pitches by—both strikes! The mob's tearing down Wrigley Field. I shake my fist after that first strike. After the second I point my bat at these bellerin' bleachers— right where I aim to park the ball. Root throws it and I hit that fucken ball on the nose, right over the fence for two fucken runs.

" 'How do you like those apples, you fucken bastard?' I yell at Root as I run towards first. By the time I reach home I'm almost fallin' down I'm laughin' so fucken hard—and that's how it happened."

The details, of course, were a bit messed up. The count was 2–2, not 0–2. The home run scored one run, not two. Perhaps some of the dialogue had been embellished. The spirit of the moment, though, was probably better preserved here than in all other descriptions by all historians and literary lions. Mrs. Lippmann soon grabbed her famous husband and they left the party in a hurry.

"Why'd you use that language?" Rice asked Ruth.

"What the hell, Grant," Ruth replied. "You heard her ask me what happened. So I told her."

The best piece of empirical evidence that *something* out of the ordinary happened was delivered by Guy Bush the next day. He was the Cubs starter for what turned out to be the fourth and final game. With runners on first and second, nobody out, first inning, he drilled the Bambino with a fastball on his very first pitch.

CHAPTER TWENTY-TWO

A DISCUSSION ABOUT Babe Ruth's money took place in the third week of March 1933 at the Gold Dust Lodge, a shelter at 40 Corlears Street run by the Salvation Army to house and feed 2,000 homeless, destitute, and jobless men in New York City. The discussion started to get warm, pro and con—the Babe was the last Yankees holdout in St. Petersburg, fighting a major reduction in his $75,000 salary—and adjutant Andrew Laurie, director of the shelter, decided that maybe there should be a vote. If nothing else, it would kill a little time.

How much should Babe Ruth earn? More than half of the residents, 1,171 men, voted. The figure they decided was $48,999, an average of all the numbers submitted. One man said the Babe should make a million dollars a year. Another said he should make a dime, and yet another said he should work for free. Some suggested he should be paid by the home run, $1,000 per homer.

It was mentioned that once upon a time (two years ago) the slugger had made $80,000 per year. A second vote was taken on whether any person in any job was worth $80,000 per year. This was close: 599 men said yes, and 572 said no.

The 599 men who had said yes were then asked who they thought should receive $80,000 per year. Each man had one vote. The results were as follows:

1. Any president of the United States (185 votes)
2. Babe Ruth (140)
3. President Franklin Roosevelt (97)
4. Former Governor Al Smith (12)
5. Former New York Mayor Joseph McKee and Jack Dempsey (5)
6. Herbert Hoover (4)
7. Henry Ford, Charles Schwab, and comedian Joe E. Brown (3)

A number of candidates received one or two votes. Among the single vote getters were Albert Einstein, William Randolph Hearst, Gene Tunney, Tom Mix, Enrico Caruso, Thomas Edison, Walter Winchell, John D. Rockefeller, and Lou Gehrig. No women were mentioned.

The average pre-Depression salary of the 1,171 voters had been $49 per week. The Salvation Army said the cost of keeping each man in the shelter with two meals per day was $1 per week.

Two days after the vote, the Babe officially signed a contract in a ceremony in the St. Petersburg sun for $52,000 for the 1933 season, a $23,000 pay cut from 1932. He squealed, but not too loudly. This was 17 days after Roosevelt had declared a bank holiday as a last-gasp effort to save the remaining banks in the country. Kenesaw Mountain Landis had set a precedent for baseball, dropping his own salary $10,000 to $40,000 after lopping off $15,000 a year earlier. Virtually all of the Yankees had taken pay cuts. Lou Gehrig dropped $5,000 to $22,500.

"I've had three ambitions," the Babe said. "I've wanted to complete 20 years of baseball and I'll do that this year. I've wanted to play in ten World Series and I realized that ambition last year. And I hope to boost my home run total to 700. I hope to do that by hitting at least 48 this year."

"You must hit 61 this year, Root, and give us a new record," Col. Ruppert said.

The twentieth season began.

The Babe made a nice show of friskiness for a young Associated Press writer on the day before the opening game at the Stadium. Fresh out of the clubhouse shower, naked, vigorously drying his hair with a towel, the Bam proclaimed that he felt better than he had in five years. Take away a sore throat that had stuck around for five weeks, he was in great shape. He said he had become a runner in the spring, ran more miles than he ever had, trying to bring life back into his legs, and they felt *ten* years younger.

"There," he said, wiping his chest now with the towel. "Those guys are crazy again. I may be 39, and I may have slowed up some. I'm not trying to kid anybody, least of all myself. But through? Not by plenty, kid."

The writer scribbled down his words.

"They say I won't play 100 games," the Babe continued. "Why, listen, I'll play every single game this season. I'd have been in there all the time last year but for injuries and sickness. That's part of the game. Everybody gets into tough luck streaks like that sometime or another."

The Babe kept talking as he dressed, all the way to his familiar camel's hair coat and matching cap, all the way onto the street where Claire was waiting for him in the car. ("The missus," he said. "All right, honey. I'm coming.") The writer, whose name was Edward J. Neil, went back to the office, typed out all the positives for distribution on the wire across the country, but couldn't keep out his overriding thought about meeting the Babe. Especially the naked Babe.

"There is plenty of weight around his middle," Edward J. Neil typed. "Enough so that in a baseball uniform he still looks as if he'd stuffed a watermelon under his shirt."

The great rush to metaphor and hyperbole to describe his exploits during the grand days was now focused on his age and size. He waddled and creaked and lumbered, an aging bull elephant left to roam in a right-field pasture. He huffed and puffed and still blew houses down, but simply not as many.

The running, the exercise for the legs, didn't work. They soon felt like lead. He pounded out his first home run off young Merritt Cain of the A's in a 7–3 win in the third game of the year, but he was lost in the outfield, lost on the base paths. He simply couldn't move like a young man anymore. He still could hit, but even at the plate he had problems.

The longest home run drought of his career stretched from April 30 until May 23, when he told McCarthy, "I feel good. I think I'm going to bust one today," and busted one into the right-field stands. There had been reports that his eyes were starting to fail, but he said the reports were "bunk."

In the midst of the drought, on May 19, he visited six orphans in Pas-saic, New Jersey. The orphans had made headlines as heroes when they signaled an engineer to avert the crash of an Erie Railroad train at a washed-out bridge near the Passaic Home and Orphan Asylum. The Babe brought bags of Babe Ruth caps and neckties and tickets for the next day's game at the Stadium.

"I promise to hit a home run especially for you," he said. "It will be one of the deepest regrets of my life if I don't send one into the stands for you."

The best he could do was a liner that fell several feet short. This was a called shot—stop the presses—that didn't materialize. There seemed to be a certain symbolism.

Not that he didn't have moments. Not that he couldn't still draw a crowd. Five days after the drought ended, in a May 28 doubleheader against the White Sox at the Stadium that attracted 50,297, he homered and singled to lead the Yankees to a 2–1 win. In the nightcap, he homered twice more to lead a 9–7 win.

Everything in 1933 was just hard, though, harder than in 1932. He benched himself for the first time in his career for the second game of a doubleheader in Detroit on June 25 after going 0-for-6 in the first game. He was in a 2-for-17 slump, another drought, and it was a hot day.

"The heat is terrific and Babe just asked for a little respite," Joe Mc-Carthy explained.

He didn't run out ground balls anymore. He left most games early for his defensive replacements. He played a measured game with measured movements.

"It's the legs, kid, they're what count," he said. "I'll last just as long as the old pins hold out. On the field, as you must have noticed, I take it easy if there isn't much chance of my reaching first base on an infield hit. I must watch the pins carefully because a 'charley horse' or two will mean the end of me as an active player."

What else could he do? In December 1929, National League president John Heydler had showed up at the major league meetings in Chicago with a proposal he thought would add energy to the game, a proposal that would have been perfect for the 1933 Babe. Heydler had called it "ten-man baseball."

The tenth man in the suggested ten-man baseball would be a perma-nent pinch hitter for the pitcher. Every time the pitcher's turn came to go to the plate, the tenth man would take his place. The pitcher never would hit. The tenth man never would play in the field. The game would be given a revolutionary, immediate injection of offense.

"With the exception of two or three, practically all pitchers are weak hitters and weaker base runners," Heydler, a former umpire and sportswriter, said. "When they come to bat, they literally put a drag on the game. No one expects them to do anything, and they literally suspend the action of the play."

Heydler had hoped the proposal would be put into action for the next season, 1930, by both leagues, but it found little support. Though traditionalist John McGraw surprisingly liked the idea, most baseball men had found it hilarious. The measure was tabled, never even brought to the floor for discussion.

"With a rule like this," Yankees scout Paul Krichell said derisively, "Babe Ruth could play until he's 50."

Ten-man baseball, alas, was not in effect. Not yet.

A fact that had to be remembered in all of this was that the Home Run King was not an old man in a real-world sense. In any other occupation, from tax accountant to construction worker, he would have been moving into his prime years at age 39. The baseball field was the only place where he was old.

He still charged the night when opportunities arose. Claire didn't make all the trips, and when she didn't, the wet blanket of moderation was removed. He still liked a drink.

"With the Babe, drinking helped him relax," said John Drebinger of the *Times,* who would cover baseball for three more decades after the Babe left. "Physically, it in no way handicapped him. He could drink, gurgle it. He was fine. I've always said that if Mickey Mantle could have handled drinking like the Babe did, he would have broken all the records. Mickey just couldn't drink. He'd take a few drinks and just get silly."

Drebinger, who always said his father had left him two legacies, a fiddle that he didn't know how to play and a drinking education that he used extensively, sat with the Babe in a speakeasy in St. Louis during this time, just the two of them. The Babe got talking about his problem remembering names.

"It's damned embarrassing," he said. "I can remember every ball ever pitched to me and what I hit and what I didn't hit, but names don't stick. A guy came in to pitch the other day, I've known him for ten years, and the fans are hollering down to me, 'Who's this guy?,' and jeez, I yelled over to whatchamacallit in center field (that would be Earle Combs) and he didn't remember."

Terrible.

"The wife" (that would be Claire), "she's raising hell. But I'm getting better, Joe" (that would be *John* Drebinger).

"I almost slid off the couch," Drebinger said.

The Babe's trouble with names was an ongoing source of humor. Stories always were told about how he was introduced to "So-and-So" and said, "Glad to meet ya, kid," and later was told that So-and-So had played for the Yankees the past three years. Or had pitched for the other team yesterday afternoon, in fact had struck out the Home Run King himself.

The Babe's own sense of humor ran toward the practical joke. He might laugh at a vaudeville routine, but would laugh harder if seltzer water was involved. Marshall Hunt always said there was no sense in telling the Babe a joke that involved any subtle play on words. He would never get it. The Babe himself didn't tell jokes. He would forget the punch lines if he did.

His best practical joke was described in a book entitled *Circling the Bases* by Billy Werber, a utility infielder who played with the Yankees in 1930 and 1931. The other party in the joke was Ed Wells, a left-handed pitcher who played with the Yankees from 1929 to 1932. The setting was Detroit.

The Babe suggested to Wells that they venture out to see two very well endowed women he knew in the suburbs. Wells agreed. The Babe brought along a bottle of gin. Wells brought a sack of oranges for a mixer. They took a long cab ride, and at a dark house on a dark street in a dark neighborhood, the Babe rang the doorbell. A man answered instead of a well-endowed female.

"So you're the ones who are trying to date my wife!" the man shouted.

With that, he pulled a pistol and shot the Babe in the stomach. The Babe fell down in a heap and screamed that he had been hit. He told Wells to make a run for it.

Wells, no fool, ran and kept running. He finally returned to the hotel about two hours later. Half the Yankees team seemed to be in the lobby.

Tony Lazzeri told Wells that the Babe had been shot, hurt bad, and was up in his room asking for Wells. The pitcher hurried to the room, which was dimly lit. The Babe was stretched on the bed in a coma. The talcum powder on his face and the catsup on his white shirt looked awful.

"He's dying," Earle Combs told Wells.

The pitcher had the desired reaction. He passed out.

"The Babe was always doing something," Marshall Hunt said. "Perpetual motion. That about describes him. I don't think I ever saw him sitting around except maybe if we were waiting for a train or something. He always had something in his mouth. A cigar. Gum. He was always busy."

The advent of Claire had changed some things in the Babe's life. His age had changed other things. A lot also remained the same. The Babe was still the Babe. Perpetual motion still ruled.

"Did Claire crimp the Babe's style?" Marshall Hunt was asked.

"Not that I ever noticed," the sportswriter replied.

Pitcher Red Ruffing, who joined the team in 1930, told a story about coming back from a walk one night in St. Louis. As he approached the front door of the Chase Hotel, he saw that some dinner or dress ball was being held at the hotel and people just now were arriving. The men on the stairs and in front of the hotel door were in tuxedos, and the women were in evening gowns. Ruffing felt underdressed and conspicuous. He decided to walk fast. His chances for embarrassment deepened, alas, when he noticed the Babe sitting in a parked car directly in front of the well-dressed people. Two women were in the car with him.

Ruffing decided to put his head down and keep walking. Maybe the Babe wouldn't notice him. Maybe the people wouldn't notice him. He walked past the Babe's car and was into the crowd of people when he heard a gruff voice behind him.

"Hey, Red," the Babe shouted. "You want a piece of ass?"

So much for avoiding embarrassment. Ruffing kept walking, straight into the hotel.

Two events stood out as the big man finished the 1933 season with 34 home runs and a .301 average and the Yankees, a universal pick for first place, finished seven games behind the Washington Senators in the American League race. (Jimmie Foxx, the A's slugger, not only was first in home runs, with 48, but also was first in batting average, at .356, and RBIs, with 163, to win the rare Triple Crown. Ruth's 34 home runs were still second in the American League. Gehrig was third with 32.)

The first event was the inaugural All-Star Game, dubbed "the Game of the Century," which was played in Chicago on July 6 at Comiskey Park. This was a grand event, never seen before, only imagined, the best against the best. McGraw came out of retirement in Pelham, New York, to manage the National League, while 71-year-old Connie Mack managed the Americans. There was all the appropriate hoo-ha and excitement, and 49,000 people were in the seats.

In the third inning of the first All-Star Game in history, with Charlie Gehringer on second, Ruth poled the first home run in All-Star Game history, a line shot into the lower pavilion in right. The home run off Cardinals ace left-hander Willie Hallahan propelled the Americans to a 4–2 win. Ruth also preserved the win in the field, his leaden legs carrying him back to the right-field fence in time to take a potential home run away from Chick Hafey in the eighth inning for the defensive play of the game. It was all typical Babe Ruth, rising to the occasion, capturing it, putting it in his pocket.

"He was marvelous," John McGraw said. "That old boy certainly came through when they needed him."

The second event came in the final game of the 1933 season. Babe Ruth pitched again. In an attempt to pump up attendance in a game at the Stadium that meant nothing, he made a well-publicized start against the Red Sox.

This wasn't the Yankees' idea; it was his idea. He had last pitched in 1930, the same situation, end of the season, stopping the Red Sox, 9–3, with a complete-game victory at Fenway Park. Before that, he hadn't pitched a major league game in a decade. On barnstorming tours, though, and even in exhibition games during the season, he took the mound. He'd pitched once in 1933 in Indianapolis when 300 fans signed a petition asking him to take the mound.

He prepared himself for this finale, throwing batting practice in the preceding days and weeks. He had Doc Painter, now the Yankees' trainer, ready to work on his left arm between innings. The Yankees made the occasion festive with preliminaries like a fungo-hitting contest (winner: G. Herman Ruth, 395 feet), a 100-yard dash, races around the bases, and a contest for catchers that involved throwing the ball from home plate into an open barrel at second base. (None of them did it.) Twenty-five thousand people came to watch the proceedings.

Ruth then came out and mowed the Red Sox down, at least for a while. He pitched shutout baseball for the first five innings as the Yanks grabbed a 6–0 lead. Part of that lead was Ruth's 34th homer in the bottom of the fifth, a shot that sneaked into the right-field stands. He faltered in the sixth, giving up a walk, five singles, and four runs, and he surrendered another run in the eighth, but hung on for the 6–5 win.

It was a remarkable achievement—39 years old, stepping in from the outfield to pitch a complete game—probably as remarkable as "the Called Shot" homer of a year earlier. Again, he created the situation that begged for failure. Again, he succeeded. It was the last big league game he ever pitched. He would finish 5–0 on the mound in a Yankees uniform.

His left arm throbbed after the game, and his immediate euphoria was dulled to the promise, "Never again." (He said a month later that he hadn't been able to comb his hair for a week.) Marshall Hunt was giddy in the *Daily News*. He typed out whimsical appraisals of the Babe's multi-task performance in four- and five-paragraph bursts with the aid of different experts from other parts of the paper. The best was under the name of A. T. Gallico, Paul Gallico's wife, who was the fashion editor.

"The Babe wore a plain everyday white flannel Yankees uniform as he carted his huge bulk to the mound for his pitching ordeal," Hunt/Gallico wrote.

> His slender calves were encased in blue wool stockings. A blue cap with a chic white "NY" embroidered above the peak sat jauntily on his head.
>
> Babe completed his apparel with a pair of kangaroo hide shoes with imported spikes of Bethlehem Steel. The sleeves of a white sweatshirt showed as he warmed up for the battle.
>
> When Babe knelt in the dirt while awaiting his batting turn, he had his left arm encased in a navy blue Yankees windbreaker. . . . In the Yankee dugout, the Babe used a dozen nice, clean, white towels to swab his perspiring face between innings.

It would have been a nice, sweet way to end a career. Of course, it didn't happen that way.

Reports that Babe Ruth would become the manager of some major league team for 1934 appeared often. He was linked in the coming weeks and months to any team that had a sudden opening in the position, an easy headline without much research. He had been mentioned for the Red Sox job, a logical location, as early as 1932, but he had said then that he wasn't ready. Now he was ready, but no one else seemed to be. The Red Sox had a new owner in boy millionaire Thomas A. Yawkey and a new general manager in Eddie Collins . . . the Tigers had an opening, and Chicago looked promising . . . Cleveland was a possibility, and then Cincinnati showed interest and finally . . . nothing happened.

Another candidate always seemed to surface. Another opportunity always seemed to be lost.

"I wouldn't be choosy about what club it is," the Babe said in all interviews. "The lower the club, the better for me. If I improved it and got it up in the race, I would get credit for it."

The job he really wanted, of course, was the one Joe McCarthy owned. But Ruppert wasn't budging: McCarthy was his man. The manager had a contract through the 1935 season. He had won a pennant and finished second in the past two seasons. Why should he not be the manager? Ruth had to be handled delicately, owing to his great popularity and his great service to the Yankees, but the truth was that Ruppert and Ed Barrow didn't want Ruth. Headaches were worthwhile when the man was hitting 60 home runs, but without the homers, headaches would be a bundled nuisance.

Ruppert and Barrow mostly wished the Babe would fade away without a lot of noise. If he received an offer from another team, they encouraged him to take it. The best one seemed to come from Frank Navin, owner of the Tigers, who was interested in Ruth as a potential manager. Ruppert encouraged Ruth to pursue the job. Ruth, booked by Christy Walsh on a barnstorming tour of Hawaii after the 1933 season ended, said he would see Navin when he returned. Ruppert told him he was making a mistake. Ruth didn't listen.

"There's time," the Babe said. "The baseball season doesn't start for six months."

The maddening part about this exercise was that he and Claire and Julia went to the World's Fair in Chicago before proceeding to Los Angeles to catch the boat to Honolulu. Why didn't he call Navin from Chicago, simply slide over to Detroit for a meeting before proceeding to California? How hard would that have been? Why didn't Claire push him?

Maybe he didn't know what he was supposed to do. Maybe Claire didn't know. He was Babe Ruth, dammit. He never had applied for a job in his life. People came to him with their offers. That's the way it always had worked. Why didn't it work that way now? Maybe he simply didn't understand.

At the World's Fair, he was introduced to the crowd at the A&P Carnival by a middle-aged man who said, "I've been a fan of Babe Ruth since I was 'that high.' " "I wasn't playing when Mr. Rector was 'that high,' " the Babe grumped in his remarks. He felt his age, but didn't necessarily want to hear about it.

He saw a marionette show that featured a Babe Ruth marionette. He took the tour. Somewhere in the day, he refused to throw at the African dodger, the racist character out of that stellar 1926 comedy *Headin' Home.* The Babe said he knew too many guys who had thrown their arm out trying to dunk the black man. He said he still had uses for that arm. There were chances he still could play.

"I'm not through yet, but I couldn't play many over 100 games," he said. "Funny thing, they had me all through going into last year, and I felt better than I had for several years. I played with my ankles wrapped in tape, and that strengthened them a lot."

He finally did make a call to Navin from San Francisco. The timing was not good. Not taking the two-hour time difference into account, Ruth awakened the Detroit owner in the middle of the night. Ruth said he needed to have an answer about managing the Tigers; was it going to be yes or no? The sleep-deprived Navin said no, and went back to bed.

The not-to-be manager of the Tigers sailed west and was greeted by a crowd of 10,000 when his ship, the *Lurline,* docked at Honolulu. Schools were closed for a half-day so local children could see him play. He had two white-and-yellow leis wrapped around his neck the next afternoon as he hit a home run, struck out, and had to shift from right field to first base and then the pitcher's mound because the out-of-school kids kept swarming the field.

His popularity was obvious. How could the magnates of baseball not see what an attraction he would be as a manager? When he returned, Ruppert and Barrow suggested the possibility that he manage the Newark Bears, the minor league team that Ruppert also owned. Ruth rejected that idea immediately. Both Christy Walsh and Claire backed his decision.

"To ask me," he said, "after twenty years of experience in the major leagues to manage a club in the minors would be the same, I think, as to ask Colonel Ruppert, one of the foremost brewers in the country, to run a soda fountain."

He was Babe Ruth, dammit.

On January 15, 1934, he signed a contract for the coming season at Ruppert's Third Avenue brewery for $35,000, which was a $17,000 pay cut from 1933. No razzamatazz was involved, no Florida standoff. Ruppert laid out the contract. The Babe signed. The $35,000 was the smallest salary for Ruth since 1921, although he still was the highest-paid player in the game.

Any sense of celebration was missing. The parties basically were locked together for one, last fractious year of a marriage that already was done. Every writer who went to Artie McGovern's gym to report on the Bambino's progress noted a sadness in the proceedings that never had been present in the past.

An attack of the flu disrupted the big man's training, then kept him from traveling to St. Petersburg until the day after his birthday. No party at the Jungle Club this year. He turned 40 in the apartment with the sniffles. When he got onto the train, he was bundled in overcoats and hurried to his compartment.

"Pretty cold, this, for an old man, eh, kid?" he said from under all his clothes. "Pretty cold."

The highlight of the spring came on the trip back when he went with outfielder Sammy Byrd, who later became a professional golfer, to play in an exhibition with Bobby Jones in Atlanta. The baseball highlights were harder to find. The season opened, and he hit a home run here, another there, hit three in two days in one momentary return to glory, but every day was a fight against embarrassment.

He benched himself for a doubleheader on June 8 against the Red Sox because he heard reports that his teammates didn't think he should be in the lineup. McCarthy said the decision was totally up to Ruth. Ruth said he felt hurt.

"I don't think that is the way to treat a fellow who has given as much to baseball as I have," the Babe explained. "I have been having some trouble with my ankle, but I don't think I'm washed up yet. This is going to be my last season as a player, but if I thought I was hindering the Yankees, I could not throw this uniform fast enough."

He had his own radio show now, three times per week for the entire summer, and the irony was that in every show one section was devoted to a dramatization of some famous moment from his career. He sat at one microphone with producer Norm Sweetser while two or three actors stood at a second microphone and read dialogue from "the Called Shot" or the Johnny Sylvester homers or whatever was the topic of the night, each page of the script dropped noiselessly to the floor when completed. A third microphone hovered over the band and also could pick up the studio audience reaction.

The only moment for the script this season came on July 13 when he unloaded on the Tigers' Tommy Bridges in the third inning in Detroit for home run number 700, the long-desired goal. It was not a particularly dramatic blast—the game would be won by catcher Bill Dickey's homer in the eighth—but it traveled 480 feet, high over the right-field wall at Navin Field, an example worthy of its 699 predecessors.

Only two other players in baseball history—Gehrig at 314 and Rogers Hornsby at 301—had hit even 300 homers. The number promised to stay on the wall for a long time, maybe forever. Ruth, rounding third base, told coach Art Fletcher, "I want that ball."

A 16-year-old kid named Lennie Bielski had pulled the ball from under a car on Plum Avenue and was surprised to be surrounded by policemen and ushers who led him inside the park and to the Yankee bench. He wound up with a box seat for the rest of the game, a signed baseball from Ruth, and $20.

"Lou," Ruth said to Gehrig, "I don't have my wallet. Give that boy $20."

The next day the Bambino hit number 701, his 15th of the season. Three days later, the action moved to Cleveland, where he walked twice to reach 2,000 bases on balls in his career, another record that would be tough to break. It was estimated that he had walked 34 miles in those 2,000 bases on balls. The day after the record, he couldn't walk at all, dropped in midstride between first and second by a Gehrig rocket that hit him on his right leg, just above the ankle. He was carried off the field, his injury diagnosed as hemorrhage between the shinbone and the skin. He was told to rest for ten days. It was that kind of season.

"I'm getting out before I'm carried out," the Babe said as he awaited transportation back to the hotel. "If I don't quit now, I might get some injury that will be permanent. I thought my leg was broken when that ball hit me. Gosh, how it hit. And how this leg pains.

"I've been getting banged up more now than I ever have been before. This is the third accident this year."

He declared in Boston on the Yanks' last trip in August that he was done as a full-time player at the end of the season. He said he would like to be a manager, maybe do a little pinch-hitting on weekends to help the gate, but would not play in the field. The people of Boston, always attracted to this character they thought had unjustly been sent from their town, paid attention to his words.

A crowd of 48,000, the largest in Fenway history, appeared for the final doubleheader in the series. The overflow was allowed on the field, standing behind ropes from right to the center-field flagpole. It was a total Ruth crowd, cheering every move he made. He doubled and singled in the first game, walked twice in the second, and then, when he grounded to first in what everyone knew was his final Fenway at-bat, received a standing ovation. The Babe was as touched by the moment as the people were.

"They all stood up," the Babe said. "Do you know that some of them cried when I left the field?

"And if you wanna know the truth, I cried too."

He clearly had become convinced that this was his last full loop around the circuit. He had signed to take a trip to Japan with an all-star team put together by Connie Mack after the season ended. Claire and Julia would come along, and they would take the long way back, traveling through the Suez Canal and then through Europe. A strange thing had happened when he looked up his birth certificate to obtain a passport for the trip—his birthday was given as February 6, 1895, not the February 7, 1894, he always thought it was. But that didn't matter. Even if he really was 39, he felt like he was 40. He felt like he was 100.

He would take a trip around the world and see where he landed at the end. He knew it would not be right field.

"I am getting too old for the game and know it," he told one interviewer. "There's nothing sadder than to see a fellow trotting around the diamond and hear his legs creaking for want of oil. If I kept playing much longer, I'd be tripping over my whiskers or putting on a pair of specs to see the ball."

He was asked what he considered his greatest moment in baseball. His answer was surprisingly introspective for a man not prone to self-analysis. He chose the first professional game he ever played with Jack

Dunn's Baltimore Orioles. That was the open door that he never even had known existed.

"I was in a daze," Ruth said. "Here I was being paid for doing what I wanted to do. I was to get $600, and that seemed an awful lot of money to a kid who never had any and whose one ambition was to own a bicycle."

His final appearance at Yankee Stadium—and it never was announced as that, though writers mentioned the strong possibility that he never would play for the Yankees again—was curiously quiet. It was a Monday afternoon, and a crowd of only 2,000 appeared, and the Babe played only an inning. He let a single drop in front of him in the top half of the inning, a ball that any average outfielder would have caught easily. He walked in the bottom half of the inning and received polite applause as he was replaced by pinch runner Myril Hoag and went to the dugout. It was an anticlimax after a career of crescendos. The Babe was not happy.

"You would be sore, too," Paul Gallico wrote in the *Daily News,* "if you were the most popular man in the country at one time and came to your funeral, or sat up and peeked out of the wagon and saw no more than three carriages trailing."

The Yankees played three games in Washington to finish the season. The Senators put together a much better good-bye production. The band from good old St. Mary's Industrial School for Boys played music. A large scroll bearing the signatures of President Roosevelt and all of his cabinet members and thousands of citizens was presented. A crowd of 15,000 spectators watched as the Home Run King went 0-for-3 on his way out the door. The Senators won, 5–3. The Yankees finished seven games behind the Tigers, managed by catcher Mickey Cochrane, who took the job that could have belonged to the Babe.

The big man finished with only 22 home runs, his lowest total since he stopped pitching. He batted .288.

Marshall Hunt, who had witnessed most of the Babe's moments and tracked him so well through these 16 years in New York, did not see his man's final game in a Yankees uniform. Hunt's sportswriting career, which had followed the same arc as the Babe's, ended at exactly the same time.

As Ruth played his final game as a Yankee, the Giants were locked into a winner-take-all final series against the Cardinals in St. Louis for the National League pennant, and the *Daily News* chose to send him to St. Louis. A plan was involved. If the Gashouse Gang Cardinals of Pepper Martin and company beat out the Giants—and they did—Hunt was supposed to stay in St. Louis and cover the opening games of the World Series between the Cards and the Tigers.

This did not happen. He disappeared.

"Marshall Hunt was a very peculiar fellow," John Drebinger of the *Times* said. "When I first knew him, when he was coming up with the *News*, about the same time I came to the *Times*, he was a terrible alcoholic. He was a brilliant writer, but the alcohol had him."

Following the Babe down the buffet line of the perpetual free lunch in the twenties, diving deep into the glamorous Manhattan hum, had its perils. How much fun is too much fun? The Babe's pace was a record pace. Who else could handle that? Kenesaw Mountain Landis, of all people, had interceded somewhere during the fun, putting up some money to send Hunt away for the cure. It seemed to take.

"Funny thing, when he wasn't drinking, he never thought of drinking a drink," Drebinger said. "I used to drink in front of him, and it never bothered him. I was kind of leery of doing it, but he was fine."

Hunt had moved back to beer by 1934, but had it under control in the last Yankees season of the Babe. He drank beer with Drebinger after the Giants games in St. Louis. Then he started to drink hard liquor, and when the Series arrived, he didn't show up at the ballpark. Paul Gallico, not only the columnist but also the sports editor, was at the games.

"Jesus Christ, where is he?" Gallico said. "Now I've got to write the lead for him."

Hunt eventually appeared, but was fired. It was a bottom-out moment. He left New York, went back to the state of Washington, took the cure again, and later became the editor-in-chief of the *Daily Olympian* in Olympia, Washington, for 22 years. He had an entire second life.

The timing was oddly perfect. Babe Ruth was gone from the Yankees. Marshall Hunt was gone from the *Daily News*. The first life was done.

CHAPTER TWENTY-THREE

THE 666-FOOT *Empress of Japan* departed Vancouver, Canada, on October, 20, 1934, for Yokohama, Japan. The Babe, Claire, and Julia were among the 1,137 passengers who waved good-bye from the decks of the four-year-old ocean liner as the twin turbine engines kicked into action and the first smoke appeared from the three funnels that were painted in the trademark yellow of the Canadian-Pacific Line.

The beauty of ocean travel, appropriated forever by mystery novelists and then screenwriters, was that stories lurked behind each cabin door, plot lines to be spun across the high seas. The somewhat portly passenger from New York, New York, the one in the camel's hair coat and the trademark cap, a member of the All-American All-Stars baseball team, was as interesting as any of the characters listed on the ship's manifest.

What next for the Babe? That was plot number one.

He had left New York angry after finally stopping at Ruppert's office at the brewery for a showdown with the Colonel and Ed Barrow. The meeting did not go well. He pushed the two men about replacing Joe McCarthy as manager of the Yankees. Could they say they were happy with McCarthy after two years out of first place? They said they could. Would Joe McCarthy manage the team again in 1935? Yes, he would.

"That's all I wanted to know," the Babe said.

He stomped from there to the World Series between the Cardinals and Tigers and, while "covering" the games for the Christy Walsh syndicate, he blurted out his dissatisfaction to sportswriter Joe Williams while waiting for a train in Detroit. Williams hurried the words into print. The Babe was done with the Yankees. He would not, under any circumstance, be back for 1935 as a player. He would be a manager or nothing. He would not sit on the Yankees' bench, or anybody's bench for that matter, only to pinch-hit. That was the story.

The Babe was now a man without a country, available to anyone or no one, let other people decide. While the newspapers hummed with speculation about what would happen, he was off on this trip of a lifetime. The All-American All-Stars would stop in Honolulu for a game, then proceed to Japan, arriving on November 4 to play 17 games in a month in different cities around the country. A game in Shanghai and two games in Manila on December 9 and 10 would complete the schedule.

The team would then sail back to the United States, but the Babe and Claire and Julia would head for Europe. This second half of the trip pretty much would be the first vacation of his life, a time to travel only for fun. Julia was included, the Babe said, because this was her present for graduating from high school. Dorothy was left at home in public school, not happy.

"If that's her graduation present," Dorothy said, living with Claire's mother and two brothers in the New York apartment, "then it was about her 15th graduation present in five years."

The status of Dorothy was given as a reason for another plot line on the ship: the Babe and Lou Gehrig, also a member of the All-American All-Stars, no longer talked to each other. Publicly cast for years as home run–hitting Bobbsey Twins, the two men never had been that close, but had shared a solid, friendly workplace relationship. They had traveled together, celebrated great moments together. Ruth had been a visitor many times at the home of Gehrig's parents and was a favorite of Gehrig's mom, to whom he once gave a Chihuahua pup which she immediately named Jidge in his honor. Now the men were quiet, hurt enemies.

Claire always claimed that the problem came from idle conversation sometime in 1933 at one of those visits to Gehrig's parents. Mom Gehrig supposedly looked at Dorothy, who was wearing shopworn hand-me-downs, and asked aloud why Julia, Claire's natural daughter, always was dressed in the latest fashions. Why was Dorothy treated differently? The remark reached Claire, and she said she reacted badly. The feud stretched to the men.

The truth of the split ran deeper. Gehrig finally had gotten married at the end of the 1933 season. His wife, Eleanor, was from Chicago. Like Claire, she was a worldly-wise, ambitious woman. Before she had known Gehrig, she had known the Babe. She met Gehrig, in fact, at one of those free-flowing sessions at the Babe's suite in Chicago. To have known the Babe at that time was, well, to have known the Babe. He didn't suffer many platonic relationships with women.

"I'm not knocking Eleanor, but very few women went into Ruth's room for sightseeing," sportswriter Fred Lieb said, telling why Gehrig's mother, whom he took to the wedding, did not like Eleanor. "And I don't think Babe welcomed very many that he didn't want to get in bed with. So that's in the back of Mom's mind all the time."

It also had to be in the back of Gehrig's mind. When he found his bride, half drunk, talking with Ruth in Ruth's stateroom on the *Empress of Japan*, the barrier between the two Yankees stars grew nearly insurmountable. He would not talk with Ruth. He also did not talk much with Eleanor for the rest of the way to Japan.

"The Babe and Lou, after they took part in that Japanese trip, were never together anymore," Fred Lieb said. "I think it started over the two ladies, Claire and Eleanor, and it was about five years before they spoke again to each other."

Another situation was whirring aboard the ship, a situation that the Babe did not know existed. He was being studied. This was his audition as a manager. Owner-manager Connie Mack, now almost 72 years old, was thinking about retiring as manager of the A's. The effects of the Depression had landed heavily on baseball by now, and most of all upon the A's. Forced as an owner to dismantle his once-great lineup to remain solvent, Mack needed a change of fortune at the box office. He still hung on to slugger Jimmie Foxx, and the possible crowd appeal of Ruth as manager (and as another bat in the lineup with Foxx) was enticing. Maybe owner Mack should fire manager Mack for the good of the operation.

The old baseball man had made Ruth the manager of the All-American All-Stars for the trip. He wanted to see what happened. If all went well, he was prepared to make an offer.

"Babe Ruth will manage the Philadelphia Athletics next year," one premature report out of New York stated on October 25, 1933. "The glamorous Babe, the most colorful figure in baseball for upwards of a

decade, whose career ended with the close of the 1934 season, will succeed Connie Mack."

The news, alas, was wrong. The audition ended quickly. The old baseball man watched Ruth and, more importantly, watched Claire's domina-
tion of him around the ship. When she barked, the Babe jumped. The old
baseball man would later tell friends, "If I gave the job to him, she would be
managing the team in a month." Mack went back to his original stated plan
that he would manage his baseball team until he was 80. (Which he did.)

The job was not open. The Babe was still a man without a country—
except, of course, for Japan.

The welcome was overwhelming in Tokyo, the site of the first four games.
The Babe and the All-Stars drew the full Lindbergh treatment in a ticker-
tape parade through the Gînza witnessed by a crowd ranging in estimates
from 100,000 to half a million people. A cold-shoulder diplomatic testi-
ness that had developed between Japan and the United States, primarily
over naval and trade issues, was missing. There was only warmth for the
Babe. Polite little boys would knock at the door to his hotel room and ask
Claire if they could meet "the God of Baseball."

He was Babe Ruth, dammit. Yes, he was.

"We had come expecting a welcome from you," he said that night at
a dinner at the Hibiya Amphitheater, "but we did not expect a welcome
of such magnitude."

It was a triumphant tour. In the first game, the Americans battered
their hosts, 17–1, at the huge Meiji Shrine Park before a crowd of 60,000
to set the tone. The Americans never lost a game, winning mostly by huge
scores against players who never had played against this kind of competition. To the fans, it didn't matter. They were excited to see the foreign-
ers play. The fans in Tokyo mostly waited for the Babe or for anyone to
belt a ball out of Meiji Shrine Park, since it never had been done. They
cheered every well-hit ball, but, alas, the fences simply were too distant.

The Babe didn't hit a home run until the fifth game of the tour. Then
he seemed to hit one every day. He finished with 13 home runs in the last
13 games in Japan. He played a lot of first base (Gehrig was in the outfield) and clowned with the fans. In one game he played seven different
positions. In another game, the only real contest of the tour, his homer in
the seventh off 17-year-old Eiji Sawamura was the only run either team
scored. Eiji Sawamura became an instant Japanese legend.

In Shanghai, China, the next stop, the Babe bopped three home runs in a 22–1 win over the Shanghai All-Stars on a freezing day. He reported that he wore a set of long johns and four shirts and still froze. In Manila, after a 7–3 win, he proclaimed that he had changed his mind and "will play baseball until I'm 100 years old."

The Japanese organizers presented four brass urns at the conclusion of the tour: for the highest batting average, for the longest hit, for driving in the most runs, and for the best pitcher. Ruth received three of them. Lefty Gomez won the one for pitching. Connie Mack said Ruth looked better on the tour than he had at any time during the previous two years. The crowds kept him excited, and he kept the crowds excited. It was an even trade despite the prevailing anti-American sentiment across the country. Baseball was a common language.

"When we landed in Japan, the American residents seemed pretty blue," Mack said. "The parley on the naval treaty was on, with America blocking Japan's bid for parity. There was strong anti-American feeling throughout Japan. Things didn't look good.

"And then Babe smacked a home run, and all the ill feeling and underground war sentiment vanished like that."

There seemed to be little doubt that trouble was ahead for the two countries. All-American catcher Moe Berg of the Cleveland Indians took a lot of pictures on the trip. A graduate of both Princeton and the Sorbonne, conversant in ten languages, and able to hit a hanging curve, he had been recruited by the OSS as an American spy. His pictures cleverly showed military and industrial installations in the background and would become valuable in future years. The Japanese became suspicious of his constant attention to his camera, searched his room, but could not find the film he had hidden. They did confiscate film from other members of the All-Stars, including the Babe, and when it was returned, black ink had been added to individual shots to blot out buildings the hosts did not wish the world to see.

In another indication of the tensions, the Japanese promoter of the trip, newspaper publisher Matsutaro Shoriki, was stabbed nine weeks later. His attackers were sword-wielding members of the Secret Warlike Gods Society, a nationalist group upset that American baseball players had taken Japanese money out of the country. Japanese money should stay in Japan to help Japanese people. Shoriki, left for dead in an alley, recovered and lived to be 84 with a 16-inch scar on the left side of his bald head.

The *Empress of Japan*, the boat that had carried all of this drama to the country, all these plot lines, eventually would become a plot line herself. Seven years later, her name would be changed. Very few international ships are allowed to change their names, and the process is costly and complicated; English prime minister Winston Churchill himself, however, would sign the order for this one. The *Empress of Japan*, now an Allied troopship, would become the *Empress of Scotland*.

The Babe, Claire, and Julia left on a German liner, the MSS *Tjinegara*, from Manila on December 13, 1934, bound for Java, then Bali, then the Suez Canal, and then France and England. Lou Gehrig and Eleanor also were headed to Europe, but took a different boat with a different itinerary. (Moe Berg went from Japan to Moscow. Everybody except the OSS wondered why he'd do that.) The Ruths did not reach Paris until January 18, 1935. The Babe promptly declared that he had not been too impressed with Java and Bali.

"For one thing," he said. "I don't like Bali and Java women. They are too chesty and too black. They're billed as the most beautiful women in the world, but you see them walking down the street chewing that red tobacco."

He also was not impressed with Paris. The city was a harrowing look at anonymity. Nobody knew who he was. He could walk for an entire day, straight down the Champs Elysées, visit the old churches and museums, and never hear someone shout, "Hey, Babe." He couldn't remember a situation like that. They'd known who he was in Bali. How could they not know in Paris? A notice from the American consulate appeared in the Paris *Herald-Tribune*, his name in a list of people with unclaimed mail. Unclaimed mail? He received mail at home with no address, no name, only his picture drawn on the front.

The French people, it seemed, knew nothing about baseball. Even the kids he visited at the American School, nice lads, didn't know how to throw a ball. He found that incredibly sad. He advised them to get back to the United States in a hurry because the old guys were being pushed out of the picture and had to leave their shoes behind. There were "a lot of shoes to fill."

The next stop was St. Moritz, a trip down the bobsled run, a funny picture right there, a big man thump-thumping through the long, icy chute, yelling all the way. That was much better. He went skiing, an even funnier picture. Can a man ski while smoking a cigar? Also better. The final stop was London, the one city that measured up to his expectations.

Jimmy Walker, the former mayor of New York, now deposed in scandal, apparently unmindful of the famous advice he once gave the Babe, was in London. Other friends were there. The Babe liked London.

He made a well-publicized trip to a cricket grounds on the banks of the Thames. Fitted with leg pads and handed a cricket bat, Ruth went to work. Two fast bowlers bounced the red ball at him off the green grass, and the Babe started swinging. He had trouble with the cricket stance, switched to his baseball stance, and did fine. The red balls started flying around the grounds.

"I wish I could have him a fortnight," former Australian star Alan Fairfax said. "I could make one of the world's greatest batsmen out of him."

The Babe vetoed that idea when he learned that the top cricket players earned about $40 a week. That didn't seem like much for a great batsman. Did Col. Ruppert know about this? He did like the game. By the time he finished, his bat was destroyed, chunks of wood gone from both edges. He said he'd like to use a bat that fat in baseball. He'd be able to play for five more years.

He also tried pitching—bowling—with less success. He was skeptical of all suggestions that some bowlers could throw a ball faster than Walter Johnson. He also was skeptical of suggestions that some batters could hit a ball 550 feet. He and the American reporter from the Associated Press debated with the hosts. It all was fun, a hoot.

"I don't want to go," he said, only half serious, on February 13, 1935, when he bid good-bye to Jimmy Walker at Waterloo Station, where he and Claire and Julia caught a train for Southampton and the trip home. "We had the best time here of our whole trip."

On February 20, he stepped down the gangplank of the USS *Manhattan* as a band played "Take Me Out to the Ball Game" to welcome him back to New York. He had been gone for over four months, traveled over 21,000 miles, seen places that were not even rumors when he was inside the walls of St. Mary's Industrial School for Boys. It was a spectacular trip. How many people in the United States had traveled around the world in 1935? He was now one of the few.

"It was great," he told the reporters who waited for him at the dock. "But I wouldn't do it again for $100,000."

His description of Paris, alas, was not preserved for future generations. Only the description of his description saw print.

The day after the Babe's return to New York, Paul Gallico reported in the *Daily News*, "I do not think the French care very much about baseball and, hence, probably were not much concerned about Le Gros Bebe when he was in Paris. All I know is that coming up the bay on the USS *Manhattan* somebody asked Ruth how he liked Paris and Babe answered in 10,000 well-chosen words and never repeated himself once. In short, he does not like Paris." These 10,000 words never appeared in print.

The world traveler was back, ready to find out what his future might be. He didn't have to wait long. Seven days later he was a Boston Brave.

The deal had a stench to it from the beginning. The Babe was the only pure heart in the entire proceeding. He had said he wanted to be a manager. Period. That was his goal. The other parties in the transaction took that desire and bent it to fit their needs. The Babe never knew what hit him.

The around-the-world trip, wonderful as it was, had hurt him in the job market. The only offers that had surfaced for his services while he was abroad had been from the promoter of the House of David bearded barnstorming team and from Zack Miller, who ran a Western-themed circus called the "101 Ranch Show." Zack was offering $75,000 for the Babe to ride an elephant every day for a year. He said Tom Mix, the cowboy, had made $110,000 on the same tour. The real jobs—the managerial jobs in baseball—had been filled without the Babe ever being placed in consideration.

Enter Judge Emil Fuchs, owner of the Boston Braves.

The good judge, 57 years old, was a glib and politically connected character who had started out as a millionaire from New York and then, in partnership with Christy Mathewson, bought the team in 1923 and steadily worked his way to the edge of bankruptcy. Matters were so bad that he had petitioned the owners from the National League at the last winter meeting for the right to bring dog racing to Braves Field on nights the team didn't play. Denied that request, he needed some other drastic move to revive his team's finances. The Babe was his new greyhound.

He wanted the Babe to sell tickets to a Boston public that had packed Fenway Park, remember, at the Babe's last appearance. He wanted the Babe to play, hit home runs, fill seats. That was all he wanted, an attraction. He wanted the Babe to ride the elephant. The question now was how to get him to do it.

Working with Col. Ruppert, who more than ever wished to see the

Babe gone from the Yankees without a lot of commotion and unfavorable press, Fuchs devised a plan while Babe was at sea that would help both Ruppert and himself. The Judge would offer a bunch of fine-sounding but hollow inducements that contained phrases like "vice president" and "stock options" and "opportunity to manage." The Colonel would say that he couldn't stand in the way of a man bettering himself. Voilà, everyone would be happy.

The best part was that they would keep all of this a secret. Fuchs met with the Babe and Claire and laid out his offer as if it were new. The Babe called Ruppert and told him about the offer. The Colonel, acting like he was hearing about it for the first time, said the Babe should take it. Voilà.

The press conference was held on February 26, 1935, at Ruppert's office in the brewery. Ruppert, Fuchs, and the Babe, all in blue suits, stood in front of the gathering.

The Judge talked of Ruth's greatness as a player, his impact on American children, the great regard the people of New England had for him. He talked—but without specifics—of the great opportunities that awaited the Babe in Boston. The Colonel seemed overwhelmed at those opportunities.

"It would have been unsportsmanlike of me if I didn't grant Ruth's request," Col. Ruppert said with the straightest face. "Opportunity knocks but once at the door of any man, and I saw here the greatest opportunity Ruth ever had. It would not have been fair to stand in his way."

The specifics of the offer were these:

1. A straight contract ($25,000)
2. An executive position as vice president of the Braves
3. A position as assistant manager of the team, serving as an aide to manager Bill McKechnie
4. A share of the profits
5. An option to purchase stock
6. An opportunity to become a part owner

Air whistled through every item except the line that gave the Babe $25,000 (another $10,000 salary cut, in fact). The Babe bought it, though, and the fans in Boston bought it. When he arrived at Back Bay station two days later to sign the contract, he was greeted by a madhouse. Police lines broke down. He was hustled through the crowd saying the word "jiminy" and holding his cap in the air so no one could steal it. At

a dinner that night, attended by every political freeloader in the commonwealth, he was welcomed as a returned hero.

The one touch of reality came from Charles C. Adams, a Braves vice
president. The owner of the Boston Bruins hockey team and a developer
of the Suffolk Downs racetrack, Adams had been installed in the Braves
operation by the bank to protect its interests. He brought the big loophole
in the Babe's situation to the front.

"No one is fit to give orders until he can take them himself," Adams
told the crowd. "Judging from Ruth's past career, we can hardly consider
him of managerial caliber now. I certainly hope he will merit promotion
as manager of the Braves. He has much to learn within the next few
months. He must prove himself to be a good soldier if he is not that already, and he must gain the loyalty of his teammates."

Two days later the Babe left for St. Petersburg and spring training. In
an odd coincidence, the Braves trained six miles from where the Yankees
trained. He soon would learn that his number 3 pinstriped uniform (numbers were first used in 1929 according to a player's spot in the batting order) had been given to his replacement in right field, George Selkirk.
Though his locker had not been reassigned, his name had been scraped off
the top, and the space was now used to store firewood.

A misguided blush of euphoria touched everything when the new vice
president hit the field at Waterfront Park on March 5, 1935, wearing
Hank Gowdy's pants, Shanty Hogan's socks, and a bright yellow sweatshirt because his own uniform hadn't arrived. The vice president hit a
home run in the first intrasquad scrimmage, and his uniform came, and
the Braves soon beat the Yankees, back to back on two exhibition days,
take that, and after only eight games had made more money and attracted
more fans than they had in all of 1934's spring schedule.

Maybe this would work. . . .

On the road north, the Babe whacked his first homer in a game as a
Brave, pounding a shot over the right-field fence in a 13–1 rout of Southern Georgia Teachers College in Savannah. In a particularly gratifying
stop in Newark, he pounded out two more against the Yankees' top farm
club, the Newark Bears, before a crowd of 10,000, mostly Yankees
fans who had come across the Hudson River to see the odd sight of their
hero in different clothes. The second home run was a monster blast. With
two strikes, the Babe stepped out of the batter's box, tightened his belt,

stepped back in, and unloaded a 500-footer over the right-field wall and onto the street, the longest home run in the history of, take that, Ruppert Stadium.

Maybe . . .

And on opening day, Braves Field, 25,000 people in the stands, including the governors of five of the six New England states, snow falling, a band playing "Jingle Bells," he blasted a fifth-inning shot off Carl Hubbell of the Giants. He added a single, made a terrific diving catch of a sinking Hubbell line drive in left, drove in all the runs in the Braves' 4–2 win.

So, maybe . . .

No.

The realities of the situation soon landed. The Braves manager, Bill McKechnie, whom Ruth was supposed to replace eventually, had no plans of being replaced. Ruth was another player on his roster, not someone to consult about team matters. The vice presidency? The duties seemed to involve attending store openings, sitting behind a desk, and autographing 500 tickets for the first 500 patrons. The stock options? The team's finances were in terrible shape. Stock options were worth nothing. Stories were abundant that Judge Fuchs was trying to sell the team.

The baseball too had been a mirage. The Babe caught a cold and couldn't shake it. He always had been troubled by colds, a big man, prone to sweat, no matter the weather, prone to colds. This was a doozy. He had played in only four games by the middle of May. He also had realized Fuchs was a fraud, realized he'd been duped. An even sadder realization was that he was an old man, overmatched now in the game he had played all of his life.

"I've played my last inning of baseball," he shouted, loud enough for the Braves Field fans to hear as he came back to the dugout after being struck out by the Cubs' Lon Warneke on May 12. "I'm through."

The next day he asked to be put on the voluntarily retired list. Fuchs asked him to at least make the coming western trip. In every city, a Babe Ruth Day was planned. Tickets already had been sold. Maybe he should take the trip, see how he felt at the end. The Babe already knew how he felt, but agreed to take the trip. He went back to New York for a day with Claire, then proceeded to St. Louis.

He told friends in New York that he was done, and his words made the papers, but he backed off in St. Louis. He said he never told anyone, "I'm all washed up." He said, yes, if he couldn't shake the cold, he would request to be put on the voluntarily retired list. The cold was what was killing him. His batting average was .155.

"One result is that my eyes have been giving me a good deal of trouble," he said. "They water considerably, and my failure to hit up to my past records undoubtedly is due to this ailment. If I can break this cold, I believe I can carry on without any trouble."

The Braves played three games in St. Louis, two in Chicago, where the Babe hit his third homer of the year, then hit Pittsburgh. This was where, during the third and final game of the series, the sun shone on his large head for one last day in the major leagues.

Waite Hoyt, the old student of the Babe in the Murderers' Row days, had done some traveling since then, playing for four different teams since 1929, landing finally in Pittsburgh with the Pirates. He was in the clubhouse on May 25 as starting pitcher Red Lucas tried to assemble a last-minute strategy to handle the famous Babe. The other pitchers told Lucas not to worry because the Babe was done. Lucas still worried.

"Never mind him being through," he said. "I'm the guy pitching to him, and he might start again."

The pitcher suddenly remembered Hoyt was in the room. Hoyt, the former Yankee, would know what to do.

"The best way to pitch Ruth is to pitch behind him," Hoyt said. "He has no weaknesses except deliberate walks. You have your choice—one base on four balls or four bases on one ball."

The other pitchers laughed. Ruth was done. Guy Bush, the Babe's dugout antagonist from the 1932 World Series, also had landed with the Pirates. He said he had handled the Babe with sinkers in the Series. Red Lucas nodded. Sinkers.

"Charlie Root threw him a sinker in the '32 Series," Hoyt warned. "The Babe hit it into the center-field bleachers."

Lucas, armed with all of this conflicting information, took the mound against the doddering old man. One pitch later, the doddering old man was circling the bases. The baseball was in the right-field stands. Hoyt, in the bullpen, nudged right-hander Cy Blanton.

"Should have pitched behind him," Hoyt said.

Bush, of all people, replaced Lucas. Bush faced the Babe in the third and threw a sinker. The Babe promptly blasted it out of the park. Home run number two on the day. Bush then faced him again in the fifth, and the aging slugger ripped a single. Finally, in the seventh, Bush and the Babe squared off one last time. This time Bush worked more carefully. The sinker was gone from the arsenal. The Babe would receive all fastballs now.

Bush hummed a strike past the doddering old man and was pleased with his change of strategy. Fastballs worked. He then tried to hum another one past. The pitch was about two inches farther over the plate than it was supposed to be. It was between the knees and at the waist. It was a perfect hitter's pitch. The Babe smacked Guy Bush's fastball straight into the air, high, like a pop-up, except it kept carrying, far, far, over the right-center-field fence at Forbes Field, bounced in the middle of the street, and rolled into Schenley Park. The estimated distance the ball traveled was well over 500 feet, the longest home run ever hit at Forbes Field.

Hoyt nudged Blanton again.

"It was the longest cockeyed ball I ever saw hit in my life," Bush said years later.

He said he was mad at himself, mad at Ruth when the ball went over the fence. He stopped being mad when he saw Ruth circle the bases.

"The poor fellow, he'd gotten to where he could barely hobble along," Bush said. "I ain't mad no more then. So, when he rounds third base, I just look over at him and he kind of looked at me. I tipped my cap just to say, 'I've seen everything now, Babe.' "

This was homer number 714, the third of the day, the last of a career. The Pittsburgh crowd of 10,000, not knowing the exact implications of what it had seen but knowing this was pretty darn good, applauded as he left the game. He was Babe Ruth, dammit.

That night everyone he knew urged him to quit. Claire urged, Christy Walsh urged, everyone urged. The Babe said he had to go to Cincinnati for another Babe Ruth Day, then to Philadelphia.

He never had another major league hit. He struck out three times and pulled a muscle in the outfield on Babe Ruth Day in Cincinnati and had to leave the game. He pinch-hit the next day, then had the worst experience of his major league career in the third game. In the fifth inning, the Reds attacked him in left field. Every batter purposely hit the ball to left in a five-run inning. Ruth, unable to move, was hopeless as he tried to field the balls. When the inning ended, he went directly toward the clubhouse, not the dugout, as the fans jeered him. It was a pitiful sight. A small boy approached. Ruth picked up the boy, hugged him, then set him back down and kept walking.

In Philadelphia, on Memorial Day, first game of a doubleheader, he batted in the first inning, grounded out softly to Dolph Camilli at first, went back to the dugout, took himself out of the game, and his major league career was finished, just like that. He had played 28 games with the Braves, with six homers, seven singles, and a .181 batting average.

He didn't know he was finished, but he was. The experiment officially was closed with great rancor back in Boston on June 2. The Babe had sat out the opening doubleheader at Braves Field in a series against the Giants, dressed in a suit on the bench with a towel wrapped around his neck. The game the next day was rained out, and June 2 was the finale.

The Babe told Fuchs that he couldn't play and his knee was going to need some rest. He said he would appear at an exhibition game in Bridgeport to make the fans happy, but he would have to miss the games that week against the Dodgers. Since he was going to miss the games, he said he was going to go to New York with Claire to a party aboard the ocean liner the *Normandie*, to celebrate the completion of its maiden voyage. The *Normandie* was a modern shipbuilding marvel. The party was a big New York social event, and he had been invited, and he said he would go to "represent baseball."

Fuchs refused Ruth's request. The Judge too had had enough of the grand experiment. Ruth obviously was not going to be his financial savior. The team was terrible, the Home Run King couldn't stay healthy, and Fuchs's bank note was due on August 1. What else could go wrong? The two men quarreled, and Ruth quit and Fuchs said he was fired, and that was the end. All that was left were the press conferences.

Ruth, upset at some knocks about his play in the Boston press, called "the New York writers" to the clubhouse after the Braves beat the Giants, 2–0. He used all of the words in his vocabulary—many of the same ones he had used about France—in describing his relations with Fuchs. He used the phrase "double-crosser" often. The contract he signed, he said, was meaningless.

"He can tear that up," the Babe said. "I don't want a thing from him—the dirty double-crosser. I don't want to have anything more to do with a man like that. He's no good. He gave out wrong statements about me, then denied it. He treated me rotten since I've been here."

A reporter asked whether Ruth had invested any money in the Braves. That had been a rumor.

"Have I any money in the club?" the Babe said. "Don't make me laugh. If I did, it would be gone by now."

How about his position as vice president?

Ruth spit a stream of tobacco juice onto the clubhouse floor.

"You know what they can do with that," he said. "I never did find out what it meant anyway."

Fuchs fired back from his office that "nobody but an imbecile would act the way Ruth did." He said he was firing Ruth on the advice of Mc-Kechnie, who long had complained about Ruth's late-night drinking and carousing, a bad influence on his sinking team. The argument over the party on the *Normandie* was the final factor.

The Babe and Claire packed the car and drove home to New York the next day, a seven-and-a-half-hour trip. She said that her husband cried on the trip and that June 2, 1935, was one of the blackest days in their lives. Two days later, the Babe called the New York writers to the apartment to deliver his final words on the Braves and Judge Emil Fuchs.

"He's a double-crosser," the Babe said, pacing across the living room. "He would double-cross a hot cross bun."

There were rumors for the rest of the season that maybe he would be back in Boston. Fuchs soon left the operation, broke, and other buyers were suggested, buyers who might want the Babe back. Sophie Tucker, the last of the red-hot mamas, and comedian Joe E. Brown were listed among possible candidates, but nothing ever happened. The National League took control of the team at the end of the year.

No one from baseball except a minor league team from Palatka, Florida, stepped forward with another job offer. The Babe declined Palatka. Col. Ruppert, just to make sure his team's situation was clear, gave Joe McCarthy a two-year contract extension. The Babe was left to get healthy, play a lot of golf, and see what might happen next. Another circus called, but again he declined.

He went to see the Braves play at the Polo Grounds. He went to a couple of Yankees games. Ford Frick, now the president of the National League, presented him with a lifetime pass to National League games. Nothing came from the American League. The Yankees made him pay for his tickets.

He had a couple of automobile accidents. He was seen at heavyweight fights. He went hunting. On September 1, he played baseball again. A promoter asked him to travel to Minneapolis to play for the Minneapolis police department against the police department from St. Paul. The Babe went 1-for-4, a line-drive double, and the Minneapolis police prevailed, 10–4.

On September 29, 1935, just as the major league seasons ended, he played again. For $3,000, he played with an all-star team of semipros and former minor leaguers against the New York Cubans of the Negro League at Dyckman Oval in Washington Heights in the Bronx. A crowd estimated as high as 10,000 came to the 4,600-seat ballpark that was the home field for the Cubans but also used for boxing matches and motorcycle races.

Tom Meany, the sportswriter from the *New York Telegram*, showed up at the game to write a feature story. He contrasted the atmosphere here, at the end of the baseball season, with the excitement that had surrounded the Babe six months earlier when he homered off Carl Hubbell on opening day in Boston. Meany found it quite sad.

"The spectators seemed to sense they were watching something pathetic, almost as if they had come across [famous Irish tenor] John McCormack acting as a singing waiter," he wrote. "There were neither newsreel nor still cameras in evidence and no telegraph keys clattered brassily in the press box, which had less than half a dozen occupants. No civic dignitaries, not even an alderman, could be observed in the crowd."

Meany missed the point. This wasn't pathetic; it was perfect. If this was to be Babe Ruth's last baseball game, or maybe one of the last, it couldn't have been at a better place. The ticket prices were inexpensive, $1.10 for box seats, 55 cents for grandstands. The day was warm for late September. The stands were filled with just folks.

He was the people's player, playing for people. He had done this forever. In the past 22 years, he had played baseball in big cities, small towns, a bunch of places in between. He had played between 200 and 250 ball games every year, 154 in big league parks, but the rest at the Dyckman Ovals of America.

In how many towns and cities had he hit the longest ball anyone ever had seen? The news reports back to New York from the barnstorming road would be a paragraph, maybe two, and most of the time they would mention his one or two homers and half of the time would mention the longest home run ever seen in Rutland or Binghamton or Minneapolis.

His best records weren't recorded in books; they were kept in individual memories of an astounding sight witnessed on a warm afternoon, the memories transferred by word of mouth. There were no rules in many of these games he played. Sometimes he would bat every inning in these small towns. Sometimes he simply would stay at the plate, swinging until he hit one out. Sometimes batting practice would be as exciting as any local game ever played. He was the Bambino, the Bam, the Home Run King. He was the show.

"You know how you're supposed to pitch to Mr. Ruth, don't you?" Christy Walsh would say to the starting pitcher of the small-town team.

"Yes, sir," the pitcher would reply. "Right down the middle."

The Babe had played with black teams against black teams, with white teams against black teams, with white against white. He was a nondenominational, nondiscriminatory belter. He played with the old guys against the young guys, with the young guys against the old. A 17-year-old girl named Jackie Mitchell struck him out once in Chattanooga, Tennessee. If you were a pretty good baseball player in the twenties, professional or amateur, big-city or small-town, the chances were pretty good that you played against Babe Ruth at least once in your life. If you didn't, it was your fault. You probably missed the invitation.

Dyckman Oval? This was home.

The pitcher on the mound for the Cuban all-stars was Luis Tiant, called "Cuba's Carl Hubbell." Kept out of the big leagues for color, he would later have a son who would do quite well in major league baseball. Tiant battled the Babe, and the Babe battled back. There was a walk, followed by two fly balls to right, followed by a double. That was his day. The Cuban all-stars won, 6–1, the first game of a doubleheader.

The Babe, scheduled to play only the first game, went to the plate while the teams rested between games. He thought the people deserved a little bit more for their $1.10 or 55 cents. Clyde Barfoot, who once pitched a couple of times for the Pittsburgh Pirates, took the mound. Barfoot pitched. The Babe swung.

Maybe a half-dozen balls went out of the park in the next five minutes, and finally, as if it were planned, he really caught one. It went over the center-field fence, crashed onto a garage. How far? Word of mouth would decide. Might have been the longest ball ever hit at Dyckman Oval.

The Babe smiled and waved. Worn out, he went home to Claire for dinner.

———

CHAPTER TWENTY-FOUR

H E QUICKLY BECAME a man who played golf and drank in the afternoon. The life and times of Babe Ruth had ended. He wasn't dead, no, but he was an inhabitant of that strange twilight that exists for men who have accomplished all they can early in life and will accomplish no more. The energy still ran through him, the need to move, do, be active, but there really was nowhere to go.

"I played 365 rounds of golf last year," he would say. "Thank God for whoever invented golf. I'd be dead without it."

He golfed. He bowled. He drank. He attended to the little bits of personal business of each day. He traveled. He went hunting. He went to Florida in the winter. A personal appearance here, a radio show there. He golfed. He bowled. He drank.

He tried to kill the energy.

The stories about him invariably were touched with melancholy. They were easy stories—the Tom Meany approach at Dyckman Oval, talking about John McCormack as a singing waiter—but now they were true. The athlete, no matter who he is, once removed from his uniform, looks much older. The Babe also looked lost.

"Polo Grounds, N.Y., Sept. 30—George Herman Ruth has finally faded into legend," the Associated Press reported when he and Claire appeared at the first game of the World Series between the Yankees and Giants in 1936.

> He was the most forlorn figure in the Polo Grounds today, snapped now and then by a photographer who noticed him in a box down the first base line near Mayor [Fiorello] LaGuardia and Jimmy Walker.
>
> But there was none of the fanfare that attended him at the Series last year. He sat with his wife and daughter and Kate Smith, the singer. And when the urchins came round for signatures, most of them wanted Kate's.

The Babe did nothing to brighten the picture. Two minutes into any conversation he started talking about his desire to be the manager of a major league team. He was fixed on the topic. As soon as he started to talk, sadness crept into his words. Bluster turned into bewilderment.

"I wanted to stay in baseball more than I ever wanted anything in my life," he would say about his frustration. "But in 1935 there was no job for me, and that embittered me."

The managing job never came. There were rumors, his name continued to appear often on lists of prospective candidates, but there was never even an interview. Col. Tillinghast L'Hommedieu Huston resurfaced once, announcing great plans to buy the Brooklyn Dodgers and install the Babe as his man in charge, but Huston's wife put her foot down, and he retreated back to his manse in Georgia. The Babe coached first base for part of the 1938 season for the Dodgers, but that also didn't work out. He was there to ride the elephant, help fill the many empty seats, not to inherit the manager's job, which went to Leo Durocher.

No one ever put a finger on why he wasn't asked to manage. Was it because of his lifestyle, the way he had roared through the nights when he was young? Was it because he wasn't cerebral, because he tripped over names and forgot facts? Did the owners think he was flat-out stupid? Was it because, simply, he was Babe Ruth? His presence still commanded any room he entered, heads turned. Was that it? Was he overqualified, too big for any owner or general manager to endure every day? How do you argue a point with the Home Run King?

Maybe it was simple circumstance. The one logical place, the place where he should have gone, Yankee Stadium, was closed. Joe McCarthy was there until 1946, winning pennants and World Championships with this Joe DiMaggio kid and a new generation of players. The other possibility, Boston, the Red Sox, also was closed. Eddie Collins, the general manager, never wanted him. Tom Yawkey, the owner, listened to Eddie Collins.

The other teams in the major leagues all had characters from their own histories, local names, to consider. There were managers too coming up from the minor leagues with proven records. The Babe never went down, showed what he could do. He turned down a couple of chances, and when he decided he would go to the minors, it was too late. No one was interested.

Managing baseball, unlike playing baseball, is a political job. He was not a political person. He was Babe Ruth, dammit. The part he never understood was that the name, the carryover, was not enough. The aspiring manager had to hustle, call, charm. That was not his style. He waited. The call never came.

He golfed. He bowled. He drank.

Time blurred together. There was a family tragedy when one of Claire's brothers, Eugene, 43 years old, gassed during the war, never healthy afterward, threw himself from the window of the Babe and Claire's new 11-room apartment on Riverside Drive, 15 floors to his death, in January 1936. The Babe and Claire were in Florida, and he came back to handle the arrangements. There was a family emergency: Julia, in medical trouble with a severe strep infection in the summer of 1938, needed a transfusion. He rushed from a Dodgers game to the hospital and gave his blood. There were weddings and funerals, the ever-present car accidents, bumps in the routine, but mostly there was the routine.

"I'm 43 on the head," he said to sportswriters he invited to the apartment on his birthday in 1937, "but I can't tell yet whether I'm just beginning to live. If it's okay with everyone, I'd just as soon be 21 again."

Dorothy, the forgotten daughter, described an increasingly unpleasant everyday situation at home in her book *My Dad, the Babe*. No fan of her stepmother, Dorothy said Claire had developed a serious drinking problem. She said Claire sometimes would start the day with a shot of gin in her morning milk or soda and proceed from there. The arguments with the Babe at night came often, a matchup between Babe's "you've ruined every friendship I ever had" and Claire's "you'd be nowhere without me."

"Not only were her mental capacities for anything but baseball statistics and money slipping, but her lush beauty also was rapidly deteriorating," Dorothy wrote about Claire. "Yet, though she was miserable, and made all of us around her miserable, it was still sad to stand by and watch this happen. My father and Claire had only been married for seven years, but she looked as though twenty horrendous years had passed. In her younger days, Claire could look terrific when she rolled out of bed in the morning; now she was overweight, wan, and desperately in need of help to pull herself back together again."

The Babe took refuge in his activities. He had been gone from the house all day most of the time when he played baseball, and he was gone all day now.

He bowled five days a week during the winter when he was stuck in New York. The closest alleys to his apartment were two lanes in the basement of the Riverside Plaza Hotel. He would arrive at one o'clock in the afternoon, leave at five. If no one showed up, he would bowl alone. The manager of the establishment said he would bet there were weeks when Babe Ruth bowled more strings than anyone else in all of New York.

Not a good bowler, only fair, a 177 average, the man with time to kill didn't care. He liked strikes, yet bowled mostly straight at the head pin, rather than trying to hit the pocket. Spares were a nuisance. Waiting for the ball to be returned by the pin boy was a nuisance. He never would sit down at the bench and table with the score sheet. The energy had to be killed. He would stand and wait. If he became tired after a couple of strings, he simply would sit on the ball return and catch his breath.

"The Babe showed no interest in his average," P. J. McDonough, another bowler, said. "He was more impressed with his pin total. I would drop in from time to time and bowl with him. When I first mentioned average, he replied that he had knocked down more than 7,000 pins in four or five weeks."

Hunting and fishing took up more of his time, ate at the energy. He always had hunted, and he hunted more now. He hunted anything, anywhere. He came back from a trip to Nova Scotia in 1937 and drove his Stutz Bearcat off the boat from Yarmouth with one deer tied onto the front bumper, two more tied onto the front fenders, and a large, dead bear sitting in the rumble seat. The bloodstained car, not to mention the bloodstained passengers, made quite a sight in midtown Manhattan.

He was either a good shot or a bad shot, depending on which hunting companion gave the appraisal. His choice of guns, they said, tended toward firepower more than accuracy. That was not a surprise. One of his favorite destinations became Greenwood Lake, a small resort town 50 miles northwest of New York City. He often fished and hunted in the area. He owned a speedboat and whirred around the lake and was known at the local taverns. Claire was never seen at Greenwood Lake.

Dorothy reported that sometimes the hunting and fishing trips really weren't hunting or fishing trips. The Babe would leave for three or four days, go wherever he went, stop at some market on the way home, buy a bunch of fish, then come into the kitchen, unshaven, and slap the fish on the counter at Riverside Drive as evidence of his good work. This procedure fell apart one time when he turned the bag upside down to pour out the fish and they were all individually wrapped in shopping paper.

"That took some explaining!" Dorothy said.

For all his hunting, fishing, and bowling, his favorite recreation—his prime energy killer—was golf. It had become his life. He was a very good golfer, a three handicapper, good enough to play in the top flights of club championships. He was long, but erratic, off the tee, solid with his irons, bedeviled by his putting. He played out of the St. Albans Golf Club in Queens but was available to tour any course at any time.

"I never saw a man who could drive a ball as far as the Babe did," Buzzie Bavasi, a longtime baseball executive with the Dodgers and later the California Angels and San Diego Padres, said. "In those days the clubs had the wooden shafts, and in the backswing you could see the bend in the Babe's driver."

Bavasi was 18 years old when he played golf with Ruth. He was a friend of sportswriter Ford Frick's son. They went to college together at DePauw University. Frick, the father, called to see if Bavasi could sponsor Ruth for 18 holes at St. Andrew's Country Club in Scarsdale, New York. He also asked if Tony Lazzeri could come along. Babe Ruth? Tony Lazzeri? Frick didn't have to ask twice. Bavasi invited Frick, the son, to fill out the foursome.

"Just before we teed off, the Babe asked if he could get a highball," Bavasi said. "No problem. The Babe had two quick ones. We played the first nine and had lunch. Babe had two more highballs, and then we played the back nine. Even with four stiff drinks in him, the Babe shot 78.

"After the game, he had another highball, but was the most pleasant person I had ever been around. Signed autographs and sat around chatting with club members."

The Babe did have a question. Where were the women? Bavasi told him St. Andrew's was a men's-only club. The Babe nodded.

"Buzzie, many thanks for a wonderful day," he said at the end. "You have a great golf club here, but it ain't for me. No broads around."

That was a typical Babe Ruth day.

The public was still fascinated by him, even if the headlines had disappeared. If his name was attached to an event, the event usually drew a crowd. A few months after he retired, he appeared at a water circus staged by Paul Gallico for the *New York Daily News* at Jones Beach. The circus really was a series of swimming races attached to some events that Gallico thought might be more exciting.

Two shows were held, in the afternoon and evening. They attracted a total of 60,000 customers. The Babe's role was to stand on the stage and hit baseballs into the water with a fungo bat. For the night show, the balls had been dipped in white phosphorus, so they glowed as they went through the air.

An impromptu wackiness occurred at the night show. Some of the swimming contestants jumped into the water to swim after the balls for souvenirs. The Babe noticed and asked for more balls. He hit them faster and faster, two and three balls in the air at the same time, fireballs cutting through the night toward maybe 1,000 swimmers all in the dark water. The crowd was howling.

The Babe thought it was wonderful. Where had he seen this act before? He looked exactly like Brother Matthias at the end of a long workout at St. Mary's Industrial School for Boys.

In November 1937, he played a golf match that set a record for bad crowd behavior. He was paired with Babe Didrikson, the famous woman athlete, and they played 18 holes for charity at Fresh Meadow on Long Island against Mrs. Sylvia Annenberg, a noted women's amateur golfer, and a character called the Mysterious Montague. No one ever had seen Montague, whose real name was LaVerne Moore, play a competitive round of golf, but he had been built into legend on the West Coast.

Friends with Hollywood stars like Bing Crosby, Oliver Hardy, and Guy Kibbe—he lived at Oliver Hardy's house—Montague supposedly could play a par-busting round of golf with a rake, a shovel, and a baseball bat. He supposedly could slice and hook the ball as if it were on a string, direct it to wherever he wanted, make it stop or have it roll as if he were playing pool. He supposedly had whipped Gene Sarazen for all three bets in a Nassau in Hollywood, shot 66 at Pebble Beach, refused to play Craig Wood because he didn't want to make Craig Wood look silly. No buildup ever had been better.

"I was playing in a foursome at the Fox Hills Country Club," Montague said, not afraid to pad his legend. "At the tenth tee, I said to the other golfers, 'See those birds on that telephone wire? Watch me pick off the one farthest to the right.'

"I teed up an old ball, took a brassie, and hit a full drive. It struck the bird in the neck, snapping its head off, 170 yards away."

A crowd of over 12,000 people, at a buck-ten per head, showed up for the match. The fact that Montague's notoriety had also brought a warrant and his arrest in Jay, New York, for a 1930 armed robbery did not detract from the thrill. (He was acquitted.) He was a show, and the Babe was a show, and the two women weren't bad either.

The match lasted only nine holes because the crowd was so wild. People came closer and closer to the action with each hole, until they were actually standing on the green. People hung from and fell from all available trees. So many people crowded the tee boxes that often one or two of the competitors couldn't even get through to tee off. The Babe and Didrikson were declared the winners two-up, but it was an arbitrary score. It couldn't even be determined whether Montague was as good as he said he was.

Ruth gave Didrikson a ride home from the match and crashed his car. Neither Babe, it was reported, was hurt. Vowing to win the U.S. and British Opens, Montague later shot 81 at Open qualifying, missed the cut badly, and never was an attraction again.

"Shucks, this was nothing," Didrikson, who came from Texas, said at the end of the strange day. "You ought to see the cattle stampede down home."

On the Fourth of July 1939, the Babe—the male Babe—had a poignant public moment. The 1927 Yankees team was brought back to Yankee Stadium to honor Lou Gehrig, who was dying. The 36-year-old first baseman's debilitating, incurable disease, amyotrophic lateral sclerosis, or ALS, was known to everyone now, including the definite sad end ahead.

The Babe and Gehrig hadn't talked in five years, and the big man was late arriving. Would he show? When he finally appeared, he was almost as majestic as he ever had been, stuffed in a white suit, wearing two-toned shoes, sporting a dark tan, looking like the somebody he always was. Posed in the middle of a picture of the 1927 returnees, minus Gehrig, he looked like the grand leader of a dour, dark-suited band.

He stood with all of them, Hoyt and Dugan, Lazzeri and Pennock and little Benny Bengough, for the progression of sad moments in the ceremony staged between games of the holiday doubleheader with the Senators. The saddest moment, of course, was when Gehrig spoke. Convinced to talk by Joe McCarthy, he gave a speech that became famous, naming the people he'd known with the Yankees, finishing with the words that made all hearts break in the crowd of 61,808.

"What young man wouldn't give anything to mingle with such men for a single day as I have for all these years?" Gehrig said. "You've been reading about my bad break for weeks now. But today I think I'm the luckiest man alive. I now feel, more than ever, that I have much to live for."

At the end, he began to cry. Ruth was nudged to the microphone. He walked to his longtime associate, if not friend, his brother in long-ball history, grabbed him around the neck, and broke their five years of silence with a whispered joke that made them both smile. He then told the crowd that he thought the 1927 version of the Yankees was better right now than the present version and intimated that he wouldn't mind playing against them right now.

"Anyway," he said, "that's my opinion, and while Lazzeri here pointed out to me that there are only 13 or 14 of us here, my answer is shucks, we only need nine to beat 'em."

And so it went. The Babe lived his retired, energy-burning life, came out for these public moments, then went back again to the golf and the bowling and the tracking of wild animals. He was something like a famous retired statesman, a professor emeritus, a president who had been voted out of office. Except he was much younger.

Both of his daughters married. Dorothy, of course, left home when she was 18 after an argument with Claire and ran away to get married. Julia, of course, went the social route, the Babe as the father of the bride in top hat and tails. Col. Ruppert had died at the beginning of 1939, an emotional scene in the last days when he asked to see "Root" and actually called him "Babe" for the first and only time. Ruth cried. A month after the Gehrig Appreciation Day in 1939, he went to Cooperstown, New York, and was inducted along with Ty Cobb, Honus Wagner, and Christy Mathewson as the first class in the Baseball Hall of Fame. Cobb was the leading vote-getter, Ruth second.

He played a publicized series of three golf matches with Cobb in 1941 in Boston, New York, and Detroit for charities. (Cobb won two of the three.) He played himself in *Pride of the Yankees*, a 1942 movie on the life of Gehrig, who finally had died on June 2, 1941. To look athletic for the part, Ruth lost 47 pounds in 60 days and almost killed himself, ending up in intensive care, but he did look good in the movie. He became so excited in the scene showing the wild train ride back from St. Louis after beating the Cardinals in the 1926 World Series that he punched his fist through a window and cut himself.

The Second World War came along, and he was a fund-raiser on assorted fronts. He played his last actual baseball at the Stadium in a benefit for the Army-Navy Relief Fund. Between the benefit game and the Yankees game, Walter Johnson pitched, and the Babe hit and on the 21st pitch lofted a long shot to right that curved foul at the last moment but clanked into the stands. Close enough. He went into a home run trot. He bowled against New York Giants football star Ken Strong in a series of matches to raise money, umpired softball games, refereed wrestling matches. He went to veterans' hospitals.

The story came out that Japanese soldiers were shouting, "The hell with Babe Ruth," or some derivative when they attacked, and he became so mad he destroyed most of the treasures he had brought back from Japan after the big trip. ("I hope every Jap that mentions my name gets shot," he said. "And to hell with all Japs anyway.") A friend told him that because of his popularity in Japan, one plan had been submitted that he be flown to Guam and put on a destroyer to broadcast to the Japanese people about the wisdom of surrender before the United States unleashed its nuclear bomb. Nothing ever came of it.

He took his final shots at getting back into baseball in 1946, after the war ended. He tried to land the Newark job, the same minor league post he had spurned long ago. Ruppert's estate had sold the team to a new set of owners. The Babe called new Yankees boss Larry MacPhail, the owner who ran the club, and made his pitch, but was turned down. He then took a nice trip to Mexico with Claire and Julia and her husband to investigate the new, renegade Mexican League, expenses paid, but found millionaire owner Jorge Pasquel mostly just wanted him to ride the elephant. How could Babe Ruth live in Mexico anyway? He came back to New York and called MacPhail again, looking for *any* kind of job in the Yankees organization. He heard nothing, then received a letter on Yankees stationery in early October.

"Bad news," he told Claire. "Good news, they call. Bad news, they send a letter."

MacPhail had proposed that Ruth work with sandlot baseball in New York, with kids. Claire said Ruth cried. Kids? They wanted him to work with kids? The door was shut and now it was locked. He never would get back into baseball.

CHAPTER TWENTY-FIVE

_____

THE BAD TIMES began on November 26, 1946, two months after the letter from Larry MacPhail. The Babe checked into French Hospital on 29th Street for "observation." He had been suffering from headaches and pains above his left eye for the past few months. His voice had become increasingly hoarse. The left side of his face now was swollen, and his left eye was closed. He couldn't swallow.

Dorothy, his daughter, said the pain had become so bad that he had threatened to kill himself a few days earlier.

"About 11 o'clock in the evening I received a frantic phone call from a friend telling me to rush over to Babe and Claire's apartment on Riverside Drive," she wrote in her book.

When I arrived, his bedroom door was locked and I could hear my emotionally distraught father threatening to jump from the 15th floor window. I got on my knees and looked through the keyhole, only to discover Babe trying to break the window guard by jumping up and down on the chain. I felt completely helpless, trying to console him from out in the hallway; I just wanted to throw my arms around him and tell him how much he meant to me. I don't know what I said, but thank God he finally came to his senses and opened the door.

He had cancer.

The optimistic approach in the first few days was that he was suffering from a sinus problem and maybe was troubled by three bad teeth. The diagnosis was soon changed. A tumor had developed in the nasopharynx, a part of the air passages behind the nose. It sat in a place near the under-surface of the skull that was inaccessible to surgeons. As the tumor had grown, it had pressed against nerves from the brain that supplied the motor function of the throat and larynx. This was what made him hoarse and made swallowing difficult.

He was doomed. That pretty much was the case. The tumor now had grown into his neck. He was off on that long forced march of the cancer patient through surgery and radiation and experimental drugs. He was a pathfinder, really, one of the first cancer patients to receive both radiation and drugs at the same time, his name and fame bringing him to the front of the list. He still was doomed.

For the last 21 months of his life, he never would feel well again. He would feel better on some days, would play golf a few times and travel, would work with American Legion baseball for the Ford Motor Company, a job that sent him around the country, but he never would feel well. Health, survival, became his primary consideration.

The "observation" stretched into 82 days in room 1114 at French Hospital. He first was treated with radiation, then had surgery on his neck that was characterized by his doctors as "serious" on January 6, 1947, an attempt to alleviate the pressure on the nerves to his vocal cords. He was still in the hospital on his birthday on February 7, 1947. He received over 30,000 pieces of mail, including a bottle of water from Lourdes. He rubbed the water on his body. He pinned a miraculous medal to his pajamas.

"How old are you?" his nurse asked, confused by the old birthday problem. "Are you 52 or 53?"

"What difference does it make if you feel good?" he said.

This was one of the better days.

He left the hospital nine days later. This was not one of the better days. He was helped from the hospital door to the car, unable to walk on his own. He looked terrible, a thousand years old, his weight down to 180 pounds on his 6-foot-2 frame. He cried as 100 bystanders wished him well. His daughter Julia read a statement that her father wanted to go home to Riverside Drive to "look at the river from my apartment window." An unidentified nurse told the *Times* the Babe was "still a very sick man."

The newspaper writers, all of them, did a nice thing: they never mentioned the word "cancer." They described how he looked and quoted what the doctors said, but they never said the bad word. The doctors never said the bad word. No one said the bad word.

The idea was to keep the news from the Babe that he was doomed. Maybe this worked. Maybe it didn't. There was no doubt, though, that he knew he was "a very sick man."

A Babe Ruth Day was held two months later on April 27, 1947, not only at Yankee Stadium but everywhere in baseball by order of new commissioner Happy Chandler. The Babe was at the Stadium, bundled into his camel's hair coat, wearing the cap. He frightened people. They hadn't seen him since he became sick. Even with a good tan, the result of weeks of recuperation in Florida, where he had fished and even tried golf, he was a sadly shrunken version of the man who once walked from the same dugout and made pitchers nervous.

The similarities to the farewell to Gehrig, eight years earlier, were obvious. Ruth thought about them the entire day. The differences also were obvious. The robust figure that put his arm around the dying first baseman and made him laugh now looked far worse than the dying first baseman had.

Like Gehrig, Ruth had no prepared, written-out speech when he approached the microphone. The crowd of 58,339 cheered at his introduction by Yankees announcer Mel Allen, and he started to cry and then started coughing, and for a moment it looked as if he wouldn't be able to speak. He composed himself.

"Thank you very much, ladies and gentlemen," he said in a terrible rasp. "You know how bad my voice sounds. Well, it feels just as bad. . . ."

"You know, this baseball game of ours comes up from the youth. That means the boys. And after you've been a boy and grow up to know how to play ball, then you come to the boys you see representing themselves today in our national pastime.

"The only real game in the world, I think, is baseball. As a rule, some people think if you give them a football or a baseball or something like that, naturally they're athletes right away. But you can't do that in baseball. You gotta start from way down at the bottom, when you're six or seven years old. You can't wait until you're 15 or 16. You've gotta let it grow up with you. And if you're successful and you try hard enough, you're bound to come out on top, just like these boys have come to the top now.

"There's been so many lovely things said about me, I'm glad I had the opportunity to thank everybody. Thank you."

The words weren't nearly as compelling as the "luckiest man" speech by Gehrig, but the words didn't matter. The delivery, the sound, the gravel and pain in each syllable was sent across the country and broadcast through loudspeakers at every ballpark before every game of the day, providing a window to the famous man's struggle. He went back to the dugout, where he had another prolonged fit of coughing.

He then watched the first eight innings of the Senators' 1–0 win over the Yankees. He was back in the hospital two months later.

The radiation had worked, allowing him to speak and to swallow a bit, to go to Florida, appear in public, make assorted stops for Ford, but the effects had worn off. The same symptoms had returned. His jaw hurt if he even tried to eat eggs. He now tried the new science, chemotherapy.

The drug, called teropterin, was basically a stronger, synthetic version of folic acid. Tests had been run on mice with mixed results, some of them encouraging. The Babe was one of the first human subjects, maybe the first. In these early days of chemical testing, there were very few rules. He consented to take a drug he knew nothing about for a disease no one had told him he had. There were no forms to be filled out. He simply nodded his head.

"There was a chance it would prove nothing, and there was a chance it might prove harmful to me in my condition," the Babe said. "I was in pretty bad shape. The matter was left up to me. It wasn't an easy decision."

He took daily injections for six weeks. He didn't stay in the hospital for all of that time, but came in every day for his shots. The teropterin seemed to work. His symptoms quieted a bit. He could eat some soft foods. He started to regain some weight. His hair, lost during the radiation treatments, came back. The lymph nodes in his neck shrunk down to nothing. The doctors in the study were so excited that they rushed out a paper that was delivered at the International Cancer Congress in St.

Louis. They thought they had cured this form of cancer. They mentioned a "52-year-old man" but didn't mention Ruth's name. His case was seen as a scientific miracle.

He'd signed a contract for a ghostwritten book, *The Babe Ruth Story*, so he spent stretches of time with the writer, Bob Considine. A top general columnist with the Hearst syndicate, Considine had become famous with *Thirty Seconds over Tokyo*, written with Ted Lawson, a flier who had lost a leg in the bombing raids on the Japanese city during World War II. The book was a great success and was made into a movie starring Spencer Tracy and Van Johnson.

Considine didn't have much more luck with the failing Ruth than previous famous writers, working as his newspaper ghosts, had had with the healthy Ruth. A half-hour into an interview session, Ruth would suggest that they take a ride, hit some golf balls, maybe play nine holes, do something. Off they would go to the golf course in the Babe's Lincoln Continental.

They would stop at a butcher shop on Ninth Avenue to pick up some hamburger that he would have cooked for lunch at the golf course. Some days he could eat it. Some days he could eat nothing more than a two-minute egg. The golf was sad. The same drives that went for 300 yards now went for 100, 150. The wooden shaft did not bend anymore.

This was no way to write a book. Ruth was far too sick to concentrate and tell his story. Considine realized he was in trouble, so he brought in Fred Lieb. The sportswriter from the *New York Telegram* became the ghostwriter for the ghostwriter.

"I wrote the book," Lieb said. "I dictated that book for about a week to ten days before the 1947 World Series. Considine didn't know enough about Ruth. See, I was with Ruth from 1920 to 1934. Considine didn't come to New York until around 1933."

The Babe went to the 1947 World Series with Claire, the Yankees matched against the Dodgers. He became a focus of attention. People noticed when he arrived or exited. The new medium—television—focused its cameras on him often. His discomfort was obvious.

In January he returned to the Neurological Institute for 17 days and was cleared at the end to go to Florida with Claire and his male nurse, Frank Delaney, to resume as much of his life as he could stand. He still felt awful when his birthday came on February 7, 1948, but at least he wasn't in the hospital.

"I'm full of aches and pains," he told a reporter on the doorstep to his surfside bungalow at the Golden Strand Hotel in Miami Beach. "My arms hurt, and I can't stretch them out. My neck hurts, and I'm hopeful the sun will do the job."

The sun did turn out to be good medicine, although no papers would be written about it for any scientific journals. By the end of six weeks, the patient said he felt "100 percent better" and a "new man" as he returned to New York. The book was about to be published, and he felt well enough to go to a book-signing party at the offices of the publisher, E. P. Dutton.

"A lot of publishers were there because it was obvious the Babe's days were numbered," Considine said. "Bennett Cerf stood in line to get the Babe's autograph. Ernest Hemingway was there. The books were just about running out, the end of the line near, and I said, 'Jeez, I'd like to have one too.' Babe opened a book and wrote, in his marvelous Spencerian handwriting, 'To my pal, Bob. . . .' And he looked up and said, 'What the hell is your last name?' I'd spent two months with him."

The book was being made into a movie, also titled *The Babe Ruth Story*, the screenplay written by Considine. The Babe had been hired as a "technical adviser," supposedly to teach William Bendix, the star, how to hit 60 home runs a year. Or to look like he could hit 60 home runs a year. The real job, though, was publicity. The Babe and Claire and Julia and her husband went to Hollywood at the end of April, arriving on May 1.

Joe L. Brown, son of comedian Joe E. Brown, had been hired by Allied Artists Studio as "special sports publicist" for the picture, a job that basically entailed helping the Babe. Brown appeared at nine in the morning and stayed with him until he went to bed. Every day started with a visit from a doctor who would swab some medication in the back of Ruth's throat. The Babe would have to say, "Ahhhhh."

"Take a look at this," Babe said one day to Brown after the procedure.

"Don't show him," the doctor said.

"It's okay," Ruth said.

He opened his mouth and said, "Ahhhhh." Brown looked inside and saw a large hole. The cancer had eaten away the back of the Babe's throat.

The movie people only needed one day of publicity shots—Ruth posed with Bendix and co-star Claire Trevor—so the rest of the time Brown took him wherever he wanted to go. They wound up one day at Twentieth-Century Fox, watching Betty Grable make a movie. They sat in two director's chairs at the side of the set. Grable did some scene.

"Look at that babe, will ya?" the Babe said. "If I'd only known her when I was younger. We'd have had some fun."

On June 13, 1948, he was in a baseball uniform for the last time. Yankee Stadium was now 25 years old, and the Babe's number 3 was retired as part of the silver-anniversary celebration. A two-inning old-timers' game was played between the gray and bald 1923 Yankees, the first team to play in the Stadium, and a team of more recent alumni before the start of the regular game between the Yankees and the Cleveland Indians. The Babe was the manager of the 1923 squad. Ed Barrow, his old nemesis, now 80 years old, was the manager of the later alumni.

The day was rainy and cold. The ceremonies were maudlin, and wreaths were placed in front of center-field monuments that had been erected for Ruppert, Miller Huggins, and Gehrig. "Taps" was played for all deceased members of the Yankees family. Six of the Murderers' Row Yankees of 1927 already were gone. Gehrig, of course, and Huggins and Urban Shocker. Tony Lazzeri had been found at the foot of the stairs in his home in 1946, dead either from a heart attack or from an epileptic fit. John Grabowski, a backup catcher, had died in a fire, and finally, Herb Pennock, the Squire of Kennett Square, had died five months earlier in January of a cerebral hemorrhage.

There was little doubt that Ruth would soon join the list. He arrived at the Stadium later than the other players, accompanied by a friend and his nurse. Again, he was frail and shrunken, wrapped in his big overcoat. He slowly changed into the pinstriped uniform, the whole deal, including baseball shoes and stockings, posed for pictures, then added the overcoat again.

"What took 'em so long to retire your uniform?" Waite Hoyt asked. "They retired mine in 1930 when they sent me to Detroit."

The Babe smiled.

Everything was an effort. He waited in the runway that ran from the dugout to the clubhouse as the ceremonies began, but his nurse suggested that he should go back to the clubhouse where it was warmer. When his time was near, he came back through the runway and sat in the dugout. He picked up a fielder's mitt that some present-day player had left on the bench and said, "Christ, you could catch a basketball with this." He talked a bit with Mel Harder, now the Indians' pitching coach, remembering a day when he had gone 5-for-5 against Harder. It was a thousand years ago.

He stepped out of his overcoat and went onto the field when his name was called by Mel Allen—"George Herman Ruth . . . Babe Ruth"—and used a bat as a cane as he walked toward his old teammates and the crowd noise churned around him. Again he went to the microphone. . . .

"Ladies and gentlemen," he said in the battered, painful voice, "I want to say one thing. I am proud I hit the first home run here in 1923. It was marvelous to see 13 or 14 players who were my teammates going back 25 years. I'm telling you it makes me proud and happy to be here."

He never would be back.

Eleven days later, he checked into Memorial Hospital. Amazingly, during those 11 days, he had been to three last stops—St. Louis, Sioux City, and Sioux Falls—for Ford Motors. He ran into John Drebinger, the *Times* sportswriter, in the hotel in St. Louis. Drebinger saw him, didn't want to be a bother, but Ruth lit up.

"Hey, you old bastard," he said to John Drebinger. "How're you doing, Joe?"

The cancer was everywhere now, in his liver, his lungs, his kidneys. A young Dominican priest, Father Thomas Kaufman from St. Catherine of Siena Parish, was assigned to him. Father Kaufman had a link to Ruth because he was from Baltimore and for one day during a family crisis he and his brother had been residents of St. Mary's Industrial School for Boys. Ruth liked that. He knew by now he had cancer. He also knew that he was dying. He was resigned to his situation.

The room on the ninth floor quickly filled with boxes of mail. People also sent good luck charms, many of them religious icons that had worked in their own situations. A statue of Blessed Martin DePorres, known as the Negro saint, stood on the Babe's nightstand. On July 21, Ruth's condition worsened, and Father Kaufman gave him the Last Rites of the Church. It was a strangely controversial move. The priest received a lot of positive mail, but also some hate mail from Catholics who thought that Ruth's profligate life didn't deserve forgiveness. One was written entirely in ecclesiastical Latin.

Ruth rallied the next day. On the night of July 26, he even left the hospital, taken to the Astor Theater for the premiere of *The Babe Ruth Story*. This was another controversial move. Dorothy was irate.

"I was totally taken by surprise," she said. "When I had left Dad that

afternoon, he was sedated, and I had no idea that he would be at the theater that night. . . . It occurred to me there was only one person who
could have bypassed the security guards so easily—Claire. When I confronted her, she admitted she was responsible. She told me that it was necessary for him to be there and, after all, no harm had been done."

He arrived at the theater with no expression on his face, a sick man in
a place where he shouldn't have been. He was taken back to the hospital
halfway through the movie. The movie was so bad, so cliché-filled and unbelievable, that people said they wished they also could have left. *The
Babe Ruth Story* was killed across the board by the critics.

"No home run," Wanda Hale of the *Daily News* said. "It's no more
than a scratch single, a feeble blooper back of second base."

The wait for Babe Ruth to die began. He was beyond treatments, and
all efforts made now were to make him as comfortable as possible. The
visitors' list to the ninth-floor room was cut down to family and closest
friends. No ballplayers were on the list. Dorothy was surprised one afternoon to arrive and find a tall, attractive, redheaded woman in the room.
The woman introduced herself as Loretta. She said she had been the
Babe's girlfriend for the past ten years.

Dorothy was stunned, then pleased. She liked the idea of Loretta.

"She was his constant companion and catered to his every need—she
even went hunting, fishing, boating, and golfing with him," Dorothy said.
"I'm glad that at last he was able to find some pleasant female companionship. Lord knows, he deserved it."

The fog settled in for one last time. Loretta? What else did nobody
know about the life of Babe Ruth? What else would nobody ever know?

Dorothy would claim, years later, that she was his natural daughter,
born out of wedlock to a family friend, Juanita Ellis. True? False? There
were no documents to prove what she said. There also were no documents
to disprove it.

The question of race would linger. Was the Babe, by legal definition, a
black man? He had heard the bad words for as long as he played. He had
been handed the wrongful stereotype that would be attached to the black
athlete—the natural talent, abilities transmitted by the touch of God, not
acquired through industry and intelligence. He never had the chance to
manage a team. So many of the pieces fit. If not a black man, he had been
touched by the prejudices against a black man.

The truth? The fog settled in for one last time.

On August 9, the Babe signed a revised will that Claire and his lawyers had drawn up. On August 11, it was announced that he was on the critical list. Major League Baseball asked that a minute of silence be observed before all games to pray for his recovery. Neighborhood kids and photographers clustered outside the hospital.

On August 16, at 8:01 P.M., the Caliph of Clout, the Monster of Mash, the Home Run King, the Sultan of Swat, the Bam, the Big Bam, the Bambino, the Babe, George Herman Ruth, 53 years old, but thought he was 54, died in his sleep. There were no last words.

"The Babe died a beautiful death," Father Kaufman said to reporters outside Memorial Hospital. "He said his prayers and lapsed into a sleep. He died in his sleep."

The first suggestion was to hold the wake at the Universal Funeral Home on Lexington Avenue. That was soon changed. The Babe instead lay in state for two days and nights at Yankee Stadium. An estimated 77,000 people came past to pay their respects. Another 75,000 watched the funeral cortege as it left St. Patrick's Cathedral on August 19, 1948.

The morning had been rainy, but the sun broke out when the services ended and the long procession drove slowly through the city.

B ABE RUTH is buried in a hillside plot at the Gate of Heaven Cemetery in Valhalla, New York, next to Claire, who died in 1976. His statue stands at the entrance to the Baseball Hall of Fame in Cooperstown, New York.

The fascination with his career and life continues. He is a bombastic, sloppy hero from our bombastic, sloppy history, origins undetermined, a folk tale of American success. His moon face is as recognizable today as it was when he stared out at Tom Zachary on a certain September afternoon in 1927.

If sport has become the national religion, Babe Ruth is the patron saint. He stands at the heart of the game he played, the promise of a warm summer night, a bag of peanuts, and a beer.

And just maybe, the longest ball ever hit out of the park.

ACKNOWLEDGMENTS

———

THANKS AGAIN to Bob Creamer, Kal Wagenheim, and Jerome Holtzman. Thanks, too, to the late Marshall Smelser. The raw material from four books is not a bad start in writing one book. The generosity and encouragement from these writers, who followed the trail of the Babe when it still was reasonably fresh, was a wonder.

Thanks to Jeff Idelson, Claudette Burke, and Jeremy Jones at the Baseball Hall of Fame. Thanks to Faigi Rosenthal and Scott Browne at the library at the *New York Daily News,* and to Luisa Tuite at the *Boston Globe* library. Thanks to the staff at the Boston Public Library, the Winthrop, Massachusetts, Public Library, the Enoch Pratt Free Library, the library at the University of Notre Dame, the libraries at the *Baltimore Sun,* the Society for American Baseball Research, and assorted other libraries. Thanks to writers Harry Rothgerber, Paul F. Harris Sr., Jonathan Eig, Chris Martens, Matthew Crenson, Allan Wood, and Wayne Coffey. Thanks to Marty Appel, Esther Newberg, Jenny Choi, and Jason Kaufman.

Also, Clarke Booth, Kevin Connolly, Tommy Shea, Ian Thomsen, Mark Linehan, Kevin McGonagle, Paul Doyle, all members of the Garden Street Athletic Club; my son, Leigh, and my daughter, Robin Moleux, and her husband, Doug. And thanks to anyone else who helped, held my hand, and/or listened to me talk about all this stuff that happened long ago.

BIBLIOGRAPHY

BOOKS

Allen, Frederick Lewis. *Only Yesterday: An Informal History of the 1920's*. New York: Harper & Row, 1931.

———. *Since Yesterday: The 1930s in America*. New York: Harper & Row, 1940.

Allen, Lee. *The American League Story*. New York: Hill & Wang, 1965.

Barrow, Edward Grant (with James M. Kahn). *My Fifty Years in Baseball*. New York: Coward-McCann, 1951.

Beim, George (with Julia Ruth Stevens). *Babe Ruth: A Daughter's Portrait*. Dallas: Taylor Publishing, 1998.

Berg, A. Scott. *Lindbergh*. New York: G. P. Putnam's Sons, 1998.

Breslin, Jimmy. *Damon Runyon: A Life*. Boston: Houghton Mifflin, 1991.

Chapman, John. *Tell It to Sweeney: An Informal History of the New York Daily News*. Garden City, N.Y.: Doubleday & Co., 1961.

Creamer, Robert W. *Babe: The Legend Comes to Life*. New York: Simon & Schuster, 1974.

Crenson, Matthew A. *Building the Invisible Orphanage: A Prehistory of the American Welfare System*. Cambridge, Mass.: Harvard University Press, 1998.

Daniel, Dan (with anecdotes by H. G. Salsinger). *The Real Babe Ruth*. St. Louis: C. C. Spink & Son, 1948.

Eig, Jonathan. *Luckiest Man: The Life and Death of Lou Gehrig*. New York: Simon & Schuster, 2005.

Fowler, Gene. *Beau James: The Life and Times of Jimmy Walker*. New York: Stratford Press, 1949.

———. *Skyline: A Reporter's Reminiscence of the Twenties*. New York: Viking Press, 1961.

Frick, Ford. *Games, Asterisks, and People: Memoirs of a Lucky Fan*. New York: Crown, 1973.

Gilbert C.F.X., Brother. *Young Babe Ruth: His Early Life and Baseball from the Memoirs of a Xaverian Brother*. Edited by Harry Rothgerber. Jefferson, N.C.: McFarland & Co., 1999.

Goldman, Herbert G. *Jolson: The Legend Comes to Life.* New York: Oxford University Press, 1988.

Harris, Paul F. Sr. *Babe Ruth: The Dark Side.* Glen Burnie, Md.: Self-published, 1998.

Holtzman, Jerome. *No Cheering in the Press Box.* New York: Holt, Rinehart & Winston, 1974.

———. *Jerome Holtzman on Baseball: A History of Baseball Scribes.* Champaign, Ill.: Sports Publishing, L.L.C., 2005.

Keene, Kerry, Raymond Sinibaldi, and David Hickey. *The Babe in Red Stockings: An In-Depth Chronicle of Babe Ruth with the Boston Red Sox, 1914–1919.* Champaign, Ill.: Sagamore Publishing, 1997.

Kelley, Brent. *In the Shadow of the Babe: Interviews with Baseball Players Who Played With or Against Babe Ruth.* Jefferson, N.C.: McFarland & Co., 1995.

Lardner, Ring, Jr. *Some Champions, Sketches, and Fiction by Ring Lardner.* New York: Charles Scribner's Sons, 1976.

Leuchtenberg, William E. *The Perils of Prosperity: 1914–1932.* University of Chicago Press, 1958.

Lieb, Fred. *Baseball As I Have Known It.* New York: Coward, McCann & Geoghegan, 1977.

Meany, Tom. *Babe Ruth.* New York: A. S. Barnes & Co., 1947.

McCarthy, Kevin. *Babe Ruth in Florida.* Haverford, Pa.: Infinity Publishing, 2002.

Miller, Ernestine. *The Babe Book.* Kansas City, Mo.: Andrews McMeel Publishing, 2000.

Morley, Christopher. *Christopher Morley's New York.* New York: Fordham University Press, 1988.

Pilat, Oliver. *Pegler: Angry Man of the Press.* Boston: Beacon Press, 1963.

Pirrone, Dorothy Ruth (with Chris Martens). *My Dad, the Babe: Growing Up with an American Hero.* Boston: Quinlan Press, 1988.

Reichler, Joe (editor). *The Baseball Encyclopedia.* 7th edition. New York: MacMillan Publishing, 1988.

Reisler, Jim. *Babe Ruth: Launching the Legend.* New York: McGraw-Hill, 2004.

——— (editor). *Guys, Dolls, and Curveballs: Damon Runyon on Baseball.* New York: Carroll & Graf, 2005.

Rice, Grantland. *The Tumult and the Shouting: My Life in Sport.* New York: A. S. Barnes & Co., 1954.

Ritter, Lawrence S. *The Glory of Their Times: The Story of the Early Days of Baseball Told by the Men Who Played It.* New York: Macmillan & Co., 1966.

Robertson, John G. *The Babe Chases 60: The Fabulous 1927 Season, Home Run by Home Run.* Jefferson, N.C.: McFarland & Co., 1999.

Rubin, Louis D., Jr. *Babe Ruth's Ghost and Other Historical and Literary Speculations.* Seattle: University of Washington Press, 1996.

Ruth, Babe (as told to Bob Considine). *The Babe Ruth Story.* New York: E. P. Dutton & Co., 1948.

Ruth, Babe, Mrs. (with Bill Slocum). *The Babe and I.* New York: Avon Books, 1959.

Ruth, George Herman. *Babe Ruth's Own Book of Baseball.* New York: G. P. Putnam's Sons, 1928.

Smelser, Marshall. *The Life That Ruth Built: A Biography.* New York: Quadrangle/New York Times Books, 1975.

Smith, Mortimer. *My School the City.* Washington, D.C.: Regnery/Gateway, 1980.

Smith, Robert. *Babe Ruth's America.* New York: Thomas Y. Crowell, 1974.

Sobol, Ken. *Babe Ruth and the American Dream.* New York: Ballantine Books, 1974.

Stevens, Julia Ruth. *Major League Dad: A Daughter's Cherished Memories.* Chicago: Triumph Books, 2001.

Stevens, John D. *Sensationalism and the New York Press.* New York: Columbia University Press, 1961.

Stout, Glenn, and Richard A. Johnson. *Red Sox Century.* New York: Houghton Mifflin, 2000.

———. *Yankees Century.* New York: Houghton Mifflin, 2002.

Terkel, Studs. *Hard Times: An Oral History of the Great Depression.* New York: Pantheon Books, 1970.

Trachtenberg, Leo. *The Wonder Team: The True Story of the Incomparable 1927 New York Yankees.* Bowling Green, Ohio: Bowling Green State University Popular Press, 1995.

Wagenheim, Kal. *Babe Ruth: His Life and Legend.* New York: Henry Holt, 1974.

Walsh, Christy. *Adios to Ghosts.* New York: Self-published, 1937.

Weldon, Martin. *Babe Ruth.* New York: Thomas Y. Crowell, 1948.

Werber, Bill. *Circling the Bases with Bill Werber.* Self-published.

——— (with C. Paul Rogers III). *Memories of a Ballplayer: Bill Werber and Baseball in the 1930s.* Cleveland: Society for American Baseball Research, 2001.

Wilson, Nick. *Voices from the Pastime: Oral Histories of Surviving Major Leaguers, Negro Leaguers, Cuban Leaguers and Writers, 1920–1934.* Jefferson, N.C.: McFarland & Co., 2000.

Wood, Allan. *Babe Ruth and the 1918 Red Sox.* Lincoln, Neb.: Writers Club Press, 2000.

WEB SITES

A Note About Web Sites
The Web brings an entirely new dimension to book research. A few taps of the fingers instantly can bring up facts ranging from the spelling of a middle name to the life story of, say, New York mayor Jimmy Walker. Any list of the Web sites visited during this project would be incomplete. Following are some notable ones.

www.baseballlibrary.com
www.highbeam.com (*Sports Illustrated*, etc.)
www.baseball-links.com

www.paperofrecord.com (*Sporting News*, etc.)
www.indiejournal.com (*The Baseball Tragedy of 1920* by Jeff Youngblood)
www.angelfire.com/pa/1927 (the unofficial 1927 New York Yankees home page)
www.stevesteinberg.net (Miller Huggins, Urban Shocker)
www.asms.k12.ar.us/armem/richter/index.html (Hot Springs, Ark.)
www.sfsu.edu/~mpmott (*Making the World Safe for Baseball* by Michael Mott)
www.sabr.org
www.aafla.org (*Baseball* magazine)
www.geocities.com/flapper_culture (the Jazz Age)
www.yankeeclassic.com/miskatonic
www.violetville.org/neighborhoodhistory
www.irishlegends.com (Knute Rockne)
www.celiatan.com
www.wikipedia.com
www.xroads.virginia.edu (*The Babe Ruth Times*)
www.thedeadballera.com
www.rauchway.ucdavis.edu/altercations.html (*The Red Sox Curse* by Eric Rauch-
    way)
www.firstworldwar.com

The search engine ProQuest, accessed through membership in the Society for American Baseball Research, was invaluable. ProQuest was the entry to the back pages of the *New York Times, Boston Globe, Atlanta Constitution, Chicago Tribune, Los Angeles Times,* and *Chicago Defender.*

INDEX

COURTESY OF THE AUTHOR

ABOUT THE AUTHOR

Leigh Montville, a former columnist at the *Boston Globe* and former senior writer at *Sports Illustrated*, is the author of the bestselling *Ted Williams*, *At the Altar of Speed*, *Manute*, and *Why Not Us?* He lives in Boston.

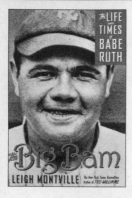
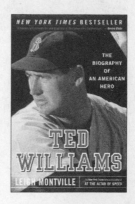
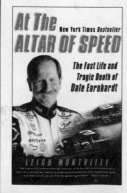